GREECE in the Bronze Age

GREECE

in the Bronze Age

EMILY VERMEULE

Chicago and London

THE UNIVERSITY OF CHICAGO PRESS

To Mary Hamilton Swindler

THE UNIVERSITY OF CHICAGO PRESS, CHICAGO 60637
The University of Chicago Press, Ltd., London

Printed in the United States of America
94 93 92   *12*
ISBN: 0-226-85353-5 (clothbound); 0-226-85354-3 (paperbound)
Library of Congress Catalog Card Number: 64-23427

Preface to the Fifth Printing

Enormous progress has been made in Aegean studies since this book was first written, and parts of *Greece in the Bronze Age* are now naturally considerably out of date. New excavations and important new publications have partly changed the balance of impressions, or have extended historical and artistic knowledge in important ways.

The Mesolithic and Neolithic periods are becoming far better known, as predicted; excavations in the Franchthi Cave on the Gulf of Argos (T. Jacobsen, *Hesperia* 38 [1969] 343) provide good radiocarbon dates for solid settlement by the middle of the eighth millennium B.C. (7627 ± 134) and sea voyages to Melos for obsidian; the Alepotrypa Cave in the Mani is receiving overdue investigation, developing the Neolithic sequence in the southwest (G. Papathanassopoulos); D. Theochares and V. Miløjčič continue with significant finds in Thessaly and Euboia. Early Bronze Age culture in the Cyclades is increasingly illuminated by J. L. Caskey's work on Kea; idols are being better

v

classified (Chr. Doumas, *Goulandris Collection* [1969]; C. Renfrew, *AJA* 73 [1969] 1), and Anatolian links more precisely explored (D. French [1968]; C. Renfrew [1971]). Early Helladic towns (Pavlopetri) and megaron houses (Akovitika) in the southern and western Peloponnesos help expand the maps. The Middle Bronze Age continues to be found in new places, often with good stratification (Pefkakia-Magoula); the tumulus burials in Epeiros and at Marathon, and other evidence of vigorous culture, make the epoch more interesting.

The contents of the Shaft Graves at Mycenae have not yet been studied as art. In this period the major concentration has been on the Cyclades and Crete, with the important excavations at Akrotiri on Thera (S. Marinatos, C. Doumas) stirring the public imagination by their wealth of finds, lovely frescoes, and recoverable furniture (*Thera* I, II, III, *Deltion* [1967–]; *AAA* [1969–]; *Connaissance des Arts* and *Smithsonian* [1971]; *Time* and *Life* [1972]); Thera's close artistic ties with Late Minoan I Crete, and the relations between its volcanic eruption and the destructions of Cretan towns explored by almost everyone (e.g., J. V. Luce, *Lost Atlantis* [1969]; A. Galanopoulos and E. Bacon, *Atlantis: The Truth Behind the Legend* [1969]; D. Page, *The Santorini Volcano* [1970]; N. Platon, *Zakros* [1971]; S. Hood, *The Minoans* [1971]). Precise publication of the sequences of pottery from Knossos, at long last, have helped make the end of chapter V here happily obsolete (M. R. Popham, *The Destruction of the Palace at Knossos* [1970]; cf. S. Hood, "The Last Palace at Knossos," *SMEA* 2 [1967] 63). The transition between Minoan and Mycenaean is becoming better known overseas, at important towns like Miletos (G. Kleiner, *Alt-Milet* [1966–]); Rhodes still needs more precise excavation.

For the palace age the most important events are the publication of the Pylos volumes (C. W. Blegen and M. Rawson, *The Palace of Nestor I* [1966]; M. Lang, *The Palace of Nestor,* II: *The Frescoes* [1969]); the discovery of the shrines by the Citadel House at Mycenae with their frescoes and strange idols with snakes (W. Taylor, *Antiquity* 43 [1969] 91; 44 [1970] 270; *AAA* 3 [1970] 74), and G. Mylonas's fine frescoes of a woman and a shield (best in Ἱστορία τοῦ Ἑλληνικοῦ Ἔθνους [1970] 273, 315). The excavations at Thebes continue through probes, with new tablets (T. Spyropoulos). A painted chamber tomb at Thebes is a welcome oddity. Nichoria in Messenia will yield the first complete town plan (W. McDonald). Work on Linear B has settled into more stable patterns; one might single out C. J. Ruijgh's *Études sur la grammaire et le vocabulaire du Grec mycénien* (1967), or the papers in the *1° Congresso Internazionale di Micenologia* (Rome, 1968), or the increasingly valuable series in *Studi Micenei ed Egeo-Anatolici,* as well as reports in *Nestor.*

The later periods are extremely well served now, with the monumental, meticulous publication of the *Perati Cemetery* (Περατή : τὸ Νεκροταφεῖον [1970]) by S. Iakovides, the careful work at Leukandi by M. R. Popham and L. H. Sackett (cf. *Lefkandi, A Preliminary Report* [1968]) and the publication of the cemetery vases from Kos (L. Morricone, *Annuario* 27 [1965–66]). LH III C is getting more popular, as it should; cf. C. Styrenius, *Sub-Mycenean Studies* (1967); E. Vermeule, "The Decline and End of Minoan and Mycenean Culture," *A Land Called Crete* (1968); R. V. Nicholls, "Greek Votive Statuettes and Religious Continuity," *Auckland Classical Essays* (1970). Late Mycenaean art continues to be interestingly represented by the painted larnakes from Tanagra (excavated at last, T. Spyropoulos) with scenes of mourning, the dead inside their sarcophagi and bull-jumping. Mycenaean connections overseas are illustrated in the exemplary excavations at Kition in Cyprus (V. Karageorghis), and new collections of materials (V. Hankey, *BSA* 62 [1967] 107).

Among the more important and interesting new books are G. Mylonas, *Mycenae and the Mycenaean Age* (1966); R. Higgins, *Minoan and Mycenaean Art* (1967); P. Dikaios, *Enkomi* (1970); S. A. Immerwahr, *The Athenian Agora XIII: The Neolithic and Bronze Ages* (1971); N. Scoufopoulos, "Mycenaean Citadels," *Stud. Med. Arch.* 22 (1971); volumes in several continuing series are indispensable (*Corpus der Minoischen und Mykenischen Siegel; Archaeologia Homerica; CAH* [2-3]; *AAA*); the superior text and illustrations of Ἱστορία τοῦ Ἑλληνικοῦ Ἔθνους, Προϊστορία καὶ Προτοϊστορία (1970) make one wish for a speedy rendition into English. When all this wealthy material is harmonized, our vision of Greece in the Bronze Age will have new life and color.

MARCH 1972

Not even those who lived long ago before us
and were sons of our lords, the gods, themselves half-divine,
came to an old age and the end of their days
without hardship and danger, nor did they live forever.

SIMONIDES
(translated by Richmond Lattimore)

Introduction

This book is probably written at the wrong time by the wrong person. As always in archaeology, solid popular interest runs about ten years behind excavations; ten years ago we suffered for good general books about Minoans and Mycenaeans, but now a whole group of competent, stimulating books has appeared, either inclusive and descriptive, or exploring special fields and theories. There is a common body of knowledge and there is fair agreement about its outlines, its chronology, and how it relates to other parts of the Bronze Age world. But while descriptions coincide, interpretations have been so different lately as to draw blood. Certain stubborn problems have resisted solution by appeals to stratification, philology, common sense, or emotion. Is Linear A Canaanite or Luvian? Is Linear B Greek, an unknown tongue, or a great bitter joke? Did Knossos fall in 1400 or 1200 B.C. (or in 1405 in the spring or 1187 in the fall)? Did the spiral come from the Balkans, the megaron from Anatolia? Did the Mycenaeans build Stonehenge? Did the Trojans take their chariots to

North Africa? How did the princes of the Shaft Graves get so rich? Was there a Trojan War at all, or is Homer only a blend of misty memories tempered by poetry? What happened in the Dark Ages? And who were the Greeks as we know them?

These are the common puzzles, or some of them, that a student of Aegean archaeology meets today. One can neither avoid them nor settle them. In ten more years many of them will be differently expressed, or clearer in implication. In a way we know less than we did before World War II; the rich new material which studs each year's excavation reports is not yet digested or co-ordinated. Lerna and Linear B and the new Grave Circle at Mycenae, Nea Nikomedia and Keos and Pylos, have precipitated a period of critical re-evaluation long before their results could be fully published. While this phase lasts, any effort to re-create a rational view of the tremendous long stretch of Aegean prehistory is inevitably personal and incomplete, like a novelist creating fiction from a private experience of impressions, memories, insights, or predisposition toward certain shapes in history. Any reconstruction which must be based on mute artifacts—palace design and painting and pots and foreign imports—invites a great play of mind over what is not included in the record. It cannot be astonishing that so few of the recent reconstructions agree in detail. Some authors have more experience in the field, some in philology; some believe more in myths and genealogies, some in stratification and the synchronisms of patterns on pots. Generally, all make the first copper tools and build Mycenae and destroy Troy at about the same time, learn about the horse and imitate the Minoans in the proper periods through reasonable channels. In offering a very selected arrangement of significances tempered by prejudice, one can only try to be reasonable.

The scope of this book is deliberately limited. It does not try to list in detail all the kinds of objects to be found on each site at each period. It has no room for major digressions into Linear B or Homer or the Near East. It tries only to give an impression of specific qualities in each phase of civilization on the Greek mainland between, roughly, 6500 and 1100 B.C., five and one-half millennia of tentative starts and achievements and disasters. The goal, hopeless to reach, would be a modernization of that great and lucid book of 1897, *The Mycenaean Age,* by Tsountas and Manatt. The Mycenaeans do not appear in the present title, although they occupy most of the text, because the term must be reserved for the latest phase of the Bronze Age, after 1600 B.C., and may be as misleading even for that slot of time as "The Athenians" would be for a book on Greek classical culture. There are local differences in style and inheritance all over the Aegean world which should not be hidden beneath a common label.

The original editorial decision to treat Minoans and Mycenaeans in separate volumes was a wise one. The two cultures used more often to be combined, and one of two things happened: the mainland peoples became rough tectonic imitators of a Crete delicately refined in art and cult, with few authoritative developments of their own apart from some architectural and military habits; or Crete became a refined and pastel brothel where the sturdy mainlanders found experience and sophistication which they put to more manly uses after destroying the corrupters of their adolescence. In separate books Greece and Crete may each enjoy its own qualities without disturbing comparisons of worth. The problem of how to separate efficiently two areas so linked in history and art is presently being handled as follows.

M. J. Mellink, author of the projected volume on the Minoans, will deal more extensively with the Near Eastern and Anatolian history and influences to which Crete responded. As closer to the mainland orbit, the early Cyclades are partially included in my volume. In the two phases of strongest attraction or hostility between Crete and the mainland, the Shaft Grave period at Mycenae and the Late Minoan II palace period at Knossos, we have each made an appreciation from more or less local, partisan points of view. In the three areas of strongest cultural intermingling—art, religion, and writing—we have deeded each other monuments which seem to originate in one place but are found in the other. For example, the Vapheio Cups are discussed by Miss Mellink as expressions of Minoan art, in this book only as examples of imported richness. Documents in religion and writing have been divided with more difficulty. In both fields the genesis and formal tradition are specifically Minoan for centuries, then adapted to varying degrees by Mycenaeans for special needs. Religion will be more emphasized in the Cretan volume, because it is more fully documented and understandable there in terms of physical survivals. Tomb rites (as opposed to shrines and cults) are described here because they are so conspicuous on the mainland. Religion in the Linear B tablets is touched upon as well. Bronze Age writing receives more space here than in the Cretan volume because only Linear B has been deciphered to general satisfaction so far, and its information concerns Mycenaean, not Minoan, activities. An initial desire on the part of the authors to interleave their books, or arrange them like two ends of a telephone with continuously open connection, was suppressed for practical reasons. We can only hope that each culture will be presented as independently and meaningfully as possible, without ignoring the strength or presence of the other.

Homer has been rejected as evidence, with a pang. He is every Mycenaean scholar's passion. All the other great ancient cultures have their quotable, instructive contemporary literature—Sumerians, Akkadians, Hittites, Canaanites, Egyptians, nearly everyone but the Minoans. From such texts in law, cult, folktale, and historical narrative a far sounder, more lively reconstruction of civilization can be made than for the Mycenaeans unfairly deprived of Homer. The danger comes when Homer gets more quoted for the Mycenaean world he never knew than historically contemporary texts for other cultures. Scarcely anyone can approach a Bronze Age tub without thinking of Telemachos' pleasant bath at Pylos, or a complex megaron system without seeing Odysseus hiding the suitors' weapons in the glow of Athena's lamp. This classical habit is so ingrained, it colors our view of hearths and food, chariots and rafts, embroidered robes and helmets, drinking cups and vineyards, besieged island cities and the gates of Troy. We say in justification that large parts of the poems incorporate Mycenaean traditions, that the five hundred years separating the fall of Troy VII A from the Homeric version of its fall have wrought only minor innovations, a few misunderstandings of the past and adaptations to more modern experience. We hope that the core of those great poems has not been terribly changed by successive improvisations of oral poets—surely poets will guard for us the heritage of the past. We are tempted to use whatever corresponds to our excavated knowledge or imagined re-creations; led ever backward, Homer is found apt for times as remote as the Shaft Graves, nearly a thousand years before the text we have. But if one thing is more certain than another in dealing with Greece, it is that every generation, let alone century or millennium, saw changes more profound than the simple classicist sometimes likes to acknowledge. It seems more honest, even refreshing, not to invoke Homer either as decoration or instruction.

In a work of this kind a thousand debts may be acknowledged with pleasure. Aegean experts who offered early training and later enlightenment should be listed at least in ideographs of gold, but as on a terse and broken Pylos tablet only a fractional tribute of gratitude is inscribed here. The following scholars have been wonderfully generous with their time, ideas, information, experience, and tours of their excavations: E. Akurgal, E. P. Blegen, J. L. Caskey, Sp.

INTRODUCTION

Iakovides, G. M. A. Hanfmann, W. S. Smith, and H. A. Thompson and E. Vanderpool, who first put me inside a Mycenaean tomb. Above all, the kindness of Sp. Marinatos calls for great grace of thanks; his teaching in the field on his excavations near Pylos and his stimulating interpretations of Aegean difficulties have been unforgettable. To three scholars who have nearly exhausted themselves offering courteous suggestions for improving this book, I can only offer appreciation: M. L. Lang for her instruction in Greek, English, Linear B, and the mysteries of the Pylos frescoes; M. J. Mellink for her wide-ranging scholarship and intelligent advice at every stage; C. C. Vermeule for his patience and lucidity. S. Chapman gave her time and skill for several drawings, J. McCredie took special photographs, M. Comstock neatened the manuscript, and Ch. C. Bey and M. Brenman contributed in ways they know best.

In conclusion, I should like to thank the following institutions, excavators, and scholars for their benevolence with photographs and their permission to reproduce illustrations: the Agora Excavations, Athens, and L. Talcott, H. A. Thompson; the Allard Pierson Museum, Amsterdam; the American School of Classical Studies; the Ashmolean Museum, Oxford, and J. Boardman, S. Benton; H. Biesantz; E. Borowski; the British Museum, London, and R. Higgins; the British School at Athens and J. M. Cook, M. S. F. Hood, W. Taylour, H. Wace; H. Cahn; the Danish National Museum, Copenhagen, and M.-L. Buhl; K. Deppert; the Deutsches Archäologisches Institut, Athens, and E. Kunze, J. Dörig; L'École Française d'Athènes, and G. Daux; A. Frantz; the Gennadeion Library, Athens, and F. Walton; Sp. Iakovides; H. Kantor; N. Kontoleon; Le Musée du Louvre and J. Charbonneaux; Sp. Marinatos; the Metropolitan Museum of Art; the Museum of Fine Arts, Boston, and W. S. Smith, C. C. Vermeule, S. Chapman, E. Moore; the National Museum, Athens, and S. Karouzou, B. Philippaki, O. Alexandri; the Nicosia Museum and V. Karageorghis; the late J. Papademetriou; E. Sjøqvist; the late J. Threpsiades; the University of Cincinnati, and J. Caskey, M. Rawson; the University Museum, Philadelphia, and G. Bass; N. Verdelis; N. Yalouris; C. Weickert; S. Weinberg.

August, 1962

Two Technical Notes

The quality of illustrations in this volume is uneven, principally because of the difficulty in obtaining recent photographs of material in the National Museum, Athens. There is also a certain amount of inconsistency in spelling, as in most books combining ancient and modern Greek names. Familiar place names like Attica, Corinth, and Crete are spelled traditionally, but modern sites are spelled as written now, e.g., Karditsa, Souphli. Place names deriving from saints are shown a little more formally than in demotic Greek, Hagia Eirene for Ayia Irini.

Because of the long, unavoidable delays of this volume, the bibliography has not always taken into account new material published in 1963. Perhaps the most important among the many books and articles which appeared too late to make proper use of are V. Desborough, *The Last Mycenaeans and Their Successors* (1964), J. Chadwick *et al.*, *The Mycenae Tablets III* (1963), L. Palmer's *Mycenaean Greek Texts* (1963), F. Matz's *The Art of Crete and Early Greece* (1963), and P. Ålin's *Das Ende der mykenischen Fundstätten auf dem griechischen Festland* (1962). The most important excavation results which are too new to be fully represented are probably those of N. Platon at the palace of Zakro in Crete, those of J. Caskey in the town and shrine of Hagia Eirene on Keos, the full study of the Pylos frescoes to be published by M. Lang, and the new treasures from the Mycenaean palace at Thebes.

CHRISTMAS 1963

Note to Second Printing

Since this was written, a number of excavations and publications have illuminated difficult Aegean problems and periods. Of special interest are: the Paleolithic rock shelter at Asprochaliko in Epeiros, which has yielded over 75,000 artifacts in 7 m. of stratified Middle and Upper Paleolithic habitation ending in 22,950 ± 1,100 B.C. (S. Dakaris, E. Higgs); the Neolithic finds from the Cycladic island of Saliagos (J. Evans, C. Renfrew) and the lake-filled caves of the Mani; the discovery of massive Early Helladic buildings at Thebes (N. Platon, E. Touloupa); a Middle Helladic shaft grave at Volimidia near Pylos (Sp. Marinatos); exploration of a Minoan colony on Kythera (G. Huxley); two spectacular treasures of gold and jewels in tholos tombs, at Peristeria in western Greece (Sp. Marinatos) and at Arkhanes near Knossos in Crete (I. Sakellarakis); continuing publication of the crucial late material at Knossos which may eventually clarify the date of its destruction (S. Hood, *Kadmos* 4 [1965] 16, M. Popham, *Studies in Mediterranean Archaeology* 5 [1964], *Antiquity* [1966] 24); many probes in isolated areas of Mycenaean Thebes which have yielded splendid frescoes, ivories, armor and chariot trappings, and chamber tombs (N. Platon, *ILN* 28 November 1964, 859 and 5 December 1964, 896; E. Touloupa, *Kadmos* 3 [1964] 25); the cylinder seals will shortly receive final publication by E. Porada; new fresco fragments from Zakro (N. Platon), Arkhanes (I. Sakellarakis), and Keos (J. Caskey); new tholos tombs in Aitolia (E. Mastrokostas); new rich chamber tombs, with gold rings near Iolkos (D. Theochares) and with wooden coffins in Athens (H. Thompson); and, at last, a site completely stratified from Early Helladic through Geometric with Dark Age continuity, at Leukandi in Euboia (M. Popham, H. Sackett).

Several important books have been published: L. Bernabo Brea, *Poliochni* (1964); P. Demargne, *The Birth of Greek Art* (1964); A. Sakellariou, *Corpus der minoischen und mykenischen Siegel* I (1964); F. Schachermeyr, *Die Minoische Kultur des alten Kreta* (1964); W. S. Smith, *Interconnections in the Ancient Near East* (1965), which pays special attention to Aegean art forms; W. Taylour, *The Mycenaeans* (1964). Among surveys and articles the most valuable may be: R. Ehrich (ed.), *Chronologies in Old World Archaeology* (1966); R. Hope Simpson, *A Gazetteer and Atlas of Mycenaean Sites* (*BICS* Supplement 16 [1965]); F. Stubbings, "The Expansion of Mycenaean Civilization," *CAH*² II, xxii (1964); K. Syriopoulos, Ἡ Προϊστορία τῆς Πελοποννήσου (1964); S. Weinberg, "The Stone Age in the Aegean," *CAH*² I, x (1965).

EASTER 1966

xiv

Contents

CONTENTS

CONTENTS

Illustrations

ILLUSTRATIONS

Chapter I

The Land

Greece is a land of many separate countries. They are often as alien to one another in scenery and gifts as they are locked apart by difficulties of terrain. Prehistoric men saw the same bony structure of the peninsula as we do now, although without the advantage of knowing what a map was or how the whole land looked in perspective (see Fig. 1). They made their adaptation to local conditions along much the same lines as their classical and modern descendants, and from the beginning differed among themselves as each district began to shape their habits uniquely. Greece has roughly twelve great natural divisions: Macedonia (northeast); Thessaly (north central); Epeiros (northwest); Phokis, Boiotia (central Greece); Attica, Megara, Saronic gulf (central coastal); Corinthia, Argolid, Troizen (eastern Peloponnesos); Lakonia, Messenia (southern and southwestern Peloponnesos); Arkadia (inland Peloponnesos); the Ionian islands and Achaia (west); the Cycladic and Sporadic islands (cen-

Greece
in the Stone Age

tral); the Dodekanese (southeast Aegean); and the Anatolian islands (northeast Aegean). These areas are defined by immovable geographic barriers like mountain masses and rough open water.

Although communication between some areas is easy (the Argive plain to Lakonia by land, Attica to the Cyclades by sea), they have as a general rule such different qualities of weather, earth, pasture and timber land, mineral deposits, and accessibility that they form natural units which could only be joined with great trouble or political adroitness. The physical basis for Greek sectional politics has been explained by many able observers; and yet there is a tendency to believe this applies only to classical history and that prehistoric Greece was a land of simultaneous and harmonious experiences. In fact, it offers an even more diverse picture than classical or early modern Greece.

Prehistoric Greece has never been considered one of the "fertile nuclei" which

Fig. 1.—Neolithic and Early Helladic Greece

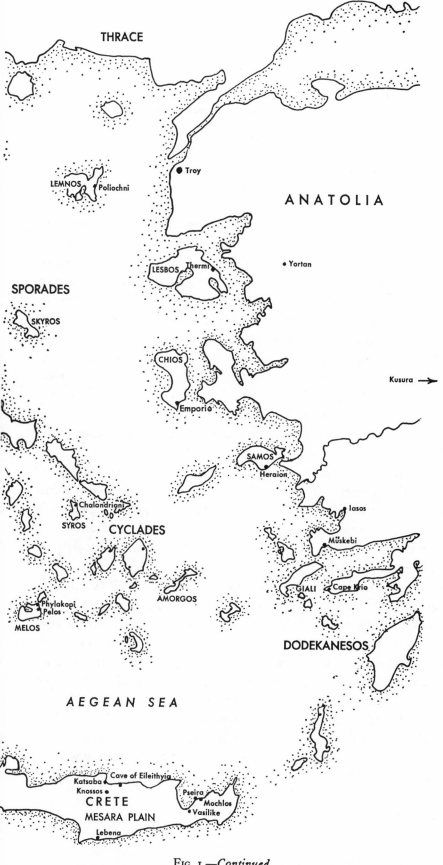

THRACE

● Troy

ANATOLIA

LEMNOS ● Poliochni

LESBOS ● Thermi ● Yortan

SPORADES

SKYROS

CHIOS

Kusura →

● Emporio

SAMOS

● Heraion

● Iasos

Chalandriani ●

SYROS

CYCLADES

● Müskebi

AMORGOS

GIALI ● Cape Krio

Phylakopi ●
Pelos

MELOS

DODEKANESOS

AEGEAN SEA

Cave of Eileithyia

Katsaba

Knossos ●

CRETE

Pseira

Mochlos

Vasilike

MESARA PLAIN

Lebena

Fig. I.—*Continued*

helped man down out of the trees in Africa or supported his earliest attempts at community life in the Near East. It is not benign enough. Although it is a healthy place for the hardy, one needs agricultural experience to subsist there and find out what will grow best in the narrow twists of fertile land or which animals can be fattened on the mountainside scrub. The first attempts to live in Greece were made in relatively open, watered country to the northeast where there were forests, cold winters, and grazing land. Central Greece and the plains areas of the Peloponnesos also attracted hunters and, later, farmers who traveled overland or sailed in from the east. Penetration was slow because the deep soil and large rivers of southern Greece are counterbalanced by a lack of really good harbors and by high mountain barriers. Attica had a tendency to thin soil and summer drought; her settlers needed to be sailors, like settlers in the islands which were rich in minerals but generally washed bare of soil. Arkadia was too high and cold for intensive cultivation except under extreme pressure. The northwest coastline was isolated from the rest of Greece by the mountains behind it. Even now it is not well understood as a prehistoric center, for, unlike the rest of Greece, it looked toward the west and Europe. The eastern islands within view of Anatolia linked themselves more naturally to her culture than to developments in Greece. In many periods they were alien to the mainland.

Across these differences in landscape and position plays a great range of climate, from the severities of central Europe to the aridities of the North African coast, and from snowy wooded heights to hot, dry plains. The sea is usually in sight from any peak, the rainfall adequate if not exuberant in autumn and winter, the winds constant though fluky, prevailing westerly or northeasterly according to the calendar.

The basic crops of the prehistoric age were hardy and rather dull (see Appendix I): wheat and barley, beans and peas, figs and pears. Knowledge of how to grow grapes and olives was brought in by progressive farmers from the east. Certain common domestic animals adapted well: goats and sheep, and pigs in oak-forested districts. Cows were rarer because they needed open grazing land. Horses were a late and expensive innovation at the start of the Mycenaean age; the famous breeding regions were Boiotia, the Argolid, and Lakonia, although Thessalian horses and Messenian horsemen also had a certain reputation. Of all these animals the goat lived best, nourishing himself by destroying the young growth in the woods. The first charcoal fire under the first goat stew was the beginning of Greek deforestation which, though often exaggerated in the imagery of intense old ladies, proceeded fast enough to assure us that prehistoric Greece was richer in timber and poorer in cleared land than fifth-century Greece. The forest meant good game to hunt, and the early Greeks were skilled hunters who, in their paintings, sometimes illustrated themselves in pursuit of red and fallow deer, wild boar, hare, and birds. From the start of Greek civilization, the "weapons" of archaeology were more often turned against beasts than human enemies. Hooks, nets, and fishbones testify to skill at the waterside too.

Greece was usually entered in antiquity through one of three gates: by land from the northeast to Macedonia and the Thessalian plains; by sea from the east to the good ports of the Cycladic islands, the Gulf of Pagasai, or the Saronic and Argive gulfs; much more rarely by sea from the west to certain outposts on the Ionian islands. The land route was probably used earlier, but sailors from the east were not far behind.

Before the First Villages

The oldest man we know of in Greece was Neanderthal. He is represented by a single broken skull, turned fossil, found in a seaside cave in northeast Greece in 1961. This skull, and some Palaeolithic bones found in Thessaly in 1958, push back the history of Greece by sixty or seventy thousand years. It had long been thought that Greece was one of the latest parts of the old Mediterranean world to be entered and, in fact, was not settled before developed Neolithic times. These relics demonstrate how ignorant we still are of the high antiquity of civilization on the mainland. There is no trace yet of the extensive kind of Neanderthal culture known through much of Europe and in Anatolia, Palestine, and Iran, but certainly wanderers were beginning to penetrate the country by Middle Palaeolithic times, probably before 70,000 B.C. Their industrial arts are best seen at Pantanassa in Epeiros; more central staying places may still be found. The extinct cave hyena was one of their neighbors and other wild game was rich.

In the next phase of the Stone Age, the Upper Palaeolithic, wanderers came farther down into Greece, reaching the Thessalian and Boiotian plains where great rivers and inland lakes among the grasslands were to encourage every succeeding attempt at settling the country. Some even went into the hillier Argolid or the coastal plain of Elis. Stone tools of hunters following prehistoric game trails have been found at over twenty sites along the banks of the Peneios river in Thessaly and in a cave at the edge of Lake Kopaïs in Boiotia. There are red flint blades from near Olympia and dull black ones from the Argolid promontory, thus bracketing the Peloponnesos. The fossilized bones of the kill lie mixed with the flints, but the human skeletons themselves are elusive. These finds are still quite new and have not been co-ordinated with better-known patterns elsewhere, yet it is clear that the newcomers had the same level of stone-chipping industry as the Levalloiso-Mousterian and Aurignacian phases of Europe. Apparently they withdrew in the face of a climatic change, which flooded some of the hollow valleys of Thessaly and which may have affected the wildlife of the Peloponnesos too seriously for continued hunting.

The connections of these pioneers were probably with Balkan Europe rather than with the East. There is no direct link between them and later Greeks; their traces are buried under layers of sterile flood-clay as deep as five meters,* or found in caves which were rarely occupied later. In the sparse evidence for the Mesolithic Age which follows we see a similar European orientation but more attraction to the sea. There are flint factories on the beaches of the western islands, Kephallenia and Zakynthos, and in the Aegean proper at Skyros, which means that rafts were crossing open water from still-undiscovered mainland sites probably before 10,000 B.C. Such camps suggest a more settled and purposeful way of life. More of this material will probably be found within the next decade, and its significance for Greece will grow clearer. At the moment, these first three phases of Stone Age culture look tentative on the mainland, the traces of splinter groups from more intensively populated regions. Greece was not less fertile for the settlers' purposes than other Mediterranean countries, but there was little pressure on men or animals to move very far into its mountains.

Neolithic: The First Villages

The Neolithic settlers of Greece played a tremendous role in developing the country's potential wealth and stamping a character upon its culture which, in some pockets, probably has not died out yet. They cannot be thought of as a united group, or even as sole proprietors of a cleanly defined segment of centuries. In some places the cultural habits of the Stone Age continued well into Middle Bronze, and the people themselves, particularly of the northern villages, surely survived as a stock even after they learned the uses of bronze or iron

---

* All measurements in this book are given in meters. One meter equals 39.37 inches.

tools. Only since 1958 have discoveries demonstrated how old Neolithic peoples really are in Greece and how various the skills they brought with them.

The oldest village we know is Nea Nikomedia in Macedonia. A radiocarbon-14 date has been obtained from three samples there, suggesting that pottery was already in use by 6218 ± 150 B.C.[1] That a farming village should have been organized in Greece before the end of the seventh millennium is something of a surprise—by two thousand years—but it brings Greece into line with the even more spectacular discoveries in Anatolia, where towns of some elegance were flourishing at Hacilar and Çatal Hüyük by 5600 B.C. Cyprus, too, had its Khirokitia, a town of perhaps one thousand houses and a people ignorant of pottery, by 5500 B.C. Farther east, the disturbing antiquity of Jericho in the eighth millennium has long been familiar. The limestone spines and difficult valleys of lower Greece kept Neolithic pioneers out of the south for some time. The first date for a village in central Greece is 5520 ± 70 at Elateia (Drach-mani), and in the Peloponnesos settled civilization seems to begin about the same time. It is no accident that those who settled first did so in the territory where the Palaeolithic hunters had been most successful: Macedonia, Thessaly, and Boiotia.

Nea Nikomedia is a low mound on the plain between the Haliakmon and Axios (Vardar) rivers. This is now the richest part of Macedonia, irrigated for fruit orchards and grain fields, but in those days the new settlers lived surrounded by Mediterranean "maquis," a ground cover of evergreen oak and scrub pine. The whole region had once been sea, but then silted and tilted to form a brackish inland lake. The first houses were built about one hundred meters above sea level on the lake shore.

The Early Neolithic Age at Nea Nikomedia is a long one, a period of unbroken development. It is too soon to generalize about the village as an entity. The architecture is almost entirely gone, but traces of it are being recovered by experimental archaeological techniques: the mound is scraped in very shallow layers, and the discolorations in the earth which appear are drawn on a master plan. The outlines of houses, hearths, pits, postholes, and graves are recovered in this way, and the phases of remodeling and rebuilding become clear as the village changes.

Several houses of large size are surrounded by a wooden palisade. The houses are crooked; they have rectangular or curved irregular walls. These walls are constructed by sinking posts in the ground, slapping mud around and between them, and covering the outside with wattle. One house even has a veranda. The roofing system cannot be reconstructed, but by analogy with other Early Neolithic sites one imagines thin round poles, made of saplings, covered with clay and brush. The floors in the early phases are beaten earth; later they are thick unpainted plaster set on a bed of pebbles. The hearths are built up of mud in a circular form. Outdoors the villagers dug large storage pits and rubbish holes. As time passed they learned to build ovens, high cylindrical structures, a sure sign that they harvested regular grain crops and converted them to bread.

These seventh-millennium farmers knew both barley and wheat, and kept sheep and goats like their contemporaries in Anatolia. They ate pig and a small kind of bull too, though the animals may have been wild game still, not domesticated. From their lake came fish and shells (the cardium shell so popular for Neolithic ornament); their fishhooks are small curved bone splinters. Hare and birds supplemented the diet. Fruit trees, either apple or pear, and poplar trees grew nearby. There may have been dogs trained to hunt and guard the food animals; one early canine skeleton is known from Thessaly, and another from southwest Anatolia.

Nea Nikomedia has pottery and tools from its very beginning. There is no pre-pottery phase. Pre-pottery civilizations have been found at one or two points in Thessaly; a similar stage of Neolithic is represented at eastern sites like Hacilar, Khirokitia, and Jericho, both before and after Nea Nikomedia according to radiocarbon-14 dating. Perhaps the conflicting dates may be reconciled soon. On the face of it, the Nea Nikomedia villagers had already passed through the painful stage of the Neolithic revolution before they reached Macedonia.

Four fabrics of pottery are made in Nea Nikomedia:[2] plain burnished wares in red, gray, brown, and black; coarse brown wares impressed with fingernail patterns; off-white pottery painted with red in geometric patterns like the famed pottery of Neolithic Thessaly; and white designs painted on a red ground which resemble certain products of the Balkans. These classes are all contemporary. The vases themselves range from very large and impressive storage jars to miniatures, which must have been toys or votives, in such shapes as frying pans or four-legged altars. The common shapes are bowls whose rims curve slightly inward, flat dishes with shallow ring bases, and tall bowls with lugs instead of handles. On occasion a playful spirit among the potters expresses itself by modeling human faces or animal heads upon the greater pots. The faces are flat and moonlike, the eyes are slit across the center, the lips are thin ridges, and a stringy beard conceals the chin.

Two other kinds of clay productions are important: stamp seals and idols. The seals, also called *pintaderas,* have a short clay handle and a round or oval base on which patterns of a simple geometric nature are incised. The idols or figurines are made both in clay and in soft stones like steatite or greenstone. Like 99 per cent of all Neolithic idols they represent plumply fertile women; they have long heads, sharp noses, slit eyes like coffee beans, prominent bellies and buttocks. They are not so beautiful at Nea Nikomedia as at Hacilar in Anatolia, but the larger ones are of excellent quality and are unmistakable signs of active religion and art.

In stonework Nea Nikomedia is not very different from its peers. Tools are made by chipping flint or chert; there is no obsidian in this part of the country and none is imported from distant volcanic regions yet. There are various types of cutting blades: beautifully polished greenstone celts and adzes, chisels and grinders, and sickles made by setting small flints at angles along the axis of a horn. Awls and needles for sewing clothes are fashioned by sharpening the leg bones of sheep or goats and hardening them in the fire. The villagers must have defended themselves and killed their game from close at hand with stone weapons or slingshots; there are no bows and arrows yet.

Finally, the people. They buried their dead in the pits outside their houses, sometimes jumbling them in a tangled pile of bones or crowding three children in together. In one storage pit outside a principal house they buried an adult woman lying on her side in the foetal position, with two children in her arms. The skeleton makes an uneasy impression (Pl. I). It is because her back is badly broken, and this apparently happened before she died. If she is typical of the villagers, they were fairly tall and had long skulls, fine features, and splendid teeth.

THE SEQUENCE IN THESSALY

In the Thessalian plains near Larissa, and just inland from the Gulf of Pagasai by later Iolkos, rises a great series of Neolithic mounds (*magoules* or *toumbes*) whose most famous members are Sesklo and Dimeni. This is well-watered country, historically excellent for raising grass-eating animals, and at sites like Sesklo or the more newly explored magoules—Gremnos, Otzaki, and Souphli —the record of prosperous habitation goes deep. The oldest known Neolithic civilization in Greece used to be called "Sesklo," characterized by capacious houses and stiffly geometric red-on-cream vases of high technical quality. Now as many as four earlier phases in Neolithic life have been distinguished, at some lag after the Mesolithic small-flake culture which is so scantily known in Greece. The Thessalian expert Miløjčič calls these phases Pre-pottery, Early Pottery, Proto-Sesklo, and Pre-Sesklo, and has arranged a careful sequence of pottery to characterize each one (see Appendix II).

The pre-pottery level is nearly one meter deep at Gremnos, suggesting at least several centuries of what looks like an important, developed agricultural society with all its household utensils of stone, gourd, basket, or leather. Obsidian (hard volcanic glass) is used for the first time as a cutting tool. The typical house is square or rectangular, with rows of postholes and a brushwood roof as at Nea Nikomedia; the farmers have storage pits and hearths and an effective range of stone tools. Their huts were burned. Above them lies the first

Fig. 2.—Neolithic pot fragment with a painted human(?) figure. Otzaki Magoula. (After Miløjčič, *NDA* 229, Fig. 2.)

pottery-using level with red-burnished simple bowls or an ornamental red-on-white ware. Among the fragments is the first "painting" of the human form in Greece—it looks like a demonic kangaroo in an apron (Fig. 2). Stone vases in white marble or red porphyry continue along with the new clay ones. There are clay stamps here too, one with a leaf pattern.[3] Houses are built of mud-brick for the first time, though the old post-and-mud style persists too. There follow, according to Miløjčič (the system seems rather refined), three phases almost without painted pottery, but with plenty of polished or impressed sherds. Then, without any real break, the Neolithic world of Thessaly emerges into the classic Sesklo phase. The time may be about 4800 B.C.

Sesklo and Neolithic A

These successive layers of deposit preceding Sesklo speak eloquently of how slow generations were to change and experiment in the Stone Age. Although depth of earth has no scientific relation to lapse of time, it is generally true that debris accumulated more rapidly in Neolithic houses than in later, neater cultures. There is more significance to these depths of experiment and development than simple carelessness in throwing bones and fruit rinds on the house floor. Sesklo itself has three meters for its early phase (Neolithic A); Elateia in Phokis has over three stratified meters in which the long, slow development of red-on-white painted pottery can be watched growing and yielding to black-polished and polychrome. Lerna in the Argolid has 3.00 m. and 13 building levels for all Neolithic; Eutresis, Orchomenos, probably Tiryns, show similar depths. Even the most "primitive" achievements of early Neolithic were of course the fruit of centuries, even millennia, of discarded technologies, and by the Sesklo period one can say of these people that whatever they did, they did extraordinarily well by contemporary standards. They were efficient pioneers from a competent, ingenious, and experienced stock, well-developed socially and technically, with a strong aesthetic flair and a religious tradition. Now, after the long genesis, two things impress us about them: how quickly they learned modern methods and new styles from one another, and how locally distinctive in quality of production they still remained. The art of Sesklo can be distinguished even by novices from contemporary work in the Spercheios valley (Lianokladi), in Boiotia (Chaironea), in the Peloponnesos (Corinth and Lerna); yet they were all in roughly the same phase of social development, for which we can continue to take Sesklo as typical (see Fig. 51).

The houses are closely grouped. A single village rarely exceeds twenty houses and the population was probably not more than one hundred and fifty. Each house is independent: a single square or oblong room or perhaps two or three rooms set together without much concern for straight lines (Fig. 52 *a*). These rooms may be as small as modern closets, or, in the next phase, as grand as eight meters square. Foundations are made of small stones from the fields; walls are either of river reeds and clay made waterproof, or mud-brick roughly shaped with stone and wooden tools. Roofs are usually reeds laid while still green and leafy on a bed of clay, rising to a little gable. The floor surface is often renewed without signifying any cultural break. Most houses have fixed hearths, in the center floor or against one wall, for roasting cuts of meat from domestic animals or making quick cakes like tortillas; out in the courtyards domed ovens are for baking loaves of bread, and probably pots too, since there are no separate kilns.

Food was rich in variety though probably hard to get enough of. The Sesklo peoples had wheat, barley, millet, peas, bitter vetch, almonds, figs, pears, and acorns. Wild vines and olives grew in the country around, and we may assume there were wild boar, deer, wolves, and perhaps lions in the hills. But these were not primarily hunting people; they were shepherds and farmers, fishers and sailors by the sea, fruitgrowers and industrialists at lakesides. Their tools were chipped stone and sharpened bone as before, but obsidian was increasingly familiar—the local flint was less hard grained and efficient.

One cannot take this spread of obsidian lightly, because it implies not only technology but trade. However common obsidian may seem on Neolithic sites, it is a truism in Aegean archaeology that the best grade of this volcanic glass comes from the Cycladic island of Melos and must be brought over great distances to the mainland by ship. There are also small deposits of less fine quality on Giali (it is pale and recognizable) and other islands and at several points in Anatolia and Cyprus. Probably the old volcanoes around the Gulf of Pagasai yielded some veins much nearer to Sesklo, but the deposits have not been found yet. The labor of building rafts or log ships with stone tools, and the danger that accompanied the acquisition of sea knowledge and astronomy on these waters, enlighten us further about Neolithic character. Ships mean woodworking skills, navigational techniques, commercial instincts; obsidian means knowledge of extracting the nuclei. If the islands were already settled, satisfactory arrangements had to be made with the islanders who would use the glass as a form of wealth against whatever the mainlanders could offer: something untraceable like food, slaves, or immunity from raids. If, as we now believe, the islands were empty until almost the end of the Thessalian Neolithic Age, it still means that long sailing voyages had to be organized and the crew put to work in the mines to bring back lumps of the material. The finished blades would be flaked back home. The Cretans and the mainlanders may have met each other for the first time on these island expeditions. We cannot view any Stone Age community as primitive when it is organized to the degree of arranging these exchanges or hazardous expeditions, and preferring their difficulties to using poor local flint.

This active, experimental character seems as typical of the contemporary Neolithic settlers in the south as of their more artistic counterparts in the north.[4] Discounting local differences and continuing to use Sesklo as a model site, one can develop from small clues an extraordinarily vivid image of Neolithic A culture. Inside the mud-plastered houses the main colors would come from woven textiles and painted vases. There would be beds of piled skin or brush, perhaps raised from the damp on benches of clay or stones. By day these beds or chipped stumps would serve as seats; by night the whole family would retire to sleep in the same room, calling in the more valuable animals especially if they were pregnant, warmed by glowing charcoal or dung on the hearth. As in all Greek village life for the next seven thousand years the outdoor court or street was a principal part of the home. The village itself was so small that it was essentially a family unit, perhaps conceiving of itself as a *genos* with traits distinct from other villages even though its social relationships and blood links were not formally analyzed by any code. It controlled and apportioned neighboring fields and sources of fresh water. It maintained casual contact with other villages in the district but made no attempt to organize into larger groupings. It was independent, apparently, in terms of politics, agriculture, and the normal needs of social behavior.

To them, a stranger's origin would immediately announce itself through small signs like clothing and dialect. To us, ignorant after the passing of millennia, pottery must perform this function of distinguishing one Neolithic group from another. In the plain setting of a Sesklo house the painted vases would stand out brightly, their strong color and clear shape the first thing noticed by visitors. The pride of Sesklo and of all contemporary red-on-white painting villages is this highly finished and technically superb ware which develops gradually from the simplest stiff step-designs to controlled flames, stepped pyramids, and filled diamond lozenges (Fig. 51). At Sesklo flames and triangles are favored, at other sites checkerboards (Tsani) or curved spikes (Tsangli); there are many subtle variations from mound to mound. Shapes are never fancy, but are more clearly articulated than the simple rounded bowls of earlier periods: cups sprout handles, bowls have low flaring bases, there are four-legged braziers or altars, and elegant collared jars. Storage and household pieces reach great size. This pottery is historically informative as well as aesthetically pleasing. It confirms the high artistic level of this oldest stratum in Greek population, it suggests racial affinities with the Near East, and it speaks of a social organization which was complex enough to assign specialized tasks through the village and secure enough to associate with other quite distant village units during visits, trading parties, and festivals (see Appendix II).

The family likeness of vases from any particular mound suggests that a master potter or traditional potting family worked in each village who shaped local taste in fine wares and so contributed to the "identity" of the group.

The women would make some coarse pots for their household and, perhaps, toys for their children. If potters were professional, we may guess that carpenters, weapon makers, basket weavers, and probably weavers of textiles were also partly specialists; again, each village would have its own peculiar style, different only in scale from the "styles" of classical cities. In some places these traits even survived the disruption caused by newcomers—the second Neolithic group called Dimeni after its type-site near Sesklo—and contributed directly to the culture of the Bronze Age imposed upon them.

Dimeni and Neolithic B

Dimeni mound, neighbor to Sesklo, represents a disruptive event in Neolithic history. After the long promising developments seen in Sesklo, new people invaded the eastern valleys of Thessaly; some of the established villages, which had never fortified themselves, were burned, and many were overlaid by a characteristically alien though connected culture. This may have been early in the fourth millennium B.C. In many ways the Dimeni people are less advanced than their Sesklo predecessors. Defensive, suspicious, ambitious but careless in art and architecture, they certainly possessed some military or political authority which gave them the entrée on the coastal side of the plain. That authority probably was given by their new long-range weapon, the bow. A flying arrow is a terrible thing to people who have always fought with knives or slings.

The newcomers' typical pots are less well made than before but impressively rich in decoration (see Fig. 51). They use complex meanders, checkerboards, pyramids, or isolated spirals jammed into a geometric background, all painted in brown or black on a golden buff ground. More rarely and later, there is a fascinating three-color technique in which angular or spiraling designs are drawn in thin ribbons of red or white, edged with fine black lines, on a red or cream ground. There may be playful faces and fancy handles on their plain gray wares, as on those of the early Trojans. The most acclaimed novelties of this culture have been found only at the type-site Dimeni: a fortification wall five or six rings deep and a long rectangular kind of house which is often taken as the ancestor of Mycenaean megaron architecture (Figs. 3, 52 b).

The Dimeni people were not numerous, but they were apparently mobile and compactly organized. It is not known where they came from.[5] They entered Thessaly from the open plains of eastern Macedonia and Thrace. They may have come around by the land bridge from Anatolia or the Caucasus, or down from the north along the Axios (Vardar) river valley. The strong feel-ings which have accompanied past analyses of this problem seem partly senti-mental. The Dimeni stock was more influential for northern Greece than the Early Bronze Age settlers in their brilliant interlude in the south, and some aspects of the subsequent Middle Bronze Age seem like throwbacks to the Dimeni period. Because the Middle Bronze Age is widely accepted as the first truly Greek phase of culture in Greece, many scholars have tried to discover whether this earlier wave, perhaps a less enduring penetration by the same stock, was ultimately "European" or "Asiatic." In terms of Neolithic economy, such issues of race and culture are not quite relevant. All Europe, the Near East, and Africa were populated by small, varied groups of Neolithic farmers whose powers and particular habits seldom extended beyond some geograph-ical pocket of fertile land. These groups kept pushing, receding from, or by-passing one another; borrowing new ideas, imposing their own systems, or staying dumbly out of touch. By the beginning of the Bronze Age, as it moved jerkily from the Near East to Britain, there are so many layered mixtures of cultural traits that one could scarcely find a family of "pure culture" for three thousand miles in any direction. Certainly in Greece the physical racial types were mixed from the beginning.

"Dimeni" is really a shorthand label for expressing a variety of changes in Late Neolithic Greece which must have resulted from a very fluid historical situation in which many groups of Neolithic farmers moved on from their own homelands—responding to external pressure or having exhausted the land —and found Greece a pleasant, thinly settled place to camp in. The pots of different settlements in this period are scarcely more alike than in the pre-ceding Sesklo phase, suggesting that the newcomers had had corresponding differences of experience and development en route, and perhaps even spoke different dialects. Again, so few skeletons of the period have been discovered that it is not possible to analyze the newcomers physically with adequate statis-tics, but preliminary studies point to their distinctiveness. The change is not limited to Thessaly; Athens, Corinth, Lerna, and other southern villages also experience a change of life and physiognomy.

The links of the Dimeni culture are both with Anatolia (the long megaron, the walled village, the animal handles, the fruit bowl, the spiral ornament so typical of the Early Bronze peoples who are shortly to occupy Troy and the Cyclades) and with groups of European Neolithic farmers who use the so-called *Bandkeramik,* disjointed geometric patterns including spirals. The Balkan parallels with Dimeni range all the way from Yugoslavia (the Starčevo-Körös culture) across toward South Russia (the Tripolye and Maikop [Kuban] cultures). Fine Neolithic figurines looking like Aegean ones occur at both ends of this diffusion. There are some independent links between Caucasia and the Near East, and between Hungary and west Greece, which have nothing to do with Dimeni; we must visualize intermediaries and trade attractions we know nothing about yet. Obviously, the Dimeni people did not move very fast across Thrace or directly from their original homeland. They had neither carts nor draft animals, and they probably stopped to harvest crops every year. This is why their predecessors are already in some ways more advanced, for they had been steadily settled and in contact with other organized centers. There was plenty of opportunity on this long migration for slow diffusion of aesthetics and technologies, and for tribal mingling, before some of the immigrants turned down toward the Gulf of Pagasai and others split off toward Europe proper.

Dimeni mound has been aptly described by Hood as looking "very much like a large sheepfold." An impressive series of low concentric ring walls rises on the mound sides to enclose a beaten dirt crown no more than 15 m. long (Fig. 3). The walls were not all built at once; at first the three inner ones sufficed, then there was some crisis and the outer walls were added rather hastily. This "fortified town" is not so dramatic a creation as it may look on the finished plan. The broad stone walls had brick tops, perhaps only high enough to provide cover for archers or to keep animals from jumping out.

Within these walls, the main house at Dimeni occupies the rear of the open crown; around the inside walls are sheds or porches for animals and storage, probably dependencies of the principal building. There are traces of smaller houses outside the walls, but it looks as though Dimeni was architecturally organized around one ruling family or village headman. There may have been a single open-air altar in the center of the plateau before the main house for community ceremonies. The houses are little improvement over earlier Neolithic types; small field stones are set in mud, with stone-pebble thresholds, floors at different levels, and slender posts to support the roofs or the projecting porches. Some walls are curved, as they will be later in Middle Helladic "apsidal" buildings, to fit into the round of the village wall. The megaron at Dimeni is not so impressive as that of the corresponding period at Sesklo, in which the main room is 8.50 by 8.25 m., larger than many modern living rooms.

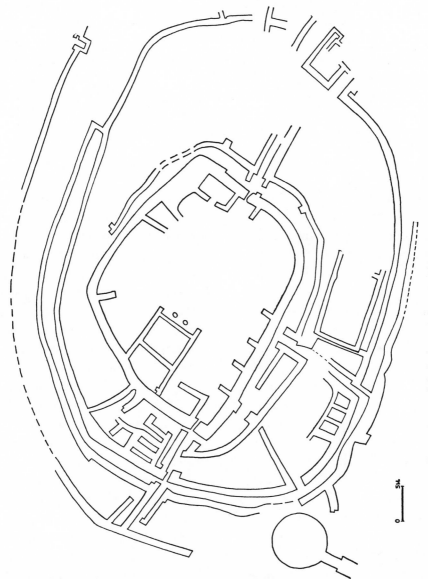

Fig. 3.—Simplified plan of Dimeni. (After Tsountas, *D–S*, Pl. 2.)

The late period introduces experiments in architecture everywhere, and it would certainly be incorrect to claim its diversity as foreshadowing the famous Mycenaean megaron (that word itself means no more than chamber, covered space, house, the big house). Dimeni did not necessarily predict Mycenae; it is simply an interesting, small northern village with solid, intelligent architecture, perhaps overrated in significance because we have so few other completely excavated sites for comparison and illumination. Dimeni represents, for historical purposes, a major shock to the earlier Neolithic civilization, which is transformed and will, in a few centuries, disappear from Greece altogether.

Neolithic Civilization

Language

Two fundamental Neolithic contributions to the formation of Greek culture lie in spheres of uncertain knowledge: language and religion. A third, the contribution of physical racial stock to the ultimate Greek population, is also hard to diagnose accurately because no large groups of intact Neolithic graves have been found (see Pl. I), although Angel's work has shown with fascinating clarity how mixed the Neolithic peoples were by the end of their tenure in Greece.[6] In these three areas we are deprived of the classic modes of description which a Greek anthropologist like Herodotos would have applied to foreign peoples: what they spoke, whom they worshiped, and what they looked like. Of the three, the language is the hardest to recover, and yet there do exist archaeological techniques for making informed guesses about lost ancient tongues which should be considered briefly, because the language problem grows increasingly acute as Greek history progresses in complication.

When a group of human beings which flourished seven thousand years ago and was grossly illiterate is absorbed in succeeding waves of settlers so completely as to leave practically no characteristic sign, deducing its dialect is the most sophisticated kind of parlor game. In general, one tries to isolate alien elements in the final tongue of the nation and see if these can be attributed sensibly to one or more earlier layers of culture. Such alien survivals normally include the names of landscape features, tribes, plants and animals, and gods. Later comers found these things in the land and took over their titles without worrying deeply about what they meant. This happened in Greek with many antique words, such as *olympos* for mountain and *argos* for dog, which survived without recognized meaning through a number of population changes to become imbedded in the final Greek language. If scholars can decide which layer of population contributed them, and what class of original language they represent, they have a preliminary basis for analyzing the nature of the lost language.

In the case of Thessalian Neolithic we know only this: many families arrived by sea from the east and by land from the north, and their cultural affinities (this is guesswork based on pottery styles) were with Anatolia and the northern Levant in the earlier stages, with Anatolia and the Balkans in the later stages. These families held the land first and longest of any group in Greece. Their language, tempered by local dialect, was widespread and had an excellent chance for survival in isolated places which were not overrun by later invaders. Even in classical times the Greeks were aware of alien groups in their midst who spoke an old language, or languages (Herodotos grouped these rather uncritically under the label *Pelasgian*). These Pelasgian languages are not all alike, and either reflect very antique mixtures with other things or represent two or three different pre-Greek languages.

Historically the name *Pelasgiotis,* or country of the Pelasgians, belongs only to the region of Thessaly bounded roughly by Sesklo on the east and the Peneios valley mounds on the west (Fig. 1). Regions of this country stayed Neolithic until the Middle Bronze Age, and even then contributed a markedly provincial color to the local civilization. It was not broadly settled by the peoples of Early Bronze with their influential language, so that chances of Neolithic vocabulary survivals are better in Thessaly than anywhere else. Another point of interest is that the oldest cult center in Greece specifically linked to the Pelasgians, Dodona in Epeiros, possessed a primitive prophetic ritual to which the Greek Zeus was definitely a late intruder and which struck even the most liberal Greeks as blindly archaic. But the Pelasgians have been the hottest subject in linguistic detective work for one hundred years and have been forced to many purposes of which they would not have approved. It is no longer fashionable to discuss them as a soluble problem.[7]

Religion

The nature of Greek Neolithic religion is much clearer. It was of a type absolutely characteristic of Neolithic cultures all over the European-Mediterranean world, expressing itself primarily through female idols, secondarily in the use of caves. The idols of Sesklo are usually clay, built up of small pellets or separate limbs pinned together, and modeled with free originality. More precious ones may be cut and polished from large attractive pebbles: serpentine, greenstone, marble, limestone (Pl. II A). Like obsidian, marble usually comes from the Cyclades and is rare and late on the mainland. As the Neolithic period grows old and is mixed with other elements, we see two trends: a complication in form and decoration, and a decline in quality. The beautiful series of figurines from Anatolian Hacilar has shown us how splendid the earliest Neolithic creations can be. Sesklo does not reach that standard, but the earliest and best examples preserve for us an antique and enduring trait in mainland attitudes toward divinity—a loving endowment of the god with the happiest and most elegant features of man. The Sesklo figurines are normally of the wellknown steatopygous "mother goddess" type which implies, with its emphasis on fleshily swollen belly and buttocks, a poignant envy and hope directed toward a divinity who has always enough to eat. This goddess, who can offer thick crops, a full belly, and a line of working children if she wishes, is modeled in various ways: usually a long oval head and neck, prominent rich breasts, slender shoulders and legs, emphatic pubic triangle, arms pressed to the breast or folded across the womb. She may stand with her toes turned out (Pl. II D) or sit with drawn-up legs (Pl. II A); she may wear her hair knotted short or in long ringlets or a tied braid; she may have a necklace (Pl. II C) or be lightly tattooed like her living models. In later Neolithic phases, the figurines are more elaborately striped with paint and the forms more adventurous, as when the goddess cradles a child in her arms. A few male figures appear which are no more representative than the women, with their sketchy faces and standard gestures. They, too, are usually naked, sometimes ithyphallic; some wear a little conical cap. We cannot be sure whether these male idols reflect a change in religious emphasis, showing the young consort of the mother so familiar in later Aegean religion, or whether they are merely sculptural experiments to relieve the tedium of the eternal female through other life studies.[8]

The Late Neolithic period also created more clay animals and model altars and thrones. Probably more of the "late" rare types were made in Early Neolithic, too, since the Hacilar figurines include a boy held tenderly during intercourse with a woman three times his size, a goddess seated on leopards, and brilliant studies of boar and deer—all before 5400 B.C. A fine marble youth of island type has been discovered in an Early Neolithic stratum at Knossos. The fundamental conceptions are modified but not altered by the incoming peoples of Late Neolithic. Consider two standard types of figurines and two very queer variations (Pl. II A–D). The standard ones are quite beautiful: a little green amulet from Malthi in west Greece, with the goddess' plump legs drawn up under her chin (Pl. II A); and a terracotta figure from Lerna in the Argolid of slim proportions and suggestive elegance (Pl. II D). No one could call the variations beautiful, but they are unforgettable. The first is really a vessel (Pl. II B), made in the shape of a woman's lower body and mounted on four stumpy legs, geometrically ornamented and crusted. The clay is polished to rich black, the incised legs are filled with deep red, and the interior is washed white with red bands. This is Middle Neolithic from Elateia in Phokis, contemporary with Sesklo, and it represents a class of idol vases known also through the Balkans, cult vessels connected with female worship or water. The second monument is unique: a *menhir* or stone pillar figure from Souphli in Thessaly, it is our only example of large-scale sculpture from the Neolithic period (if it is really Neolithic, not Mycenaean or medieval) (Pl. II C). It is well over life size and crudely expressive of a lady with a great necklace standing demure and frontal, her hands pressed against diaphragm and belly above a short embroidered skirt. She is now marvelously mounted inside a nineteenth-century Turkish prayer niche in the Larissa Museum.

The representations make it certain that all Greece worshiped the same type of fertile earth mother, using similar idols and probably similar ceremonies, sacrifices, and hymns. Apart from language differences, these ceremonies would have been recognized equally by visitors from Anatolia, Syria, Mesopotamia, the islands, Bulgaria, and Hungary. The extraordinary power and insistence of this religion so deeply rooted in agricultural life is clear from the fact that it never died out in Greece. It may have been outlawed, made unofficial, transformed, suppressed, harnessed, set in political balance with newer religions, but any archaeologist of religion will recognize in it one of the primary gifts of the Neolithic civilization to its heirs in Greece and the Near East. Because the goddess was the same in all places and yet locally powerful and individual in each, we may perhaps look here for the origin of that custom, so conspicuous in Linear B texts of the late Mycenaean world, of naming each "lady" with a local epithet to distinguish her from the "lady" of another village. Naturally, some epithets became titles and then incarnate deities, like the later "nymphs" or brides of cities: Mykene at Mykenai, Thebe at Thebai, Athene at Athenai. But Neolithic cults were not entirely local. The multitude of pottery and broken idols in great caves like that of Pan at Marathon or Eileithyia near Amnisos in Crete comes surely from more than one settlement. One may guess that certain places with a "holy" feeling about them attracted Neolithic peoples from quite distant places on occasions like fairs or annual ceremonies of seeding and harvesting. Such opportunities for broad contact may have contributed to the rapid spread of innovations.[9] Thus Dimeni bowls turn up at Prosymna and Corinth in the Peloponnesos. Early Cycladic fragments are discovered in what may be a late Neolithic stratum at Eutresis, southern Urfirnis near Volo. The seals and copper of Sesklo are probably imitated from Anatolia, and there are also less traceable exchanges like textiles and words. This active, hybrid character of Neolithic civilization in Greece seems typical also of all later phases and deserves attention. Local divisions are never really fixed, nor are the breaks in time phases clean. Population, beliefs, and language survive into new eras, with the old peoples probably exerting a continuous underground influence on the newcomers from positions as slaves, as exiles to less congenial plots of land, or as coexisting tribal units. While each phase and area expressed itself in characteristic productions, to which we can assign an approximate set of centuries, surprising reminiscences of things past keep emerging to disturb the clean charts of scholarship. The Greek Neolithic Age, which endured in some parts as long as four thousand years, may not be really well known yet, but it is surely of extreme and controlling importance.

Chapter II

The Chalkolithic Revolution

People in Greece never live without change for very long. The Neolithic Age is the longest uninterrupted stretch in Greek history, over three thousand years ruffled only by a local invasion or two and a mixture of human types. This is ten times as long as the classical period in Greece, three times as long as the entire span of her literate ancient history. These Neolithic civilizations could not have continued as they were beyond the third millennium B.C. even if no new people had landed on the coasts. Too much was being invented in the East for a nearby Stone Age economy to survive in competition, and we have seen that the Neolithic villages were far from being isolated or passive in such competition, at least near the shore and along the major inland passes to the plains.

Some innovations of the Chalkolithic and Early Bronze ages beyond the Aegean had already affected Neolithic Greece by trade or imitation: the first

Early Bronze Age
Greece and the Islands

awkward seals in early Sesklo, the copper blades hidden for safekeeping in her later phase. Metal was passing out of the rare-ornament category of discoveries into the category of economic necessity. Greece's own few veins of silver and gold were not going to be fully discovered and exploited for many thousand years yet, and she was never to be rich in copper, iron, or tin. The great advances in metallurgy were made in the regions of natural resource: the Caucasus, coastal Anatolia, the highlands of Mesopotamia, Cyprus, and southern Egypt. Even in the full Bronze Age of the Greek mainland, the new copper tools were rare for many generations, and most workers went on using obsidian or flint. Still, new things were known, imported, and justly valued: tanged or leaf-shaped dagger blades, axes, fishhooks, an occasional chisel or saw for woodworking, nails, and pins.

Some Cycladic islanders in the third millennium were already prospecting and mining their mountaintop wealth: copper on Paros, silver and lead on Naxos and Kouphonisi and Keos, gold on Siphnos. We cannot be sure how early these mines were worked, but most mainland metal creations of the period have parallels in the Cyclades, and by about 2400 B.C. there were very fine silver and gold diadems ornamented with animals (Fig. 9), chased bowls (Pl. VI B), silver-wire and bronze pins topped by birds, spirals of a kind known also in Troy and on Lemnos (Fig. 8), and, from the little explored island of Euboia, gold and silver vases which are simpler counterparts to the treasures of Troy II. There is even an iron ax at Asine, two thousand years ahead of itself in Greece but contemporary with iron daggers at Troy and Alaca Hüyük. We would immediately learn more about the metals of the age if we could find important burials, which have been hunted for generations without much success.

A specialized metal technology absolutely affects social structure in villages even where metal itself is not particularly common. Those who are not trained to mine and forge must either produce surplus agriculture to buy the new tools or continue less effectively with traditional stone tools. Those who can cope with the new technology develop a commercial pattern of life quite beyond plain Neolithic farming organization. This development of specialized trades and increase in personal wealth, plus, apparently, a sudden population growth before 3000 B.C., created the impressive city structures of the Near East. It affected peripheral regions in two ways. Architecture and industry in settled places became more complex as villages grew into towns. Also, mobility increased among tribes which knew something of the new developments (and felt the access of power accompanying them) but had no safe land of their own. This led to the colonization of new coasts and islands. A variety of movements spread from Anatolia across the Aegean islands (Lemnos, Chios, Syros, Aigina) to the eastern half of Greece in an arc from Orchomenos and Eutresis through Attica into the Argolid and even into Arkadia. Messenia and Lakonia have their own local variations (see Fig. 1). In west Greece another group of Early Bronze colonists occupied the islands of Leukas, Ithaka, and Kephallenia. Crete perhaps received a group of Anatolian sailors, and Anatolians almost certainly settled the largely unexplored mounds of Macedonia and Thessaly. They were not all the same racial stock—if there could be such a thing after the blending of families in the Stone Age—nor did they all speak precisely the same language or make the same objects. Troy, the Cyclades, Lerna, and Leukas each had its uniquely characteristic art; but they had all reached similar levels of culture or potential to create culture.

THE EARLY HELLADIC AGE

General Features

The new characteristics of Early Bronze towns in Greece are in general: a choice of a low hill quite near the sea to build on (less often inland by fresh springs as in Neolithic); houses of two rooms organized en bloc with graveled or cobbled streets outside, the whole area sometimes surrounded by a defensive wall; a habit of digging storage pits (*bothroi*) all over the site at the start (this habit disappears and again revives in later phases); the use of herringbone masonry for the foundations of houses, a characteristic manner of leaning fieldstones against each other at supporting angles instead of piling them flat; a differentiation in status of houses with some quite large central building sometimes a focus for the rest; general use of good mudbrick for walls and even tiles for roofs; a pottery which is often monochrome and burnished at the beginning, next glazed with a dark paint (EH *Urfirnis*), and a characteristic shape, the so-called sauceboat (Fig. 51; Pl. VI A); an active trade overseas and a variety of imports and influences; a strange absence of the figurines of the earlier period; and the increasing use of copper and silver. A few sites develop a rich mastery of carved seals; there may even be marks on pots which resemble signs in later writing systems (Fig. 6). Some of the architecture is on a grand scale, and at every level the potentialities for a highly organized and sensitive civilization are apparent.

Chronology

With Early Helladic begins the traditional chronological system of triads for the Bronze Age, dividing it into Early, Middle, and Late Bronze with special labels for each area (Helladic for Greece, Minoan for Crete, Cycladic for the central Aegean islands). Each period is further subdivided into three segments, I, II, and III. Subdivisions may be still more subtly calculated (Late Helladic III A:1 early) with such refinement that, if absolute dates were available, it would be much more convenient to write 1420–1390 B.C. than to memorize such labels (Fig. 51). Two thousand years of Bronze Age civilization are thus divided into nine major phases, and every effort has been made to force them into harmony with the original scheme which Sir Arthur Evans worked out for Crete. But Crete was never seriously invaded as the mainland was, and its archaeological history is much easier to describe in terms of transitions in pottery styles. Outside Crete the system is a straitjacket at certain times; and the connotations of destruction, population and language change, and periods of primitivism or flowering that it should carry are blurred. It is one of those superimposed logical orders of an essentially poetic nature which are our inheritance from nineteenth-century humanism, like the whole concept of Stone, Bronze, and Iron ages.

Early Helladic lasts most of the third millennium B.C. It corresponds pretty accurately to the Old Kingdom and First Intermediate Period in Egypt; to Proto-literate, Early Dynastic (Ur I), Akkadian and neo-Sumerian in Mesopotamia; to Troy I–II, for the first phase, IV–V for the second in Anatolia; and to the distinctive phases of Pelos and Kampos pottery, and later to the Chalandriani fort on Syros and Phylakopi I on Melos in the Cyclades. Naturally, the histories of the new towns vary from place to place. Troy was probably founded about 2900 B.C., Poliochni on Lemnos a century or two earlier, Lerna in the Argolid a century or two later. In chronological charts these five or six generations do not seem important; in human or historical terms they must have been very important, but beyond our recall. Until a family or group settles permanently, long enough to make successive houses and import recognizable objects from abroad, their special experiences are lost to us.

Each new Early Helladic town in Greece had a rhythm and history slightly different from those of its neighbors. Central Greece showed affinities to Thessaly and to the region around Troy, the northern Peloponnesos had a distant likeness to Crete, Attica was tinged by the culture on the islands. Individual town histories depended a great deal on local circumstances: wars, intermarriages, language fusions, whether the new settlement was primarily geared to farming or maritime trade. There were, to be sure, three main phases of this third millennium civilization in Greece, but they do not correspond to those in Crete. EH I was comparatively scanty and has been found most recognizably in Central Greece. EH II represented a strong, wealthy period with new vase forms and technologies. EH III was brought by new people who sometimes destroyed EH II sites and sometimes merged into them without violence. The EH III people had a culture which anticipated the Middle Helladic Age in some ways.

Reconstructions of the history are entirely based on successions of house strata and pottery styles, which are accurate only for a particular site. Occasionally, a town may be tied to its neighbors through simultaneous use of a single seal, similar imported objects known from abroad, or related building styles. The family likenesses in pots which characterize the three phases are as follows (see Fig. 51): EH I: red polished bowls and collared jars, saucers, lug handles. EH II: dark lustrous glazed ware, sometimes in patterns; yellow mottled ware; sauceboats, little saucers, askoid jugs. EH III: patterned ware, more light-on-dark in the north, more dark-on-light in the south, especially in tankards and metallic-looking bowls; "ouzo" cups; chevron patterns; the first signs of the potter's wheel.

The sequence is quite well stratified at Lerna in the Argolid and at Eutresis in Boiotia, both with a relatively light overlay of later ages, both lucidly related by the excavators to other sites and to the outside world. Orchomenos and Tiryns also have fine architecture. Other towns contribute features of interest: Hagios Kosmas its cemetery and its links with the Cyclades, Zygouries its private houses, Asine its seals, Askitario and Aigina their walls. Because Lerna is the most recently dug (1952–58) and the most impressive in buildings, it may serve to illuminate the basic character of the age.

LERNA AND EARLY HELLADIC HISTORY

Lerna is at the farthest corner of the Bay of Nauplion (Gulf of Argos) as you sail west toward the Argolid. It was not settled before EH II. An old Neolithic village on the site showed twenty historical levels of activity some centuries before the new people came, but there was no contact between the two. The newcomers tidied up the mound, graded the humps, filled the hollows, and built their first houses on the enlarged crown (Pl. III A). These had thick foundations of stone, up to 1.20 m., laid in the herringbone style. Upper walls were crude brick, and the architects were clever at truing their lines to make stable, square rooms of good size. These rooms were strung together, perhaps facing an open court or graveled street, and exhibit a stronger sense of organization than before. In the center of the plateau rose a monumental structure, Building BG, which lies obliquely under its more famous successor, the House of the Tiles, and is technically similar. Thick mud walls formed corridors running the length of the building, framing large central rooms; the roof was made of fine schist plaques. This house and the smaller ones around it covered several earlier levels below, and must itself have lasted more than a generation, so that we may perhaps allow some two hundred years for the opening development of the town (Lerna III). The whole place was surrounded by a defensive wall (Pl. IV A) which passed through four phases of changing architecture, the last two or three being contemporary with the central "palace." There are three perceptible changes of pottery and perhaps six levels altogether; then the palace and fort both burned down violently.

The people of Lerna took a while to recover from this setback. Small houses and a graveled street ran over the old palace site. Yet there was no change of people; they revived and built a greater building in the center of town. The House of the Tiles is the most completely preserved expression of Early Helladic II culture in Greece, continuing the innovations of the earlier period in a fine monumental style (Pl. III B). It was designed in a period of intricate stamped sealings and metal tools as well as contact with the Cycladic islands. Late Lerna III had every potential for developing a high degree of civilization, much as Early Minoan Crete presaged the power of Knossos. But like so many other promising sites, it was not left to develop in peace.

Shortly after the basic construction of the House of the Tiles was completed, and before any new fortification wall rose, Lerna III was subjected to a savage fire which left a deposit of black-and-orange calcined debris all over the central part of the site. There were no skeletons in the houses or on the streets, but one rarely does find such dramatic evidences of battle on destroyed Greek sites—everyone usually departs in time, and the most valuable things are removed before, or by, the enemy. There is no doubt that enemies came to Lerna. After an accidental fire, life would have gone on as before with repairs and new buildings, but after this fire a totally new culture took possession of the town. This was EH III (Lerna IV).[1]

There were five or more building periods in this phase, but throughout them no new house was allowed to build over the middle of the old House of the Tiles: the debris of that building was heaped over the center and graded down into a sacrosanct shield-shaped tumulus whose perimeter was marked off by a circle of stones. This unique event in Bronze Age archaeology is difficult to interpret—was it motivated by respect or fear? Obviously, the EH III conquerors felt some strong emotion connected with a destroyed building whose architecture they never matched themselves, for they kept it as a monumental, useless mound in the heart of their own settlement, domed four meters above street level.

The EH III peoples built small irregular buildings. Their houses have only one or two rooms; some have apsidal ends as in the following period. They used no seals and had very little foreign contact, although one man owned a horned jar made in Troy. Their pottery is painted in linear patterns (mostly dark-on-buff in the Argolid [Pl. VIII B]). The characteristic shape is the two-handled drinking goblet (see Fig. 51), and there are no more sauceboats. A few pots made toward the end of their tenure show signs of being turned on the wheel and there are increasing amounts of simple gray ware, both features being typical of Middle Bronze Age repertories. The villagers dug bothroi and graves even on the edges of the House of the Tiles and defended themselves behind a slim wall and a gate with wooden posts.

These Patterned-ware intruders were clearly still in the Early Bronze phase of development, although different in stock and background from their Early Bronze predecessors. At Lerna and several other sites there was no destroying break between their arrival and growth of Mycenaean Greek civilization in the later second millennium. There is no evidence that they were themselves Greeks and no way to contrast their language effectively with the languages of EH I–II or MH. Present theories explore the possibility that all three groups were Indo-European and that the Greeks of the Late Bronze Age had a complex variety of relatives and forerunners in the land before them. The EH III peoples were not, perhaps, so numerous as their EH II predecessors, and they were certainly not so sophisticated in physical culture; they were marauding destroyers who stopped one of the most potentially civilized societies Greece ever had. Their conquest was permanent in many places, reinforced by other invasions in the Middle Bronze Age, and alleviated later by fruitful contact with Crete. This break between EH II and EH III must have been exciting and shocking while it was happening. It is partly hidden by both the invaders and the defenders being termed Early Helladic; their sequence is not so harmonious as in Crete.

THE FLOWERING OF EARLY HELLADIC II

Fortifications

The discovery of the wall around Lerna III consolidated a new conception about the nature and power of Early Helladic II Greece (Pls. III A, IV A). The town aligned itself with such other princely fortified sites as Troy and

Mersin in Anatolia; Poliochni (Lemnos), Thermi (Lesbos), and Emporio (Chios) among the great eastern islands; the Cycladic forts of Syros, Siphnos, Melos, and Aigina; the newly discovered town of Askitario in Attica. All these places are coastal. Inland towns like Eutresis and Orchomenos, which were probably just as rich, felt no need to protect their possessions and lands in this way, undoubtedly because they were not menaced by pirates at sea.

None of the Greek or island towns has been completely cleared, and one cannot tell how the wall relates to the whole plan: it may just rim a vulnerable area (Syros; see Fig. 4) or surround the whole site in an ellipse or rectangle. Some fortifications have projecting angles or horseshoe towers, some have cells attached inside as barracks. The ground level is usually much higher inside than out, so that the defenders could see over the upper mudbrick walls and shoot from breast height, while the attackers would be several heads below at an awkward angle.

Lerna's wall was rebuilt four times in early Lerna III. At first it functioned more as a retaining wall for the mound than as a defense, although the brick part rose free to some height. Then a hollow horseshoe tower and a guardroom were added in herringbone masonry. A stair rose outside the tower in broad flagstone treads. Next the whole system expanded and covered the stairs and the old tower was replaced by a solid rectangle. Then it grew again and was made round as before. Some of these changes, which are essentially minor adjustments or experiments, were accompanied by fire. The wall seems to have started earlier than the big central Building BG and to have burned at the same time. In the interval afterwards, and during the House of the Tiles, the town was left undefended—perhaps the work was too expensive to undertake again or perhaps the men of Lerna were seduced by a false sense of Aegean peace.

Town walls at other sites have not been published in such stratigraphic detail, but they must have gone through phases too. The settlement by the harbor on Aigina, under the classical temple of Apollo, looks strong on paper; on the site itself, its wavering lines hidden under the rubbish of picnickers seem less impressive. One rectangular tower sticks out beside the earliest gate. The gate is an example of that bending passage with traps like canal locks which was brought to high perfection in the later military architecture of Mycenae, Tiryns, and Athens. Its purpose was to expose attackers to missiles from above and to the right, unshielded, side as they jammed into these narrow boxes between high enclosing walls. The Cycladic fort at Chalandriani on Syros (Fig. 4) was designed in a developed phase of Early Cycladic roughly contemporary with late Lerna III. The double fieldstone wall ran along part of a cliff which was naturally protected from attack by difficult ravines. An ellipse of 70 m. has been preserved, with five horseshoe hollow towers on the inner wall. To attack, one had to slip through a narrow slot in the outer wall and pass within arm's length of a jutting tower to break into the main gate (left) or minor gate (right). In both cases, one passed through the wall into an inner compartment which itself had a door onto the little acropolis

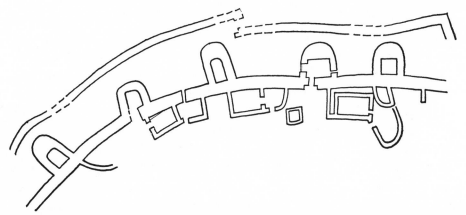

Fig. 4.—Walled fort at Chalandriani, Syros. Early Cycladic. (After Tsountas, *Ephemeris* 1899, 118, Fig. 32.)

plain. A normal man could only crowd through the little gate sidewise; in the big gate, he had to climb a stair to the tower and force three successive doors. Clearly, the architects of Syros were not naïve in these matters. Yet something happened, for the acropolis was abandoned while still filled with storage jars and valuables like the unique silver diadem from Tower B (see Fig. 9) and a Trojan drinking cup; it lay deserted after the third millennium.[2]

Syros' towers are slightly more spacious than Lerna's, which are judged to be too cramped to draw a bow inside. Perhaps in both places the normal fighting style demanded hand-to-hand skirmishing with daggers, not long-range archery. Comparatively few arrowheads are reported from Early Helladic and Cycladic sites, but leaf-shaped or slotted daggers and spears of good quality are favorite weapons. Whatever had to be attacked or defended demanded close, dangerous contact. Lerna, again, offers the clearest image of what Early Helladic Greece possessed to make these walls worthwhile.

The House of the Tiles

A repeated combination of mobile raids and vulnerable wealth must have existed to create this architectural novelty of the walled coastal town. In the Aegean one thinks naturally of pirates. Ordinary pirates attack, not for land but for portable loot, food, or women. These are all naturally missing from the archaeological record, but there are two assurances that wealth was concentrated at Lerna: the ambitious House of the Tiles, and the sealings from the stores kept inside it (Pls. III B, V).

The House of the Tiles is the only completed building of its period at Lerna; no smaller houses were found around it. It takes its name from the mass of fallen roof tiles, both terracotta and blue-green schist, which slid into the building when it finally burned and collapsed. Like its predecessor, BG, it is just over twice as long as it is wide (25 m. × 12 m.), with doors on all four sides; the ground-floor plan consists essentially of two large rooms divided and flanked by corridors (Pl. III B). These corridors run the length of the building on both sides. Sections of the corridors were walled off to form small rooms, some of which could only be entered from outside, or halls opening on stairs to the upper floor. A smooth surface of yellow clay was spread all around this "palace" outdoors and on the ground floors inside. Red clay benches were set along the outer faces of the long walls north and south, where the villagers could sit and be partly protected from sun and showers by the projecting eaves. The roof had a gradual pitch; the terracotta tiles (slightly coarser than in the earlier period) were laid without fastenings in a clay bed, and the schist slabs were used at the eaves where the water ran off most vigorously.

Indoors, the walls downstairs were coated with reddish lime plaster or stucco roughed by some comblike tool to grip a final coat of smooth plaster which was never applied. The walls were finished only above the stairs. The largest apartment (6.43 m. × 8.05 m.), toward the east and the sea, was prepared with "a certain sober elegance," the excavator reports: stucco walls grooved in rectangular panels like an eighteenth-century library. Doors were set in wood-sheathed jambs flush with the surface of the thick adobe walls. The stairs were wood planks sheathed in clay, with solid clay steps at the bottom where one would land most heavily. There must have been windows to light the great interior apartments. The building is set on a solid platform of stones, and the pains the architects took to make it fine and sturdy is demonstrated by the accurate lines and true corner angles of its walls. When it burned, the House of the Tiles was practically empty; only a few saucers and seal impressions show it was ever used at all.

There are other Aegean towns with buildings to rival Lerna in size and quality, although none of them could be completely excavated. The three foremost are the huge round building under the Mycenaean palace at Tiryns, the central megaron at Troy II, and the House on the Hilltop at Vasilike in eastern Crete. These last two are outside our territorial limits and are mentioned only as comparable structures in places which traded with Early Helladic Greece. The Trojan megaron is a little wider and deeper than the House of the Tiles (13 m. $\times$ 30 or 40 m.); it has a single room with a central hearth and a spacious porch between antae. Trojan technique and ambition is ahead of Greek at this time; the walls of Troy II, with their height, fine masonry, and intelligent layout, make Lerna or Aigina seem provincially haphazard. The group of parallel megara on the Trojan acropolis obviously formed a genuine "palace" complex for several responsible and wealthy leaders, while Lerna and Tiryns with their single great buildings have a curiously communal aspect. Vasilike illustrates yet another plan, with small basement store chambers set around two, probably originally four, sides of a square. These rooms have few doorways, but one assumes that the apartments on the first and second floors were larger and connected more easily. Vasilike resembles Lerna in certain technical details, such as the hard red plaster on the walls. The normal Cretan habit of inserting a timber framework in the brick wall for strength and elasticity caused the great house to burn so disastrously that the brick turned to "cement," and the whole plan may never be cleared.

Tiryns, Lerna's near neighbor in the Argolid, provides a fourth plan of construction which is as mysterious as it is impressive. For the sake of saving the Mycenaean palace above it, only a segment of its circle could be cleared, but that segment is of a truly gigantic building. The outer stone foundation is three times as thick as anything at Lerna (4.70 m.; the wall proper is 1.85 m.); the original proportions of the circle have been calculated as a 27.90 m. diameter, 88.0 m. circumference, and a probable domed height of 26.40 m. The House of the Tiles would fit neatly inside it. Its foundations are composed of three concentric rings with doorless corridors between; the walls are sun-dried brick strengthened with frequent half-ellipse insets. If this building was ever used as a palace, there must have been a ramp leading to a higher level. There is also the suggestion that it served as a communal granary for the whole Argive plain; such half-egg domed granaries are known on a smaller scale in Orchomenos, the Cycladic islands (imitated in the famous green steatite model from Melos [Pl. VIII D]), and in Egypt. The tholos might more romantically have been a ceremonial structure whose design clearly distinguished it from ordinary secular buildings. Inside the tholos were quantities of roof tile and schist slabs. It was an extraordinary feat for the time to link these into a conical dome, but it must have been achieved—perhaps at a very low-grade pitch since the building is so broad. Tiles and an oval wall have also been found nearby at Asine on the bay; this type of construction may have been a specialty of Argive architects.

Many Early Helladic towns had no large central building but only groups of two- and three-roomed houses along paved or graveled lanes. Eutresis (Fig. 52 c) and Zygouries provide good examples. A small fixed hearth and an open courtyard were usual; sometimes the roof was supported on a timber post for large spans. At Hagios Kosmas, a small obsidian emporium on the southern Attic shore, rooms tended to agglomerate. The excavator suggests that when sons married and could not afford a separate house they moved into one room and walled it off for privacy from their in-laws. There is no link between these normal dwellings and the great houses, which are so strangely isolated or at least not found in recognizable connections with private houses. Lerna is particularly unusual, with its outdoor benches but no internal furniture and its rooms blocked off from the inside. Perhaps we are too quick to think in terms of "palaces" and "kings" in the later historical sense; these anonymous buildings may have been something more in the style of village granges to which all citizens had equal access. The concept of a community farm with a large centrally defended building harmonizes with other facets of Early Helladic civilization. Yet the architecture makes an impression of concentrated power which must somehow reflect the organization of EH society.

Life and Art

Like the classical polis but on a smaller scale, each town controlled farmlands and coastal approaches within a radius of about ten or fifteen kilometers. Farming was probably more efficient than in Neolithic times. Early Helladic was an agricultural and trading society, and the period was settled enough for farming experiments to be tested over several generations. Wheat was a good crop, barley even more important, and its several varieties suggest that strains had been deliberately crossed. The farmers knew olives, both to eat and probably to press for oil. Figs were very popular. Curiously, the EH II people were particularly fond of figs and the EH III people had the skill to plant vineyards and raise grapes, but at Lerna the two fruits are never found together. Mostly people ate vegetables: peas, beans, and lentils were staple items as everywhere in the early Mediterranean; nuts and dried chick-peas were marginal delicacies. Farmers kept the same domestic animals as before—primarily sheep and goats, some pigs—but they were less of a daily dish and were probably conserved for their wool and leather as long as possible. Early Helladic women were busy weavers to judge by the loom weights which survive. Oxen were certainly uncommon and probably very expensive, although one famous beef bone was found cooking in a stewpot at Zygouries, left behind when the house caught fire. Red deer and boar were still in the hills to be hunted—as they were until the Roman period—and their antlers and tusks were adapted for tools. If the pre-Greek language with -*nthos* terminations should be ascribed to Early Helladic (see p. 60), these people also had words for mint and marjoram, for pomegranates and parsnips, for bees and honey and beer, as well as for useless flowers like hyacinth and narcissus, and for the cypress tree. They also knew an astonishing number of words for manure.

Farm products were very likely the "treasures" stored and sealed inside the House of the Tiles. Until it was dug, only a handful of seals were known on the Greek mainland (Fig. 5) and were thought to be imports. Only at Lerna do the sealings, the stamped clay wads impressed with seal marks, survive in such numbers as to convince anyone that a native industry in seal-carving flourished to satisfy a strong sense of private property (Pl. V). No actual seals were discovered. This discrepancy has been noted at other sites, and suggested to earlier excavators that the sealings came on goods shipped from Crete. Carved seals of a high order are a special manifestation of Early Minoan artistic sense, and are preserved in good numbers in tombs. The sense of design employed on them seems more open and fluid than at Lerna, however (Fig. 5 *d*), and most Cretan seals are slightly later.

Seals were used for many purposes in the Bronze Age. They were pierced by string holes and worn around the neck or wrist, thus constantly available in a world without pockets, and ornamental as well. They put personal guarantees on local property like storage jars and the doors of locked rooms, and they vouched for the contents of goods exported in jars or chests. Mainland sealings traveled as far as Troy (Fig. 5 *e*). Sometimes the seals served as dies for repeated decorative patterns on clay (Pl. IV B) or, presumably, on textiles; they might also tattoo the skin. Sometimes they were jewels of an amulet character in themselves, in which case they were likely to have a handle in a special shape like a bird's head or a human foot. The few existing mainland seals are porphyry, serpentine, steatite, or clay (Fig. 5). Probably a greater number made in ivory or wood have disintegrated; the patterns sometimes show that angularity of execution so common in chiseling grained wood.

What the seals were actually used for in particular cases can sometimes be guessed from the marks on the backs of the sealings, the wet clay into which they were impressed. At Asine one clay lump covered a door bolt made of two

Fig. 5.—Some Early Bronze Age seals: (*a*) Amorgos (after Dümmler, *AM* 1886, Beil. 11); (*b*) Asine no. 7 (after Frödin and Persson, *Asine,* Fig. 172); (*c*) Lerna S 46 (after Heath, *Hesperia* 1958, Pl. 22); (*d*) Mesara, Crete (after Kenna, *Cretan Seals,* Fig. 34); (*e*) Troy II B (after Blegen, *Troy* I, Fig. 408); (*f*) Zygouries (after Blegen, *Zygouries,* Pl. 24, 4).

saplings fastened at right angles; another sealed a wooden stopper in the neck of a jar. At Lerna sealings closed wooden boxes and wicker baskets which had been corded with string over a projecting peg; they stopped the mouths of jars which probably held liquids such as oil or honey. Two deposits of sealings were found, one hundred examples from a burned house contemporary with the end of the fortification wall, and one hundred twenty-four examples from seventy different seals in the debris of the House of the Tiles. In the older house, which has not been fully published yet, they came from a downstairs storeroom which had wooden shelves piled with a variety of pots, tools, copper and flint knives, whetstones, basins, a baking pan, and a jar holding charred wheat. The deposit in the House of the Tiles was in a small room (XI) open only to the outside and too small to contain the proper number of storage containers, so that the excavators judged them to have fallen from a safer place above. Such quantities of farm goods could not possibly all have been imported, nor the seals to guarantee them with.

The variety of carved patterns on the seventy original seals is stimulating. A selection of the impressions is shown in Plate V. Compared to the plainness of Early Helladic vases, their sense of design exceeds our expectations. There are angular, rounded, and crenellated enclosing lines; the central motifs employ loops and double loops, sophisticated fragmentations of the spiral, swastikas and meanders, trefoil and other abstract plant motifs, and the more naturalistic forms of spiders or tall jugs. Most designs are fully closed and highly organized but not static. Each one is distinctive though it may show a generic likeness to others employing variants on the same formula. Rich conceptual imagination plays with seemingly unbounded originality over a basic repertory of angles and curves. It is too easy, and unfair to Early Helladic art, to hold that the best designs were copied from Cretan seals. Few convincing parallels exist, and those mostly from the slightly later period of the Cretan tholos tombs (Early Minoan III–Middle Minoan I). The Lerna sealings guarantee the existence of a local school of Argive seal designers whose preference for symmetry and self-contained geometric forms is reflected on a larger scale in architecture.

Occasionally, a cylinder or seal was pressed on the wet clay in a repeated band or pattern to ornament a vase or a fixed hearth. One good example from Lerna has running spirals with angular animals in the interstices (Pl. IV B). Curiously, the same cylinder was used on another pot found at Tiryns and another at Zygouries; all three towns patronized the same workshop, perhaps in the same year.[3] Such carved, impressed design is more congenial to Early Helladic artists than expansive drawing or painting; only rarely do they make quick sketches on pots, such as the incised baying hound of Raphina. Although the impressed technique is best suited to small surfaces, it is also used as subsidiary design on larger monuments. A fine example is the great ceremonial hearth from Building BG at Lerna, which has incised chevrons running around the rim and stamped triangles bordering a cavity for ashes shaped like a double ax —the whole thing measures nearly four feet across (Pl. IV C).

With the exception of such rare pieces of potting which dwarf Neolithic work, most EH II pots are small and rather delicate, like the sense of design.

They are seldom painted, except for the iridescent dark glaze which coats their lower bodies or rims. A plain fine surface is preferred, gray or buff or a special yellow or mottled class. When patterns are attempted, they are refined (Pl. VIII A). The potters excel at shapes. Of all shapes, the sauceboat is most characteristic (see Fig. 51). It has a long neck with a flaring rim, a round body, and a handle at the tail, and is sometimes turned into an animal by modeling the spout like a horned ram or other beast. No one is sure what the sauceboat was used for: perhaps some runny preparation of cheese, perhaps a lamp or a drinking cup. It is extraordinarily popular at all sites in and near Greece in this period. A splendid example from Arkadia, in the Louvre, is hammered of pure, thin gold (Pl. VI A). The range of other vase forms suggests a quite sophisticated society and cuisine: spoons, ladles, saucers, flasks, jugs, jars, boxes, stands for grilling meat, and fruit bowls. Like contemporary pottery in Crete, especially at the comparable site of Vasilike, clay "rivets" at rim or handle seem to imitate lost counterparts in metal. Some day a treasure of these may turn up to assure us that Greece was not behind the Cyclades or Troy in such arts.

A last feature of life at Lerna which deserves mention but not overestimation is the existence of pot marks on perhaps two dozen pots or sherds (Fig. 6).[4] A pot mark is a simple sign scratched into the clay, either before the vase is fired if it is made by the potter or afterwards if it is made by the owner. It is a shorthand declaration of production or property. Because the signs are so simple, usually straight lines or crosses, they inevitably look like the simple signs later used in Aegean writing systems. The intellectual jump between the two is still very large; in the first case the symbol functions like a thumbprint on the object, in the second it functions as a substitute for sound. Pot marks begin at Lerna in Late Neolithic; they become quite common in Middle Bronze (Lerna V) and in the Shaft Grave period (Lerna VI). Egypt and Mesopotamia had been writing for centuries before Early Helladic II, but there is little impetus in the Aegean to do so before the middle of the second millennium, another eight hundred years. Yet a primitive concept of expressing meaning through a sign is already embryonic and is a natural by-product of the use of seals. Some seals use abstract signs as part of the ornament (Fig. 5 f; Pl. V). Crete is experimenting in the same manner during Early Minoan II and III, when detached symbols first appear as decorative elements on seals. Perhaps, if Greece had not been invaded, the spiders, jugs, or "imitation signs" would have developed similarly toward script. The EH III invaders also use pot marks, but

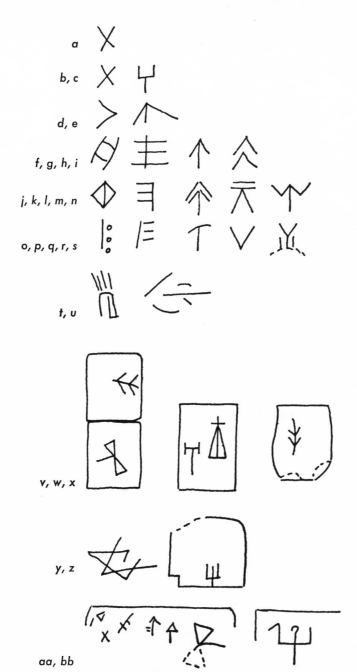

FIG. 6.—Pot marks and masons' marks in Greece: (*a*) Neolithic, Lerna; (*b, c*) Early Helladic, Lerna; (*d, e*) Early Helladic, Orchomenos; (*f–i*) Middle Helladic, Lerna; (*j–n*) Middle Cycladic, Phylakopi; (*o–s*) Shaft Grave period, Lerna; (*t*) Linear A on bronze cauldron, Circle A, Grave IV, Mycenae; (*u*) Canaanite jar, Menidi tholos tomb; (*v*) façade, Peristeria tholos tomb; (*w*) façade, Kephala tholos tomb, Knossos; (*x*) krepis block, Treasury of Atreus; (*y*) graffito, Marathon tholos tomb; (*z*) block near South House, Mycenae; (*aa*) graffito, chamber tomb at Enkomi, Cyprus; (*bb*) Protogeometric foundation block, Iolkos.

no seals. There is no external reinforcement of the groping toward writing until the Shaft Grave period brings stronger contact with Crete.

People, Religion, and Burial

As in Neolithic, Early Helladic graves are curiously elusive. Our ignorance of them means also ignorance about the personal appearance of the people, their racial affiliations, and their important art which comes in all periods mostly from unrifled burials. This loss is particularly disappointing because the third millennium in the Near East and Egypt was the period of splendid royal tombs or concealed treasures: Schliemann's Treasure of Priam and related hoards in late Troy II; the tantalizing Dorak Treasure of Bandirma, also Troy II, which is temporarily lost; in Crete the stone chamber tombs of Mochlos and the corbeled tholos tombs of the Mesara plain and Lebena with their attractive small finds in gold and ivory. Farther off, beyond the strict Aegean, there are the famous hoards of gold and furniture from the tomb of Queen Hetepheres in early Fourth Dynasty Egypt, the Royal Tombs of Ur with their jewels and musical instruments, the Royal Tombs of Alaca Hüyük whose inlaid bronzes and weapons look forward to the Shaft Graves of Mycenae. The multiplicity of specific funeral customs and tomb types in these scattered areas does not altogether disguise a general Early Bronze love of burying gold work and weapons with the bodies of princes. Early Helladic Greece will probably never produce spectacles on the same level as the East, but there must have been wealthy men and leaders whose graves would astonish us unless their burial customs were entirely different from those of the contemporary outer world.

With three exceptions, there are only about two dozen graves known on the whole east mainland, a number insufficient for even one prosperous settlement.[5] The exceptions are coastal sites: two strongly influenced by Cycladic practice (Hagios Kosmas in Attica and several graves in Euboia), one a local western type of community round grave best known on Leukas. Two types of burial seem peculiar to the mainland and not very elegant: simple inhumation, and the habit of dumping several bodies down clefts in the living rock. A deep shaft or well at Corinth held twenty skeletons. The Cycladic method adapted by some eastern coastal sites is to make single burials in a stone-lined box or cist covered by a slab, and the mainlanders also use this type for multiple burials or family graves. Hagios Kosmas shows very clearly how the two ethnic groups mingling in a shore town produce a fused set of funeral customs. The Cycladic cist is the normal shape, the multiple skeletons the normal number (see Fig. 11 *a*). About half the cists are sunken pits lined with stones; half are built up in a similar box-shape out of fieldstones and include rough imitations of a door slab or lintel. They are irregularly shaped, from rectangular to nearly round, and are grouped into two definite cemeteries.

In Euboia, around Chalkis, the tombs are also grouped, but they differ from those of Hagios Kosmas in being rounded underground chambers with a rectangular entrance hall plunging shaftlike from the surface of the earth (see Fig. 11 *c*). They are odd precursors of Mycenaean chamber tombs and a reminder of local variations throughout Greece which are partly concealed from us by likenesses in pottery. The grave gifts in Euboia, like those in Hagios Kosmas, are primarily of Cycladic character, although they also include curious local pottery. Considering the gold vases and unusual architecture from here, it is a special pity so little professional exploration has been done.

The third extensive Early Bronze cemetery, on the Ionian island of Leukas, looks entirely different. The settlers were probably of another stock, and their connections were closer to the northern Adriatic coast than to the rest of Greece, although they used mainland types of pottery including sauceboats. They built communal graves in clusters of twenty or more (thirty-three are known at Nidri). These are round platforms of fieldstones heaped up to nine or ten meters across with hollowed-out cists in them where a single skeleton crouched in each hole. Earth was spread over the whole construction. This kind of grave has no strict parallel on the mainland so early, but the Leukas graves are hard to date; they may belong in the later transitional phase, EH III to MH I. There are MH stone circles of a similar kind both in Leukas and farther down the west coast toward Pylos (Fig. 15). They contrast with the round tombs of central Crete of the same period (EM III–MM I), which are hollow, corbel-roofed in stone, and have their dead spread out on the floor rather than in cists. The grave gifts on Leukas are what one would expect: mainland and local gray incised pottery, bronze blades and obsidian arrowheads, a few bits of jewelry like coiled bracelets, and a dagger with spirals on the golden hilt to show that the westerners had sailed around to the Cyclades or even Troy.

All mainland graves with gifts of any quality in them show the influence of the Cycladic islands, or at least have the same kinds of little offerings which are better known from the Cyclades. There are scraps of gold earrings and silver diadems; marble or slate palettes for grinding powdered colors to paint the face with; Cycladic "frying pans"; daggers or knives with light stone and bone pommels for the men; and copper tweezers, pins (see Fig. 8 *f*), thin silver bracelets, or chalcedony beads to be worn by both sexes. Hagios Kosmas shows how simple and island-oriented such burials were. The pottery is of strongly island character, although sauceboats are common to both cultures. There are locally made versions of Cycladic marble idols, the palettes, tweezers, and frying pans, a few beads, a few seashells, and flakes of obsidian. These are standard minimum equipment for the afterlife, whatever an Early Helladic fisherman thought that might be like. These gifts and the crude efforts to turn graves into little house models shed some dim light on the religion of the age.

Other evidence for religion is hard to find and harder to put together. Early Helladic Greece did not make female idols in the number and high style of Neolithic Greece, which suggests a change of religious ceremony. There are only a few little terracotta figurines which look oddly like their late Mycenaean counterparts, stubby dressed figures with beaked faces, striped casually in glaze paint. There is nothing especially religious about them, any more than about the few quadrupeds which try to look like bulls and fail. The lack of sculpture contrasts strongly with Cycladic idols and animal-shaped clay fantasies (see Pl. VII, Fig. 8 *a*). One would guess that whatever ceremonies Early Helladic people practiced were public and large scale, not involving a private god image in every farm kitchen. The hearth from the earlier monumental house at Lerna (Pl. IV C) is grand beyond mere usefulness, nor was there any practical reason for shaping its cavity like a double ax. Another queer structure was discovered recently at Eutresis: the Chasm, a huge circular "building" with a stone wall around it and a deep funnel inside. It lies outside the later House L, long interpreted as a religious center (Fig. 52 *c*). The hole is 6.40 m. across and the funnel at least 3.20 m. deep. Only God and the architect know what it was meant to be; it is obviously abnormal. Perhaps there is a connection with the other round or oval buildings on EH II sites, or with the chthonian worship for which later Greeks use bothroi so that sacrifices could penetrate to gods under the world's surface. The Chasm is obviously neither a grave in the center of town nor a practical kind of building; as so often, ritual must be the temporary explanation. Another find at Eutresis is a white marble *baetyl,* or stone pillar, perhaps phallic, whose context gave no clue to its use. No one would be justified in re-creating Early Helladic religion from such enigmatic survivals, except that the strong impression made by Neolithic fertility worship and matriarchy has faded away, and the personal toilet articles in the graves speak of an urge to comfort and supply the dead.

THE CYCLADES

Tsountas and Blegen pointed long ago to the very peaceful nature of mainland relations with the Cyclades, especially in EH II. The islands have none of the red-polished simple vases of EH I, but share a number of common traits with EH II: sauceboats and askoi, a linear sense of design, and similar houses on a small, rough scale. The number of island imports into Greece, the actual fusion of groups in places like Hagios Kosmas, the intermediate character of cultures in Euboia and Aigina, the mainland imitation of Cycladic grave types, all suggest that the two peoples were not alien in stock or civilization and that they could probably communicate without interpreters during their commercial or piratical meetings.[6]

FIG. 7.—The Cyclades

45

The Cyclades (Fig. 7) are so little explored that even now we cannot tell how early they were settled. There are at least local Neolithic cultures on Saliagos, Christiana, and Kea. Mainlanders surely met islanders on their journeys to collect obsidian, but left only faint signs of this intercourse. It now seems that the islands began to be sparsely settled while northern Greece was still in a late phase of Neolithic B, at a moment when southern Greece would soon receive her first Early Bronze explorers. A few steatopygous idols in island marble, and reflections of Cycladic idol types at Dimeni, speak of tentative commerce with Thessaly, Attica, and the Peloponnesos before the full establishment of the Early Helladic Age, and some primitive-looking pots from cemeteries at Pelos in Melos and at Kephala in Keos connect the islands with genuine late Neolithic. As a whole, however, the Cyclades develop no authentic culture before the middle of the third millennium, contemporary with the flowering of Early Helladic II. This island civilization continued, adventurous and attractive, without a serious break until the end of the Bronze Age. Its greatest danger was from earthquakes, only secondarily from foreign conquest.

Origins and Livelihood

Early Cycladic is in a sense the best period on the islands, when they are freshly settled and still unaffected by fashions or political control from Crete. Scattered sailing parties crossed from the coasts of Asia Minor to harbors they doubtless already knew well by reconnaissance. They turned to a double life of farming and sailing and went "native" very quickly, adapting to local conditions and making the most of each island's natural gifts. Since the Cyclades are so strategically looped across the central sea (they form the northern sea bridge of antiquity as Crete and the Dodekanese form the southern sea bridge), there was tremendous maritime potential from the start, and the islanders continued to be in touch with both mainland ends at least until the close of the millennium. But they were not imitators, and in fact their balance of payments must have been very sound, since they exported in quantity and imported practically nothing. Clearly much of their living was made as carriers and middlemen.

They were not entirely dependent on sailing. However forbidding the islands may look from out at sea, many of them are extremely fertile inland. Their metal deposits of copper, silver, lead, and gold were a basic element in the new Greek metal revolution. The marble of Paros and Naxos is still almost legendarily desirable. The obsidian of Melos kept the Early Bronze Age alive all over the Aegean world. Where the soil is volcanic it is excellent for grapes, and dry climate and steady sun assist in creating those famous wines—Samian, Chian, Naxian, Peparethian, Theran—which Roman connoisseurs could distinguish at a sip, and probably prehistoric connoisseurs too. The grape seeds at Hagios Kosmas might have come from Cycladic cuttings. Some of the upland valleys will support cattle and wheat, and on the larger islands—Naxos is the size of the entire Argolid—it is not surprising that as many as a dozen or even twenty sites and cemeteries have been observed. "Site" may mean no more than a family steading which was occupied for only two or three generations before the farmer moved on to less bony soil; sherds may come to the surface in such places, but it has proved hard to find any substantial architectural remains. From the maps, it looks as though most islands were settled in a scattered style, not drawn into substantial communities like Lerna. The walled fortresses of Chalandriani (see Fig. 4) and Phylakopi are exceptions.

Only three village sites have been excavated in a manner one could call informative, in contrast to nearly two thousand known or suspected graves. They are: in pride of place, Phylakopi on Melos, which continues with rich art through three definite archaeological phases until the end of the Mycenaean world; Chalandriani on Syros, discouragingly empty on an eroded cliff but architecturally a bright spot; and Thera (Santorin), whose villages are poorly published but extremely interesting both before and after the great explosion of the late Bronze Age which covered them in pumice like Pompeii (see Fig. 52 *e*). The early town at Hagia Eirene in Keos is just starting to be exposed. Still, no settlement is completely known, either in area or in stratified depth, which could solve the many puzzles posed by Early Cycladic graves and exports.

The earliest art has affinities with the art of early Troy, of the Yortan cemeteries on the west Anatolian coast, and even with styles at Tarsus and Mersin in southeast Asia Minor. The homeland of the mariners was once somewhere on Near Eastern coasts, and the language of some of them may be the same as the language of some Early Helladic Greeks (the *-nthos/-ssos* language of which more will be said later). They may not originally have been all one racial stock. As in Greece, we must visualize mildly contrasting histories on different islands, borne out by some difference in skull types and taste in pottery. Syros, for example, with its dolichocephalic skulls, fondness for frying pans and spiral ornaments, and indifference to covered toilet boxes, presents another aspect from Amorgos with its incised wares, huge idols, and interest in copper weapons (Pls. VII A, C; VIII C). Yet these are only modulations within a total likeness which is conditioned by the nature of island life and which suggests an underlying common quality, allowing us to distinguish the Cycladic peoples as a group from the mainlanders.

Architecture and Art

On every island the people built in the handiest material, stone. Fieldstones are used for entire houses, not just foundations. Often the schist flakes away from outcroppings in long natural plaques so that it is usable for walls or roofs without much trimming. The same plaques make the box graves where stones at one end imitate the doors and lintels of the houses. The most superior example of island stone architecture is Mycenaean Keos, which still stands two or three floors high and probably expanded an old tradition (p. 118; Pl. XVI A). Early Cycladic houses, like mainland ones, are normally two rooms, with crooked walls, sometimes on a courtyard, probably dark, with dirt or stone floors, and cool because the walls were never plastered. When such houses collapse, there is no telltale brick or stucco to notice; the stones simply revert to cluttering up the fields. One interesting feature is the round-ended or apsidal house on Syros and Paros, apparently before it comes to Greece with the newcomers of EH III, although after its use in Troy I. Because the settlements were small and scattered, we cannot tell how the whole village was laid out or whether there was some central feature. Although an oval wall on Paros recalls the enigmatic round or oval buildings of the mainland, and the original of the greenstone granary model from Melos must have been very large (Pl. VIII D), and although Cycladic sailors must have seen the sights of almost every major Greek coastal town, apparently they did not learn to build in brick or make tiles. Either technique or ambition failed them in the construction of monumental buildings.

Their aptitude for stonework extended to harder, finer stones for all forms of art. Slate, green and black steatite, colored breccia, and marble are trimmed, ground, and polished for the grave gifts found on the mainland and in their own graves. Palettes, pestles for grinding color, cosmetic saucers, stone boxes with conical lids, and stemmed bowls are common offerings (Pl. VI C). Above all, marble is the normal material for the famous idols (Pl. VII). Naxos was a natural center of production, because in addition to marble it possessed the corundum mines on the northeast coast, the best natural crystalline carbon in the Mediterranean world. With this supremely hard abrasive (Greek *smiris* or *smuris,* our emery) and bone or copper tools, the islands could create the most elegant shapes of any contemporary culture. It is no wonder that their exports in this field circulated widely. The basic outlines are simple and formal, to avoid the danger of splitting the large-crystalled stone or spending tedious time in polishing.

Marble vases are normally better made than the corresponding shapes in clay, at least in the earlier period. The repertory includes simple saucers and bowls, bowls on high flaring stands, buckets and boxes, and conical vases like the later Minoan rhyton (Pl. VI C). In pottery the clay is often full of mica or not very clean, nor is the firing temperature in Cycladic kilns as high as in Greece. The fifth classical enemy of the potter, *Omodamos* (crude baking), was familiar in Cycladic workshops for centuries, and may have encouraged their preference for lugs instead of articulated handles which would not stand much strain. In the graves, there are even vases merely dried hard in the sun without kiln-firing, a compromise between furnishing the dead with useful gifts for the afterlife and a suspicion that the use would not be very demanding. This habit extends to the mainland at Hagios Kosmas. All through the history of Cycladic pottery the forms are reminiscent of prototypes in marble or metal, and they are decorated in a dry metallic way.

Because the tradition of grave gifts is so conservative, it is hard to be sure whether different styles in Cycladic pottery belong to different islands or are actually different in date. The most primitive types come from the so-called Pelos culture, named after a cemetery on Melos: rounded, collared jars and bowls like gourds, dark grey and soft, incised with grooved or herringbone designs. Sometimes the incisions are filled with chalky white, a trick more firmly established in western Asia Minor in the middle of the third millennium. Crete uses the same style in sub-Neolithic. Next in time, perhaps, is the Kampos cemetery on Paros where S-hooks and embryonic spirals are used decoratively.

Early Cycladic II–III has its northern center on Syros, perhaps a southern center on Naxos. Vases are larger and better made; there are flaring stems and curving necks and mainland forms like the sauceboat and the askos. A streak of fantasy in Cycladic pottery produces double or triple sauceboats, jugs in the form of such animals as bulls and hedgehogs (Fig. 8 *a*), and complicated *kernoi,* which consist of a row of little vases mounted on a ring over a high openwork stem. The mysterious frying pan (Pl. VIII C) and the classic Cycladic spiral belong especially to this developed phase. Patterns on pans are incised or stamped out with carved blocks: representative like female genitals

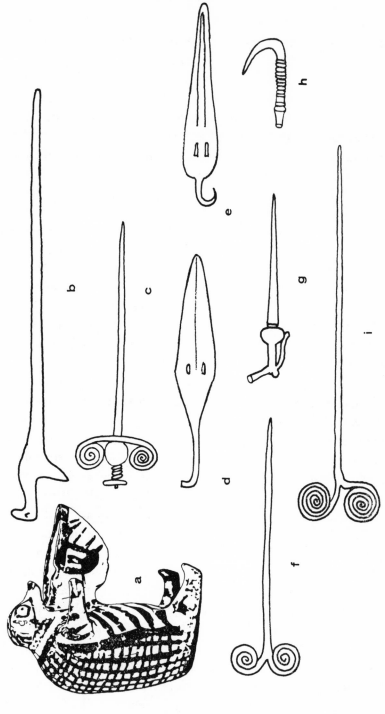

FIG. 8.—Cycladic and Trojan minor arts: (*a*) terracotta hedgehog holding a porridge bowl(?), from Syros, in Athens (after Hood, *Dawn* 199, Fig. 13); (*b*, *g*, *h*, *i*) pins and a fishhook, from Syros (after Tsountas, *Ephemeris* 1899, Pl. 10); (*c*, *d*) pin and dagger from Troy II (after Schmidt, *Troianischer Altertümer* no. 5842, and Blegen, *Troy* I, Fig. 356); (*e*) dagger from Amorgos (after Zervos, *L'Art des Cyclades*, Pl. 103); (*f*) pin from Zygouries (after Blegen, *Zygouries*, Pl. XX, 9).

above the handle, or abstract like triangles, stars, concentric circles, or spirals. The spiral may be set in a single running band, or in a square of four. At its most distinctive it may spread across a broad field with each spiral linked to all its neighbors by tangent stems (see Pl. VIII D). Backs of frying pans are a favorite field for the design; ships may intrude among the spirals as though they were waves (see Fig. 10).

A good deal of nonsense has been printed in the past about the ethnic significance of the spiral. It is a simple design but one difficult to do well. Its nearest model in nature is a coil of rope on a ship's deck. It comes most naturally to people whose artistic tradition is either in paint or wire metal work, not in woodcarving. Cutting a spiral across wood grain invites frustration. A painted spiral appears in pre-Dynastic Egypt, and another in Dimeni Neolithic, but Cycladic artists do not paint at all in the beginning. When they start, they imitate straight-line incised designs, never painting spirals until they have been in touch with Middle Minoan Crete. The Syros spiral idiom helps to confirm the islanders' status as gifted metallurgists like the Trojans and the Lemnians.

Later Greek myth associates dwarfish supernatural smiths with several islands: the Telchines and Dactyls on Crete and Keos or Hephaistos on Lemnos. Their real counterparts made the spirals into brooches and pendants in silver wire, bronze, steatite, and gold (Fig. 8), and the loss of their finest metal vases is a bitter one. A broad silver dish in New York illustrates their level of performance from quite an early phase, in its design of alternating vertical and slanted blocks of grooves (Pl. VI B).

More popular than any other product, in antiquity and in modern times, are the marble idols found in Cycladic graves and distributed beyond the strict Aegean in all directions (Pl. VII). They must have satisfied some international disposition for religious symbols then, as they do for aesthetic forms now. They are as different from fat-bottomed Neolithic clay figurines in character as they are in material: an abstract harmony of geometric volumes presenting nature as a concept rather than in its shifting daily aspect. The simpler ones have well been called "the ideogram of the ideal woman," the fuller ones "empreinte(s) de décence et d'une extrême finesse de sentiment." They have also been slightly overrated as art. Their restrained forms are a response to the technical difficulties of shaping the stone without splitting it.

The idols vary in size from an average of eight inches to one or two giant specimens over five feet tall which had to be broken at neck and knee to fit them into the grave. They do not vary so much in scheme although, if we had more certified material, connoisseurs could surely detect different schools of island carving. As things are—so many idols being stolen from unknown graves or forged and sold abroad—one can only stress the repeated features. They are flat from back to front, with long cylindrical necks and elongated oval heads tilted backward. Shoulders are broad, hips slim, legs bent slightly at the knee, and feet often pigeon-toed. The arms are folded in low relief across the belly or even abbreviated to incised scratches or stumps. The breasts are only lightly modeled; usually the only jutting feature is a long arched nose rising at ninety degrees from the tilted facial plane. Incisions accentuate folds of flesh at the neck, belly, groin, knee, and ankle; the female sex organs may be drawn on as a slit triangle or omitted. Within this scheme there are variations, some figures more starkly triangular, some more ovally rounded, but it is rare to find any dramatic departures. Red paint sometimes indicates a diadem on the head or tattoos on the cheeks. This art has a comfortable self-imposed limit, partly technical, partly illustrating the appeal of standard forms in antique religions, where tradition and security are mutually reinforcing.

A second abbreviated class of "fiddle-shaped" idols seems now not necessarily more primitive, but a reduced version of the fuller sketch, in which only the long conical neck and flat oval body are made. They may have incised necklaces and genitals. This flat kind is common at Troy and resembles the products of workshops as far off as Kültepe; a dumpier kind is manufactured locally in north Crete in EM III and in the eastern islands. Harbor towns along the south and west coasts of Greece also yield a few coarse figures, perhaps bought cheaply from passing Cycladic ships. A third class of "sports" shows two joined figures, mother and child, women with crescents on their heads, men, or musicians (see Pl. VII D). The antiquity of some of the latter has been questioned, especially the players on double flutes or panpipes. But standing men with little ridged caps, and marble phallus models, are known from excavations on Naxos and Paros. Two of the more discussed lyre players come from Karos and from Cape Krio in Anatolia, which are almost totally unexplored—it is possible the southern islands had a more protean imagination than we give them credit for.[7]

The real religious value of these idols is not clear, as little in the Cyclades is clear owing to lack of excavation. They come from graves, but not from every grave, and some of the very large ones must have stood elsewhere before burial, in houses or even shrines. They are more than dolls and probably less than sacrosanct images. The protective goddess was welcome company in life and

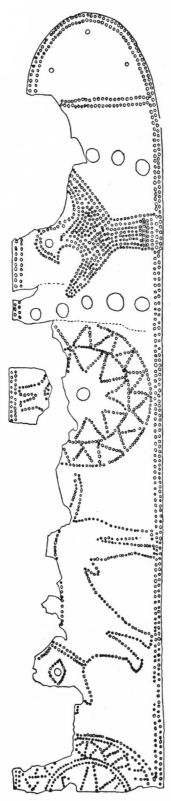

Fig. 9.—Silver diadem punched with bird goddess and collared beast, Syros. (After Tsountas, *Ephemeris* 1899, Pl. 10.)

death, but we cannot say whether her replicas were regarded as amulets, ikons, cult statues, or funerary gifts. She appears in quite a different form on the silver diadem from Syros (p. 33; Fig. 9), standing like a bird among collared beasts and wheels (or mirrors?) in a design which testifies to the fresh symbolic imagination of the islands. The incised female genitals on frying pans (Pl. VIII C) are fertility symbolism in a more obvious vein.

Maritime Trade

The resources and products of the Cyclades are only half of their double life; to the outsider their sailing activities must have been even more impressive. The waters connecting the islands are tricky to sail. The sea is shallow enough for waves to be characteristically choppy and sudden; irregular land forms funnel the prevailing north winds in a fluky way. Yet one is never out of sight of land for very long, except in the stretch between the islands of Amorgos and

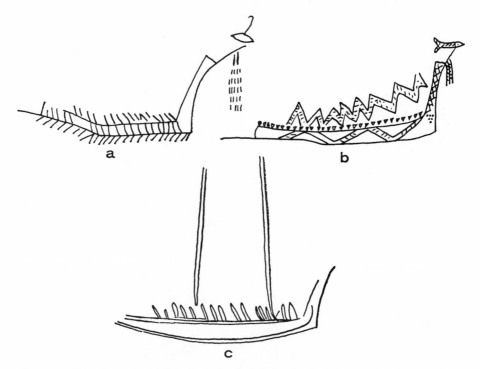

FIG. 10.—Ships from Cycladic frying pans and an Early Helladic pot: (*a, b*) Syros (after Tsountas, *Ephemeris* 1899, 90, Fig. 22); (*c*) Orchomenos (after Kunze, *Orchomenos* III, Pl. 29, 3).

Kos or in the Andros-Ikaria-Chios triangle (see Fig. 7). Crete is much more isolated by sea than any of these and survived it happily.

We have a better notion of Cycladic ships than others of the age, for artists were fond of sketching them on the frying pans (Fig. 10). The craft looks very long for its beam, with a high stern post and a low blunt prow fronted by a beak for probing shoals or for ramming competitors. These ships were probably undecked. They were steered by a pair of long wooden rudders, often topped by a fish emblem, and powered by a double bank of oars which are always sketched sticking out like fish spines. Where oars can be counted in the drawings, they range between twenty and thirty-five: the numbers are never even on both sides, but the artist was not making blueprints. There is never any notation for mast and sails although pre-Dynastic Egypt made full use of this new invention. Perhaps the islands could not support enough flax to make them; wool or leather would be too heavy and expensive. These ship drawings were imitated as far inland as Orchomenos where the sketcher added a mast (Fig. 10 *c*). They were not the only trading ships at sea, of course,[8] but they were among the most active and adventurous.

One should not think, anachronistically, of a fleet of Cycladic merchantmen. Voyages were probably loosely organized by two or three local shipowners, with family or poorer farmers for crew, who coasted over to Aigina or down to Mochlos with small goods they had manufactured during the winter. These goods included the more popular shapes in pottery like frying pans and lidded boxes, the same in marble, palettes and tubes and tweezers for cosmetics, idols and pins, obsidian and copper, and silver. The jewelry and tools could have been in finished form, although lumps of obsidian and metal ore might be put on board in a crude state, to be worked by customers at the other end, or to their order by the smith-sailors as they camped on the beach. This tradition of traveling metalsmiths seems to have persisted for small tools all through the Bronze Age. The late-thirteenth-century wreck off Cape Gelidonya preserves such a floating tinker's shop complete (p. 228).

Cycladic work was good and probably eagerly awaited as the seas opened for sailing in the spring. Island products were distributed all through the maritime world, from Bulgaria to Crete, from Troy to the Dalmatian coast and Sicily. Some were genuine imports and some were local imitations in handier material. Certain weapons and pins must have passed through several hands before reaching the final grave. Some may have been produced in small local factories set up overseas, extensions of the situation at Hagios Kosmas. This spread of recognizable artifacts is one of the most valuable chronological signals an archaeologist could hope for, offering rough cross checks in time among a number of fringe Aegean cultures (p. 64). What the islanders themselves took home in return is not so clear. Their graves hold practically nothing from abroad. Perhaps it was higher-grade copper from Cyprus, tin for alloying bronze from Anatolia, cloth and meat from Crete, or grain from the mainland. Some food probably had to be brought in, but since they had their own granaries, their own wine and oil, their own sheep and goats and fish, we must imagine their need for something else, an important but perishable staple like grain, which was one of the perpetuating factors in the cycle of third-millennium intercoastal trade.

Cycladic Graves

In contrast to the situation in Greece, over two thousand graves are known in the islands and practically no settlements. On most islands, the graves come in clusters of about a dozen—apparently family cemeteries near some farmhouse. Only Syros draws them together in common plots of greater extent, but even there the sections are maintained separately. The smallest section was composed of 65 graves, the largest of 242. The same two standard variations of type as at Hagios Kosmas are most common: the dug-out pit lined with plaques or fieldstones, and the built-up cist with fieldstone walls and a plaque roof (Fig. 11 b). Normal examples measure about one meter long, three-fourths of a meter wide, half a meter deep. This is just large enough to hold a single dead person if he is laid on his side with his knees drawn up to his chest. Most Cycladic dead lie on their left side although there is no rule about this any more than about the orientation and shape of the grave. He may have a bed of pebbles below him and a stone under his head, a few gifts laid by his head or hands. The graves are usually not marked by stones or mounds on the surface. Occasionally, a more elaborate form of double grave serves a whole family and may be repeatedly opened; it has upper and lower cists like ship bunks and holds up to seven bodies (see Fig. 11 d). Rarely, a rough stone precinct accents part of the cemetery.

The survivors seem to have offered no food and burned no ceremonial fires at the simple funeral. The gifts are those used on the mainland but probably made in the islands: marble or clay vases (especially the saucer, the jug, and the pyxis), perhaps a bronze pin or a dagger, lumps of red and blue coloring matter, some obsidian, a pigment tube, a seashell necklace. Graves are the source of practically all Cycladic idols, although not every grave has one and some have several with a single body. A hoard of objects was found in the hollow of a wall in one of Syros' richest graves; a list of its contents shows not only what is typical, but also what kinds of Cycladic art are found together in closed contexts and therefore presumably made at nearly the same time.

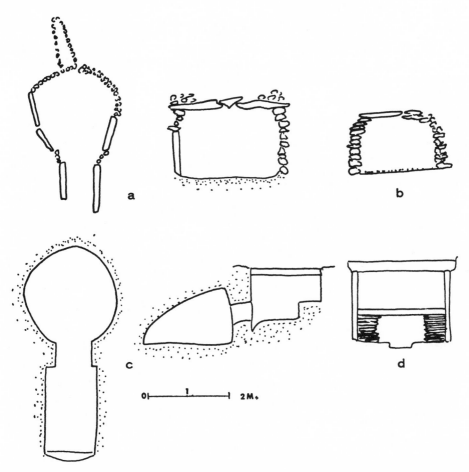

Fig. 11.—Diagram of Early Helladic and Cycladic graves: (*a*) Hagios Kosmas no. 3 (after Mylonas, *Aghios Kosmas,* Drawing 18, plan and section); (*b*) Syros, cist grave (after Tsountas, *Ephemeris* 1899, Fig. 5); (*c*) Euboia, chamber tomb (after Papavasileiou, *Archaion Taphon,* Pl. 1, 1, plan and section); (*d*) Paros, double-decker cist (after Tsountas, *Ephemeris* 1898, Fig. 5).

GREECE IN THE BRONZE AGE

From Syros:

Chalandriani 468: Rectangular cist 1.38 × 0.82 m. No bones recorded. To the right of the door, a bronze awl, a stone plaque, a pebble polisher, a clay cup with a leaf impression on its base. In the wall hoard, a clay bowl with stamped and incised designs, two scallop shells, three bronze daggers, a bronze pin with a double-spiral wire head and another with two circles of joined wire loops; three bronze needles, two bronze awls, six stone beads each of a different shape, two bone rings, ten murex opercula pierced to be strung as a necklace; one flat fiddle-shaped idol.

From Amorgos:

Dokathismata 14: Rectangular cist of normal size. One skeleton. On the right of the door, two marble idols with triangular faces and slim triangular bodies, a clay gourd-shaped jar and a saucer. Inside, two marble saucers, one with lug handles and a lump of red color; a bronze spearhead; a slim bronze dagger with four silver rivets toward the hilt; a fragment of a little silver bowl.

Without such graves we should know nothing of Cycladic art in its most original period, nor even recognize its elements abroad in foreign contexts. Yet graves give us the art without the history, and offer too emphatic a view of small portable objects, a view which deceives us when we project it back onto the missing settlement life. The real life, and the history, of the early Cycladic civilization is still almost blank and therefore perplexing.

INTERNATIONAL RELATIONS AND CHRONOLOGICAL DEVELOPMENT

The achievements of the Early Bronze Age in Greece and the Cyclades are very much those of contemporary civilizations farther East. The basic steps forward are identical: professional understanding of metals and an increase in their distribution and quality to a high point in the third quarter of the millennium; organization into towns; collective storing and defense of wealth which involves agreement on a political system; the first tentative concept of how conventional symbols may carry a message, whether in carved seals or in pot marks; unfrightened trade over long distances especially by sea, which meant exposure to new languages and response to alien cultures. Of course these developments in Greece are on a minor scale compared to Sumer and Egypt, or even Troy. Yet they are negligible neither by any real standard nor by the restricted standard of Greece alone. The length of time these hopeful evolutions lasted is hard to tell precisely, but the great era seems to be between 2500 and 2300 B.C. A slower, simpler EH I might be dated from 2800 to

2600, followed by a transitional century in which new concepts of metallurgy and monumental architecture developed. The consolidation and fruition of EH II, 2500 to 2200, would bring the bright span of Early Helladic civilization to six hundred years or a little more. Tentative radiocarbon-14 dates from Eutresis have fixed a mature phase of EH I at 2670 ± 59, an early phase of EH II at 2431 ± 58 B.C. Charcoal samples from the burning of the House of the Tiles at Lerna vary curiously, but one sample harmonizes with theoretical chronology, 2283 ± 68 B.C.; another is as late as 2041 ± 68 B.C.

Like its contempories in Anatolia, this talented society suffered the shock of invasion by less advanced tribes. The date may be 2200 or 2100 B.C. While EH III is not yet well understood, it simultaneously interrupted growth and imported a radically different aesthetic and architectural tradition into Greece, which persisted there until the crucial time of Minoan influence nearly eight hundred years later in the Shaft Graves. The new ways were stabilized by the Middle Helladic invaders of the following period. We might imagine two waves of partially related newcomers who attack or make alliances according to local circumstances, since some sites are burned after EH II and some after EH III.[9] The two phases are separated by a few hundred years, long enough for EH III houses to be built and repaired four or five times over. In absolute terms, EH III may last from *ca.* 2200 to 1900 B.C., MH I may begin immediately thereafter. While the EH II, III and MH peoples are archaeologically distinct, they have general likenesses to certain groups of Anatolians. We now tend to see Anatolian backgrounds in many more phases of Greek life than was fashionable a generation ago. Fashions may swing back, of course, or the rich new discoveries of Anatolian archaeology may come to be considered as expressions of parallel achievement without implying hereditary relationships. Fortifications, apsidal houses, and the potter's wheel appeared in west Anatolia first; then they are found in the Cyclades and finally Greece, as though carried by westward sailors, but none of the Greek peoples are transparently from Troy or Tarsus—or Syros or Macedonia or any other familiar place. Local coloring and small-group traditions obscure for us at this tremendous distance of time what must have been essentially simple historical motions.

After the House of the Tiles was burned, it took Greece over half a millennium to approach the same point of civilization again. The islands never did, except where their local arts were revitalized by Crete—their arts and maritime adventures seem less special later. EH II had had a chance to create a stable, uniform culture in Greece. Although its development was slow and subject to mischance, Lerna lasted five hundred years without serious failures and thus managed rather better than most modern cities. After the disruption, the five or six invasions which had by then taken place in Greece created such a variety of races, living conditions, and languages that a new uniform culture would have demanded tremendous military authority or political tact on the part of some energetic minority. A movement in this direction took place in the Shaft Grave period, and the Mycenaean "empire" almost succeeded in making Greece one nation. The potential was offered by the broad overlay of Middle Helladic culture on earlier individual differences, and perhaps through similar language.

The Language Problem

The major language to leave its mark on Greece, before Greek was generally spoken there, was a language with distinctive possessive or locative suffixes in *-ssos* or *-nthos*. This language left signs of itself in later Greek, lending place names, common words for trees, birds, and agriculture, and a small number of mythological or heroic personal names. This original "pre-Greek" language was not necessarily homogeneous in different districts; it may have been a whole family of related dialects rather than a single tongue. At some period of the prehistoric world it spread through Greece, the islands, Crete, Anatolia, and possibly north and west into the Balkans. Such a series of contiguous cultures, speaking in a way each neighbor could understand, must have found in language a wonderfully stabilizing factor for civilized exchange. The dialects could only have spread so widely in a period of diffuse contact, of international koiné.

The Neolithic period was one of likeness among separate geographical regions, but there was such marked local color in the expression of its culture that the common features seem to be the result of many tribes reaching similar technological levels at the same time, rather than of direct relationships in language and race. Most archaeologists view the Early Bronze Age as the more truly international one, an age when explorations by many groups perhaps stemming from a single original stock created a new range of related cultures in various parts of the Aegean world. The period of greatest international likeness is Early Helladic I and II, between about 2800 and 2200 B.C. After the intrusions of Early Helladic III and Middle Helladic there are too many special developments, and when international links are detectable they seem to result from trade or political domination rather than from an underlying cultural unity. For example, Middle Minoan Crete and Middle Helladic Greece were radically unlike and were not even in touch with each other for several centuries after 2000 B.C. Any spread of related dialects in Crete and Greece must have taken place before the Middle Bronze invasions of Greece. It cannot easily have occurred later, because the next intrusion was made by small numbers of new dynasts in Greece in the late seventeenth century; they did not reach Crete as a group, and even in Greece the linguistic remains are far more widely spread than the newcomers. In the Late Bronze Age, Mycenaean Greece and Hittite Anatolia show certain areas of likeness, as Greece and Crete do in other ways, but Crete and Anatolia have almost nothing in common. Greek and Hittite are certainly related as branches of Indo-European, and may each have links to the *-ssos/-nthos* family with its legacy of names, but neither seems responsible for its spread and neither is closely related to the Cretan tongue. One must look for the diffusion of the pre-Greek language in earlier times.

The proper names in question are clustered most densely along the south coast of Anatolia, curving up to the Troad in the northwest. In Greece, they are peculiarly concentrated through central Greece and Attica; they also occur sporadically in the Peloponnesos, north Greece, coastal Crete, Cyprus, and the Ionian and Adriatic seas. Typical names are Tirynthos (Tiryns) and Korinthos (Corinth) for villages; Parnassos, Erymanthos, Lykabettos, Hymettos for mountains; Kephis(s)os and Ilis(s)os for rivers; and a dozen or so hill forts named Laris(s)a. The Cyclades contribute Koressos on Keos, Apeiranthos on Naxos, Amarynthos on Euboia, Eressos on Lesbos; in Rhodes one finds the eastern dialect form, Ialysos or Lindos, matching Ephesos or Halikarnassos on the opposite coast. These are certainly places where "the Minyans" never came, not even the Patterned-ware peoples of EH III as far as the pottery shows, and it would be difficult to attribute the spread of such names to any period after approximately 2200 B.C. where Greece is concerned.

The first archaeological connection to Early Helladic was made by Haley and Blegen in 1928; their arguments still persuade most archaeologists. The linguistic evidence has tripled; each new map adds names, particularly from Hittite historical documents. The names in Greece cannot all be matched against Early Helladic remains although the important ones can. Some names are known primarily from classical and Roman sources, or from coins and inscriptions; some may have been transferred with people in motion or have been applied to a place much later out of sentimental and antiquarian impulses. Since Greece was so fully populated in all periods of prehistory, any

61

scholar seeking to equate the place names with a particular period will likely enough find the proper sherds at hand. Yet the broader considerations sketched above still suggest Early Bronze as the period of dissemination.

The perplexities surrounding this language problem in recent prehistoric studies come from two tendencies: to oversimplify it by assigning all "non-Greek" forms to a single "pre-Greek" language, and to identify that language with Luvian. Luvian was one form of Indo-European spoken in Anatolia during the days of the Hittite empire. It employs similar suffixes and seems particularly at home with the -nthos/-ssos names, in the mountains of Lycia and Caria and along the southern coast. Luvian probably does not develop autonomy so early as used to be thought and is characteristic of the later part of the second millennium without clear archaeological antecedents. It shares the odd -assos/-nda terminations with Hittite, and both languages incorporate roots from older languages to which they add these typical suffixes. The chronological difficulties of relating Luvian to a third-millennium language in Greece are plain even to optimists; the archaeological difficulties of understanding the spread of the pre-Greek dialects to Greece at any later period are also plain.

Two rather undocumented theories of recent years identify both the Cretans and the mainlanders of the Middle Bronze Age with the Anatolian Luvians, and interpret the opening of the second-millennium cultural epoch as springing from a Luvian invasion of Greece. These propositions are mutually contradictory for Crete and Greece, of course, since they had quite different histories from 1900 B.C. on. The theories are based on a facile comparison of names and endings which conceals a real complication of events in those times and ignores the underlying populations which affected language in each region. In fact the hypotheses are wrongly stated. The Cretans are not Luvians; they are Minoans, whatever they called themselves. The man who first called the mountain behind Delphi *Parnassos,* whether he did so in Early Bronze or Middle Bronze (there are villages of both ages at its base) was not a Luvian but a mainlander. The man who says *monte* is not identical in race, religion, art, or time with the man who says *mons,* any more than Massachu*setts* is a linguistic cousin of Dor*set.* The architecture and script of the Aegean are as yet not matched in Luvian territory, and when the two areas emerge into full historical light the Greeks, Cretans, and Lycians obviously regard one another as different races.[10]

In the five thousand years between Nea Nikomedia and the Shaft Graves there were constant interplays among Greece, Anatolia, Cyprus, the Levant, and Crete. There could not be enough radically alien languages to supply each moving people with a fresh tongue. The movements were bound to create many local members of one or two broad linguistic families, and resemblances among their vocabulary words are not archaeologically identifiable with invasions. There is a good chance that the *-nthos/-ssos* terminations were disseminated locally by distantly linked people. There is also a possibility that some second-millennium names of this type in Anatolia came from Crete or Greece, instead of going toward them. By "pre-Greek" one does not, or should not, imply "non–Indo-European." In archaeological terms, the Early Helladic peoples would then be genuine forerunners of the Mycenaeans, and would have racial affinities with the Luvians who emerged into national identity half a millennium later under the Hittite empire. The implications of this theory for the Cyclades and Crete should be very interesting. Now seems a good moment to maintain a cautious attitude and not leap into the dark with massive theories of migration or kinship. But on the mainland, at least, there is no great difficulty in visualizing the architects of the House of the Tiles, the users of seals and pot marks, as members of an Indo-European tribe who are constantly receptive to new ideas from the older tribes of Greece and the contemporary civilizations of the east.

Some of the "pre-Greek" words surviving into classical Greek help reconstruct lost images of the early Aegean world. The cult and myth personalities *Narkissos* and *Hyakinthos* are among the most colorful of those half-divine youths who insist on dying young. *Marpessa* is equally admirable for having the courage to refuse a god in marriage. Food words are particularly rich: *olynthos*, the wild fig; *kerasos*, the cherry tree; *apsinthion*, wormwood; *minthe* and *kalaminthos* for varieties of mint; *kolokynthos*, the squashy gourd; *erebinthos*, the pea; *terebinthos*, the turpentine tree; *kissos*, ivy; and *bussos* or *karpassos*, flax, over which hovers *melissa*, the bee. Birds of the land and the sea were named now and transmitted to later Greeks: *phassa*, the ring-dove; *aiginthos*, the linnet; *skinthos*, the diver; there are various edible fish including *brussos*, the sea-urchin; and mammals later extinct which seem to appear in the *bonasos* or *bolinthos*, the European bison (no bones have been found). Objects of daily use include the wicker basket (*hurissos*), the brick (*plinthos*), pitch-tar (*pissa*), glue (*glitton*), the hunting javelin (*hussos*), the famous Cretan bathtub (*asaminthos*, borrowed later from the *labyrinthos*), and after the bath the game of draughts played with *pessoi*. The survey should climax with words for two things no Greek could ever live without, *thalassa,* the sea, and *glossa,* the tongue.[11]

Trade and Chronology

Early Bronze is a world of coastal contacts. From the thousands of products traded back and forth, regrettably few survive in clear contexts which could align the parts of the Aegean littoral in time. Judging by what turns up in graves or in hastily abandoned buildings, the most fashionable exchanges were jewelry, metal weapons, and marble idols. Pottery was secondary, except when it held something desirable and so was sealed for shipping abroad; occasionally the amusing and popular types such as the sauceboat and frying pan were exchanged. A steady trade was surely carried on in perishables like grain, wine, or cloth.

The first cross-influence that can be cited is the importation or imitation by Late Neolithic villages of fiddle-shaped idols that look like Cycladic or Anatolian models and are alien to the plump Neolithic tradition. Then comes the casual spread of stamped and white-filled wares by trade or infiltration. In the days of Lerna's greatest prosperity there were links across the whole Aegean. Some of the similarities grew out of common traditions rather than the admiration of traders—urban architecture, fortification walls, clever metal creations. Trade is really active only between the Greek mainland and the neighboring islands, where the Cycladic trinkets like idols, diadems and pins, cosmetic apparatus, and some pottery are exchanged in shore towns, probably for farm products. The islands share with Troy II the use of tweezers, bone tubes for holding coloring matter, schist molds for casting copper weapons and pins, and an occasional seal impression guaranteeing the transshipment of valuables in pots (see Fig. 5 *e*). A silver spearhead at Troy is a twin to one in copper on Amorgos, the closest of the Cycladic metal centers to the Anatolian coast (see Fig. 8 *d–e*). Spiral-headed and bird-headed pins are common to Greece, the Cyclades, the eastern islands like Lemnos, and Troy; there are inland Anatolian variations on the same jeweler's theme. Twisted arm rings like Trojan ones reach as far west as Leukas. The Trojans sent their typical tall jugs and the famous *depas* westward too—the jugs to Euboia, the *depas* to Syros and Orchomenos—although one cannot be sure how late in the millennium this happened. The potter's wheel and apsidal house come to the Aegean more slowly, in Early Helladic III, from the same direction. None of these regions can match the civilization of Egypt or the East yet. They are perhaps more isolated from one another than we realize in our excitement over trade exchanges.

The combination of the few known imported pieces and the general tenor of activity permits an equation in time among the walls of Lerna, early Troy II, and the Chalandriani fort. The House of the Tiles was built in the age of Troy II *g* and EM II Vasilike. The round graves of Leukas and the granary of Melos also belong to this phase. Then come the duck askoi from the Cyclades at Samos, Troy, and Tarsus in the epoch of EH III, and the winged jar from Troy IV in Lerna IV. Red-cross bowls unite Troy V, Tarsus, Eutresis, and Zygouries. Beneath the imports and resemblances one marks the movements of peoples, especially clear in EH III. All the minor trade goods need to be better stratified at home before a positive chronology can be given, but even slightly floating in time they allow us to inspect the commercial and migratory patterns of the third millennium through different small view-holes, and promise that the chronological fixes are not too far wrong.

Chapter III

Disturbance in the Aegean

The period 2200 to 1900 B.C. is framed by two major intrusions into Greece of similar invaders: the Patterned-ware people and the Minyans. These three centuries are not very interesting in Greece (Fig. 12) and scarcely more so in the Cyclades, but abroad they are the stage for a dramatic series of wars and movements which, by establishing strong interactions of incoming and surviving nations, produced the political states of the Middle Bronze Age. At the beginning of the period there were sweeping changes in pottery, and in control, through all Anatolia from Tarsus to Troy. The Akkadians had the invading Guti to cope with on their southern frontiers. The Levant's polite exchanges with Egypt stopped, and Egypt herself coasted along with diminished respect for her royalty and disturbed by the rise of powerful provincial families; she would soon slide into the darkness of the Seventh and Eighth Dynasties and the First Intermediate Period.

The Opening
of the Middle Bronze Age

By the end of the period new dynasts have established themselves in Troy, founding the great Sixth City which would endure with its walls, its monumental buildings, its wheel-made pottery, its textiles, and its horses until finally brought down by earthquakes and the Greeks toward the end of the millennium. The dynasts conquered Troy V without burning it, and a radically new civilized panorama spreads out in this corner of Anatolia. At the same time the eastern islands and Thrace seem to lose their inhabitants almost without trace. Farther south, in the interior, after the Assyrian colony at Kültepe is burned out, two strong kings create stability by 1800. The Hittites are entering the fringes of their future empire and will shortly consolidate their control. Syria and the Levantine ports open up to Egypt once again, and the palace at Mari evolves its courtly, frescoed splendor. Egypt, which revived early, begins to link herself strongly to her foreign neighbors with the accession of Amenem-

FIG. 12.—The Middle Helladic and Early Mycenaean periods in Greece

ANATOLIA

Troy

Poliochni
LEMNOS

SKYROS

Kusura →

Hagia Eirene
KEOS

SYROS   DELOS

Miletos

SIPHNOS

Phylakopi
MELOS

Trianda
Ialysos

THERA
Akrotiri   Thera

RHODES

AEGEAN SEA

Tylissos   Katsaba
Knossos   Amnisos   Mallia
Kamares
Cave   CRETE
Gortyna
Hagia Triada
Phaistos

Palaikastro
Gournia   Zakro

FIG. 12.—Continued

het I and the opening of the Twelfth Dynasty. Like Troy, Minoan Crete begins a phase of monumental architecture and harmonious arts across the island; there is no sign of a break, but suddenly, as elsewhere in the world, a new energy expresses itself in princely, territorially extensive rule. In all these centralized political formations writing comes naturally, almost routinely, although none of the new Middle Bronze kingdoms had unbroken literary traditions of their own except Egypt; they borrowed and converted older scripts.

These fluid changes were not confined to the Aegean, of course. The megalithic cultures of the West shared in establishing a new tone, predominantly military and princely, for a Europe still languishing in the wattle and bone-tool phase of Neolithic. The Beaker Peoples, the Corded-ware bringers, the gold-braceleted princes of Ireland and Denmark, the nuraghi-architects of Sardinia—these are old familiar figures in the archaeological pantomime who take their first bows after 2000/1900 B.C. Two interesting aspects of their dominance which concern Aegean developments are their openness to contact with the old Mediterranean world and the fact that at least some of these nations in motion spoke Indo-European tongues.

THE LANGUAGE PROBLEM

The diffusion of recognizable Indo-European languages in the second millennium B.C. is one of the most complex historical processes in linguistic archaeology. They spread from India to the Hebrides, and rouse the most peculiarly nationalistic emotions of any archaeological "facts." Luckily, only a narrow segment of the diffusion concerns us here, that bounded on the west by the Adriatic and on the east by Armenia. Between these two frontiers the two classic Indo-European languages of the Aegean Bronze Age, Hittite and Greek, grew into recognizable form. Although no language records survive from the earlier years of infiltration, it seems fairly clear that the texts, when they do appear in each "empire," reflect a tradition of some centuries in both dialect and culture. After the Hittites set themselves up in Anatolia, and "the Minyans" make their dull way into Greece, there are no more interruptions on a large scale until the Sea Peoples of the thirteenth century and the Dorians of the twelfth. The slight possibility that Greek was not spoken in Greece until much later will be reserved for the discussion of the manifold problems of Linear B.

At least two factors combine to differentiate the various languages of the Indo-European family. First, the philological distinction between the eastern and western cousins, the *satem* and *centum* groups, is one that apparently goes back to a split in some aboriginal racial homogeneity long before Greek and Hittite, both branches of the *centum* family, reach the Aegean. Second, each incoming group met people speaking earlier, perhaps richer, languages which could not help affecting their own. Whether the influence came from subjects or equals, the Early Bronze peoples had so much higher a technology, and had so long understood the land and how to live off it, that we should be astonished if words were not borrowed, even words of an active or emotional kind. So common nouns for tools or vegetables, shapes of pots or buildings, proper nouns for neighboring tribes, landmarks, or old gods haunting the land, and names for concepts of quality and error, color the configurations of each intruding Indo-European dialect in a different way.

There seems to be a greater diffraction of this nature in Anatolian speech than in Greek. Hittite developed in company with two other Indo-European languages in Asia Minor, Luvian and Palaic; it was also affected by some underlying native language which had branched into geographical variants before its speakers were organized into a single political unit by the Hittite invaders. Greek is more consistent, to judge by the eventual linguistic product. It may have become more strictly formed by a smaller number of speakers outside the land, and have been less touched by indigenous languages inside it. Two major Greek dialects were spoken during the Mycenaean period, Ionic and Arkado-Cypriote. Aeolic Greek may well have been a third dialect in Thessaly, although no texts survive to prove this. These dialects almost certainly evolved from Middle Helladic speech. They share a clear inflected structure and a relatively pure vocabulary. No doubt they assumed their final form inside the Greek mainland, and no doubt the language which the invaders first brought with them was modulated by Early Helladic and even Neolithic speech, but the settled parts of Bronze Age Greece were so closely in touch that strong provincial coloring did not fragment the ultimate shape of Greek, which was remarkably logical and consistent.

Of course, words continued to be borrowed by the Greeks once they had reached Greece, not only from local populations but from Mediterranean neighbors who taught them about new materials and technologies, or ideas. The Cretans, the Canaanites, and to a lesser extent the Egyptians were influential. Thus the words φοῖνιξ, "phoenix" or "palmtree" or "griffin," χρυσός, "gold," χιτών, "tunic," σησάμη, "sesame" are probably Canaanite; Homeric ἄμωμος, "blameless," seems a negative form of Semitic *mûm*, "physical blemish"; μακάριος, meaning "blessed" or "dead," perhaps derives from Egyptian *makheru*, "justified-by-a-voice-before-god," i.e., deceased and safe in the afterlife. There are many interesting borrowings of this sort, but they are essentially ornamental flourishes borne on the wings of trade, like sofa and mañana, and not influential deviations. In general the Greek of the Bronze Age, though a flexible and adapting instrument of behavior, preserved itself intact at the core and only enriched its periphery by contact with aliens. Since language is as much a product of historical accident as of pure formal endowment, the primary task is to see what happened in Greece historically during the Middle Bronze Age.

THE "MINYANS" ARRIVE IN GREECE

Schliemann called them Minyans because he discovered them first at Orchomenos in Boiotia, where fabulously rich King Minyas and his daughters had trouble later with the god Dionysos. Orchomenos was one of the great dynastic centers of the Late Bronze Age, and Minyas himself is related to a great range of early heroic figures active in Greece and abroad before the Trojan War. Pelias, Athamas, and Jason of Iolkos link Boiotia to Thessaly; Neleus and Nestor of Pylos are the most prominent colonists in the west (p. 163); the legendary Argonautic expedition symbolizes Minyan exploration of north Aegean waters. The Minyans were a large race or tribe whose unity in speech or blood was recognized by other Greeks and whose fortunes were chronicled by epic and lyric poets after the Dark Ages. They were almost certainly not the original creators of the gray pottery which we still name after them through Schliemann's mythology. The tribal name Minyan must be strenuously distinguished from the archaeological label "Minyan" for the invaders who bring the Middle Helladic Age to Greece. We have no idea at all what these newcomers called themselves. They are generally assumed to be the first wave of true Hellenes in Greece, but we understand their culture only in the narrow terms of physical remains. They shall be called "Minyans" here for convenience.

Typical Minyan ware is unmistakable: wheel-made, in sharp shapes like the thick-stemmed goblet (Pl. VIII E) or the low bowl with two ribbon-like handles looping up over the rim (Fig. 51). The lips and bases are profiled with such clarity they seem cut with a knife; the characteristic rings around goblet stems were sliced with a stick held against the turning pot. When Minyan ware is good, it is one of the three best prehistoric mainland fabrics (the others are

Sesklo, and Mycenaean III A). It looks hard and polished as hematite, its glossy blue-gray surface slightly softened by the "soapy" feel by which students learn to recognize it, its iron elegance of outline often persuasive that the original models of its few shapes were made of metal. Unluckily, the best Minyan is rare, and the range of shapes is dull: goblets, two-handled bowls, fruitstands.[1]

Far more important than the pottery pieces themselves is the national culture they have been taken to represent. Since the coming of the Greeks to Greece is obviously a crucial historical event, and most students associate this arrival with the arrival of Minyan ware, all the promise of Greek civilization, one feels wistfully, should somehow be implicit in these first pots. So, qualities of rationality, precision, sense of organic design, clarity, authority, and freedom from surface fuss have been seen in Minyan vases. In the absence of decent architecture or art, they substitute as symbols of national psychology. In fact, of course, the ouzo cups and garbage pits of EH III, or the crooked walls and pathetic stone tools of MH I, would be equally realistic symbols. The need to see something expressive of Greek spirit in Minyan ware grows strong only in places Homer sang about.

Indeed the early stages of the Middle Helladic Age are spiritually very poor. There is almost no architecture from the period when EH III is being transformed into MH I, only levels of mixed pottery as the older gray wares yield to the new. Almost every site has this transitional moment, whether the town was burned or not. It takes a while, perhaps generations, for the Minyan character to establish itself across the country. As it does, it picks up contact with the Cyclades, and maintains some sort of relation with the Balkans, to guess by a few imported pots from the sea and the north. Perhaps this means that, now as later, the new civilization will develop its own character only when it is in touch with others, and that when it is isolated or uncertain it withdraws so far one can scarcely see it. This extreme poverty and sense of marginal existence make the early days of the Middle Bronze Age difficult to connect in the imagination with theories of princes from Anatolia or the north carving out new military provinces in Greece. And yet as invaders they must have had talent or sheer numbers to take over from EH III so effectively. Perhaps the effort of moving into Greece so exhausted them that they remained convalescent for two centuries. The new people do not conform to our traditional stereotyped vision of slashing northern barbarians who sweep down by road from the Balkan (or Russian or Trojan) plain, bringing with them the horse and chariot, the long bronze sword, the ruthless nomadic politics, the cold-climate megaron house, the fortified feudal citadel, and the potter's wheel. Indeed this picture is neither internally consistent, nor demonstrable archaeologically. Nomads on horseback are not likely to be ceramically fussy and carry their wheels with them; unbreakable vessels, of skin or gourd or gold, would be more practical and characteristic. Conversely, there are no horses yet, no chariots, no swords, and precious little metal; no fortified hill-towns appear until the Aegean world opens up, some time in the late eighteenth century.

SETTLEMENTS, ARCHITECTURE, AND POTTERY

The aspect of an established Middle Helladic town seen from out on the plain is not perceptibly new. The sites are usually the same as Early Helladic sites, except that the mound has grown a little higher; a road leads up to it from the nearest pass or from the sea. On top is a chaotic arrangement of houses, no longer divided into blocks as before, but set by the whim of the owner-builder. Streets wind their way among crooked façades, a concession to existing facts. Houses are set on stone foundations as before, but the walls are thinner, often piled up in the "potato" style of masonry; the mudbrick upper walls are usually left unplastered inside. These are narrow buildings, often three rooms in a row, with a long lean line—the "kennel" look, Miss Goldman called it— which will persist through Mycenaean times (see Fig. 52 *d*). Sometimes the ends are rounded into apses as in EH III, sometimes rectangular; they probably had ridgepole roofs, and the owners often set jars under the eaves to catch the drip.

The indoor scene gives an impression of considerable industry. Some houses have ovens in the main room, almost all have a little round hearth, perhaps off center out of the draft from the door. There is no evidence yet for the great central hearth circled by four pillars which marks the megaron of the Mycenaean world, but there is very likely a wooden pole on a stone base to hold up the beams. In the back room the stores were kept: clay bins full of chick peas, which they loved inordinately or found easiest to grow, and other products of their farms. More sheds and stalls may frame a little dirt yard along one side of the house (Figs. 14, 52 *d*) recalling the "palace storerooms" of ancient Dimeni (Fig. 3). There are no palaces yet, or even spacious houses, although excavators are always hopeful. The "palace" at Malthi is five higgledy rooms of which the largest would fit inside Sesklo's big house; at Asine the "palace" is made of two houses side by side with a party wall, for an expanding family one supposes, scarcely royal in scope. Some efforts at community specialization are suggested by installations out in the open village: a big domed bake-oven at Eutresis, an oven or kiln and possibly a metal foundry at Lerna, a professional smith's shanty at Malthi (or is it Mycenaean?) with a collection of scrapmetal and broken bits for odd jobs. In less specialized households there is at least a certain neat routine for arranging the basically agricultural domestic economy, as though village institutions had been fixed by long experience and a conventional turn of mind. The tools used are pathetic. The peasants rely on flint, a little obsidian (less than in Early Bronze, being poorer sailors at first), and stag antlers. A few metal weapons turn up in the graves, but nothing to match Early Helladic even without graves. One feels that the Minyans had only recently emerged from a real Neolithic stage, and that although they were clever at pottery they were at this point still behind in other techniques of civilization. They learned from those they had conquered or displaced, and by the middle of the period their own formal pottery tradition has been modified by other styles.

Pottery is the clearest index to the complex crosscurrents which make Middle Helladic end as a broadly civilized era though beginning in a dark age and a mystery (Fig. 51).[2] The Minyan ware, at first the dominant pottery of the new era, is soon competing with other fabrics like Matt-painted ware, and is itself modified in local schools as it comes slowly to the far reaches of Greece. While villages seem architecturally similar across the whole country, it is improbable that industry and customs were also alike. The newcomers were relatively few, and the survivors of the older regime too clever and numerous to disappear quietly. We do not know precisely who was responsible for Matt-painted ware, which has vague similarities to simple patterns from Neolithic, Early Helladic III, or the Cyclades. It comes into focus in Greece later than the first true Minyan, in a phase sometimes labeled MH II (see Fig. 51). This is the foundation period for some sites but a mature phase for others. The designs are executed in brown-lilac or green-black on buff grounds. This fabric eventually fuses with Yellow Minyan to form the basis for all Mycenaean pottery, and brings color back into the repertory (Pl. IX A, D). One dramatic sherd from the great production center on the island of Aigina shows a sailor in a helmet balancing on the deck of a fish-prowed ship, unless he is riding a whale precariously (Fig. 13), a prehistoric "boy on a dolphin."

The vignette reminds us of the Cycladic and coastal contributions to Middle Helladic culture, with tentative sea voyages providing merchant contacts that steadily increase to a high point in the Shaft Grave period. Ships are painted with eager skill (Fig. 43 *a*). Lerna offers proof of early, rare contact with both north and south: Balkan pots of the Bubanj culture and undistinguished Cretan cups of Middle Minoan I A. One grave at Lerna held both a Matt-painted drinking cup and a Middle Minoan bridge-spouted jar of Kamares ware, imported from Crete during the eighteenth century B.C. (Pl. IX A–B). Such imports are limited to eastern coastal sites and islands, but are signs of things to come. Slightly later, in Athens, potters are making the Minoan shapes in their own Matt fabrics, illustrating the growing power of Crete to mold

FIG. 13.—Sailor riding a fish or ship; Matt-painted sherd from Aigina

the mainland minor arts (Pl. IX D). One must not be lured into the easy belief that all Middle Helladic Greeks were Minyans, or that the Minyans themselves were a conforming group; one should not underestimate the contributions of the outer Aegean to their slowly increasing wealth and sophistication. This wealth remained primarily agricultural, and was minor compared to what followed, but possessing it encouraged changes in the economy and in architecture.

Because they had little to guard, or felt safe until the commercial world began to activate itself again near 1750 B.C., most towns were at first unwalled. It is significant that the sturdiest new walls were built once more in the islands where Cycladic civilization had to a large extent turned away from Greece and toward Minoan Crete. Phylakopi and Aigina both refortified themselves, and Siphnos' fort was perhaps newly designed at this time. In Crete the historical epoch is Middle Minoan II to III A, an energetic age of palaces and sea adventures, with foreign connections as far as Byblos in the Levant and Abydos in Egypt.

It was only natural for Melos and Thera, the islands closest to Crete's north shore, to be drawn persuasively within the political and cultural sphere of their greater neighbor. The walls suggest island fears rather than the influence of Cretan architecture, for Crete herself was still unwalled. Pirates and rival traders made such renewed defenses desirable. On the mainland these dangers could not have been so strongly sensed, for some coastal sites like Lerna and Asine lay undefended. Brauron in Attica had a walled hilltop, but houses rose fearlessly outside its protection. Perhaps there were walls at Mycenae, Argos, and Tiryns already, but their outlines are hidden under the later defenses of the Mycenaean age, and what used to be considered Mycenae's MH acropolis wall now proves to have been constructed in the thirteenth century. In fact the classic wall from which the image of the feudal Middle Helladic citadel has been drawn surrounded one of the most provincial possible west coast sites, Dorion-Malthi in the Triphylian hills.

Dorion-Malthi

Malthi conforms agreeably to our otherwise unfulfilled expectations of the early Greeks, and like Dimeni it looks more impressive on paper than in stone (Fig. 14). An acropolis 138.0 m. long was enclosed during the later part of the Middle Bronze Age (MH II led directly into LH I), by small rough blocks laid on the uneven stony contours of the hill without a dressed bed. Much of the wall is missing, having slid down the hill or been robbed; what is left changes in thickness from 3.50 m. to 1.60 m., as it goes, and has four or five narrow passages through it. The main gates lie at the north and south; the others are little more than doors which are converted into cattle passages in later times. The farmyard quality of this citadel is noticeable. In a few places the wall is thickened or juts out in lateral spurs, presumably for defense platforms. Inside, a whole small village is preserved, with a natural spring on the top of the rock as its original attraction, and a view over a fertile valley which is still the main pass between the west and east Peloponnesos. It is a poor village but a large one, with stalls and storerooms attached to the entire inner face of the wall, and hundreds of small rooms crookedly and haphazardly adjoining wherever the acropolis bedrock did not protrude too sharply. Malthi remains the most completely excavated MH site in Greece. Being so provincial and cut off from contact with the richer east except when an occasional Cycladic ship passed up the coast a day's walk away, it represents vividly

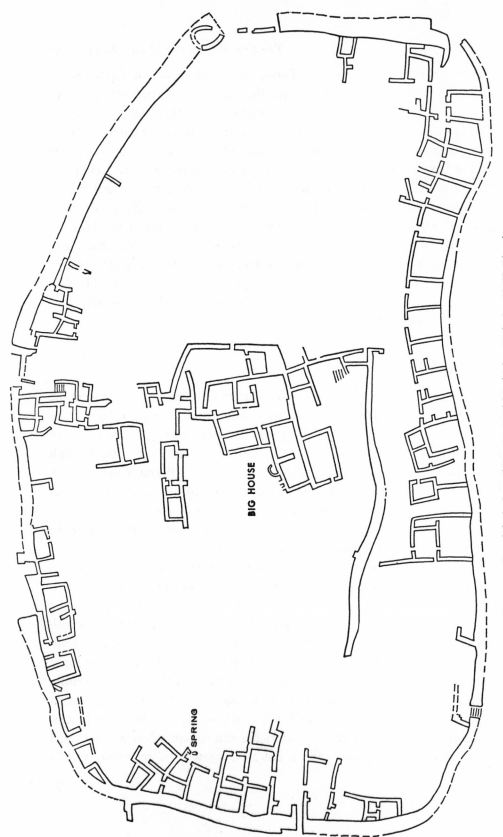

BIG HOUSE

SPRING

FIG. 14.—Simplified plan of Dorion-Malthi. (After Valmin, *SME*, Pl. 3.)

how Middle Helladic might have continued without the stimulus of excitement that the Second Intermediate Period shortly administers. Its walls do not protect treasure so much as flocks and the land, land which is about to receive new settlers from the north and east. Like Mycenae in the east, the whole west coast from Olympia to Pylos will erupt into a wealth foreign to Malthi around 1600 B.C.

THE GRAVES

The balance between houses and graves is more natural during the Middle Bronze Age than at any earlier time in Greece. MH graves are very well known.[3] The normal type, a shallow cist lined and covered with slabs, recalls Cycladic cists of the Early Bronze Age. Usually a single person is put in each one, contracted to save space in the early phases (cf. Pl. X A), more often extended in the later. Sometimes the floor is strewn with pebbles, probably not as a drainage arrangement, but as an expression of refinement, or distaste for setting one's parent directly on bare earth. Sometimes pebbles are laid over the corpse as well as under. The gifts are very poor as long as the economy is poor. In the majority of graves there are none until well on in the period when a pot or too, a string of unimportant beads, a dagger or spear, may be laid inside the grave or on top of the cover slabs under the earth crust. Along with this increase in gifts comes an increase in the number and size of known graves, and in the number of burials in one cist. They never became family repositories in the Mycenaean sense, but there may be two or occasionally three skeletons together.

An unusual feature is the practice of intramural burial, a habit new to Greece though old in the East, and upsetting to the vivid imagination. Infants and children are put directly under the house floors; even adults may be buried between or behind walls or in passages. These are not furtive concealments of family mistakes even though the graves are usually sunk below walking level, nor can it be said at this distance that any sentimental urge was operating to keep a child close to his parents. It is simply an old habit among these people. Anthropologists suggest the people hoped the spirit of the dead baby would somehow reimpregnate the mother, but this might be awkward with the adults. Sometimes an epidemic must have run through a village and two or three children are crowded into the same pit; a single poor room at Peristeria in the Peloponnesos had nine children around it (Pl. XV A). Adults are more often buried outside the village bounds in cemetery ground set aside solely for that purpose and not cultivated.

At the end of the period a confluence of imported pottery and increasing funeral display developed which cannot be accidental. All over Greece in the generations just preceding the Shaft Graves at Mycenae there seems to be a new readiness to experiment with traditional grave forms which is partly in

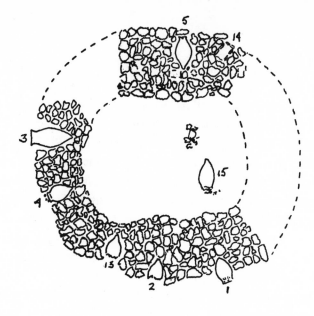

FIG. 15.—Tumulus with pithos burials, Hagios Ioannis in Messenia. (After Marinatos, *Ergon* 1954, Fig. 55.)

response to outside stimuli. Melian and Minoan vases appear in burials at Lerna (Pl. IX B); Eleusis digs larger graves for more persons and more gifts and even inserts doorways at one end, as though preparing a transition to the chamber tombs of the Late Bronze Age. Besides the cists there are un-usual burial tumuli, low mounds of earth held in shape by a stone retaining wall with several separate burials inside. Some of these may go back to the old tradition of Leukas in Early Bronze (p. 43), for the Middle Bronze colony on that island continued and grew richer. At Hagios Ioannis near Pylos in Messenia the tumulus is studded with gigantic pithoi up to seven feet tall facing outward, one or two people contracted in each (Fig. 15). Farther up the coast at Samikon is a tumulus with stone compartments probably built during the Shaft Grave era, whose 150 vases included one splendid version of the Cycladic bird style (Pl. IX F). Aphidna in northern Attica, where Theseus later raped the princess Helen, is even more peculiar; a stone wall enclosed thirteen graves in a precinct—some cists, some pithos burials, and some which almost qualify as proper shafts; the pottery is quite unorthodox Minyan. The island of Delos uses round low tombs like Cretan tholoi.

Whether these queer intrusions into the conservative burial forms of Middle Helladic Greece represent minor tribes of different background, the mute physical facts do not inform us. Because of the deep interest one feels in the Shaft Graves and tholos tombs which initiate the following Mycenaean epoch, it is natural to look for predecessors on the mainland, and yet the evidence for either architecture or funeral customs which could link up with them is very shaky. Speaking honestly, there is nothing in the Middle Helladic world to prepare us for the furious splendor of the Shaft Graves.

Chapter IV

ROYAL BURIALS AT MYCENAE

The Shaft Graves on the acropolis at Mycenae are the most familiar discovery of Bronze Age Greece, and their gold treasures are probably the most admired of all prehistoric hoards (Pls. X–XIV, XLVII A; Figs. 16–19, 48 a). Schliemann found them in the autumn of 1876 and so introduced Mycenaean civilization to the world at the point where, in a real sense, it still begins. The Shaft Graves mark the upper boundary in time of the six hundred years during which Mycenaean culture forms itself, reaches various climaxes, and disappears. The burials are frontier posts between Middle and Late Helladic; the scenery does not change dramatically as one crosses over, but the climate begins to brighten.

In the nineteenth century no one could know the real date or connections of the Shaft Graves. Knossos was still an undug mound of corridors and sherds. Only one collection of Mycenaean pottery had been brought back to a Europe which could not recognize it, the Collection de Bosset from the Ionian Islands

The
Shaft Graves

presented to Neuchâtel in 1836.[1] Early travelers in Greece had noted tholos tombs and huge antique walls before, but scholars had no sense of chronology or of Mycenaean style yet. Trained eyes were so unprepared for the peculiar art in Schliemann's graves that it was held by savants to be Phoenician, Byzantine, Celtic, or a set of incompetent forgeries. Schliemann's notes were also insufficient to explain the funeral customs of the age clearly. Now thousands of other Mycenaean tombs and dozens of excavated sites have helped relate the Shaft Graves more correctly to mainland history and artistic development, and recent Greek excavations at Mycenae have produced most of the missing information. Schliemann's graves, Circle A, still puzzle in their richness and curious style, but at least the transitional age which produced them can be described and partly explained.

Circle A was unique for seventy-five years, until the Greeks found a second circle of shaft graves (Circle B) outside the citadel walls behind the Tomb of Clytemnestra in 1951–52. An isolated pair of shafts was discovered at Lerna in 1954 and 1955, and other singletons in poor repair were noted by Wace at Mycenae, with related types at Argos.[2] The excavations of Circle B at Mycenae by Papademetriou and Mylonas were carried out with meticulous attention to details of rites and construction. Schliemann, by contrast, had failed to make sketches of the arrangements in each grave before lifting the objects, had related measurements to moving points like stelai being carted off to the depot, and had allowed certain vivid ideas about cremation, embalming, sacrificed slaves, and coffins to move between his observations and his excellent intelligence. The new evidence of Circle B, Wace's years of architectural and ceramic study, and Karo's monumental publication of the material from Circle A now all combine to allow a reconstruction of the Shaft Grave culture with much more reasonable perspective. A few points are still difficult, however: the origin of this culture, its duration, and its relation to other developments in Greece and abroad.

Circle A held six deep burial shafts and a group of Middle Helladic inhumations which were never numbered (Fig. 16). It was one focal point in a large prehistoric cemetery spreading down the slopes west of the town. There are disturbed graves under many later buildings in this section of Mycenae, which was finally made part of the inner city when the Lion Gate and southwest fortification wall were built after 1300 B.C. (p. 269; Pl. XXIV A). At that time the part of the old cemetery which contained the six shaft graves was graded into a terrace about 28 m. across. The original surface of the circle was deep underground by then, and the new terrace had to be supported by a massive retaining wall, perhaps standing on a wall contemporary with the graves. The thirteenth-century urban renewers lifted up some of the flat tombstones, or stelai, which had marked certain graves, and turned them to face west. They built an elegant new circuit wall to mark off the precinct, to be entered from the north and the Lion Gate. This wall is now one of the conspicuous landmarks of Mycenae. It is a fine double ring of upended limestone slabs forming a parapet around the graves. The core of the ring wall was filled with earth, and the two rows were capped by limestone plaques resting on wooden beams. Schliemann at first called this ring the agora of Mycenae, because the wall reminded him of the polished benches on which Homeric elders sit for public duty. As Tsountas remarked, the sitting here could have been comfortable only for giant Cyclopes—the wall stands 1.45 m. high. Some shafts were left

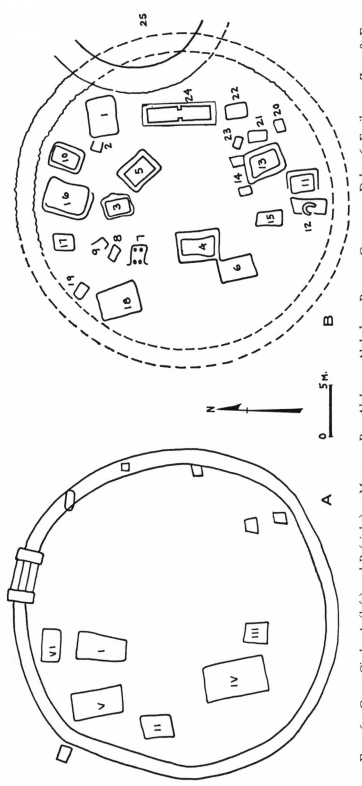

Fɪɢ. 16.—Grave Circles A (left) and B (right) at Mycenae. B 1, Alpha; 2, Alpha[1]; 3, Beta; 4, Gamma; 5, Delta; 6, Epsilon; 7, Zeta; 8, Eta; 9, Theta; 10, Iota; 11, Kappa; 12, Kappa[1]; 13, Lambda and Lambda[2]; 14, Lambda[1]; 15, Mu; 16, Nu; 17, Xi; 18, Omicron; 19, Pi; 20, Sigma; 21, Tau; 22, Upsilon; 23, Phi; 24, Rho; 25, Tomb of Clytemnestra.

outside the new circle or were destroyed by foundations for new buildings; a certain amount of gold was recovered from them later. Nineteen people were buried in the six preserved shafts, from two to five in each, a total of nine men, eight women, and two children.

Circle B outside the walls is slightly larger, poorer, and older. It was contained within a rough stone wall and was never redesigned (see Fig. 16). It held Middle Helladic inhumations in cists (Pl. X A) or in bare earth, the shafts, and one unique masonry tomb of later date (*Rho*, p. 125, Pl. XVI C). For practical purposes the distinction between cists and shafts comes at the one-meter depth; there are real differences in construction and concept. Of the twenty-four total graves, fourteen are true shafts and twenty-four persons are buried in them. Five stelai survive, one badly cut into when it was reused (Fig. 18).

The size of the circles, their enclosing walls, and the stelai are external symbols for the extraordinary quality of the burials within them. Such design goes far beyond plain Middle Helladic practice, and sets the graves specially apart in a funeral precinct. Schliemann's notes are filled with the excitement anyone still feels when he walks into the Mycenaean Room in the Athens National Museum for the first time.

There are in all five tombs, in the smallest of which I found yesterday the bones of a man and a woman covered by at *least* five kilograms of jewels of pure gold, with the most wonderful archaic, impressed ornaments; even the smallest leaf is covered with them. To make only a superficial description of the treasure would require more than a week. Today I emptied the tomb and still gathered there more than 6/10 kilogram of beautifully ornamented gold leafs; also many earrings and ornaments representing an altar with two birds . . . There were also found two scepters with wonderfully ciselled crystal handles and many large bronze vessels and many gold vessels. I telegraphed today to the *Times*. [Schliemann to Max Müller, November 24, 1876; Meyer, *JHS* 82 (1962) 92.]

In one of his earlier graves (V), at a depth of twenty-five feet he met a layer of pebbles,

. . . below which I found at a distance of three feet from each other, the remains of three human bodies. . . . on every one of the three bodies I found five diadems of thin gold plate . . . a number of small knives of obsidian, many fragments of a large silver vase with a mouth of copper, which is thickly plated with gold and splendidly ornamented with intaglio work; unfortunately it suffered too much from the funeral fire to be photographed. . . . the most remarkable wheel-made terracottas found in this tomb represent the lower parts of birds in black colour on a light yellow dead ground ... also ... a most ancient wheel-made vase, presenting on a light yellow dead ground a beautiful and fantastic ornament of plants ... in a very dark red colour. [*Mycenae and Tiryns* 150–59.]

These preliminary notes give in miniature exactly those elements which make the Shaft Graves unusual: multiple burial, the mass of gold too thin to be real, the quantity of weapons, the combinations of metals on vases and weapons, and the pottery imitating or being imported from the Cyclades (birds) and Crete (plants) (cf. Pl. IX F; Fig. 26). The obsidian knives show that the poorer past is in the immediate background but is merging with a wealthy, foreign-tinged present of extended sea trade.

The graves which held these treasures are not architecturally revolutionary except in the idea of the deep, roofed shaft. From the excavations of Circle B it is clear how they were made. A rectangular pit was dug into the soft bedrock as deep as four meters below the surface. The workmen then laid artificial walls of small stones or brick against the rock walls, to waist or shoulder height, and spread a layer of pebbles on the floor. The dead person was lowered down into the shaft on a skin or rope sling. His funeral costume was given its final trimming with gold, and his gifts were set beside him. These usually included his favorite weapons, personal jewelry, clay or metal vases, and such food as jars of oil, meat on the bone, even oysters. Log beams were then laid across the tops of the inner walls, supporting a roof of branches bound with clay. In Circle A some of these beams were shod in bronze for toughness; one grave (*Zeta*) in Circle B had four posts in the corners of the shaft to support the roof. Then the upper shaft above the roof was filled with earth almost to the top, some sort of ceremony was held which involved eating meat and drinking wine, the bones and broken wine cups were tossed into the shaft, earth was mounded slightly over the hole, and a stele was set in place if the grave was to have one. As long as the lower roof held out against the pressure of the earth above, the grave would stay empty, but if it cracked the whole weight of earth would slide down to crush the burials below. For every later burial the work had to be laboriously reversed: the stele set aside, the dirt scooped out, the roof undone. Someone had to climb down to move the first body and its gifts aside, and to steady the new body as it was being lowered; then all would be built up and filled in as before. A Mycenaean funeral was always a lot of work; no wonder the family entertained afterward in grateful payment (cf. p. 299).

The gold in the shafts was fairly well protected by this mass of earth and roofing, for a robber would be conspicuous the minute he went down from the top. This did not stop robbery; it only had to be planned beforehand. Circle B: *Lambda* gives evidence for such a plan successfully carried out. The builders dug a hole through one wall into an adjoining shallow grave, and later reached from that grave to the new funeral gifts, overlooking only a heap of swords right under the hole. In the later Mycenaean world it is quite common for the family to remove belongings from older burials, and the tholos tombs of the Early Mycenaean Age were robbed regularly.

Scarcely a tomb in the older circle, B, was as rich as the poorest in the younger circle, A. Graves *Alpha, Gamma, Nu,* and *Omicron* in the former measure up to the standard of the less spectacular in the latter, I, II, and VI, but are completely overshadowed by the great shafts III, IV, and V. The contrast between the two precincts is effective documentation for the growing wealth of this new military society at Mycenae. Circle B: *Gamma* illustrates the older level of achievement at its most interesting. Two stelai stood on the mound above the shaft; a carved one had been cut down later to serve as the base for a plain one (Fig. 18). The upper filling of the shaft held at least forty broken vases, apparently taken out of the lower chamber when extra burials were made. The grave itself held three men and a woman in extended positions. Two of the four had been pushed aside to the walls, and the third had almost no gifts of value. He was a well-grown man (1.70 m. tall) about twenty-eight years old who seems to have died after one of the earliest observed trephining operations in Greece, for his skull, fractured in life, had three neat holes bored through it. The fourth dead person, a man about six feet tall (1.80 m.) which was huge for those days, took up most of the space on the grave floor. He lay on his back with his hands on his hips, his legs curiously bowed like a rider's, a bronze sword and an ivory-handled dagger by his right thigh. The grave contained more than fourteen bronze swords, daggers, spearheads, and knives; one bronze vase and nine painted clay vases; two gold cups; gold bands which had trimmed the sleeves and hems of the funeral clothes; a wooden box sheathed in silver plate; an electrum funeral mask which was not found on anyone's face but resting against rotted wood in a corner; and the famous little amethyst gem, scarcely half as big as a finger nail, which gives the first real portrait of a Mycenaean prince (Pl. XI C; p. 95).

Grave IV in Circle A was one of the two richest in the younger group. Three men and two women were buried in it. Since Schliemann made no plan of how the gifts were distributed, and the inventory takes 395 entries in Karo with more added since, only a rough total can be attempted here. There were three gold masks (Pl. XI A); two gold crowns; eight gold diadems or head-bands; at least twenty-seven swords and sixteen more sword pommels of ivory, gold, alabaster, and wood; at least five daggers and six more pommels;[3] sixteen knives; five "razors"; five gold vases; ten or eleven silver vases; twenty-two bronze vases; three alabaster vases; two faïence vases; eight clay vases; two gold *rhyta* (Pl. XI D); three silver *rhyta* (Pl. XIV); two ostrich-egg *rhyta;* two engraved gold rings; two silver rings; three gold armbands; at least one gold necklace with animal links (Fig. 19); one gold-and-ivory comb; one large silver figure-of-eight shield. From the funeral clothes of these five people came 683 engraved gold discs and miscellaneous repoussé ornaments, gold foil cut-outs in the shape of cult buildings, bulls' heads, double axes, stars, octopodes, lilies, and other flowers (Fig. 19). There were gold knobs from the men's dagger-belts, gold straps from their sword-baldrics, gold sleeve and neck and legging bands, gold and linen from their sword-scabbards, plume-sockets from their helmets. There were arrowheads (38), boars' tusks (92), whetstones (2), an ax, a trident, nine beads of Peloponnesian amethyst and 1290 of Baltic amber, "sacral knots" of colored Minoan faïence, a crystal and faïence gaming board probably brought from Knossos. Add to this catalogue the less identifiable strips and discs of gold, scraps of ivory, bits of bronze blades, fragments of woven linen, handles off gold and silver cups whose bodies had disintegrated, rivets and nails and pins and splinters of wood, and it is hard to believe that the Shaft Graves represent simply a mild progress from Middle Helladic cists.

The numbers by themselves are impressive, and yet they cannot convey the extraordinary workmanship and expense involved in these gifts. Two of the daggers are the famous inlaid ones with scenes of a lion hunt and galloping lions (Pl. XII). One of the gold cups is the Cup of Nestor with hawks on the struts (Fig. 48 *a*); one of the silver ones is the Silver Siege Rhyton (p. 100, Pl. XIV). The gold rings have scenes of battle and stag hunts. The sword pommels are made of precious materials and patterned with lions and panthers; the hilts are gripped by griffin protomes or set with gold and lapis cloisonné; the blades are engraved with spirals and shields. One of the bronze cauldrons is incised with a sign in Cretan script, the first known on the mainland (Fig. 6 *t*). The materials are international: ostrich eggs from Nubia sent through Egypt and Crete, lapis lazuli from Mesopotamia, alabaster and faïence from Crete, raw ivory from Syria, silver from Anatolia, amber from Prussia brought down the Adriatic route or out of Odessa across the north Aegean. The techniques used in shaping these materials are mostly new to Greece, and the styles of art represented upon them are as mixed as their origins.

ART IN THE SHAFT GRAVES

Almost every object is decorated with abstract patterns or figured scenes. Many combine different materials for their contrasting color and texture. The Shaft Grave princes seem to have particularly valued small portable objects like weapons, jewelry, and drinking cups, so that surfaces are slender and the treatment intricate. Some shapes demanded symmetry, like necklace discs or sword hilts, but symmetry is by no means an artistic rule, for dagger blades and stone stelai have scenes which stream in a single direction. Because the wealth represented by the funeral gifts was not inherited or typical in mainland Greece but was somehow acquired abroad (p. 106), they were naturally ornamented in an international hybrid style. And because many of them are new to the Aegean repertory, like the masks and stelai and clothes trimmings, the Aegean could not always provide an iconographical tradition—there is experiment which sometimes fumbles, sometimes succeeds in creating models for later Mycenaean art. The peculiar art of the Shaft Graves comes from combining these factors at a special moment. It mixes the rich and the tawdry, the miniature and the monumental, naturalism and abstract heraldry, intricacy and primitive coarseness—it is both eclectic and original.

The Stelai

These tall limestone slabs are the only monumental art of the period. Not every grave or dead person had one. Two sculptured and three unsculptured examples were found in Circle B (the richer graves *Alpha, Gamma, Omicron,* and *Nu*); eleven carved and four or six plain examples came from four shafts in Circle A (Figs. 17, 18). Only six of the twenty-two are decently preserved. They range between three and six feet high (1.05 to 1.86 m.), are narrow, smooth on the back, and incised or lightly carved on the front. The local soft limestone is easily pocked by exposure to weather, and the cut surfaces flake away easily, but the scenes which can be made out repay close consideration. The principal designs are bands of ornamental running spirals and scenes of chariots or animals which are the first real examples of sculpture in Greece.

Their style used to be thought appalling. Even Schliemann, who was fond of them, felt they were "made as rudely and in as puerile a manner as if they were the primitive artist's first essay to represent living beings." Perhaps they were, at least in stone. It must have been exciting to design them.

Four types of scene have been identified in the stelai: racing, hunting, war, and animal combats. On the best-known slab (Fig. 17 *a*), a single man drives a two-wheeled chariot at a furious pace, hunched over the rail, urging on his

Fig. 17.—Grave stelai from Circle A, Mycenae: (*a*) No. V, Grave V; (*b*) No. I, Grave V; (*c*) No. VIII, context unknown; (*d*) No. IX, context unknown. (After Heurtley, *BSA* 1921–23, Pls. XIX–XX, Fig. 30.)

horse(s), while a man on foot stands placidly in front of him holding a large club or stick. Both men are naked and unarmed except for the sword hanging from the driver's shoulder (?) and the footman's stick; the driver may have a whip in his right hand and seems to wear a cap or helmet. He has usually been understood as an Achaian warrior running down his opponent with the new battle chariot. Mylonas has argued, however, that the scene is not military at all, but shows aristocrats at a funeral game, where chariot races were later the highest entertainment for trained men at the death of kings. The artist makes a "snapshot" of the dramatic moment when the chariot turns the mark (represented by the footman with his stick) before winning home. The argument is persuasive, for it is a feeble battle without shields or spears. Chariots are illustrated in funerary contexts by later Mycenaean art (p. 205), and the horse is linked to death rites in many primitive Indo-European cultures. But battle scenes are also attested, in thirteenth-century palace frescoes (Pl. XXXI) and perhaps other, battered, contemporary stelai (Fig. 17 c–d). One shows a battle wagon, four-wheeled in the Near Eastern fashion, with the warrior apparently plunging head first to the ground behind his charioteer; another, in two registers, inserts a spearhead beneath the rolling wheel above, and shows two armed warriors under a taut rein below, blunt-faced and determined.

A stele with a full-scale hunting scene (see Fig. 17 b) cannot be accurately interpreted, for the condition is too poor. A lion pursues a gazelle below; above a chariot rushes to the right over circles which have been understood as rocky ground or even (implausibly) a fallen enemy whose toes are upturned under his shield. Hunting from chariots is known as a Shaft Grave sport from a gold ring found in Grave IV, and is represented in Egyptian painting of a slightly later date. All these chariot compositions look unpracticed enough to be first attempts. The details of hitching are ignored, the powerful horse conceals his mate (?) and careens over the plain like a lion, the naked rubbery bodies and featureless faces of the actors are spread across the field without any control of perspective. The surface is as flat around the figures as around the edging ornaments which hold the scenes in geometric blocks and registers. Spirals are inserted decoratively to fill the blank ground.

This intrusion of unnatural ornament appears even in a more experienced composition, one which occurs in better style on gems and goldwork, and probably has Near Eastern models behind it (Fig. 18). This is the theme of great animals hunting each other and being hunted in turn by men, best illustrated by one stele from Circle B: *Gamma*. The center of the block was cut away to be used as the base for a new stele, but Marinatos' reconstruction is practically certain. Two lions attack a bull and are themselves attacked by hunters. One man is already wounded and lies crumpled in the pasture, but his companion on the other side has hurt the lion, who falls backward away from the bull. This scene shares features with the hunts on the dagger blades, where Schliemann immediately saw an emotional likeness to Homeric similes, hungry marauders running in on a herd and the herdsmen trying to beat them off or watching helplessly. It is the kind of situation which touched an agricultural society where it hurt most. Yet the Mycenaeans seem to have invested the bull and lion with further, perhaps symbolic, significance, and this stele is valuable in showing that their combat, which will always be a favorite theme in Mycenaean art, has already in this earliest period been tried out on a large public surface. It is handled in the normal technique for the better stelai of both Circles: the sculptor simply cuts away the background stone to an even plane

FIG. 18.—Grave stele from Circle B, Grave *Gamma,* Mycenae. (After Marinatos, *Geras Keramopoullou* 74.)

around his figures without further modeling or incision. A more primitive group is just incised, as though drawn with a stick on plasticine.

The stelai show several characteristics of Mycenaean art which will endure until the Dark Ages. Their themes are significant: the expensive militarism of warriors with chariots and horses, the large-scale violent animal combats, the atmosphere of rugged country life. The animals are all arranged in the "flying-gallop" stance which sweeps the Aegean at about this time, intruding into the older canons of Egyptian and Minoan art. All four feet are off the ground, or the animal's body stretches almost parallel to the earth with an upward kick of his hind feet toward the clouds, a shorthand convention meant to impress us with his tremendous speed and energy (Fig. 19; Pl. XII). No one is sure where this convention began or how it spread so fast. Isolated examples are known slightly earlier than the Shaft Graves, but from now on it is the highest fashion in the Mediterranean and seems typically Aegean rather than Egyptian or Near Eastern. It may have been formulated by artists working toward a new concept of representation, in which the traditional static outline of a man or animal was discarded for a characteristic pose or action which could convey a story in universally recognizable terms, however frozen. The flying gallop is essentially a narrative creation. Another persistent preference of the stelai sculptors is for organizing the picture in parallel bands, in panels of strict horizontals and verticals, avoiding natural background and treating the figure as a silhouette clearly defined through isolation. There is much in common between this technique and the rare figure studies on Matt-painted vases (cf. Fig. 13); one would not be surprised if some of the stelai had been accented originally with the simple colors of pottery. The ornaments are those of vases, too, vastly more practiced than the figure style; the whole exercise is decorative drawing on stone rather than true sculpture.

Metalwork

There are several styles in metalwork (Fig. 19). On round surfaces like sword pommels or the flat gold discs from clothing, the composition is normally interlocked or symmetrical. A number of small gold cutouts show an absolutely antithetical, heraldic treatment of addorsed animals which seems alien to any Cretan style and is more congenial to Anatolia or the Near East. At the same time themes are borrowed from Crete, like the octopus and the butterfly, but arranged in the new, stiff way (cf. Pl. XLVII A). The intricacies of formal ornament—interlocking spirals and quadrated meanders—are more "European" (meaning what will turn up in Europe centuries later as the foundation for Hallstatt work), although the elements were already current in Early Helladic and Cycladic design. Few artists have ever made more ornamental use of the spiral than the Shaft Grave goldsmiths. They confine it to neat running strips or extend it over the whole field of a breastplate or hilt (Pl. XIII A); they alternate it with dotted concentric circles or intrude upon it the new foliate bands of Crete. In every field of design they count heavily upon an exact geometry of growing or diminishing size, and enlivening simple outlines with elaborate miniature surface textures.

In the realm of figured composition, bad and good lie side by side; there is clumsy relief work on the most expensive metals, like the Cup of Nestor (Fig. 48 *a*), and excellent detail on inexpensive ornaments manufactured in Mycenae specially for the grave. We cannot decide by quality alone which things are imported and which things made at home. Often when the workmanship is best the theme is purely local; at other times themes borrowed from Crete are treated in a surprising drab clumsiness. An example of the first category is the amethyst portrait gem from *Gamma* which surely must have been made by a Minoan (Pl. XI C), since Greece had at this time no experience in gem carving, but which records the Mycenaean physical type of a middle-aged bearded man with prominent eye ridges and a thin flaring nose. The face is like those on the gold funerary masks which, in spite of crudeness and battered condition, have the same high cheek bones, thin-ridged nose, heavy brows, large ears, and thin lips (cf. Pl. XI A). This kind of study is rare in either Crete or Greece, but the gem reflects more finely the same mainland desire for royal portraiture as the masks so alien to Crete. The second category is illustrated by the little gold cutouts of the lady in a Cretan flounced skirt, or the cult building with birds perched on horns of consecration (Fig. 19). The themes are pure Cretan and the execution appalling.

Three drinking cups in the form of animals, all from Grave IV, illustrate a further curious range of style. A silver bull's head with a gold rosette on its brow should be Cretan; a parallel in black steatite from the fifteenth-century Little Palace at Knossos has the same rounded, delicately textured masses. A silver stag with branching horns is also clearly foreign, in this case from Anatolia: a traditional type, elongated, with stumpy legs, a grave motionless pose. The great lion's head cup in gold belongs to neither of these artistic provinces (Pl. XI D). Its flat facets suggest more familiarity with wood-carving and whittling than direct metallurgy; the style reappears many centuries later in the northern nomad or Scythian spheres of art where burial customs also recall the early Mycenaeans (cf. Pl. XI B).

These stylistic incongruities, drawn together in the Shaft Graves into a single artistic repertory, may be tentatively explained in three ways. The inharmonious pieces may be really imported from different foreign areas; or different styles may have become attached to different subjects, as powerful curved Minoan modeling for bulls but flat stark carving for un-Minoan lions; or the princes of Mycenae had passed through several overseas districts bringing back models, ideas, and craftsmen (or alien princesses with prejudices and craftsmen

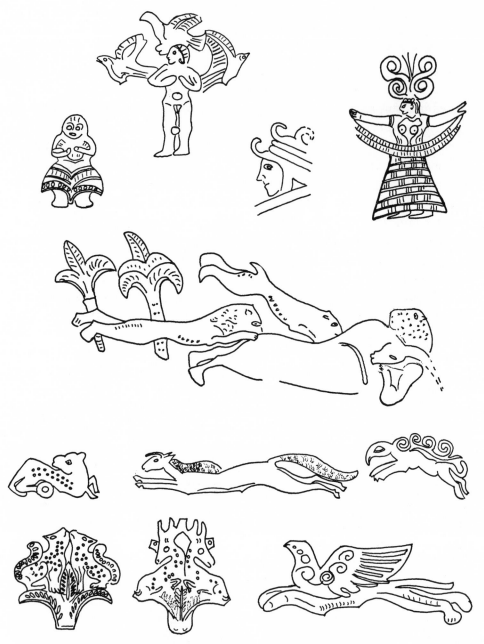

Fig. 19.—Variant styles in the art of the Shaft Graves

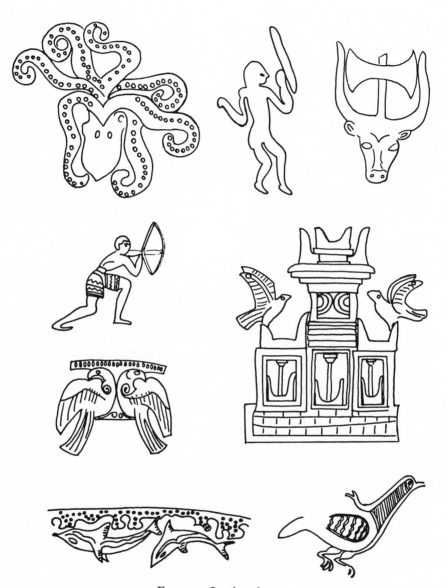

FIG. 19.—*Continued*

in their retinue) who continued to work at Mycenae for a generation or two, each in his traditional way, until a genuine Mycenaean style gradually evolved.

The most renowned metalwork of the Shaft Graves is on the inlaid dagger blades and the silver vases with war scenes (Pls. XII–XIV; Fig. 21). Here are the same paradoxes as before: work so excellent it is attributed irrationally to Crete, technique at home in the Levant, and subject matter dear to the Mycenaeans. The splash of weapons through these graves is extraordinary. Half are types not made in Crete. Long swords are known there from one hoard at Arkalochori, contemporary with the beginning of the Shaft Graves and perhaps slightly earlier, in an aristocratic model: a narrow rapier with rounded shoulders and such a short tang for insertion into the hilt that one could never trust it for anything but a level thrust (Type A). The blades are just under three feet long and there is light incising on some surfaces. The great dress sword of Mallia with an acrobat curling around the gold pommel-plating is the only really ornate Cretan forerunner of the Shaft Grave swords. The Mycenaeans also have a more efficient, broader, and stouter blade (Type B) with a longer tang and flanged shoulders for greater handle security, which does not occur in Crete at all. On both types great care is taken with the balance, by trying light pommels in wood or alabaster or faïence or ivory, and the blades are patterned with magnificent variety. The flying, wild steppe-horses or griffins stretched along the blade (Fig. 19) are not Minoan art types. The lions and griffins carved on the hilts, sometimes gripping the blade heraldically in their jaws (Pl. XIII A) are not known in Crete. Other designs are ambiguous: lilies are at home in Crete and in islands like Melos where Crete and mainland meet; figure-of-eight shields become popular in both cultures at the start of Late Bronze; the battle-axes inlaid on a fragment of contemporary blade from the island of Thera (Pl. XIII C) are almost unique but have possible prototypes in the Levant. War, beasts, and gardens laid on war blades symbolize the complex charms of mainland civilization.

The inlaid daggers draw on all these mixed sources for a brilliantly achieved effect (Pls. XII–XIII). They are done in the niello technique which is rare everywhere in the Mediterranean except in Greece but started as a specialty of Asia (the earliest pieces come from Byblos, and were made about 1900–1800 B.C.) For the three Mycenae blades (Pl. XII) the smith cut a shallow bed into the bronze and laid in a darker sheet of bronze against it, into which cold-hammered cutouts of figures and landscape elements were set. He polished the surface to remove hammermarks, oxidized the blade to darken the silver parts, engraved the details of tunics, hair, eyes, and spotted skins. Finally he filled these incisions with black niello, a copper-lead-sulphur-borax compound, heating the blade to burn it in. Different grades of metal were used for color contrast: in the Nile scene, pale gold, polished silver, and pale electrum for the fish and papyrus blooms; reddish electrum for drops of blood on a duck's breast; dark silver for the river; and bronze for the fields behind, all framed in the brighter bronze of the cutting edge. This is correctly called *Metallmalerei,* or painting in metals. The brightness is a link with Cretan polychrome vases and frescoes, the skill with Cretan metalworking skills as old as the prototypes for the Treasure of Tod.[4] The technique comes ultimately from the harbors of Syria where Mycenaeans had been trading (cf. Fig. 40), and the narrative interest and the details of weaponry are specifically Greek contributions.

The Nilotic scene of leopards hunting ducks along a river in a papyrus marsh is the least Greek (Pl. XII A). Its animals in their natural setting look like contemporary Cretan frescoes which are in turn indebted to Egypt. But the naïvely angled, unmuscular bodies are not what one would expect of a Cretan master metalsmith. The lions flying through rocky fields are a Greek or Egyptian motif in a conventional Minoan setting (Pl. XII C). The lion hunt, the most complex of the three in its numbers of figures with alternating attitudes and weapons, is a pure, beloved Mycenaean theme (Pl. XII B). Five men are in serious battle with three lions. The largest lion is covering the escape of the other two, who fly away with a backward look; he has clawed down the front hunter and, as he falls with outflung arms and curled knees, the lion passes him to charge the other four who stand tense in closed rank. Left legs are thrust forward and bent, weapons are raised to throw or shoot; there is tautness on both sides as we watch a moment of unfulfilled action where the artist has no favorites. The four standing hunters carry carefully alternated tower- and figure-of-eight shields, seen now from the front with dark splotches on the hides, now from the back where they frame the slender bodies. The unshielded archer crouches between two armored friends and stretches his bow (see Fig. 19). The figures have elegant Cretan proportions but wear a kind of embroidered trunks known rarely, and later than this, on Crete. Their hair is short or knotted up in the mainland fashion, their javelins and shields are of mainland types, and their flexed rubbery anatomy is blander than in Crete. The huge lion with open jaw and steel spring is quite another beast than the sinuous cat of an Hagia Triada fresco, Crete's closest parallel, a truer brother to the slinking mixoleopards on the Myrsinochorion dagger of the next epoch (Pl. XIII B). How can one say what is Cretan or Mycenaean in so blended a piece? The inlay technique continued for a long time at a high level in Greece and nowhere else; common sense would call it a mainland achievement. Some inlaid weapons must have been stolen from old tombs and shown around in classical Greece—inspiring Euripides'

> All along the blade of the deadly sword, hooves pounding,
> horses leap; black above their backs the dust blows.
>
> *Elektra 476*

The Silver Siege Rhyton

This battered drinking cup from Grave IV must interest any student of the period intensely, in spite of a condition which will always conceal what the figured scene once represented (Pl. XIV).[5] It is a slender, rather short, funnel-shaped vase of silver plate with repoussé reliefs, fitted with a bronze lip, handle, and foot which were overplated in gold. Too few fragments are left to restore the vase to its original height, which was probably *ca.* 0.30 m., and since the surviving pieces do not fit together exactly, the composition may be rearranged. The cup, like the daggers, blends a Cretan form and motifs with an un-Cretan style. The rhyton is a Cretan vase-shape manufactured in precious metals and stone as well as in clay, ornate examples being carried in both Cretan and Egyptian procession frescoes (see Fig. 28). Minoan steatite versions are famous but seem slightly later than the Mycenae vase. They are carved in a very different style, with beautifully outlined figures arranged in mannered genre or religious scenes, generally in registers, and with only shorthand suggestions of landscape or architecture.

The Mycenaean vase is both cruder and more dramatic. It is almost the earliest known representation of the siege scene which later became a stock sculptural theme among the Egyptians and Assyrians. This vase attempts to illustrate an entire city in its landscape, with crowded miniature soldiers and civilians. It gives the impression of being reduced from wall painting or from some other broad flat surface where the variety of figures and architecture would seem less cramped. Its only possible predecessor in the Aegean world is the faïence Town Mosaic from Knossos, which is even harder to reconstruct. There are two or three later war compositions on the mainland which may reflect the same tradition (see Fig. 20 *b*).

Toward the top of the vase, in the principal fragment, is sketched a complicated city on a hill. It is seen from below, and from a distance across the bay over which it stands guard. Its walls are irregularly bedded on a hump of rock, indicating a mountain setting as at Mycenae itself. Toward the left, where the rock falls away, is a steep stone retaining wall for a terrace projecting over the mountain side. One sees the edge of a palace three stories or more high, the rooms or houses on each story set back in stepped grades. A great city door of wooden planks is swung shut where the rock rises highest against the wall and the enemy could climb up most easily. A coastal plain separates the city from the sea, which here forms a deep irregular inlet like the innermost corner of a narrow bay or a river-mouth. Beyond the city is a grove of olive trees, on a plain which recedes infinitely toward the horizon.

At the dramatic moment of action chosen by the artist, four excited women are standing on the terraced edge of the city, and two more are leaning forward from windows or terraces above. They wear short-sleeved jackets, and wave their arms in great gestures of encouragement or terror. One looks back toward the interior of the city as though to call out reinforcements, or to turn away from something she has just seen in the plain below. In another part of the city where a stepped portico rises high with pillars and horns of consecration, we see a pair(?) of men naked on a balcony, one straining toward the fight, the other seeming to rest on the parapet.

Below the city on several types of terrain a battle or skirmish moves toward the left where the vase is broken off. On the edge of the water three naked slingers stretched full height act as a screen for four or five naked archers who squat on one hock and balance themselves with an outthrust leg as they draw their bows; a sixth archer is in the front rank facing a man who looks back toward the city, more likely a desperate or wounded compatriot than the first of the enemy. Behind this active center of the battle two men stand reserved and intent, clothed in stiff tunics from shoulder to knee, and holding staffs stretched forward toward the fight (or perhaps javelins, the line is unclear). A naked soldier comes rushing past them. This total "army" of thirteen men is all barefoot and wears its hair cropped short.

Farther below, on a smooth surface interpreted as deep sea, come the upper bodies or caps of five men, who are usually imagined as poling a boat toward shore. The steersman wears a plumed helmet and short-sleeved tunic; the others have ridged caps without plumes. They are moving up the narrow inlet, and have passed the mouth where a pair of wild trees stand on a promontory. On the other side of the promontory stretches a ledge of rocks or shoals over which are scattered the limp spread-eagled bodies of three or four men, swimming or pulling themselves from rock to rock. Since the ground is rendered in a delicate but conventional series of triple arches which also ornament the foot of the vase, and the postures are so indecisive, it is impossible to be sure of these men's role. The composition is closed, as far as the fragments reach, by two men with great clubs raised above their heads, the only figures moving right toward the city. These seem to be the only surviving figures from among the enemy. Sprawled between the two sides are six collapsed naked men, who could be interpreted as the dead. Others have taken them for swimmers, or for slingers stooping for stones. The fragment does not join anything and may be rotated.

This involved drama, where we see at least thirty-eight armed or moving figures, six trees, and a large city rising in tiers, is executed in a miniature technique, and naturally some details are blurred from the condensation into small space. Perhaps the preparatory sketch does not always coincide with the finished repoussé hammering; there are shallow lines along the shore which would scarcely have shown even when the cup was held in the drinker's hand at a normal distance. These have been taken for stones and throwing sticks, or the prows of sinking ships, but are too faint for certainty. There is no space for meticulous relief in individual figures; only the eyes, chins, stretched muscles, and buttocks are emphasized. On the other hand, the artist was talented at composing the elements of his picture so that nothing is hidden or confused. A little motion suggests tremendous activity. Figures are cross-layered cleverly against the landscape with glimpses of more distant action through the arms and legs of the front rank. There is skill in proportions (though the men are too big for the architecture as always in Aegean art) so that both crowded impressions and individual actions can be brought to the surface without muting each other. The perspective is unruly but convincing: the city is viewed from below, the boatmen and swimmers from above, and the shore-fighters from a natural height; the artist is floating in an official launch offshore.

The only sure way to interpret the story would be to find the missing pieces in Schliemann's dump. If the Siege Rhyton is a genuine historical relief, as it is often claimed to be, it is the only one in Aegean art. More likely it expresses a generalized tradition of battle imagery which may be attached to different historical events through succeeding generations. In Crete the Town Mosaic is less warlike but contains a similar variety: the faïence plaques which compose it illustrate the houses of the town with slit windows above a gate building, soldiers leaning on their spears, a ship's prow, swimmers rising with a froglike kick, goats in a pasture, branches, and waves of water. No one is fighting, but all one needs for a good siege is present. The Town Mosaic is earlier than the Siege Rhyton; other excerpts are slightly later, like the fragment of a steatite vase showing a bearded archer leaning into his shot against a sea of triple curves (Fig. 20 *a*). This is a sophisticated caricature of a non-Cretan, possibly a Mycenaean or Syrian, with flying beard and huge crooked nose.

Other fragmentary survivals of mainland art illustrate war themes in a finer but more conventional manner than the Siege Rhyton. The first is one of the most beautiful of all Mycenaean silver works, part of a great vase also from Grave IV showing warriors in combat on a hilly battlefield (Fig. 21 *a*). Here is everything one expects: tall soldiers, figure-of-eight shields, kilted tunics, and

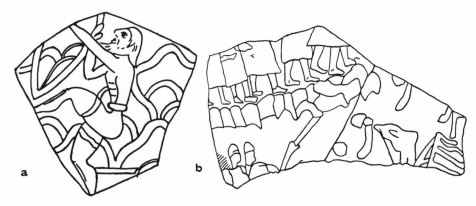

Fig. 20.—War scenes on steatite vases: (*a*) fragment with an archer, Knossos (after Evans, *PM* III, Fig. 59); (*b*) fragment with men marching through mountains; a dolphin and a ship, Epidauros (after Papademetriou, *Praktika* 1950, 200).

long spears; the artist is free from bizarre obscurities. In the thirteenth century two examples continue the tradition. The siege fresco from the megaron of the palace at Mycenae includes the city on the hill, pastoral landscape, busy soldiers, and decorative vulnerable women (p. 200; Pl. XXXI). A broken steatite vase from neighboring Epidauros represents, in the upper register, an army of soldiers marching up a rocky hillside, and in the lower register two helmeted warriors facing a seascape with a dolphin and a ship (Fig. 20 *b*). Siege scenes are known among the unpublished Pylos frescoes too. The Siege Rhyton initiates this persistent series in mainland art. It goes further than the Town Mosaic in trying to show an ancient town in its complete setting of hills, groves, and sea, with details drawn from observation, and the chosen moment one of poised emergency. This instinct to regard the whole town as an actor, or as the only setting in which individuals have significance, reappears in palace frescoes and seems very Greek.

The rhyton has been discussed at such length because the historian is in desperate need of a clue to the history of the Shaft Grave princes, and the scene looks so complicated and real that one is tempted to believe it an illustration of some recent adventure, perhaps one already circulating in poetry. It is not the kind of cup a silversmith would turn out in dozens of replicas for casual customers. Whoever ordered it, and wanted it buried with him, must have had

a   b

FIG. 21.—Silver cups of the Early Mycenaean Age: (*a*) battle scene, Circle A, Grave IV, Mycenae (after Karo, *SG*, Pl. 129, drawing by S. Chapman); (*b*) hunting scene, Dendra tholos tomb (after Persson, *RT*, Pl. 17, drawing by S. Chapman).

personal connections with such scenes. Even without this visual imagery, the swords in the Shaft Graves are evidence that Mycenae's early wealth came more by violence than merchant profiteering. No ingenuity will transform the vase into a historical document, however, or make it tell where the gold came from. Guesses have made the defenders into Hyksos or Cretans or Lycians, the attackers into Mycenaeans or nameless natives in whose quarrel the Mycenaeans come by sea to interfere. But like the artists of the dagger blades, the designer is emotionally objective, surveying impartially the troubled women, the responsible elders, the desperate swimmers; he is also necessarily working in the eclectic vocabulary of his period. The architecture is reminiscent of Crete, and the slingers might be Cretans, but not as they—who never paraded naked or wore their hair in ugly crops—saw themselves. There are no normal Aegean swords and spears, no kilts or Asiatic robes, only the single tunic on the steersman to link this foreign scene with Greece. It need not be very foreign. One thinks of Phylakopi with its Minoan houses and naked fishermen, or cities on remote rivers in Greece which are being settled by Mycenaeans in this period on top of a "barbarous" peasant stock: Kalydon, Thermon, Peristeria (p. 117). Into some quasi-historical memory of this kind the artist has inserted elements from half-recalled prototypes perhaps in paint or steatite, and by fusing the two types of memory has made a story both too detailed to be traditional, and too general to serve as a document. Its great value is in crystallizing for us a current that runs through the other representational scenes of Shaft Grave art: specific scenes pervaded by a conventional, hybrid iconography, with real actors performing timeless acts in rich detail. The two silver vases of Shaft Grave IV seem to project such memories onto a large permanent surface.

Pottery

Just as the gold and silver objects show a queer searching for style, so do the vases of both circles seem original and often without parallel.[6] It is as though in the process of creating a ceramic tradition in Greece, drawn from Old Minyan, Minoan, and Cycladic models, experimental freaks were momentarily tolerated. They are much more perplexing to date than later standard wares. Circle B pottery is the culmination of the Middle Helladic tradition, with huge ridged Minyan goblets, curiously patterned Matt-painted cups and jars (Fig. 51), and a few polychrome pieces reflecting the developments in contemporary Phylakopi and Crete. The Minyan ware is not limited to cists of Middle Helladic form, but is found also in the new deep shafts such as *Iota*. This grave held Matt-painted jars and jars with spirals in the newer Aegean styles as well, and since only one skeleton was buried in it, we see the convergence of all these traditions at a single crucial moment of time.

An astonishing feature of Circle B pottery is the wild handling of Cycladic motifs—birds, roses, suns, trailing vines, lilies, ivy, and spirals (Pl. IX E; cf. Pl. VIII F)—in some cases on local shapes in local Argive clay. Phylakopi, the leading contemporary city in the islands, is usually considered the source of this style, but obviously the potters at Mycenae are diverting and enriching Cycladic influence. Other Greek sites with Cycladic vases, like Samikon (Pl.

IX F) or Delphi, seem to react more calmly. Circle B continues past this experimental stage into real Late Helladic I pottery such as Vapheio Cups (Grave *Omicron;* p. 117; cf. Pl. XVIII A–B) but has no imported Minoan vases of that period. The only piece from Knossos seems to be a little green faïence cup with a spray of flowers on the rim, like those faïence vases from the MM III B Temple Repositories which are associated with bird jugs from Phylakopi.

Circle A offers the same Middle Helladic range but with less stylistic exaggeration, and extending much later in time into developed Early Mycenaean. There are Cycladic bird jugs, local Minyan and Matt vases, then local Mycenaean of an impressive early kind alongside Late Minoan I imports from early fifteenth-century Knossos (p. 140; cf. Fig. 26 *a–b*). The abundance of gold, silver, and bronze vessels in those graves perhaps made clay seem less interesting, and it is surprising how poor some of the ordinary pots are. The best vases of the later phase incorporate Minoan rather than Cycladic motifs— double axes, heart-shaped ivy leaves, lilies, argonauts, and heavy-rimmed majestic spirals—but begin to transform them into the real Greek idiom which inspires the next four hundred years of mainland pottery.

The Historical Setting

These crosscurrents in art are set in the decades after the Second Intermediate Period in Egypt when stable power orbits were forming in many parts of the Mediterranean. The older graves, still late Middle Helladic, mark the first major turning of the mainland toward the sea and the East, where it would always turn for vitality as long as Mycenaean culture lived. The first contacts are tentative. Crete had been trading with the Levant since the nineteenth century B.C., at important harbors like Byblos, but her first brushes with Greece in MM I A are sporadic (p. 73). Indeed, Middle Bronze trade is tenuous everywhere except in the line from Syria to the Delta and the Red Sea. Conversely, Minyan culture was slow to spread through the islands and scarcely reached Crete at all before the Shaft Grave epoch. Cycladic sailors may have mediated at first between the two cultures which would soon swamp or ignore the Cyclades. The earliest Middle Helladic expeditions went up toward Troy and the Anatolian coast (Miletos), west toward the Lipari islands, but not steadily down to Crete. When Crete finally entered the picture, the image it offered the Greeks was so attractive that Minoan fads buried the older styles under an avalanche of novelties.

Opportunities for new commerce were found in the atmosphere of internationalism and curiosity which stirred the Mediterranean after the Hyksos interlude in Egypt. The "foreign" art style of the Shaft Graves awakes after the
Hittite king Mursilis I had destroyed the first dynasty of Babylon (*ca.* 1595),
and the pharaohs Kamose and Ahmose were coping with the ill-mannered
Hyksos kings in the Delta (*ca.* 1565). As the era prospered the Mitanni
warrior kingdom in Syria grew strong, and Aegean notions were adapted for
private houses at Alalakh; Crete was rebuilding after the earthquake of MM
III B. The awakening ends with the campaigns of Tuthmosis III against the
Mitanni and Hittites in the middle fifteenth century. Those campaigns created
a new, in some ways more stable, international balance. Then developing Mycenaean Greece and wealthy Crete got to know each other very well, unhappily
for Crete. In practical terms, the beginning of the Shaft Grave era links up with
MM III B Crete, and Crete in turn links up vaguely with the Eighteenth Dynasty in Egypt after 1570. There is nothing imported in Circle B before 1550
B.C. at the earliest. Circle A begins in the same ripe Middle Helladic age, lasts
through the sixteenth century with steadily intensifying Minoan association,
and terminates (Grave I) after the accession of Queen Hatshepsut in Egypt in
1504 B.C., well into the fifteenth century.

It is strange, and a matter for regret, that no trace of the palace or town of
the Shaft Grave princes has ever been found at Mycenae. Solid architecture is
nearly a blank in this period and the succeeding one. Karo thought that the
Shaft Grave people's nomad background made them concentrate their wealth
in small jewels and weapons which they could wear on their persons or carry
in wooden chests. Indifference to earthly housing and interest in rich hidden
tombs is a trait among Scythians later; perhaps it could be projected back onto
sixteenth-century Greece too, although by Late Helladic I the land seems too
settled for a really Bedouin scale of values. Perhaps one should imagine the
Mycenaean warriors living behind a wooden stockade on the citadel, in a small
town which provided shelter though not permanent comfort or luxury. The
graves illustrate a dramatic difference in wealth between royalty and subjects.
Houses must have contrasted too, but at present the domestic architecture of
the sixteenth and fifteenth centuries is only scantily known in the rest of Greece
and not at all in connection with the Shaft Graves of the Argolid.

One must separate the idea of Shaft Grave burial from the rich Minoan
influence on the later graves at Mycenae. Technically it is wrong to call the
transitional period Middle Helladic–Late Helladic I "the Shaft Grave period"

everywhere in Greece, for other parts of the mainland pass into the Late Bronze Age with equal swiftness and delight in Crete but without such graves. The transition is independent of the grave form, and would have happened anyway. The first tholos tombs have Matt-painted pottery, and the first chamber tombs have the same experimental Mycenaean fabrics as Circle A. These vases reach islands like Keos and Melos within a few years. Coastal regions all over Greece suddenly receive new dynastic foundations where the mingling of the old Minyan and Matt-painted styles with delicate LH I pots signals a whole historical epoch forming a unit on the borderline of the two ages (p. 117). The Shaft Grave group in the small Argive plain is only one element in the new explosion.

The origin of the Shaft Grave idea has never been settled. Some scholars feel that the shafts developed normally out of older cists, when new wealth inspired more gift-giving, and family-consciousness made a multiple vault desirable. Others note the undeniable differences from previous burial customs: great depth, the wooden roof, multiple gifts and bodies, carved stelai, the passion for being buried under a heap of gold with armor and masks. A child might be dressed completely in gold (Pl. X B) as no Minyan child ever was. If the builders were native Middle Helladic adventurers one must explain how they became so rich and why they departed from tradition so radically. If they were newcomers, their links were with Anatolia and the north—princes at Alaca had been buried this way in the third millennium, and beyond the Black Sea the habit persists much later. The archaic cemetery at Trebenischte in Bulgaria continues to use royal gold funeral masks in the same severe accents one thousand years after the Shaft Graves (Pl. XI B).

The Shaft Grave era was one of mobile, highly trained soldiers everywhere seeking new stations of power. When recognizable Mycenaean civilization emerges there are many tribes in Greece, calling themselves by different titles and probably speaking dialects odd to one another's ears. Greek tradition affirms this variety in the legends of foreign princes who came from the east or south to establish new kingdoms in Greece. By imaginative classical chronology some appeared on the stage very early: Kadmos the Phoenician at Thebes, Kekrops the "earth-born" (i.e., of mysterious parentage) at Athens, were both ascribed to the sixteenth century. Danaos the Egyptian at Argos, Aiolos the Hellene in Thessaly "before the flood," and Minyas at Orchomenos might be placed historically in the early tholos period. Pelops the Lydian at Mycenae belongs to the "empire" period. Scholars have long appreciated the meaning of short or divine genealogies for such mythical princes; they are "new" people, whether arriving from abroad or lifted up out of mainland obscurity.[7] The Shaft Grave princes are too early for any genealogy at all, but their innovations are clear enough.

It used to be thought that these Argive princes gained their personal wealth in the wars of the Second Intermediate Period, perhaps acting as mercenaries helping to expel the Hyksos from Egypt. An emotional logic lurks behind this theory which is not supported by any fact. The date of the Hyksos expulsion is traditionally *ca.* 1570 B.C., which is later than the first Shaft Graves but long before their most opulent phase after 1500 B.C. Of all Hyksos products the scarabs and the button-based juglets are most typical and none appear in the Aegean at all; the Shaft Grave art which relates to Egypt corresponds to work in the Eighteenth Dynasty after the Hyksos had gone. Even this influence is probably funneled to Greece through Crete or the Levant, like the Nubian ostrich egg in a Knossian mounting of faïence and dolphins, or the flying gallop expressed in Levantine niello inlay. Neither the Egyptian nor the Hyksos kings ever displayed any interest in the sixteenth century mainland or its soldiers; even Crete was only one fringe area with which the Hyksos king Khyan tried to keep on good terms. The well-known lid with his cartouche from Knossos, earlier than the Shaft Graves, is matched by an inscribed fragment of obsidian vase from the Hittite capital of Hattušaš and by a lion from Baghdad; the mainland was a barbaric haze beyond these old powers. But the emotional links from the Shaft Graves to the expulsion of the Hyksos are based on perception of parallels in art and politics. The Hyksos king Apophis had a dagger on which the first Egyptian version of the flying gallop was drawn; Ahmose's mother Ah-hotep was buried with a model carriage and a famous griffin-inlaid ax. The loot from Kamose's campaigns against the Asiatics, won on occasions like that made poignant on the Siege Rhyton, was entirely comparable to the wealth of the Shaft Graves. Kamose says on his Karnak stele of victory:

I saw his women on the roof of his house while looking out their windows. Their bodies did not move when they saw me, they looked out from their gates and from their walls like the young of the *inḥ* animals in their holes, someone is coming? Behold, I had come. . . . O miserable Asiatic, look, I drink the wine of thy vineyard. . . . I have cut thy trees and also I have cast thy wives into the ships' holds, I have seized thy chariotry; I have not left a plank remaining of the three hundred *baw* ships of cedar filled with gold and lapis lazuli, silver and turquoise, bronze battle-axes without number, as well as olive oil, incense, fat, honey, *iwtern* trees, carob and pine(?) trees and all their precious woods.[8]

This triumphal chant is eloquent for a pattern of life that the Shaft Grave warriors must also have known to some extent, a life of raids, aristocratic battle training, and the amassing of portable loot to astonish any Middle Helladic farmer. They came to it later than Kamose and worked closer at home. Asiatic and Egyptian gold may have contributed to their burial gifts, but most were made in Greece in new ways, not imported or seized abroad. Their dominance perhaps sprang from five different skills or qualities. The princes were few, no doubt closely knit by social or family ties which helped them impose their policies on a diffuse agrarian peasantry. They knew how to exploit local metals and metal technology. They had the training in new war techniques—the battle chariot and the long sword—to be pretty redoubtable in violent conflict. They had the intelligence to capitalize on trade with newly affluent Mediterranean regions. And they seem to have been fearless in foreign contact. Whether they were an elite which rose from the old Middle Helladic Indo-European stock in response to new opportunities, or a group of related aliens who made a peaceful entry to the Argolid, does not matter much. Whatever the origin of the warrior aristocracy, it tempered Minyan society to its advantage and opened up new districts to a wider Aegean horizon as it took hold of Greece, thus laying the foundation for a recognizably Mycenaean civilization.

Chapter V

DEVELOPMENT OF A MYCENAEAN CULTURE

The years between the Shaft Graves and the fall of Knossos are best understood as a single unit on the Greek mainland. There are deep-rooted difficulties in distinguishing the two conventional phases, Late Helladic I and II, as historical periods. Roughly, the early part of the period is characterized by rapidly inflowing Minoan styles in pottery and jewelry, like those which light up the Shaft Graves; the later part consolidates these styles into a distinct Mycenaean idiom and adds the peculiar class of vase known as the Palace style (see Fig. 51). Architecturally the great achievements of the age are the tholos, or beehive, tombs which dwarf the domestic buildings in quality and grandeur. There may have been real palaces in Greece at this time but no satisfactory traces of them have been discovered.

In international affairs, we saw that the first Shaft Graves seemed linked to MM III B in Crete after the beginnings of the Eighteenth Dynasty in Egypt,

The Early
Mycenaean Age

and continued to be used during the opening of the last palace age in Crete, the renovations which followed a serious earthquake in the sixteenth century (p. 107). The latest vases in the Shaft Graves were mature creations of this second Cretan palace age, like the earliest vases in the tholos tombs. The Mycenaeans quickly caught on to the possibilities of exchanges with older, richer civilizations and began to export their own versions of Cretan vases to Egypt. It is difficult to say precisely how long this phase of first explorations lasted, or what caused it to shift into the more aggressive middle-class patterns of the "Mycenaean empire." The end of Late Helladic II is normally thought to coincide with the fall of the palace at Knossos close to 1400 B.C.; that crucial date has been challenged lately and needs re-examination (see p. 136). Evidence which is independent of Knossos suggests that the most active years of the Early Mycenaean Age are those from the accession of Tuthmosis III as co-regent with his mother Hatshepsut about 1504 B.C. to the end of the reign of Amenhotep III about 1380 B.C.[1]

During this period the Mycenaeans found their own distinctive styles in architecture and minor arts, increased their output of bronze weapons, established mainland workshops for gem carving and pottery, and to a large extent drew the boundaries for each local sphere of power in Greece (see Fig. 12). These local kingdoms do not always match the seats of later power. The early kings, who are often nameless because the genealogical traditions of later Greek poetry scarcely reach back into the sixteenth and fifteenth centuries, made special arrangements for attracting foreign wealth into their own areas. They apparently held it concentrated within the aristocracy until leveling movements after 1400 uprooted many nobles and reduced the rest to more common status. Their kingdoms are marked by a series of tholos tombs. The contents of these tholoi, where they survive unrobbed, suggest that the west coast was trading actively in amber along the Adriatic route and in liparite and obsidian around Sicily, while Lakonia and the Argolid turned toward Crete and the Aegean islands (Fig. 22). Both Cretan and Mycenaean ships traded regularly, though not heavily, with Egypt: more Mycenaean vases have been found there (see Pl. XLV A), although more Minoan precious objects and textiles are illustrated in the wall paintings of the Theban tombs (see p. 150; Fig. 28). Egyptian ships called in return at Crete, especially in the reign of Tuthmosis III when we hear of Keftiu ships (i.e., ships bound for the Keftiu land of Crete) being fitted out in the royal dockyards,[2] but Egyptian merchants seem not to have reached Greece until the fourteenth century, if at all (p. 152).

In the East, particularly north Syria, there was so much jockeying for power among the Hittites, Mitanni, and Egyptians that direct Aegean trade to Levantine ports seems shrunken from the earlier Cretan palace period. Politics were perhaps too unstable for confident traffic. During the late sixteenth and early fifteenth centuries practically nothing purely Minoan or Mycenaean appears in those regions. Although a narrow path was kept open to Byblos through Cyprus and some Aegean exports may have trickled into Egypt that way, there are less than a handful of vases in the Near East proper (Fig. 22). It is mostly in a few reminiscent decorative motifs that one senses the attraction each area still felt for the other.[3] At the same time Crete was exploring the possibility of creating trading centers in island towns or founding independent colonies in the central Aegean. The biggest center was Phylakopi on Melos, too old and secure to be taken over completely but face-lifted by Minoan fresco painters and

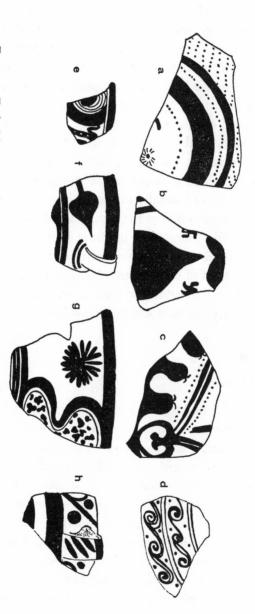

Fig. 22.—Early Mycenaean sherds (Late Helladic I–II) in foreign ports: (*a*, *b*) Miletos (after Weickert, *Istanbuler Mitteilungen, 1959–60*, Pl. 35, 3; Pl. 9, 1); (*c*) Byblos (after Stubbings, *Levant*, Fig. 10); (*d*) Lipari (after Taylour, *Mycenaean Pottery in Italy* 18, Fig. 2); (*e, f*) Troy VI (after Blegen, *Troy III*, Fig. 383); (*g*) Gezer (after Stubbings, *Levant*, Fig. 12); (*h*) Lipari (after Taylour, *op. cit*, Pl. 3, 12).

architects who represented a considerable enclave of Cretan newcomers (Fig. 23 *a*). Little Trianda on the beach of Rhodes facing Anatolia was a new settlement without previous history, and there the Minoan remains are more purely provincial Cretan (Fig. 23 *d-e*). On Keos off Attica, legend says, King Minos slept with the local princess Dexithea to found an island aristocracy; he left half his warriors behind with her when he returned to Crete (p. 154). Thera imitates Minoan vases and frescoes in the villages buried under lava after the island erupted in the Late Minoan I period (see Figs. 23 *b*, 52 *e*), and Theran style is also influenced by Melos. About two dozen hills overlooking island ports are named Minoa, at least four of them reflecting this phase of the "Minoan thalassocracy" although some are named only in nostalgia later.[4] Meanwhile the mainlanders reached out farther north and east; the oldest Anatolian "colony" is at Miletos with pottery of the Shaft Grave period (Fig. 22 *a-b*). The west coast more naturally explored the western seas where MH and early LH vases have been found in the Lipari islands (Fig. 22 *d, h*). Everywhere the two Aegean civilizations seem to move in peaceful competition without excluding each other from their overseas outposts, until a political alteration shortly before the fall of Knossos.[5] Presumably the Cretans did not yet sense any danger from mainlanders so keen to imitate them, and guided them to foreign markets they had long known themselves.

ARCHITECTURE

Towns and Houses

The paradox of Late Helladic I and II is that their high quality of vase painting and the minor arts contrast with an almost complete lack of decent domestic architecture. It is the situation of the Shaft Graves continued, and indeed aggravated, because numbers of wealthy chamber tombs as well as tholoi show that large Mycenaean communities lay nearby. The intelligent architecture of the tholoi on both coasts of the Peloponnesos proves that equally good masonry and design could have been applied to living quarters if the local dynasts had wanted it that way. Apparently they did not, but occupied their citadels in comparatively flimsy structures, although they sometimes protected themselves behind fortification walls (p. 162).[6] Most houses were built in rubble and brick as before, single rooms with earth floors and crooked lines, nothing strong enough to survive the building operations which remodeled most sites after 1400.

Curiously enough, the fullest remains of this early period are found in the north and northwest provinces: Thermon, Malthi, Peristeria (Moira), Tragana, and Pylos (Englianos). There is a small settlement at Kirrha and one room at Eutresis in central Greece, part of a house at Mycenae, and a well-preserved island town in Cycladic style on Keos. The Peristeria village is probably typical (Pl. XV A). It is one of many villages newly founded in the Shaft Grave period when newcomers apparently came to colonize a thinly populated Middle Helladic district whose peasant traditions survive in Matt-painted pottery. The settlers chose a tall, defensible cliff over the navigable Kyparisseïs river which assured their communications to the west and the sea; a broad pass in the plain below them led eastward to Dorion-Malthi and Arkadia. It was rich wooded country where cleared terraces could grow barley and wheat, olives and grapes and fruit trees; there was game in the woods: boar and deer, hare and edible birds.

The earliest houses sprawl over the hilltop with groups of crooked rooms. The walls are stone rubble bonded with waterproof clay; the floors are beaten earth stiffened with pebbles or clay. The whole ensemble has a drunken, tired look exaggerated by later earthquakes. No house has more than two stratified floors and most have only one. On these, the pottery is a thorough mixture of older Middle Helladic kitchenware and new Cretan fashions, particularly the "Vapheio" or "Keftiu" cup—a thin-walled tankard with a ribbon handle and floral, spiraled, or rippled patterns which is named after its Cretan prototype in gold (p. 128; Pl. XVIII A–B; Fig. 41 *d*). Household industries continue from the older world. The floors of the village are littered with scraps from bronze-making crucibles, obsidian, flint, shells, stone hammers, storage vessels, weaving equipment, and animal bones; yet every household has its share of Minoan gilding too.

Peristeria illustrates for many sites the solid chunk of "transitional" time surrounding new towns in Late Bronze Greece. This period, Middle Helladic III–Late Helladic I, has more definition of character and is more noticeable stratigraphically than the "pure" units Late Helladic I and II. It exactly parallels the contemporary transition on Crete from Middle Minoan to Late Minoan, though without Crete's interrupting earthquake, or any local signs of invasion and disaster except adventures like the Shaft Graves. In prehistoric archaeology it is rare to find such a peaceful, fruitful age of transition where the old lies usefully among the new through at least two generations of an experimental epoch. Since the towns of this age are almost always freshly organized upon the sites of later palaces or strongholds, they must reflect a new impulse toward centralized, industrially competent, dynastically dominated living into which the influence from Crete filters as a symptom of mainland receptivity but not as a primary cause of change. The emergence of the Early Mycenaean Age as an historical era thus involves movements of new princes or barons with small bands of followers who take over fresh territory, but there is absolutely no interruption or conflict in the growth of civilization, only a curious access of energy.

Keos in the Cyclades (see Fig. 7) offers a good physical contrast to Peristeria because its finely built stone houses still stand nearly to the second story. The main settlement lies in the inner corner of the great harbor of Koressos, on a small sea-washed promontory named Hagia Eirene, protected from the worst winds (Pl. XV B). The settlement was an old one, with Early Cycladic houses, a prosperous Middle Cycladic phase, and a series of Late Cycladic phases punctuated by earthquakes. The island of Keos seems to have preserved its ancient legends in particularly direct form, so that poets of the fifth century B.C. could recount its involvement with Crete with historical conviction (p. 154). Hagia Eirene passed through many of the same developments as Peristeria. Its Middle Bronze period was disrupted by earthquake; the Late Bronze Age began with peaceful continuity of tradition, and increased in wealth and luxury through contact with Crete all during the tholos period of the mainland. An extremely damaging earthquake knocked down this rich town at about the time of the fall of Knossos, and the next stable phase, which has strong mainland coloring (p. 285), came in Late Helladic III B. The legend of Minos' naval visit and fathering of a prince, Euxantios, on the island princess Dexithea must derive from the most interesting period of Minoan association.

This town, corresponding to Early Mycenaean foundations on the mainland, formed a compact community right at the water's edge. It was protected from land attack by a thick fortification wall with towers and gates. The princely houses faced the sea and were separated from each other by narrow paved streets (Pl. XVI A). The traditional Cycladic architecture of stone slabs is seen to good advantage, for all the alleys and courtyards are paved with flagstones; there are narrow elegant stone drains indoors and in the main streets, with catchbasins and water-breaks in the Minoan fashion. The houses themselves are made up of many adjoining rooms. The walls and stairways are built of stone, with timber chases inserted into door frames and middle walls for support and elasticity. The lowest floor is dug into the earth, forming basement storage rooms used chiefly for great jars of oil or wine and other commodities which needed to be kept cool, and local goods waiting for export. In these storerooms dirt floors are the rule; they could be reached down wooden ladders as well as formal stairs. Of the eighteen rooms excavated in the largest building (perhaps the prince's or governor's house), at least twelve are basements. Upstairs

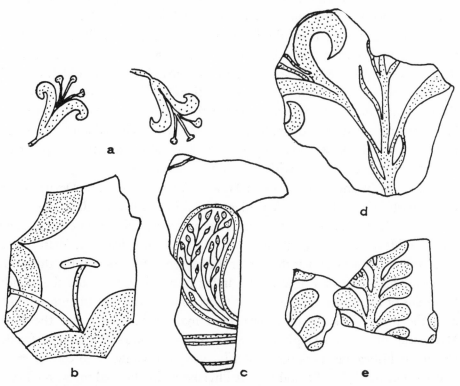

Fig. 23.—Early Mycenaean fresco fragments with Minoan plant designs: (*a*) Phylakopi (after Bosanquet *et al.*, *Phylakopi,* Fig. 64); (*b*) *Thera* (after Perrot and Chipiez, *Histoire de l'art* VI, Fig. 212); (*c*) Tiryns (*ibid.*, Fig. 239); (*d, e*) Trianda (after Monaco, *Clara Rhodos* 1941, Pl. 11).

the houses rose above ground in two stories, almost certainly stone to the roof, for the islanders did not like to build in mudbrick. The stairs rise high with shallow treads and several turns. One notes an almost unnatural delight in bathrooms and plumbing arrangements. The walls are plastered and made bright with simple frescoes, red or blue bands on a white ground. Some floors are smooth red plaster over a flagstone base. Such houses must have been pleasant to live in, their windows looking over the sea, plenty of space and light and water, decorated with luxury goods from Greece, Crete, and neighboring islands.

The town on Keos is the Cycladic counterpart of Minoan Gournia, where one glimpses an entire community in its industry and in its living quarters. No doubt the basic elements in the economy were fishing and farming, but the Keans also exported stone vessels, lead, and bastard silver (litharge) abroad. In return they acquired the finest vases of their neighbors, the Marine style from Crete, the Palace style from the mainland, bird jugs from Phylakopi. Their contacts abroad started at the beginning of the Shaft Grave period, attracted the first Cretan vases when Peristeria and other mainland towns did (Pl. XVIII A), and increased through passing generations until the second earthquake. Keans valued these imports and mended them with lead clamps when they broke, but never imitated them. The local pottery is plain red and dull. A few molds for jewels or weapons suggest that they also imported copper from abroad but forged it locally with traditional Cycladic skill.

Keos is not in any proper sense a Minoan colony, in spite of Dexithea's romance with Minos. It is an independent island in touch with all its neighbors, growing rich in a period of peaceful Aegean trade. Like Peristeria, its main phases of life are at the beginning of Mycenaean culture, from the Shaft Graves to the fall of Knossos, and at the end of the Mycenaean empire in the thirteenth century. This is true of a significant number of sites in Greece and the islands; historians of the future will surely try to account for such fluctuating intensity after the main blocks of time have been more stably fixed. For the Early Mycenaean phase both Hagia Eirene and Peristeria show the leaven of older Cretan sophistication working in sturdy provincial contexts abroad to create new local cultures. The Second City at Phylakopi, the doomed towns on Thera, and the early levels of the colony at Trianda on Rhodes all speak to the same point: how the opening of the Aegean to constant fearless shipping and the naval and artistic power of Crete are reflected in distant places in individual ways, which are yet linked through the quick spread of southern fashions (see Figs. 22–23).

Tholos Tombs

The tholos tombs of Bronze Age Greece are still about the most spectacular buildings of our Greek architectural inheritance. No picture can dramatize them falsely; they are always larger than one remembers or expects.

King Minyas' revenues were so very great that he surpassed all earlier men in wealth. Minyas was the first person we know about to build a treasury as a receptacle for his riches. Now, the Greeks are peculiar for holding foreign things in greater admiration than domestic things, since as you know famous men have turned to describing the Egyptian pyramids with extreme accuracy, but they have not even mentioned the treasury of Minyas or the walls of Tiryns, although they are no less wonderful. . . . The treasury of Minyas is a marvel as great as anything in Greece or outside it. It was constructed in this fashion: it was made of worked stone, in a circular design, with the peak blunt rather than sharp; they say the highest of the stones is the keystone for the building. There are graves of Minyas and Hesiod. [Pausanias 9, 36–38.]

Minyas' building at Orchomenos in Boiotia is not the first one, in spite of Pausanias' enthusiasm for it; a tradition reaching back to the last years of the Middle Helladic Age had helped shape its very sophisticated thirteenth-century design which included a side chamber ornamented with greenstone walls and a ceiling carved in spirals and rosettes (cf. Fig. 45).

No one knows where the concept of these domed stone-lined holes came from, for they have no real ancestors in Greece or in other Mediterranean regions the Greeks knew. All attempts to derive them from the smaller round tombs of EM II Crete constructed above ground, or the rectangular tombs of Syria built underground, have run head-on into gross divergencies of shape and date.[7] Probably a combination of factors created them: a native megalithic streak in the Mycenaeans, reports of the pyramids in Egypt, new techniques learned in Crete for cutting stone, a liking for round burial precincts, and a new sense of political rivalry which urged the local prince to dramatize himself like his foreign "brothers." Experiments in tombs of other shapes were made at the same time, like the slim rectangular stone chamber inserted in Circle B at Mycenae (*Rho*) (Pl. XVI C) or the grandiose but imitative built tombs of Knossos: the Royal Tomb, the Temple Tomb, and the tholos on the Kephala ridge (cf. Fig. 6 *w*).

The circular underground tomb is in fact the easiest kind of chamber tomb to build, whether it is simply hollowed out of bedrock or lined with stone. It is easier to reopen and more permanent than a shaft, though not as safe through the ages; sometimes pits or shafts were sunk in the floor inside the tholos chamber and roofed with slabs for added protection. It is far better as a family vault than a group of cists; it is more secure than pithos burial in a shallow mound, and more impressive to look at. Tholos tombs appear simultaneously with chamber tombs cut to look like them at the very start of the

Early Mycenaean Age, especially in Lakonia and Messenia. Later the vaulted chamber tomb fades away just as experimental forms of stone tombs do; only the tholos continues, practical and traditional in princely families (see bibliography).

Professor A. J. B. Wace, the British archaeologist who excavated Mycenae for many years, was the first to establish a clear sequence of architectural criteria for dating tholos tombs. They cannot be dated from the contents easily like many normal tombs because most of them have been repeatedly robbed and disturbed. Wace based his observations on the nine tombs near Mycenae. The system does not work quite accurately for other rich regions like Pylos and Thessaly where distance from the Argolid imperceptibly becomes an extra factor, but it is the best standard available (see Fig. 24).

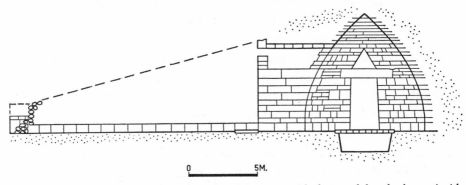

0   5M.

FIG. 24.—Section of the Tomb of the Genii, Mycenae, with door and façade shown inside chamber for convenience. (After Wace, *Mycenae*, Fig. 15.)

The most "primitive" group (Cyclopean, Epano Phournos, Aegisthus) illustrates all the architectural essentials. A deep circular cutting into bedrock is lined with small stones; a runway, or *dromos,* leads down to it from the natural surface level, passing through a deep doorway, or *stomion,* into the chamber. This stomion is framed in larger blocks of stone to make a finer and sturdier façade where the building is not externally supported by rock, but it is still fragile for the size of the tomb and the height of the entrance. The top of the door is level with the ground outside so that lintel blocks could be slid into place without any engineering troubles. From there on up the roof is built in corbeled rings of fieldstones constantly buttressed from outside by fresh earth until a keystone can plug and weight the hole at the top. What one sees, then, is an earth mound above ground level, and unless the dromos to the underground façade is kept clear the tomb is like an iceberg, only the top crust showing. The dromos was probably kept open for a certain length of time before and after a royal burial, but the stomion was walled up immediately, with stones at both ends, to discourage thieves.

Group II (Panagia, Lion, Kato Phournos) advances to building the chamber of better-cut stones on an ashlar foundation, strengthening the door and lengthening the lintels, curving the inner one to sweep around with the tholos. The weight on the cracking-point of the lintels is reduced by the "relieving triangle" in the center of the façade: a thin stone slab screening an empty space which runs through to the chamber. The façades are dressed more handsomely in large blocks of conglomerate; the dromos is lined with conglomerate or fieldstones to keep the earth from washing in.

Group III (Atreus, Clytemnestra, Genii) (Pl. XVII A; Fig. 24) expresses the perfect culmination of architectural design, and the builders have energy to spare for elaborate ornament. The Treasury of Atreus, described hundreds of times, is its most famed representative (Pl. XXVI): a tremendously long dromos (36 m.) lined with rectangular saw-cut blocks, a doorway of perfectly dressed blocks framed by half-columns of red and green carved stone in two stories and closed off by bronze double doors; two giant lintels of which the inner one is over eight meters long and weighs over one hundred tons; a chamber entirely fashioned of dressed ashlar blocks solid enough to withstand every pressure of water and earth, still rising intact under its slightly eroded mound; a side chamber with its own lintel and triangle. It is believed that the dark chamber was once studded with bronze rosettes pinned to the walls, a decoration which, like Orchomenos' spiraled side-chamber, attempted architectural perfectionism undiscouraged by dim light. The whole building is set on a square terrace in the hillside, displacing several older houses; a stone circle or *krepis* ran around the edges of the mound to hold back the earth, and on two blocks of this are lightly-carved masons' marks of branches in the Cretan style (Fig. 6 *x*). Atreus is not, of course, a monument of the Early Mycenaean Age; rather it is the ultimate development of a tradition founded then; it was built some time after 1300 B.C. (p. 216).[8]

The west coast started its own series of tholos tombs even earlier than Mycenae and in more abundance. Curious vaulted chamber tombs imitating tholoi were dug for commoners. The earliest tholos known on the west coast is at Osman Aga by Navarino Bay. It was made of crude fieldstones and contained MH pottery as well as Shaft Grave types, a sure indication that tholoi and the Late Bronze Age arrived together in this region. At Peristeria a very large tholos was cut into the houses of the LH I hill village and contrasts with them dramatically in architectural quality (Pl. XVI B). The local king of the hill did not mind destroying part of the village for his tomb. Like the Vapheio tomb in Lakonia, it has an elongated dromos (28 m.) lined toward the inner end and paved with colored pebbles. Its façade and stomion are in square limestone blocks "as beautiful as goat's cheese in the barrel," according to the locals, brought from a quarry several miles away over the hills. The inner lintel is curved (aligning it with group II at Mycenae); the chamber is built of small square stones and again paved with red, black, and white pebbles. The stomion is particularly interesting because it was lined with white plaster, suggesting that the passage may have been kept open on occasion as a public monument. The façade is made dressy with shallow setbacks and is carved upon the left jamb with two Cretan signs, the branch and the double ax (Pl. XVI B; Fig. 6 *v*).

The Peristeria tholos illustrates some peculiarities of tholoi in general outside Mycenae. It is part of a group, as these tombs often are. At Mycenae there are three groups of three; on the west coast there are pairs or whole clusters. At some centers only one tholos has been discovered so far, but only in Crete and Attica are singletons normal. Such groupings must have been created by a single ruling dynasty who considered that an older tomb had been used too frequently or was in poor condition and built a more modern example nearby. The Peristeria group, although not yet fully excavated, seems to consist of three tholoi inside a massive peribolos wall which surrounds them in an oval precinct, much as the Grave Circles at Mycenae had been set apart from ordinary ground. The group spans three centuries, from Late Helladic I to III B. This is the regular limit for tholos use. Most were built originally during the course of the fifteenth century; practically none were used after the fall of the mainland palaces in the late thirteenth century, except in the wildest provinces.

The best tholoi are characterized by Palace style pottery, particularly the handsome large jars with marine or floral designs (p. 130, Pl. XVIII D–F). The Palace style is in a sense a freak in Mycenaean ceramics, for it is much more familiar in tombs than in houses, as though it were designed for funeral gifts. It is canonically restricted to the period LH II, although in fact LH II has never been distinguished as a stratigraphic level in any mainland domestic building. Most towns with clear strata have three major living levels: Middle Helladic–Late Helladic I; Late Helladic II–III A; Late Helladic III B. Tholoi are common in the first two periods, but since Palace style pottery is not the ordinary domestic pottery of either one, a tholos tomb containing scraps of it cannot be exactly dated within a generation or two. And since Wace's architectural dating criteria at Mycenae do not work precisely in other regions, the problem of correlating Greek tholos tombs with Greek historical phases is a testy one. Some provincial tholoi, for example, have relieving horizontal bars instead of relieving triangles, or simple hollows in the stone sheathing above the door, and one does not always know whether these are fifteenth century or two hundred years later. In more remote ages it might not be so important, but between 1550 and 1380 B.C., when every other major culture of the Mediterranean is fully literate and records its experiences through king lists, campaign reports, and diplomatic correspondence, the most royal phase of Mycenaean civilization is left unfixed.

The tholos age is one of foundations for royal towns, the age of the tentative shift of power from Crete to Greece, the beginning of the introduction of such civilized tools as writing in the north, and the drift of Greek adventurers to Knossos. Tholos tombs, and the Palace style, are new features along the north and east coasts of Crete before the fall of the Cretan palaces. Mutual influence is clear, for tholoi are built in Greece especially in those places whose contacts with Crete are freshest, and the art of the princely tombs is more strongly Minoan than it ever will be again.

Crete was not the only catalyst; Egypt and the Levant contributed ideas and techniques in spite of relatively thin trade. The local Cretan counterparts of the Greek royal tombs, the peculiar masonry structures at Knossos known as the Temple Tomb (late sixteenth century) and the Royal Tomb at Isopata (mid-fifteenth century), borrow many of their features from Egypt, such as courts and stairs, crypts, and ceilings painted blue. At Mycenae the curiously experimental tomb inserted into Grave Circle B during the fifteenth century displays its debt to Canaan in the east (Pl. XVI C). Tomb *Rho* is a long, thin stone crypt with a pointed roof, built from fine limestone blocks whose joints are covered by bands of red paint. It was built inside an older rock-cut shaft, and consists of a passage and chamber about 5.50 m. long. Robbed in antiquity, the surviving scraps from its original gifts still serve to show that, like most tholoi, it was built when the Palace style was popular, and an Egyptian scarab of lapis lazuli highlights its international background. Similar underground vaults are slightly earlier at Ugarit; Mycenaeans are clearly visiting the east and imitating what impressed them there.

The startling access of wealth and energy which tholoi symbolize would perhaps be easier for us to understand if there were any accompanying destruction or signs of newcomers, but the Early Mycenaean Age was the most peaceable of any Greek age of innovation. Since tholoi were purely local Greek statements of power, only occasionally flirting with foreign techniques, one should probably explain their sudden emergence in non-archaeological terms. They may have resulted from an idea, possibly in the realm of political consciousness, which gave the Mycenaeans some sense of themselves as a people for the first time. The contacts and window dressing of the age were Cretan, clearest in tholos art, but the spirit was pure Greek.

ART IN THE THOLOI

Because they are so conspicuous, tholos tombs have always invited thieves, who have been active in them from Late Mycenaean days until now. The thieves learned quickly that they need not destroy the entire building, or labor through the walled doorway, but could often slip in over the lintel through the space behind the relieving triangle. Wace pointed out how this asocial sport has been preserved in two immortal stories of "treasury-builders": Trophonios and Agamedes who made a tholos for King Hyrieus in Boiotian Aulis, and the nameless master mason–thieves who so plagued King Rhampsinitos in Herodotos.[9] The story turns on a stone which can be removed from outside and replaced for a deceptively placid appearance. "Hyrieus was struck dumb when he saw the keys and other sealings unmoved, but the number of riches getting continually less," Pausanias records. Because of the thieves and the natural weakness of the tholos as a building (the roof almost always collapses), only two and one-half unplundered tholoi have been discovered in Greece so far out of all that were built (see bibliography). The surviving ones are Myrsinochorion, Dendra, and the cist at Vapheio. The beauty of the objects recovered from these is so startling that more of the same would doubtless spoil us. Even ransacked tholoi usually produce gold or fragments of precious stones, and the pottery, which thieves tend to ignore. Energy and royal resources spent by other nations on public temples and palaces were poured into these private monuments in Greece; the traditional title of "treasury" is ironically true.

The art of these tombs covers a number of years in the developing Mycenaean civilization, overlapping the end of the Shaft Graves and continuing just past the fall of Knossos. After that, although tholoi continue to be built in conservative provincial regions in the fourteenth and thirteenth centuries, they are generally poorer and tumbled about through reuse. The art is not always easy to date because of the unstratified, topsy-turvy nature of the contexts in the most known tombs. The collapsing roof has often brought surface material down inside, which is sometimes older than the tomb itself, if it had been cut into an older cemetery site as at Mycenae: a fine Middle Helladic vase is illustrated here from the dromos of the Tomb of Clytemnestra built nearly four centuries later (Pl. IX C). Sometimes the intrusions are later if the tomb was used by the family through many generations, or was a hangout for shepherds, robbers, tourists, or worshipers after the Dark Ages. Surviving scraps of gold and other precious burial gifts in robbed tholoi are not as precise documents of date as pottery, because their styles did not change so rapidly. A brief glance at two early and two later groups of discoveries in Early Mycenaean tholoi may, however, help bring artistic developments into some relief.

The Vapheio Prince

The Vapheio tomb is a good introduction to that mixture of ruin, wealth, and lost myths which most tholoi offer. It has been known since 1805 and was excavated by Tsountas in 1888 after much of it had collapsed and robbers had frisked through the contents on the floor. The tomb is quite large (10.35 m. diameter, 29.80 m. dromos) though not finely built, and is peculiar for sitting on top of a high hill, like a hat on an oven, instead of being cut into the base of a slope. This seems a special trait of tholoi in Lakonia, Messenia, and Thessaly. It was built for a prince who controlled an important province of Lakonia, below Sparta on the slopes of Mount Taÿgetos. He must have developed a clear trade line to Crete, down the valley of the Eurotas river to the coast, past the island of Kythera, and so south. No palace has been discovered yet at Vapheio, although an extensive site nearby at Palaiopyrgi may conceal one. Ancient authorities and modern travelers agree that the Bronze Age city was probably Pharis which, as the nineteenth-century explorer Leake remarked, "chiefly flourished before the Trojan War."

The robbers had scattered small valuables on the floor of the tholos as they left—gems, scraps of amethyst, amber, a gold-foil fish—but they failed to notice an underground pit in the chamber floor. This was slightly longer than a man, paved, lined, and covered with slabs of stones, and held the Vapheio prince with his gifts intact. The skeleton was not in good condition, but it was probably a man—one of markedly Minoan and possibly effete tastes, Tsountas thought, because he was surrounded by rings, a heap of gems at either wrist, eighty amethyst beads on his breast, a mirror, an earpick, and perfume vases. This delicacy of character was offset by a whole arsenal of weapons: a three-foot sword, nine knives and daggers, a pair of massive hunting spears, and a pair of axes. Some of this gear seemed to have been packed into a wooden chest at the head of the pit; the double necklace of amethyst and the heaps of gems where the disintegrated wrists had lain were naturally part of the costume in which the prince was buried. He had a gold-plated dagger at his side, and a gold and silver cup at either hand. The gold ones are, of course, the renowned Vapheio Cups with scenes of netting and mating the great bulls of Crete, surely made on Crete itself. Other international elements or imports are two vases of Egyptian (or Syrian) alabaster, a crescent ax of Syrian design as adapted by the Egyptians, beads of Baltic amber, and an iron ring, which is one of the first examples of the material in Greece and may have come from an Anatolian source. Tomb gifts of a more local, significantly Mycenaean, sort included sets of bronze scale pans and stone lamps (p. 298) and pottery which seems of a moment only slightly later than the Shaft Graves. The tradition of Shaft Grave craftsmanship also is continued by the dagger found next to the prince which was inlaid with silver and niello figures of swimming men. The whole group of gifts demonstrates that the eclectic fashions of the Shaft Graves were still current, and that rulers of Spartan hill towns were rich enough to procure them.

All through the Early Mycenaean Age, the south Mediterranean influences carried by trade were constantly reinforcing and redirecting native Mycenaean efforts toward a mainland art form. In the case of Vapheio, trade was attracted by the presence in this well-watered plain of someone with the presence of mind to set up a terminus for Cretan exports along the good sea lane past Kythera, and who perhaps offered in return blocks of the prized *lapis lacedai-monius,* or flecked green porphyry, which Knossos used in stone vases and seals. Another Lakonian asset was *rosso antico,* the red marble later used to such good effect in the Treasury of Atreus (p. 216; Pl. XXVI C), and perhaps the horses for which Sparta was always renowned.

There were several dominions approaching Vapheio-Pharis' stature in Lakonia at the opening of the Mycenaean Age. Many towns were expanded from their Middle Helladic foundations, and although the population was not dense it seems more active and commercial than before. Some of the valleys remained agricultural and peripheral, but on the north and west frontiers there were tholos centers comparable to Vapheio, with the same mingling of Cretan imports and local restatements of Cretan models. At Kampos in the west toward Kalamata a tholos contained two lead statuettes of a man and a woman which are certainly Cretan. At Vourvoura (Analipsis) in the north toward Tegea the tholoi held Palace style vases of the highest international quality, made in local clay (Pl. XVIII D).[10] Just as in the Pylos district, the early chamber tombs of commoners imitated tholos tombs—a cheaper version of royalty drifting through to the ranks below.

The two gold repoussé Vapheio Cups are the only surviving examples of their class, the kind of splendid, purely Minoan metalwork which is occasionally inventoried in the Linear B records at Knossos (Fig. 41 *d*) or which is carried as a royal gift in the painted processions of Egyptian tombs (p. 150; cf. Fig. 28). The cups illustrate finely the high quality of Cretan models available to the early Mycenaeans, from which their own craftsmen could learn. From their combination of pure drawing and subtle relief work the Greeks took mainly the former for their canons of proportion, gesture, and iconography. The relief carving was less congenial to them (p. 214) although they did learn something of modeling and musculature from it. The cups have more depth, more compact reality and sympathy than the Greeks generally managed, and no trace of that angular fantasy which the mainland loved.

In the Vapheio gems (Pl. XIX A–E), the most brilliant single hoard ever found in Greece (p. 223), one can watch the progress of Greek gem-cutters in various stages of instruction from Minoan prototypes and imported stones. They are still learning how to adapt small vigorous representations to the restricted field, shifting from the flat, whittled style of the Shaft Grave stelai to a more natural use of undercutting and highlights. Many of the Vapheio gems were made in Crete, but a good number also are well-designed versions of scenes which had no Cretan prototypes. Minoan religious and marine iconography is prominent: the goddess with her votary, mastering an ibex or a goat (Pl. XIX A), a pair of circling dolphins (Pl. XIX B), worship under a tree. A priest in a long robe accompanied by a griffin is a blend of eastern and mainland ideas, cut in a stark right-angled way that seems un-Minoan. Favorite Mycenaean themes are expressed with more skill than on the gold rings from the Shaft Graves: an armed warrior whirling his chariot down the road (Pl. XIX E); a pair of hunters with slim Minoan figures but short hair and kilts, giving a twisted lion the coup-de-grâce (Pl. XIX C); a single hunter dueling a boar in a rocky hollow, where the landscape is drawn from Minoan shorthand models but the figure retains the casual flabbiness of the Shaft Grave stelai and the sport is a mainland one (Pl. XIX D). The blend of Mycenaean and Minoan styles is becoming complete. The distribution of such finely conceived and developing art in regions one might later consider provincial helps to explain the broad homogeneity of Mycenaean style in the following period of the palaces. The Vapheio prince was a collector and a connoisseur, like many nobles who were astonished and delighted at what the Cretans could do with their hands. No mere passion for the privacy which gems offer could have required him to own forty-one different types.

Kakovatos and the Palace Style

About the same time as the Vapheio prince was buried, three tholos tombs were built on a low ridge facing the western sea at Kakovatos in Triphylia. Again thieves had cleared out the contents, but enough small finds of precious materials and large Palace style jars were left to convince Dörpfeld in 1906 that Kakovatos was in fact the royal seat of the family of Nestor. He named it Pylos. It is from many topographical points of view the only Pylos in west Greece which suits Homer's account in the *Iliad* of Nestor's fighting boyhood. Nestor himself lived some three hundred years after the tholoi, contemporary with the palace at Englianos a long distance south which calls itself Pylos clearly enough on its tablets; scholars have not yet agreed on how to reconcile the archaeological remains, the Homeric narratives, and the testimony of classical geographers.[11] These Kakovatos tholoi contain the Palace style at its most classical, its strongest adaptation of Cretan architectural, marine, and floral motifs to ornament tall jars of a mainland type (Pl. XVIII E). The clear painting and great range of the Kakovatos jars permit them to act as standards for most other comparable finds. There are argonauts swimming in an organized school through seaweed and rocks more orderly than their Minoan counterparts; sprays of stiff papyrus and rosettes, ivy leaves growing sidewise from rubbery stems against a dotted background, lilies and iris in both the stiff upright and naturally blowing styles, unlikely trees with leaves like tennis racquets, the mainland "ogival canopy" which was adopted later in reverse lend-lease by Crete, and large mainland spirals set horizontally like architectural friezes. It is clear that this monumental style developed in rich coastal districts trading with Crete, and redirected Cretan artistic inspiration to please mainland aesthetics.

The wealthy barony at Kakovatos was trading in Adriatic regions too, and was strategically situated to attract voyagers from the Ionian Islands and Italy. Quantities of Prussian amber in the tholoi testify to an established trade route with Europe. Amber is especially characteristic of early burials in Greece, and is much rarer after 1400 B.C. At Kakovatos it is shaped as heavy beads and engraved plaques. Many other important minor objects were neglected by the robbers. Among them are rich miniature ornaments made in a more fluent style than the Shaft Graves', such as a gold toad with a granulated back, a gold owl peeping sideways, gold rosettes inlaid with lapis lazuli, an iron signet ring, leaves and flowers in blue glass-paste, many engraved bone circlets and ivory inlays from furniture or boxes. Among the most important minor objects one would single out the little blue glass bull with clover-leaf inlays who stands stretch-legged and, though small in scale, is the only surviving counterpart of those bull statuettes offered by the Keftiu in Egyptian frescoes (Fig. 28 *a*), and also the earliest pure glass vase in Greece, a translucent blue-green bowl with rounded petal flutes. The only known gem drifted into the excavation dump, where it was rescued by an observant student in 1909 (see Fig. 25).

Myrsinochorion

The unplundered tholos tomb discovered by Professor Marinatos in 1956 at Rutsi-Myrsinochorion near the southern Pylos belongs to a slightly later phase. Its rich art looks backward to the Shaft Graves, forward to the palace epoch. It is so rare to find such a tomb intact that every detail is significant for reconstructing the burial practices of the age (p. 298). It was one of a pair, as is normal in that region, and held a series of family burials spanning two or three generations. The last burial lay in the middle of the chamber floor on a blanket or rush mat colored red and blue. He had been an active warrior like the Vapheio prince, and ten swords and daggers in leather scabbards lay near him. He also had a mirror and massed gems, including two curious cylinder seals, one in a hybrid Asiatic style (Fig. 29 *d*), and wore a heavy necklace of Baltic amber. Six more persons were buried in two cists under the floor surrounded by older objects of art: carved ivory boxes, a comb engraved with wildcats hunting ducks, a variety of fine vases and gems, and, above all, two splendid inlaid daggers which continue and improve upon Shaft Grave traditions. One resembles Palace style vases in offering a marine vignette of argonauts swimming among rocks and weeds; the other shows gracile if anatomically peculiar leopards stalking through a pastoral landscape (Pl. XIII B). It surpasses the hunting scenes of the Shaft Graves in movement and natural composition; Mycenaean minor art is losing its first flat, strained aspect. But the twists of fantasy persist and are especially clear on west coast gems of the period, which have gone farther toward mastering the material than most native Vapheio gems but keep the same interest in abbreviated, violent, or bizarre narrative. A Myrsinochorion example shows two men grasping a pair of lions by mane and tail (Pl. XIX G); another from the nearby tholos at Tragana seems to excerpt an entire battle frieze with dueling warriors (Pl. XIX H); a third from the

FIG. 25.—Sketch of gem from the Kakovatos excavation dump. (Courtesy A. Sanborn; Loeb Bequest, Munich Antiquarium.)

dump at Kakovatos, an agate, shows a hero challenging a great lion while an uncouth daimon in a long skin coat grabs at his sword-sheath from behind (Fig. 25; cf. Pl. XLIII E).[12]

Here one feels in touch with a set of stories or symbols already so codified and familiar that they could be recognized by two or three figures who hold the time sequence of a greater narrative synthesized in their postures. Some compositions may originate in the Near East, but they have probably been adapted to local tales. From the drama of the reduced scene one would guess the original theme to have been of broader scope, with the causes and results of these odd combats told in full, perhaps drawn from such a familiar stock that they could not be misread in the reducing process. The Mycenaeans of the early period display a fondness for condensed symbolism in art which will continue among their descendants because it is rooted in a habit of regarding worldly events as general, recurring crises rather than individual or irreplaceable moments. It is the poetic side of mainland tradition, quite alien to a sense of history, and welcomingly open to any foreign iconography which could serve its purpose. One begins to understand, looking at the best creations of LH I and II, how the otherwise talented Mycenaeans could have had so little real art of their own and yet were able to transform what they borrowed so uniquely: they reflect through new-found visual forms their own older inherited art of words and action.

Dendra: Metal and War

Vapheio and Myrsinochorion showed that the "provinces" were not so provincial. In the Argolid, which always used to be considered the center of Mycenaean growth, no unrobbed tholos is known before the slightly later example at Dendra-Midea near Mycenae. Midea must have been a dependent fief of Mycenae or Tiryns, for it lies east and inland from them in rolling, wooded country, and would have had to use Tiryns or Epidauros as a port. Individuals grew rich there, but the stony acropolis is no match for its greater neighbors; as Pausanias remarked, "in my time nothing was left of it except the foundations" (2.25.9). Here Persson excavated in 1926 a tholos whose keystone had fallen in during the tenth century B.C. and whose chamber had been disturbed by intruders of the Protogeometric period. Again, three cists under the floor held their skeletons and gifts safely. A small king in the third cist lay literally covered with metal vases and weapons: gold and silver cups with scenes of marine life and animal hunts (see Pl. XX A; Fig. 21 *b*); rings of silver, lead, copper, and iron soldered together in layers; five swords with their gold hilts and decayed scabbards; spearheads, knives, and carved gems. The strong point of the Dendra cemetery, both the tholos and the contemporary chamber tombs, is in this metalwork and the new bolder, flatter style associated with the close of the early epoch.

The two most acclaimed Dendra cups are one with octopodes floating over sea bottom in low relief, and one inlaid in niello with four stiff, dramatically colored bull's heads. The Minoan flavor of the first, the Levantine parallels to the second, are persuasive of Dendra's activity in Aegean trade. Even more elegant is the hoard of silver vases from Tomb 10 (Pl. XX B) which all have exact counterparts in clay. This tomb is "dated" by its Palace style vases; its ornamented metal vases show a similar controlled architectural poise. One extraordinary goblet has ducks flying in military formation (Pl. XX A). Through a complex technique of low relief and surface chasing, each duck is seen in characteristic double perspective, body from the side and wings from below, flying over a pebbled beach or the glinting ripples of the sea, isolated and accented by an ornamental quatrefoil of raised silver wire. Enormous labor went into this small goblet. Its niello-and-gold handle, and the scale convention for water, prove its direct continuation of the best craft in the Shaft Graves; the stunted rock-work and band-arrangement of the birds recall fifteenth-century Knossian fresco work like the partridges in the Caravanserai, or the stone Marine style vases in the Throne Room. It is contemporary with a charming formal composition on an amethyst gem from Myrsinochorion, two ducks flying level with the horizon (Pl. XIX I). Soon, by natural development, this tholos-period love of marshaling animals and plants into an order clearer than reality will become the "empire" style of banded, heraldic, restricted design. What is often called the "tectonic symmetry" of mainland art and explained as a reversion to Middle Helladic formality after Crete's influence fades out with the fall of Knossos may be better understood as the same irreversible process that so often affects naturalism in the arts of other civilizations: a process of codification, of easy reliance upon an established repertory, which is driven forward by increasing technical skill and increasing demands for art works by more middle-class patrons. This is not a characteristic of Mycenaean art to be generalized into theories of national culture; it happens just as clearly in Crete in Late Minoan III.

A fragmentary silver goblet from the tholos itself (Fig. 21 *b*) makes quite a different impression, its wild hunting scene spread broadly over a blank field in co-ordinated motion. Two hounds are loose in a meadow stirring up four deer; they have broken in on the flanks of the grazers and nip the heels of the stag in front; behind them a yearling checks his gallop and a stag contorts his body in a leap to break away. The bodies are curved, heavy, and playful; the flying gallop in which all the actors are caught is accentuated by sharp hooves flailing at angles and the rush of the chase is expressed by a long-legged gangling charm as the animals race over empty space. The elimination of background rocks and trees will be echoed again in palace frescoes of the next two centuries, where all is motion and role against a minimal landscape; it contrasts markedly with the Vapheio Cups and their rich natural setting. The violent action and mastery of animal anatomy links the goblet to the ivory pyxis from a royal grave at Athens (p. 219; Pl. XXXVI B–C). Of all works on the mainland this seems closest to Egyptian New Kingdom hunting scenes which have so often been felt to reflect Aegean influence.

One of the most exciting discoveries at Dendra has international implications of a different sort. In 1960 a tomb known to the Antiquities Service for several years was broken into by robbers whom the police could not quite prevent from disturbing the doorway. This chamber tomb (No. 13) was then excavated properly by Verdelis and Åström, and was found to contain a single male burial, a warrior wearing a complete bronze cuirass, surrounded by other military gear (Pl. XXI A; cf. Fig. 41 c),[13] already famous with good reason: it is the only such armor known from Greece before the Dark Ages and was buried about the time of the fall of Knossos. Many details of its construction agree with formulas in Homeric poetry which used to be thought of as post-Mycenaean innovations. It is made in two pieces, a front and back shell which fasten on the side with twisted thongs. Below the hips, like a skirt, come three flexible bands of bronze front and back with attachment holes in the lowest front band to adjust its height and give the soldier's thighs greater freedom as he ran. The neck is finished off in a tall bronze collar, and where this joins the cuirass a decorative "cravat" lies obliquely across the breast. Two shoulder guards are thonged onto the main shell, loose enough for active play with the spear or sword. A pair of bronze greaves guarded the shins. Another, later pair of greaves also in bronze was already known from a tomb in Achaia (Pl. XXI C) to confirm Homer's account of "bronze-clad Achaians" as the core of Mycenaean fighting strength; the Dendra greaves will persuade reluctant scholars that at least some Homeric material reaches back to early stages of Mycenaean culture. The rest of the warrior's equipment consisted of a boar's-tusk helmet with metal cheek-pieces, leather stretched over a wooden frame which is probably a shield, three bronze and three clay vases, and a bronze comb with gold teeth. His swords were missing, presumably taken by the robbers; an exactly contemporary pair is illustrated in Plate XXI B to complete the ensemble.

Verdelis pointed out the contrast between this suit of armor and the ideograms for *cuirass* on the Pylos tablets of the thirteenth century: the real thing seems more archaic than the sketch. Marinatos went farther and established its likeness to ideograms on the Knossos tablets of recently disputed date (Fig. 41 b). At Knossos, cuirasses are issued to special Greek troops along with a helmet, a chariot, and a pair of horses; those of the Dendra type are called *qe-ro*$_2$ (ancestor of the Homeric γύαλα) and have a *qe* written across the stomach. Although Homer knew it as a very archaic, inherited suit of armor, a nasty question arises as to whether the Knossos tablets could possibly be as late as the Pylos ones if the armor was current two centuries earlier. One can fight in an inherited suit for a generation or two; after two hundred years even a well-oiled heirloom tends to get rusty. Since a sword from the Dendra tholos is attributed to a workshop which also made swords for two warriors buried outside Knossos in the days when that palace was destroyed, and the *qe-ro*$_2$ tablets come from the Little Palace where the Greeks may have been living, it seems almost certain that the Early Mycenaean Age and the palace age of Crete came to an end simultaneously. The rich Dendra warriors with their fighting gear and their drinking cups have direct significance for when and how Knossos fell.

The Fall of Knossos and the International Scene

The bitter problem of the fall of Knossos was alluded to in the Introduction. A solution will be offered here which is not the normal one, and may not be generally accepted. In simple outline, the problem is this. The earliest Bronze Age excavations were at Mycenae. The character of the Mycenaean Age was quite well understood, as early as Tsountas' epoch-making essay Μυκηναῖ in 1893. Schliemann and Tsountas had made extensive excavations, mostly in tombs, but also uncovering the palace at Tiryns and rich private houses on the acropolis at Mycenae. The whole setting of Mycenaean life was beginning to form a harmonious total without reference to Knossos, which was still unexcavated. After 1900, when Evans' explorations in Crete had begun to illuminate a second culture of apparently much older traditions and strongly marked character, it became obvious that Crete and Mycenae were somehow related. Because the artistic power and extent of Knossos were so overwhelming, Evans naturally considered it primary, and the Mycenaean culture of the mainland secondary, perhaps developed through Minoan colonization in Greece. During the 1920's and 1930's a great deal more was discovered about the Greek mainland, and a chronology was established for its pottery by Professors Blegen and Wace, a chronology which in its general outlines, subject to minor modifications, has withstood every critical test. These two scholars also saw an increasing number of local differences between Crete and Greece, especially in architecture. Since the typical Cretan palace plan is nowhere repeated on the mainland, it became difficult to consider the great Mycenaean megaron-palaces as the buildings of colonists. There were corresponding mainland individualities in fresco work, pottery, gems, weapons, tombs, all the small significant signatures by which one civilization is distinguished from another.

Knossos was the first Aegean site to produce numbers of inscribed clay tablets. Although he could not read them, Evans made many intelligent guesses about words and forms, correctly deduced much of the content from the ideograms (drawings of objects which come at the right side of most tablets for quick identification [see Fig. 41; Pl. XLVI]), and saw that the Knossos tablets belonged to a different, slightly later, script than the tablets found at other Cretan palace sites like Hagia Triada, Phaistos, or Tylissos. The script was labeled B to separate it from the older type. It was, of course, tablets in this script that Professor Blegen found on his legendary first morning's excavations at the west coast mainland palace of Pylos (Englianos) in 1939. Up to that point, archaeologists were aligned in two camps: those who still believed the Minoans must have controlled the mainland in order to introduce so much Minoan art there, and those who, on the contrary, believed that for a special period Greeks had controlled Knossos. That period was the generation just preceding the devastation of the palace by fire, years when Knossos seemed to have a different experience from that of the rest of the island, during the ceramic phase of Late Minoan II. Late Minoan II is particularly characterized by the sudden appearance of Palace style vases (Fig. 26), just as Late Helladic II is on the mainland. The Palace style is found in significant quantity only in mainland tholos tombs and in the palace at Knossos. Other physical signs that something new happened at Knossos then were an increasing militarism in art and in the contents of tombs, the presence of horses and chariots whose shapes were clearly drawn on the tablets (Fig. 41 *b*), a new stylized and heraldic set of motifs in frescoes and in gems, and a rather un-Minoan arrangement in certain rooms including the famous Throne Room of King Minos. There was also, of course, the familiar legend of the adolescent Athenian king, Theseus, who had "slain the Minotaur in the Labyrinth" and freed Greece from its annual tribute to Minos. From cross-links to Egypt, Evans put the fall of the palace very close to 1400 B.C., shortly after the accession of Pharaoh Amenhotep III.

The Pylos tablets both clarified and complicated this historical reconstruction. Their abundance and good preservation led to the famous decipherment of 1952 by young Michael Ventris in England. Ventris demonstrated the possibility of reading so many words, phrases, and even whole tablets as an extremely archaic form of Greek that only a few bitter critics found fault with the results. It should be emphasized that the Ventris decipherment has by no means led to the easy understanding of Linear B, and that many of the earlier translations, so eagerly promoted as historical and social illuminations, have now been discarded or modified by scholars although they live on in the popular press. But it is certain that the Pylos tablets are written in the script first known from Knossos, as are the tablets later found at Mycenae, and that as a group of documents they have an extremely close relationship to those at Knossos. They are in Greek in both places. Although the Knossos texts seem tempered by Minoan vocabulary and names, there is no doubt that the Cretan palace had to administer its economy in a foreign language for some years, and that the economy was organized in the same style as at Pylos later.

Similar relationships appear between the frescoes from Knossos and Pylos, particularly the sets of heraldic griffins in the throne rooms of each palace or the procession scenes, and some of the architectural features like setbacks in long walls, columned porticoes, and bathrooms. There is very little difference in the style of script on the tablets of each palace (see Fig. 41; Pl. XLVI), and in the kinds of inventories they keep. Even some personal names seem identical in the two sets. But there can be no doubt whatsoever that the Pylos tablets were those of the series currently stored in the palace when it was burned down, and that this fire happened at the close of the LH III B period, conventionally dated *ca.* 1230–1200 B.C., or two hundred years after the fall of Knossos (Fig. 51).

Professor Blegen first suggested a systematic review of the stratification at Knossos, to see whether there might not actually be some shift downward in the 1400 B.C. destruction date proposed by Evans, so as to minimize what seemed like an extraordinary conservatism of writing and fresco painting for two centuries. Other scholars had been feeling uneasy about the situation too, especially in the Knossos sections of the Throne Room and the so-called Room of the Stirrup Jars, where a tablet listing 1,800 of this peculiar kind of Cretan oil vase was found at a somewhat lower level than a group of the stirrup jars themselves which were painted in a simple, perhaps late, style. The excavators of the British School, continuing Evans' work at Knossos under the direction of M. S. F. Hood, tested the stratification as far as they could, using the old field notebooks for comparison, which had been stored with other Evans material in the Ashmolean Museum at Oxford. At the same time, Professor Palmer, an Oxford philologist who had contributed a great deal to the further development of Ventris' decipherment, was led by a technical linguistic point to wonder whether the Knossos tablets were not actually later than the Pylos tablets. He too turned to the fieldbooks, claiming to have "discovered" them, and found enough apparent discrepancies between those first records and the later monumental and reflective publication of *The Palace of Minos* to warrant charges that Evans had falsified the evidence for the date of the burning at Knossos in order to make it harmonize with his convictions about the priority of Knossos over Mycenae. Palmer, in publicizing his beliefs through the newspapers and popular journals, and meeting bitter opposition from the archaeologists who knew Knossos firsthand, was perhaps led into an extreme position, from which he declared the fall of Knossos to have taken place in III B like the fall of Pylos, and that the critical material in the last habitation phase of the palace must be ascribed to that date, or slightly later, *ca.* 1150 B.C.

It may well be wondered why so much space is devoted here to a résumé of an academic quarrel which still continues, and which cannot be solved in the terms in which it is being played out. Linear B is a new prehistoric field demanding the utmost co-operation between linguists and field archaeologists, and when the two groups become arraigned against each other in counter-charges, the field suffers in spite of casual flashes of illumination from each side in support of its position. But the importance of the subject for Aegean history cannot be overestimated, because it is in the relations between Crete and Greece that the kernel of Mycenaean development lies, and it is absolutely necessary to view those relations in a reasonable chronological perspective. One cannot arbitrarily declare a set of objects to be LM III B rather than LM I, in rough terms to move them from the early fifteenth to the late thirteenth century B.C., without threatening the whole historical fabric so painstakingly worked out on dozens of sites in the course of the last eighty years. The Aegean would be pried loose from the framework of Egyptian and Near Eastern history, and the few stable Late Bronze Age scenes which we can recognize now in the procession of archaeological events, would dissolve in artistic anarchy.

The axiom is that chronology must be based on pots. It helps if the pots are lying with datable, preferably Egyptian, objects but mostly they have to be analyzed independently. In the Late Bronze Age, pot styles change more uniformly over a broad region than was ever true in Early and Middle Helladic; there is less purely local style in local rhythms, athough of course the workshops of each city have individual traits and material. Pottery changes may be viewed in two ways: either as a series of inevitable stylistic developments in which one repertory of design-motifs is imperceptibly transformed into the next and each may be taken as characteristic of its period; or as physically stratified sandwiches in which, without reference to aesthetic evolution, the pots below are inevitably earlier than the pots above. These two views must always be combined into one binocular vision of a period. The field tests correct the aesthetic judgment, and the aesthetic distinctions guide the field tests where the stratification is mixed up or intruded upon, as so often happens. Knossos is particularly susceptible to such mixtures because the palace building and the surrounding town are so complicated and large. The frescoes on the walls are likely to be older than the pottery on the floors which, in turn, may have fallen from rooms upstairs or have been deposited in one room during the repaving of another. It has proved extremely difficult to co-ordinate the pottery in actual use in the palace at the time of its destruction with the pottery saved in storerooms, the pottery in houses outside the palace, and the pottery in outlying tombs.

In specific terms of Knossos pottery the following sequence has been upheld for years (Fig. 26). While the Greeks were experiencing the rich transition of the Shaft Grave era, the Cretans were repairing their lives and palaces after a serious earthquake which interrupted Middle Minoan III B. The repairs signal the beginning of the last palace age in Crete when, without in any sense interrupting their natural artistic development, potters slowly changed from the richly colored, rather derivative light-on-dark wares of late Middle Minoan to the new, more delicate dark-on-light styles of Late Minoan I (Fig. 26 a). It was while this change was consolidating itself that Crete and Greece first steadily approached each other. The occasional MM III sherd in the Argolid, or slender evidence of contact like the Knossian faïence vase in Grave Circle B (p. 106), is succeeded by the strong Minoan influence in the later burials of Circle A where the first imported, spiral-ornamented LM I vases appear. Other typical motifs of this early chestnut-on-buff LM I A pottery are slender grasses or reeds like those on cups from Melos and Keos (Pl. XVIII A; cf. Fig. 26 b), or simpler ripples and dots which influence the "Keftiu cup" clay beakers of most important LH I mainland sites like Peristeria (Pl. XVIII B).

As this new style was maturing, Knossos suffered another "shock," or at least parts of the palace were remodeled again, and a new, more formal and symmetrical spirit pervaded the decorative arts. The pottery is now LM I A "mature," more solid and ornate but continuing the same naturalistic plant motifs

F<small>IG</small>. 26.—Development of Late Minoan pottery styles at Knossos: (*a*) LM I A early, pitcher (after Evans, *PM* II, Fig. 253 *b*); (*b*) LM I A mature, jar; (*c*) LM II Palace style jar; (*d*) LM II–III A, Ephyrean goblet (after Hutchinson, *BSA* 1956, 69, Fig. 1, 1); (*e*) LM III A:1, late Palace style jar, Ialysos (after Maiuri, *Annuario* 1926, Fig. 50).

and spirals (Fig. 26 *b*). This LM I A mature style is in use all over Crete with local variations, and also appears in Cretan footholds abroad like Phylakopi and Trianda. In Greece it shows up in the latest Shaft Graves and the more prominent tholoi of the early series. Next, there appears the most famous of all Minoan vase styles, the Marine style of LM I B. Not many vases of this splendid order are known; the best are so often illustrated that laymen may believe all Minoan pots look like this, with wonderfully tilted and controlled sea creatures swimming through sandy pools framed by seaweed and rocks—sponges, turret shells, argonauts, and dolphins are the favorites. There is very little of the fabric at Knossos itself although the marine motifs were used there even earlier, in frescoes and stone carving. The best examples are found in eastern Crete, at Gournia, Palaikastro, and Zakro in contexts of LM I A "mature." Most other prominent sites have one or two pieces to boast of: Phaistos, Mallia, Hagia Triada, Phylakopi, Trianda, Keos. Only Greece itself has practically none; one Attic sailor brought home a dolphin basket from Knossos as a souvenir (Fig. 27). In spite of this, the marine themes became so popular in Greece that they are reflected on the earliest Palace style jars like those from Kakovatos and Koukounara on the west coast (see Pl. XVIII F).

The Palace style is normally felt to succeed the Marine style in both Greece and Crete, with a little overlapping at its start. It stiffens the marine designs and the older plant and architectural ornaments into a more majestic symmetry, especially on the great three-handled jars which are its best expression. Evans considered it typical of the last active days before Knossos fell, and segregated the period of its use as LM II, a period unknown at any other Cretan site (see Fig. 26 *c*). Along with the great jars come a number of stemmed drinking goblets painted with a single detached ornament in the Ephyrean style of the mainland (Pl. XVIII C; Fig. 26 *d*). Finally, just before the palace is burned, a new series of vases is produced, with more spaced out and conventional plants or ornaments, and occasionally a crowded pictorialism of birds and flowers (see Pl. XVIII I; Fig. 26 *e*). The ewer and alabastron shapes of the earlier period continue; there are more stirrup jars than before, and smaller versions of Palace style jars as in Greece (cf. Pl. XVIII G). This is LM III A:1, absolutely the latest kind of pottery in the destruction debris, and in a sense the natural continuation of LM I A mature only enriched by experience of the Marine and Palace styles. It is particularly well represented in the Warrior Graves outside the city toward the harbor. Part of the confusion over the date of the fall of Knossos lies in the label for this pottery. Cretan archaeologists prefer to call it a late stage of LM II so as to keep the last days of Knossos a ceramic unit. Those looking at it from the Greek side prefer to call it LM III A because it corresponds with the mainland III A fabrics and is definitely later than the Palace style there. Whatever one calls it, it is a well-developed and perfectly recognizable kind of pottery which appears at other sites as well as

Fig. 27.—Marine style basket with diving dolphins, Varkiza (Attica). (After Theochares, *Antiquity* 1960, 266; drawing by S. Chapman.)

Knossos and is more like normal mainland styles than anything before in Crete.

Pottery is a dull and fussy subject, yet in the case of Knossos there is some excuse for lingering over it. Only pottery will tie the histories of Crete and Greece together and, with luck, link them to an Egypt fully endowed with absolute dates. The urgency of understanding the Knossos sequence is obvious, since the Linear B tablets have proved the Greeks to have been in control there for a respectable length of time before it fell and since an astonishing number of other important sites in Crete and abroad were also burned, knocked down, or abandoned during the crucial period. The questions are, when did the Greeks come? how did Greek-controlled Knossos relate to the rest of the island which had a different pottery experience? are the destructions of Cretan sites simultaneous or did the rest fall earlier than Knossos because they died using LM I? what absolute dates should be given to this Greek interlude? how did the outside world, especially Greece and Egypt, regard it? and what were the consequences of the fall of Knossos for Mycenaean civilization afterward?

The traditional allotment of time to each new pottery style is roughly one hundred years for LM I (1550–1450) with the Marine style starting a little after 1500, and fifty years for LM II (1450–1400) at Knossos, while the rest of Crete persists with LM I down to nearly the same moment. These chunks of fifty years are more convenient than real, and sometimes seduce the historical imagination into too great regularity. There is, for example, simply not enough Marine style or Palace style to account for fifty years of workshop output apiece. The Marine style was never the absolute hallmark of a period, but a very choice elaboration on the more ordinary styles of its day which were a continuation of LM I A. In the great eastern production centers, in the south, and at Knossos, this style is found in contexts of LM I A mature, stratified above the first examples of LM I A pottery but mixed with the later developments of it.[14] The two periods LM I A and I B are only one at heart, and the Marine style is a special class within the later part of that period.

A more serious paradox at Knossos is the evidence that the Palace style, which took its name from that palace, is not actually found inside the palace at all, much less stratified upon its final floors.[15] The great jars were stored in depots outside the proper limits of the palace, or used in houses and tombs beyond it, in a tracery that looks topographically significant. They turn up most densely to the west of the palace, in houses, such as the Little Palace, refurbished during the Greek period, and in tombs of the new Warrior Grave type along the road to the harbor. Some of the more important buildings have been interpreted as Greek headquarters during the final period, and most of the tombs have military gear which looks particularly mainland in inspiration. The Knossos Palace style jars were painted skillfully in local workshops just as the Greek ones were made in Greece (such big delicate pieces do not travel well), but they were not the common pottery of the palace in its final days. Evans thought they were missing in the palace either because the court people drank only from metal vessels while the lesser townspeople were reduced to using clay, or (since the jars are really rather splendid for lesser townspeople) that they were kept locked up in special west magazines when not being used.

The pottery actually lying on most floors of the palace when it was burned was an advanced expression of LM I A, as everywhere else in Crete, with a fair number of pieces in the newer LM III A:1 style. It is often difficult to distinguish the flowery motifs on one set from those on the other (Fig. 26), and the difficulty is complicated by the comparatively empty floors at Knossos and the rarity of good sealed deposits. Yet the excavation reports seem to make it clear that there are no physical levels corresponding to the Marine and Palace styles at Knossos, LM I B and LM II, and that from a pragmatic point of view the final period is a single long and prosperous unit characterized by a gradual development from LM I A to LM III A:1, between which the Marine and Palace styles should not be allowed to intrude as separate divisions of fifty years each on purely aesthetic grounds. They were there, of course, and in the sequence that Evans pointed out, but they were dramatic ripples across the face of a more leisurely stylistic growth to which they contributed their richer vocabulary of design. They were luxury pieces to the Greeks who came to Knossos in LM I at the end of the Shaft Grave period, and stayed there peaceably until the palace burned in LM III A. This was perhaps already the early fourteenth century when mainland palaces began to outshine the old Cretan centers.

If the time sequence of pottery at Knossos is adjusted slightly in this way, a clearer image of palace history may emerge. The Greeks' adventure in Crete was without doubt one of the most fruitful "emigrations" the mainlanders ever made, and they made it at a moment when Crete was reaching her own greatest successes as an artistic, civilized country. In LM I her palace architecture was at its most formal and subtle, her technical command in painting and small sculpture was of the highest order and admired by foreign contemporaries, her long training of young men as athletes and sailors brought her to a position of authority on the seas and made her the cultural model for neighboring regions. Of all Cretan towns Knossos had maintained the closest relations with the Greek Peloponnesos for perhaps three generations. It was the best port on the north coast facing Greece and had developed trade lines toward it through intermediate islands like Kythera, Melos, and Aigina (see Fig. 30). Mycenae, and to a lesser extent Pylos, were probably regular ports of call. Knossians and Greeks had felt a mutual interest since the transitional Shaft Grave era, no doubt based on mutual profit. Crete could offer technology, luxuries, and extensive knowledge of Aegean commerce and harbors, and the mainland perhaps reciprocated with horses, soldiers, and a willingness to act as companions in Cretan enterprises. Marriages between Knossos and Mycenae have often been suggested to explain the blending on the royal level of which the Shaft Graves are so eloquent; they are likely enough, though Greek myth is younger than the Shaft Graves and the first imported Cretan princesses it remembers were Ariadne and Phaidra of Knossos who charmed Prince Theseus when he killed the Minotaur. At any rate, Knossos was not alien by the time a small group of Greek soldiers went down there to live.

Late Minoan II is an expression of the Greek influence at Knossos rather than a chronological phase. Since no level is uniquely characterized by it, Knossos seems not so queer and special as used to be thought, nor so divorced from the experiences of the rest of the island. The Greeks were attracted by the splendors of fifteenth-century Knossos and did nothing to interrupt or spoil them. They only took them into their own charge, and maintained them through Minoan palace staff and artisans. While the Greek warriors were there, Knossos was, in fact, a power with a unified economy and homogeneous arts, although the vagaries of archaeological classification have made it seem to have a double image: LM I architecture, frescoes, and minor arts in the palace; LM II pottery and weapons in certain outlying buildings and in tombs. The two strains had fused into Late Minoan III A before the palace fell. This new decorative scheme could not have grown up overnight; it was the achievement of good potters who had been left in peace with active markets for a generation or more. The way other Cretan towns accept the new style so readily suggests that the whole island had had open communications before Knossos was destroyed, and this pottery does, in fact, form a solid underlayer from which Crete as a whole developed its own "empire" style after the palace age.

The Greek texts at Knossos offer the same picture, as cattle, grain, and oil come north over good roads from distant and rich parts of Crete (p. 241; Fig. 41). When LM II used to be considered a separate historical phase, and all other Cretan palaces were thought to have been destroyed in the LM I period, it was easy to construct a theory that violent Greek invaders at Knossos had destroyed rival Cretan centers and had isolated Knossos from a ravaged island milieu. Now it is clear that the two other great palaces, Mallia and Phaistos, flourished ceramically throughout the Greek period at Knossos though without having the Palace style in their storerooms, and that they were not ruined until the same time as Knossos, in Late Minoan III A. Even the apparent isolation of the Palace style at Knossos may be an archaeological accident, since new excavations in an extraordinary palace complex at Zakro in eastern Crete have revealed the Marine style, the Palace style, and the new III A pottery all together before a destruction contemporary with Knossos'. The island of Keos (p. 118) has exactly the same history and is destroyed by an earthquake at the beginning of III A. Texts and pottery together affirm that all Crete was prosperous under the domination of Greek Knossos, without interruption to its interior or exterior trade. Independent sources such as the Egyptian tomb paintings and the Minoan imports in the Cycladic islands or Cyprus also suggest that Cretan representation abroad was never broken during the crucial period, and that the island was wealthy and energetic, not filled with charred ruins and desperate refugees.

After the second shock at Knossos, in the period LM I A mature, the new ways taken by her artists and artisans created a model which would be extremely influential for the mainland in its own first palace phase in the following century. Some stylistic elements seem to reflect the same kinds of interests which were so strong in Greece during the Shaft Grave and early tholos periods. What Evans called Knossos' "sacral and conventional" aura meant in fact a shift toward large-scale frescoes without landscape and with a focus on the human actor. There is a new liking for symmetry where it would be structurally effective, and there are new motifs alien to Crete, like monsters and huge hairy shields. The griffins of the Throne Room, the rich embroidery of the procession fresco at the south entrance, the balanced postures of the drinking decadents in the Campstool fresco, have neither Minoan nor Mycenaean prototypes directly behind them. They might be explained as a blending of Mycenaean fantasy and ornate external detail with Cretan mastery in genre scenes and figure studies, both trends tempered by Aegean visits to Egypt and the Levant. Frescoes from other Cretan towns seem to retain an older and more genuinely Minoan "garden" sense, a greater purity of line and generosity of motion.

At the artisan level military fashions exert a new influence (Fig. 41). The horse and chariot become popular on gems; the crested helmet, body armor, flange-hilted "horned" sword and figure-of-eight shield, razors, and amber spread through the island, reaching the south at Phaistos and Hagia Triada. There had been excellent local Cretan equipment before, including long rapiers and hide shields, but the Warrior Graves of Knossos emphasize the cross-links with the mainland. One of these held a sword which seems to come from the same workshop as a sword in the Chieftain's Grave and the sword from the Dendra tholos tomb. The Dendra cuirass is matched by the ideogram for *cuirass* on the Knossos tablets (see Fig. 41 *c*); Knossos' first bronze helmet, boar's-tooth helmet, and one-edged knives turn up in this period. There are great thrusting spears, a fondness for ornamented blades, and chased gold cups. The first true tholos in the mainland architectural tradition is built on the Kephala hill by Knossos, and its façade is inscribed in a "mixture" of Linear A and B, recalling the façade of the tholos at Peristeria (Pl. XVI B; Fig. 6 *v, w*). Other great built tombs of the period like the Royal Tomb at Isopata are hybrids of design, with chambered forecourts and the mannerisms of Canaan and Egypt as well as Greece. They express the mixed, absorbing character of the period just as the pots and luxuries do. They are Cretan counterparts of the intrusive pointed vault, Tomb *Rho,* which was set in the center of Grave Circle B at Mycenae long after the other graves were dug and which reflected the funeral architecture of Ugarit and Enkomi (Pl. XVI C). It is a period of wide travel, of free exchange in ideas and local fashions which touch places as distant as Syria, Britain, and Germany. Knossos takes on an international look, though her own strong traditions keep on developing and affect the newcomer Greeks in permanently influential counteraction.

Egypt's vision of Crete and the Aegean in the crucial period is particularly welcome. No historical document shows so clearly as the great painted tombs of Egyptian Thebes the wealth of international contact which excited the Mediterranean world before the fall of Knossos. The tombs belong to high officials and soldiers working under Queen Hatshepsut and the pharaohs Tuthmosis III and young Amenhotep II. It was the highest fashion in fifteenth-century Egypt to decorate the walls of one's funerary chamber with exotic processions of foreigners bringing expensive gifts or bowing in humility before the might of Egypt. The painters regularly included Asiatics, Syrians, Libyans, Africans, and occasionally the rarer types of Hittites, Mitanni, and the men of Keftiu. Scholars often discuss these tombs as though their painted scenery could replace lost Aegean history if analyzed subtly enough,[16] although in truth the painters were no anthropologists, and often confused the labels on their foreigners or exaggerated the splendors of their gifts to the point one cannot recognize them archaeologically.

Among the foreigners, the Keftiu are surely meant to represent Cretans in Minoan costume, usually carrying elaborate metal vases, animal rhyta, ingots, or rolls of cloth (Fig. 28). Syrians are sometimes labeled Keftiu too, but they

Fig. 28.—The Aegean and Egypt (drawings by S. Chapman): (*a*) glass-paste bull amulet from the tholos at Kakovatos (after Müller, *AM* 1909, Pl. 12, 5); (*b, c*) objects from the Tomb of Menkeperrasoneb, Thebes; (*d, e*) Syrian and Keftiu in procession with Aegean gifts (after Davies, *The Tomb of Menkheperrasonb*, Pls. 4, 5).

can usually be distinguished by their long linen robes. There are ten or more tombs at Thebes which include Keftiu in their repertories; the principal four belonged to Senmut, Useramon or Amenuser, Menkeperrasoneb, and Rekhmire. The style of painting in other tombs, especially those of Puyemra and Kenamon, seems lighter and more sensitive in animal scenes than most Egyptian painting, as though distantly aware of the inimitable motion and color in fifteenth-century Minoan frescoes. The awareness may have been transmitted through minor luxury arts such as ivories and gems on which fresco themes had been employed, rather than through direct visits to Minoan palaces, for it had been stirring tentatively in Egypt as long before as in the reign of the pharaoh Ahmose with the first tentative flying gallop (p. 109).

The fresco series begins shortly after Hatshepsut's exploration of the novel fairyland of African Punt, which increased Egyptian delight in foreign exotica. Interest in the Aegean and the Levant grows steadily during Tuthmosis III's brilliant campaigns in Palestine and Syria when looted objects and mercenaries were circulating freely. The Syrians were more popular with painters than the Keftiu, bringing ships, chariots, copper ingots, gold and bronze vases, ivory, and bears. Both types seem to fade away in the later, less military climate of painting after the fall of Knossos, during the Amarna Age, although continued trade with the Aegean is assured by fourteenth-century Mycenaean pottery at Tell el Amarna and other Egyptian towns (Pl. XLV A; cf. Fig. 29), and the spirit of Amarna decoration may have had some influence on palaces in mainland Greece. One puzzle in the Keftiu frescoes while they lasted has always been the imbalance between the representations and the archaeological record, for it is Minoans who get painted while Mycenaeans leave their pots (p. 114). The painters take no trouble to distinguish mainlanders from Cretans or men of the Cyclades—Crete served as the model for an assortment of Aegean types because it was the longest known and most fascinating center of Aegean culture.

The usual Keftiu costume is a short embroidered kilt with a codpiece or a deep tasseled prong between the thighs, cinched at the waist by a broad, tooled belt of metal or leather (Fig. 28). The Keftiu wear elaborate sandals with high ankle straps or even turned-up toes, though Minoans and Mycenaeans usually show themselves barefoot in painting (p. 172). They wear their dark hair long, and it is distinguished from other foreigners' by its wavy strands over the shoulders and a spring of spitcurls on the crown. In gift they bring long conical rhyta of metal like the Silver Siege Rhyton (Pl. XIV), cups inlaid with silver and niello like those inventoried in the Linear B records at Knossos (see Fig. 41 *d*), tall fluted and engraved jars of gold and silver, vases with animal protomes like those made in eastern Crete, animal-head drinking cups in the form of bulls or lions like those in the Shaft Graves at Mycenae (cf. Pl. XI D), and even whole animal statues whose real counterparts have been lost to us except in dim reflections like the little bull amulet from the tholos at Kakovatos (Fig. 28 *a*). Sometimes the Egyptian painters add elements from local or Levantine vases, but their reporting is accurate enough to provide good cross-fixes between the Nile valley and the Aegean in the days before the fall of Knossos, and to illuminate its prosperous, creative activity under the Greeks. Only the artist for Rekhmire, nearly the last in the series, seems to have restyled a Minoan codpiece in favor of a plainer kilt (more Syrian than Mycenaean in fashion) as though something new in the quality of the Keftiu had struck him. This is a casual, smudgy touch it would be historically quite improper to equate with a mainland invasion of Knossos and a destruction for the rest of Crete. To the Egyptians, impartial outside observers, the Knossos problem does not exist. Relations between the two areas remained steady though not intense in the period of Greek dominion. Each region interested the other, and adapted fashions from the other. There was surely some sensible undercurrent of trade in wine, oil, timber, gold, and medicine from which the luxury items of the frescoes were thrown up as froth.

Knossos still seems to us now, as it did to Evans, the generating nucleus for Mycenaean development during the tholos period. Perhaps there has never been so dramatic an influence from one culture upon another, corrupting neither and strengthening both. There may have been little sense of "nationality" or race distinction in men's awareness then; a man came from Mycenae or Sidon or Knossos or Miletos as a potential contributor to mixed communities, with recognition of his special background but no particular prejudice. If a Mycenaean captain of soldiers became "Minos" at Knossos, the event may have been experienced by Cretans as interesting rather than threatening, so long as traditions and religion were not violated and the town continued prosperous.

No one knows how Knossos fell, or why. The excavators thought it was by human violence, since fire swept the west wing but the Grand Staircase in the east wing was not broken. Others have thought only an earthquake could be responsible for the simultaneous ruin of so many distant towns—Phaistos, Hagia Triada, Mallia, Gournia, Zakro, and distant Hagia Eirene on Keos, Trianda on Rhodes. In an earthquake foundations crack; otherwise the superficial damage from flames and falling walls quite resembles war damage, and it is not always easy to read the archaeological signs correctly.

If it was war, many explanations are possible and none can be proved. On the economic level, certain patterns are clear. Knossians were, at first, extraordinarily generous toward the Greeks, guiding them toward good trade harbors in the Levant and the West, perhaps accompanying them to Egypt and to Cretan posts in the Cyclades. Just at the time of the fall of Knossos Greek influence in these regions accelerates and the Minoan fades away. The critical sign is the new pottery of III A. Troy, Miletos, Trianda, Enkomi, Maroni, and Scoglio del Tonno by Taranto all show influxes of the ware, not coming from one distribution point but from as disparate trade centers as Athens and Rhodes. Egypt has it too, well before the Amarna Age (Pl. XLV A), and Egyptian souvenirs turn up in Mycenae itself (Fig. 29). The Crete which grew richer under Greek leadership at Knossos was competing with Greek cities on the mainland for control of Aegean trade.

The number of archaeological mixes, or "heirloom cases," between Late Minoan I and Late Minoan III A is a sign that these periods touch, as suggested above for the pottery sequence at Knossos.[17] The Crete of greatest bloom in LM I is then anterior by no more than a generation to the Crete who lost her dominance in sea trade in LM III A. At the end, Knossos Greeks seem to be thrusting hardest in just those foreign towns where the mainland Mycenaean element is becoming more obvious. The "late" stirrup jars at Knossos which so troubled Professor Palmer are matched by stirrup jars of Cretan oil found at Troy along with Mycenaean pottery of the latest Palace style (cf. Pl. XVIII H). Others turn up at Ugarit in Canaan just after 1400 B.C. when the records tell of Canaanite merchants asking to import goods from Crete without paying duty on them. The north Aegean island of Staphylos (Peparethos) receives a new prince whose brilliant burial recalls the Shaft Graves, especially in the quality of his great sword, but whose vases are matched at Knossos in the Warrior Graves and in the "late memorial cult" of the Temple Tomb. Home in Crete, two cases illustrate the blend of militarism and commerce. In a Cretan farmhouse near Gortyna lay a clay statue of a warrior in one of the new Greek cuirasses, with Late Minoan I and III vases around him together on the floor; the rustic villa was literally stuffed with huge storage jars for grain and oil. A special tomb at Katsaba, the harbor of Knossos, is the counterpart symbol for the sea trade. It was part of a cemetery where many ship captains were buried, using novel wooden coffins (p. 301) and the typical war gear of the Warrior

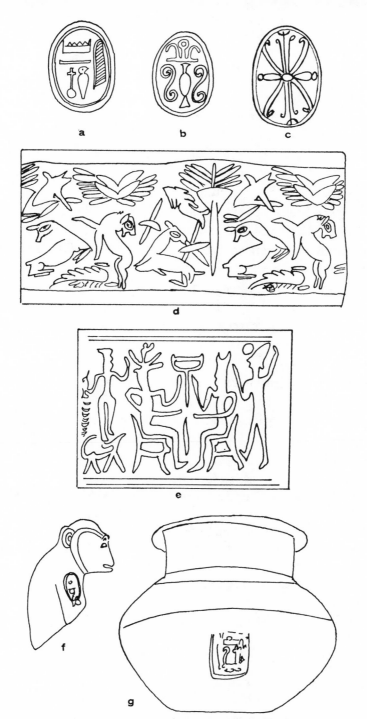

FIG. 29.—Egyptian and Near Eastern seals and scarabs in Mycenaean contexts: (*a*) scarab of Hatshepsut, Prosymna, LH I (after Blegen, *Prosymna,* Fig. 597); (*b*) XVIII Dynasty scarab, Koukounara, LH I–II (after Marinatos, *Ergon* 1958, Fig. 158); (*c*) scarab of Rameses II(?), Perati, LH III B–C (after Iakovides, *Ergon* 1958, Fig. 32); (*d*) hybrid Asiatic cylinder, Myrsinochorion, LH II–III A (after Marinatos, *Ergon* 1956, Fig. 92); (*e*) Near Eastern cylinder, Ialysos Tomb 17, LH III B(?) (after Maiuri, *Annuario* 1926, Fig. 47); (*f*) Blue glass-paste ape with cartouche of Amenhotep II, Mycenae, LH III A(?) (after Fimmen, Fig. 169); (*g*) Faïence vase with cartouche of Amenhotep III, Mycenae, LH III A(?) (after Tsountas, *Ephemeris* 1888, 154, Fig. 10).

Graves, and even Palace style vases painted with helmets like floating octopodes. In this tomb, a great alabaster jar from Egypt with the royal cartouche of Tuthmosis III was buried with a remarkable Minoan vase, a ewer with knobs on, which fuses in a single piece of clay all the decorative traits of Late Minoan I B, II, and III A. This pair expresses perfectly the uninterrupted and international character of Knossos culture in its last years.

Destruction of Knossos by war, then, would have followed some commercial friction between Crete and Greece which had become inflamed to the point of outrage. It is easy to imagine a dozen ships of jealous mainland Greeks sailing in to burn it. It is not so easy to imagine simultaneous naval expeditions against all the great centers of Crete and the islands. The evidence of earthquake at other sites might suggest that an initial natural catastrophe was quickly followed up by Mycenaean scavengers and that unaffected mainland towns capitalized at once on the removal of Knossos by increasing their own exports of oil abroad.

It would have been hard to restore Crete to her former equilibrium after such a memorable disaster. The poet Pindar tells an enlightening story about Euxantios, the son of Cretan Minos and Princess Dexithea of Keos (p. 116).

I liked the story of Lord Euxantios, who refused when the Cretans wanted him to be king there and to share a seventh part of the hundred cities with the sons of Pasiphaë. He told them of his sign from the gods:

"I am afraid of a war of Zeus, I am afraid of the deep-striking Earth-Shaker. Once they sent the land and the clustered army into deep Tartaros, with lightning-flash and trident, leaving only my mother and her strong house safe.

"Now, trying for wealth and thrusting aside the divine law of my country, utterly abandoned, am I to have a grand estate elsewhere?

"How would it be safe for me? Let it go, heart, let go the cypress-land, the pasture by Mount Ida.

"To me little land has been given, a thicket of oak, but I have no share of grief, no civil quarrels."[18]

Thirty-three hundred years after the fall of Knossos we are not in a position to know how it happened. Perhaps the final act in the play between Crete and Greece was a passive resignation of power by the older civilization, as Matz suggests. Perhaps it took place in a flare of antagonism, with self-preserving attacks by rival mainland princes, as the Theseus myth intimates. Perhaps Knossos was destroyed by Poseidon, lord of earthquakes, in an upheaval of the Aegean seabed, as Marinatos suggested in a classic paper. At this distance we

can only observe the moment of transition, when Crete imparted her unique skills of art and writing, foreign experience and religious tradition, to Mycenaeans who were beginning to recognize their own potentialities. Without knowing the details, one can see the transformation which Cretan civilization worked on the later Greek world. The ruin of the island palaces is immediately followed by the rise of several on the mainland.

NOTE, 1972

Discoveries in the town of Akrotiri on the south coast of Thera, where since 1967 Marinatos has been reopening the old French excavations, have contributed complex new dimensions to the discussion of the weakening of Cretan power. Akrotiri, buried deep under pumice from a violent volcanic eruption, was apparently deserted around 1500 B.C., in Late Minoan I A. Some observers believe that a later eruption caused catastrophic ashfall and tidal waves on Crete about 1450 B.C., when Mycenaean adventurers may have moved into Knossos to exploit a shocked political and economic situation. The archaeological connections are not clear yet, but may become so. Meanwhile, Akrotiri's premier status as a center of Cretan commerce and civilization in a Cycladic milieu has allowed a vivid recreation of the cultural levels of the beginning of the Late Bronze Age. There are rich mixtures of local and imported pottery; well-preserved architectural details; evidence for daily life, such as food, furniture, weights and measures; graffiti in Linear A; and brilliant frescoes of swallows, antelopes, blue monkeys, spiral friezes, child boxers, and a priestess. (Evans would have enjoyed it.) The volcanic theory of the destruction of Knossos is, as a consequence, in highest fashion now.

Chapter VI

The Beginnings of Domestic Architecture

As though houses and tombs were on a seesaw balance, the first great architectural complexes do not rise in Greece until tholos tombs have almost stopped being built. Perhaps only the latest tholoi, Atreus and Clytemnestra and Genii at Mycenae, are contemporary with traceable palace outlines as examples of the grand funerary style. The familiar palace-town centers of Mycenaean civilization are not designed as we know them until Greece becomes thickly settled and stable after the fall of Knossos and during the Amarna Age, and these towns conceal or have destroyed most earlier architectural phases.

The period from 1400 to 1200 B.C. (LH III A and B) is marked by many more chamber-tomb burials than before, each with greater numbers of gifts, suggesting that the population of Greece increased in these generations and that more middle-class members of society grew rich. There is no longer the dramatic contrast between the gold-guarding aristocracy and the anonymous

Life
in a Mycenaean Palace

peasantry, but apparently new merchant and professional classes developed as the supporting stratum which allowed each local prince to consolidate his power in different economic terms. The Greek palaces express this change visually. They are neither complete towns nor pure royal houses, but nuclei for centralized valley communities which are expanding in crafts and industries as well as preserving the sense of dynastic tradition. The age of palace foundations is also the age of colonists and merchants overseas: in Rhodes where they remained "Mycenaean," in Cyprus and Egypt where they became partly "native," and in Ugarit where they settled among other aliens as local agents for import and export of mainland needs. Miletos, Phylakopi, Staphylos, Ialysos, Kos, and other Aegean centers grow more active, and a spectrum of independent local kingdoms with a sense of national Achaian identity begins to emerge.

The five principal palace-towns of the fourteenth and thirteenth centuries

Fig. 30.—The Palace Age in Greece

FIG. 30.—*Continued*

are Mycenae, Tiryns, Athens, Thebes, and Pylos (Pls. XXII–XXV). We should expect others, especially where the tholoi betray earlier wealthy settlements and where old legend is concentrated. Iolkos in Thessaly is now being dug. Amyklai in Lakonia; Eleusis, Marathon, Brauron, Menidi, Spata, and Thorikos in Attica; Delphi and Orchomenos in central Greece; Delos and Keos and Ialysos among the island towns, have all afforded traces of strong Mycenaean power from an early time, although erosion, overbuilding, and lack of deep exploration have hidden their late Bronze Age urban outlines. The two "great houses" Homer spends most time in, that of Menelaos at Sparta and of Odysseus in Ithaka, have not been found yet; some which have been found have not yet been connected successfully to inherited legend, like the romantic island fortress of Gla in Lake Kopaïs (Pl. XXII B). Practically every classical polis has its layers of Mycenaean sherds; and it would be, in a sense, more rewarding now to excavate such a town completely, than to concentrate on another palace. But the lure of palace frescoes and possible tablets is hard to resist. Of excavated palaces, Tiryns and Pylos are best preserved and most interesting. Part of the palace at Mycenae fell over the hill, Athens' Acropolis was leveled and built over, Thebes' Kadmeion lies under an expensive part of the modern town. For walls and private houses, Mycenae is best (Pl. XXIV).

The general features of a Mycenaean town are like those of its counterparts in Crete and Anatolia although on a smaller scale. One major exception is that Greece builds no noteworthy temples or shrines. Towns on the east coast, near harbors, are generally protected behind a wall; the construction may be great Cyclopean boulders fitted and smoothed, or careful ashlar facings binding a rubble core (p. 264). In the west, walls are lower and thinner, or the outside wall of a palace-building substitutes for a separate citadel defense line. The citadel is usually built on a significant height, and has several gates or entrances overlooking the main roads which converge at such centers. The principal gate usually faces the principal road, and its position is therefore dictated by local traffic. The road leading up to it is normally wide enough for wheeled carts, while narrower streets or paths lead to the postern gates in patterns related to the private houses outside the citadel limits. The inner town may have several main streets as at Mycenae, and the palace lies on the highest ground above the private houses, sometimes set off from them by a ramp or stairs (Pl. XXIV A). These towns are not planned in classical Hippodamian or modern terms except by terrain and common sense.

Two engineering specialties contributed to the town's well-being, road-construction and water-supply. The Mycenaean road system was extremely advanced for its period, forming a large connecting network among the chief towns of the Argolid and Messenia, probably Boiotia and Attica too. There were stone bridges, reinforced culverts and guard-stones along the edges, and the surfaces were often graveled (p. 263). Chariots and farm carts could travel with fewer bumps than in later classical days. Water systems were equally sophisticated. Drains inside and wells outside the towns were dug through a considerable depth of rock at Tiryns and Athens. In the later nervous days of the palace period, the underground fountains of Mycenae, Tiryns, and Athens were marvelous feats of design, tapping water from distant hills and storing it safely in deep rock basins inside the city walls. At Pylos water was brought into town by an open raised wooden aqueduct supplied through forced rise from a spring a kilometer away. Washing tubs or watering places for animals were set into the main channel. The water passed through the industrial and palace quarters in terracotta pipes, and was carried off in a system of underground channels, some lined with stone. The great lake at Gla (p. 266) was apparently drained or controlled by a system of dikes and ditches, and in fact the Mycenaeans predicted almost every hydraulic achievement of classical times except the invention of waterproof cement; for waterproofing they used refined clay or lime plaster. When one looks down the corbeled tunnels of the Tiryns water passages, sloping with stepped roofs and yellow clay floors nearly 30 meters through the city wall to reservoirs hollowed in the natural rock where pure spring water still seeps, one's admiration for the palace engineers is tempered by awed respect.

Professional workshops, guardrooms, storerooms, and kitchen quarters are attached to the palaces at the rear or sides. There is still little information about lower towns of Mycenaean centers where small craftsmen must have worked in annexes to the palace industries, but there seems to have been some encouragement for private enterprise also. The palace is always the economic and industrial center of the complex, however, as well as the civil and military center. Provincial towns and villages would have had more independence in one way, and less specialization among craftsmen, although they would also have been less self-sufficient, because they needed to acquire raw materials from other towns with stronger trade lines abroad. Mouriatada, north of Pylos, is a specimen of one of these county seats (p. 182; Fig. 52 *f*). In the main towns the concentration of resources and specialized staff meant that the palace could occupy as much as half the available space inside the walls, which in turn meant a new challenge to main-land architects. No town in Greece is as big as Knossos—the Pylos palace is only a quarter the size—but Knossos and its Cretan neighbors served as models which the new dynasts adapted to their own traditions and needs.

THE GROWTH OF A PALACE

The palace at Pylos (Englianos), which is the nucleus of the larger town of Pylos, illustrates Mycenaean town design with great liveliness (Pl. XXII A). The excavations directed there by Professor Blegen have cleared one of the most complete palace plans in Greece, and the Linear B tablets from this palace offer more specific information about the function of the plan than any other site has given. As the excavations continue (1939, 1952——) they will probably reveal more dependent buildings and houses of the lower town to complete the picture. The succession of buildings is also especially clear at Pylos, so that one can watch the architectural design expanding and changing as the town grows.

At first the plateau at Englianos was only one of many Middle Helladic vil-lage sites in Messenia, less impressive than Malthi or Peristeria (pp. 77, 117). It is set on a narrow hill among gullies which tilt in deep parallel folds to-ward the sea, the rough country forcing the main road inland as it runs south-west from Mount Aigaleon to the great natural harbor at Pylos-Navarino. Englianos is thus a good morning's walk from the shore and farther from its own harbor (Boïdokoiliá), but it is placed to command a view of the road, and one can see the ships by the beach. Since the nearest sweet spring is across a valley, one supposes that the power of Pylos in the thirteenth century sprang not so much from the natural advantages of the site, so much less dramatic than at Mycenae or Athens, as from the character of the dynasts who decided to settle there.

Before 1300 B.C. Englianos had a period of anonymous florescence like richer neighboring sites (Myrsinochorion, Iklaina, Tragana). There was one respect-able fifteenth-century limestone building on the acropolis and traces of houses in the currant vineyard below. A broad road led up to the main gate with a flight of shallow steps and flanking walls, perhaps towers. A tholos tomb stood opposite the gate and another down the road southwest. But there is no sign that Pylos was more distinguished than half a dozen other early Mycenaean towns in its region. About 1400 B.C. signs of growing population are visible in the spread of a lower town around the Englianos plateau, matching the growth in other contemporary towns and cemeteries.

At Englianos, at least, this fourteenth-century town was burned, and new princes took over the hilltop. This would be two or three generations after the fall of Knossos, coinciding with the beginning of the III B pottery style and the full international phase of the thirteenth century. If history accords with legend, it was Neleus the prince of Thessaly who came into the Peloponnesos after conflict with his brother Pelias at Iolkos; they were both "sons of Poseidon," and the strong attachment to Poseidon's cult in both places, as well as certain technical architectural features, link these otherwise distant areas. We are prepared to believe in high mobility in this later Mycenaean world. What is surprising, and suggestive, is the freedom of one Mycenaean group to burn out and take over another, as late as 1300 B.C. Reckoning by generations, our poetic records reach back only two or three generations before Neleus, to the Knossos period, and so the earlier settlers at Englianos are nameless.

The Palace Plan at Pylos

The Neleid newcomers shaved off the top of the plateau and began building a palace very much like those at Tiryns or Mycenae. There is so little hesitation or experiment in its plan, we must believe the architectural tradition was already quite conservatively fixed. The older block was gradually supplemented by larger palace buildings for the next hundred years, and then at the end of the thirteenth century Pylos was burned out, like most sites in Greece, in a tremendous fire fed by the wooden struts in the walls and the oil in the storerooms. What happened next, no architectural survivals tell us, except that tombs were still being made and used near the ruined palace in the twelfth and eleventh centuries; local families survived and bred beyond the end of the empire period. A picture of a ship on a sherd from the reused tholos at Tragana is assurance that trade continued and that Messenians did not all become refugees or relapse into frightened isolation (Fig. 43 *b*).

As it stood at the end of its hundred-year occupation, the palace of the Neleids consisted of three main blocks covering nearly half the plateau (Pl. XXII A). All earlier buildings were torn down to make room for them. The principal block of the last period holds stage center (Pl. XXV A), conforming closely in design to the second palace at Tiryns (Pl. XXIII B) though a little less elaborate. Its focus is a large megaron of classic form: a deep enclosed room with central hearth surrounded by four columns which support an open balcony on the second floor (Pl. XXV B). The single door leads out through two shallow vestibules or porches to a great walled courtyard, which in turn opens through a columned entrance or propylon toward the main street on the south. As you enter this main block from the street the propylon is guarded by a jutting tower complex on your right, unshielded side, and the official archives room with its anteroom featuring a jar for tax oil lies on the left under survey from a sentry platform. The entrance thus expresses in physically symbolic terms the double function of a Mycenaean palace: military defense and civic administration.

The megaron is the focus of the main block, but the subsidiary rooms are extensive and equally interesting. Along the outer walls of the megaron two long corridors faced with limestone run back to the pantries and storerooms at the rear of the building. Doors in the outer walls of these corridors open onto another series of magazines. Each corridor connects directly with the inner vestibule outside the megaron and with the walled courtyard in front of it. Such a design allows privacy from noise and movement in the megaron itself, while permitting free circulation to the business parts of the building and supervision at restricted exits. The main block also contains a whole complex of living and private rooms on the ground floor, off to the right (north) of the court. A small megaron, called the Queen's Megaron, is connected by little passages to a painted boudoir and a genuine bathroom (a drainhole from one corner leads outdoors to the general drainage system). Another suite of apartments (the king's?) has a bathroom with a painted tub still in place, and dressing rooms and bedrooms. Outside these royal suites two small enclosed yards or garden courts were added as the century passed. They offered privacy and fresh air, protected from the street outside their walls. Tiryns had a similar double-megaron plan; it seems to have been a traditional design for handling large royal families. Flights of wooden stairs lead up from these private quarters and from the corridor to other principal apartments on the second floor. Although this upper part of the palace was totally destroyed in the ultimate fire, it must have had ladies' boudoirs among other rooms, for charming fragments of ivory mirrors and other toilet articles fell through to the ground in the destruction.

Outdoors, on either side of the central palace building, streets run back to the magazines at the rear, and isolate the megaron from the wing-blocks. At a later period these streets, like certain corridors indoors, were blocked off by

crosswalls to form courtyards, perhaps in a sudden urge for privacy or defensible isolation of the royal quarters. In the earlier plan, they permitted a
traffic flow around the central block and the southwest (oldest) block. This
southwest building is the original part of the palace, the "Neleus" plan as
opposed to the "Nestor" plan of the center. A ramp from the main southeast
street leads into a courtyard paved in stucco. Beyond this broad space one
enters the old palace through two columns, a deep vestibule painted
with a scene of mass-murder and pink griffins, then sharp left past a third
column into a principal hall with two rows of columns. This hall is not a
megaron in shape, but a long, deep, hearthless space with perhaps three columns in each row. Its approach and design are less organic, less axial than in
the newer block, and have something of Crete's impromptu planning, but still
conform to mainland canons. The hall was surely the throne room of the
original palace, and when the new block rose it must have been converted to
some other important use—some think a home for the dowager queen, some
a main reception or banquet room for the whole palace. The old block is a
self-contained unit with at least eighteen pantries and storerooms behind the
hall, each having to be entered from the one before. The arrangement is awkward but private and protective. Stairs rise between the hall and the storerooms
to living apartments on the second floor.

The old block was built on heavy foundations which hug the westernmost
edge of the palace plateau behind a thick wall. This wall is designed with setbacks, running nearly 40 m. along the course of a pre-Neleid wall; it functions
both as a retaining wall for the newly graded terrace, and as a defense barrier
on the west. Pylos was otherwise defenseless in the thirteenth century, for the
fifteenth-century tower and gate system had been abandoned.

The third block of the palace, east of the main building, is a more poorly
built "industrial quarter" with special annexes. When the street on this side
was blocked off and the king's and queen's courtyards constructed, they were
deliberately doorless toward the workshop façade, as though some social distinction were operating. These palace workshops open off two sides of a
little courtyard; they are long businesslike rooms parallel to the axis of the
main building and so apparently planned in relation to it. The focus of the
court is a painted altar, with a room behind it which the excavators see as
a stepped shrine in Cretan style. If this is so (the destruction of the palace
was too thorough to leave any religious equipment intact) it is important
(p. 283). Shrines of any sort are extremely rare in Greece; the two known

examples at Asine and Keos are not in palaces. Yet the Pylos tablets provide such an active picture of ceremonies on palace lands, that any physical evidence for their setting is precious. The courtyard could have functioned as a theatral area, its diminutive size compensated for by second-floor windows, a balcony propped by columns down one long side, and the flat roofs of the main building from which palace people could have a clear, though slanted, bird's-eye view. The workrooms beyond this doubtful area held storage jars, fragments of bronze, clay sealings from packaged goods, bits of bronze arrowheads and of decorated ivory. One section was probably the chariot repair-shop, another the armory, both vouched for in the tablets. This part of town is well drained by the elaborate channel and pipe system.

In the rear of both main palace blocks stand separate sheds, the wine stores filled with jars, a little round foundation called a "rabbit-pen" (probably the remains of a small granary tholos like the one on which Odysseus hanged his maidens). On the eroded slopes beyond the modern edge lie the remains of a potter's kiln with crumpled discards around it.

The Function of a Palace

The comparison to medieval citadels is traditional, and good if one does not press the implications too far.[1] A town like Pylos was much more than a shelter for the dynast, his family, special troops, and servants. It also acted as a safe-deposit and central goods-exchange for most products, both from the palace shops and from the county towns and villages in its economic dominion. Indeed, the prince's authority must have been based to a very real extent on how well he controlled these multiple interchanges, on the fairness and efficiency of his business routines, and on personal surveillance. The citadels by now had become much more than eyries for raiding eagles; they represented for the first time a true town milieu in mainland life. Even before the decipherment of the Pylos tablets it was clear that the power of such palaces extended broadly into the surrounding countryside. The palaces geographically closest to each other are Mycenae and Tiryns, then Gla and Thebes, but Pylos seems to have had no close rivals. In its final days Pylos mastered a lot of territory: if the place names in the tablets can be taken at face value, it probably included most of the huge Messenian promontory, from the head of the Messenian gulf to north of Kyparissia and the Arkadian Pass. Such a tract falls in size between Attica and Boiotia, not quite compact, and studded with towns of equally strategic location and families probably older than Nestor's, who would have been glad to challenge his mastery in discontented times. Much depended on his keeping the county families in firm control and insuring good trade lines with neighbors by land and sea.

In the early days of the Englianos excavations it seemed amusing, or horrifying, to find so many burned, crushed pots inside the palace, crowded into storerooms and pantries around the main megaron. One such room held 850 pots of twenty-five different shapes; another, the shocking total of 2,853 stemmed drinking cups. Other palaces and private houses were exactly the same: Thebes stuffed 250 plain pots in a single room, the House of the Oil Merchant at Mycenae was filled with oil-stained stirrup jars. Professor Blegen's audiences used to consider with some delight the un-Homeric image of Nestor as a dealer in kitchenware, and yet this "shopkeeper" symptom harmonizes well with the Linear B records kept in the archives room. The whole palace is like a miniature Hellenistic trading center; the oil and wine stores, the smiths' and masons' working quarters, the tablets and the endless pots all contribute impressions of how crammed with energetic life such buildings were before their capture.

THE PALACE SETTING: REAL AND PAINTED VIEWS

Because of its storage and exchange function, one would expect much of the palace to be stripped down to the businesslike buff. This is true in many areas, but a surprising number of rooms are highly ornamented and painted. Part of their color and nice detail is adapted from Cretan palaces. Long outdoor walls are treated with setbacks for relief and shadow, both in heavy defense walls like Tiryns' and in domestic blocks like the Pylos megaron. Pale limestone ashlar masonry faces the rubble wall cores in public areas, and into it is inserted a boxlike framework of heavy timber beams and braces which is left exposed in some palaces but plastered over in the later period at Pylos. Such timber strutting was widely used in Crete and Anatolia from the Early Bronze Age onward, because it created a frame sturdy enough for normal use, but pliant enough to yield in an earthquake where a rigid wall would snap. Often the exposed wood provided a stage on which fresco figures could walk. It turned the palaces into firetraps, for wood was used freely not only inside the walls but also for door jambs, ceiling beams, stairways, columns, and projecting balconies. Coats of painted plaster on all these projecting elements only partly protected them. There are no obvious fire precautions, yet so many drains ran under the main storerooms and passages that perhaps the staff knew places where the cover-slabs could be ripped off and the water bailed out in emergencies. As long as no malice set light to the oil stores there was no more danger from day to day than in a modern frame house with an oil tank in the cellar.

Great stretches of the palace were dark. The principal rooms were large but sealed in; the private rooms were small, and there were few windows on the ground floor. Downstairs light and heat were supplied by portable tripod hearths or braziers, by stone lamps set on tables and tall ones standing on the floor, by saucers with a wick in oil carried from room to room, and by torches in the less flammable parts of the building. A fresco fragment from a long dark stairwell at Pylos shows a man against a black background with a lamp standing beside him; one suspects the artist of an un-Mycenaean sense of humor. Upstairs may have been much airier and more pleasant with windows and roofed balconies overlooking the courtyards. The fresco painters loved to use the motif of the rich façade with balconies and windows, and the theme turns up on the walls of almost every palace. One fragment from Pylos shows diagonal ripples as though a veined marble slab or curtain was set across the opening (Fig. 32). The long fresco from the megaron at Mycenae illustrates a palace in several levels, from the grass on the slope below to the red hill behind (Pl. XXXI).

Views of the palace figured importantly in the Mycenaean palace fresco repertory from a combination of several different aesthetic impulses. The theme was inherited from the Cretans who illustrated the palace exterior in a meadow setting (Hagia Triada) or the interior filled with the people of the court (Knossos). Since the decoration of a palace was the most tangible expression of a prince's authority in an age when tholos tombs were scarcely being built any more, great expense went into its real design and decoration. Friezes and dadoes were carved in costly stones like marble, porphyry or alabaster (Fig. 31), elaborate capitals were set on fluted wooden columns (Pl. XXX C), bronze sheathing covered double wooden doors or thresholds, and ornaments were painted on every available surface (Pl. XXV B). Often the motifs reflected or paralleled motifs which had been common in vase painting from the Palace style onward and were thus familiar routine both for the sculptors and painters who put them on the palace walls, and for the fresco painters who reduced the image of the palace to miniature. A marble dado or door frame from the fourteenth-century palace at Thebes (Fig. 31) still uses the spiral and scale patterns which first appeared in Greece in the Shaft Graves of the sixteenth century, and matches the quality of the ceiling in the thirteenth-century Orchomenos tholos tomb. More familiar examples of this princely style are the alabaster-and-blue-glass dado from Tiryns or the porphyry split-rosette bands from the megaron at Mycenae. When artists re-

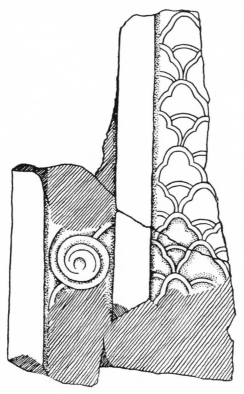

FIG. 31.—Fragment of marble architectural ornament, from a dado(?), palace at Thebes. (After Keramopoullos, *Ephemeris* 1909, Fig. 19, drawing by S. Chapman.)

create impressions of the palace setting, therefore, they accentuate these more splendid details, regularly including the colored discs over doorways which stand for projecting beam-ends, the bands of checkers along entablatures, the meticulously jointed walls, the floral capitals, and the horns of consecration at the edge of the roof (Pl. XXX C; Fig. 32). Even if the colors are not true, their work has the utmost value for reconstructing the palace in our imaginations. They choose as they do out of the ensemble because the architect had also placed his strong focus on the key points of entrance, on vistas along which the eye is drawn by aligned columns, within a framed symmetry of large blocks.

Mycenaean palaces are often contrasted with Cretan ones as examples of a sealed axiality which emphasizes authority and unity as distinguished from a more dissolved and spontaneous Minoan design. This is partly because mainland palaces were smaller and partly because they made less general use of the column, the light-well, and the partition wall with piers. The Mycenaeans saved these Cretan borrowings for public areas where they strove for monumentality. When the plan calls for only one or two megara among a

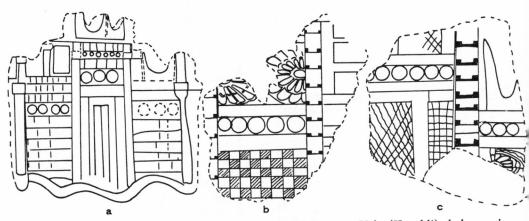

FIG. 32.—Views of palace façades: (*a*) gold foil ornament, Volo (Kapakli) tholos tomb (after Kourouniotes, *Ephemeris* 1906, Pl. 14); (*b*) fresco, Orchomenos (after Bulle, *Orchomenos* I, Pl. 28); (*c*) fresco, Pylos (courtesy M. Lang).

sea of smaller rooms, any sensible architect will emphasize the route approaching them with wider or multiple doors, columns leading in lines toward piers or openings, or in the axes of massive gates. Actually many buildings had a minimum of finesse in such arrangements—even Pylos was sparsely columned and narrow-doored, Mycenae grew off-balance, Gla almost ignored the megaron design—and the generalization about Mycenaean architecture usually springs from enthusiasm about the classic plan at Tiryns (Pl. XXIII B). Tiryns nearly doubled the scheme at Pylos: two columns between piers on either side of two massive gates, a colonnade around three sides of the megaron court, two columns in the porch in line with piers framing three bronze doors on bronze pivot poles. Most plans were less clever, and made broad concessions to the lie of the land or to accidents of growth.

One must commend even the limited Mycenaean adaptation of columns and columned balconies, one of the most attractive elements in any Greek building until the development of the classical stoa which it predicts. Earlier village houses had made only embryonic efforts to get air and shade this way, with shallow porches jutting over the front door, but of course the outdoors was more directly part of their environment than in the Mycenaean urban complexes. At Pylos the wooden columns had red rings of stucco around their feet and were often vertically fluted with as many as sixty shallow channels. From other sources in other places an enormous range of column designs is preserved: the plain down-tapered shaft of Crete used on the Lion Gate at Mycenae (Pl. XVII B), the zig-zags and spirals carved on the Treasury of Atreus' engaged half-columns (Pl. XXVI B), the broader Doric fluting used on the Tomb of Clytemnestra, or spirally fluted columns known best from small ivory inlays (Pl. XXXIX D). These shafts were topped with a corresponding richness of capital design, best preserved in ivories and frescoes (Pls. XXXIX D, XXX C). The Sphinx Gate fresco from Pylos' gateroom, a slender and fantastic design, shows the single fluted column between antae rising over a story high to a spreading floral capital. This was a dramatic entrance where the heraldic monsters and the elegant column complemented each other as attractions. In this field of architecture the Mycenaeans exhibit more taste for experiment and relaxed inventiveness than the Cretans, more than there would be again in Greece until the fourth century B.C. The influence of the experimental Egyptian city at Tell el Amarna may be somewhere behind it.

We cannot wonder that Mycenaean artists enjoyed reproducing the elegant effects of mainland palaces, filling them with typical figures—showing the ladies on their window seats watching life outdoors (Pl. XXXI), inserting soldiers into the courtyard (Orchomenos), even putting stags, horses, and sphinxes in architectural settings where they would be decoratively effective if not quite convincing as a document of palace life (Hagia Triada and Pylos; Pls. XXIX D, XXX C; Fig. 33 *b*). It may be that the palace offered these painters a more significant frame of reference than any expanse of pure nature, and that their fantasies refused to be separated from it. They also had difficulties with perspective.

Interiors: Paint and Furniture

The power of the palace to focus the imagination of people living in it probably sprang less from its aesthetic attractions than we like to think, more because it provided a social unit in which every inhabitant had his clear role. For us the significant element is the art, the painting on the walls and floors, the rare remains of furniture. For them such things were doubtless admirable but often taken for granted—at least it is curious that Homer and his poetic sources never mention frescoes at all. If Greek epic tradition contains any genuine reminiscences of Mycenaean palaces, the poets must have been blind or uninterested. It tempts one to believe that epic only gathered its true strength after the fall of the palaces and discarded elements which had dropped out of real life (p. 307). Even the poets' description of furniture is limited to special royal pieces of particular splendor. Since our only sources for understanding how Mycenaeans felt about their physical environment are poetry, which refuses to help, and painting, in which the artists practically never show interiors or genre scenes but only open their doors onto flat colored walls, all reconstructions must be based on scanty archaeological remains and on such odd items of equipment as the Linear B tablets choose to record.

Paint was used to brighten floors, walls, benches, columns, and beams in rich primary colors. Plaster floors with geometric designs within restraining squares were common in most public apartments or even outdoors. One can see in the great court before the Pylos megaron, for instance, where rain dripping over the north balcony scarred the stuccoed pavement, which had been blue with scallops and red spirals. Inside the megaron the floor around the huge central hearth was similarly painted in bright red and blue abstract motifs like a carpet (Pl. XXV B) with an octopus floating prominently in front of the throne. A smaller room off the queen's apartments employed a livelier naturalism of fish and octopodes, like those which Tiryns combined rather stiffly on its megaron floor or Hagia Triada in its shrine. Mycenae favored pure geometry in both megaron and court. A painted plaster floor strikes us as a fragile architectural investment, nor did Crete often waste good designs underfoot this way. Painted floors and dadoes are common at Amarna in Egypt, however, and the Mycenaeans seem to have chosen this kind of ornament as a substitute for woven rugs in public apartments. Since they usually show themselves barefoot in the frescoes (except for hunters in linen leggings and bulljumpers in leather sandals, who would have left off their professional boots outside) perhaps the floors were not much scuffed by the padding of naked feet.

When so much surface is already decorated, one supposes that woven hangings or rugs were not widely used. Weavers were extremely proficient in the

Late Bronze Age but most of their work went into tunics and cloaks. Major items such as curtains in doors and windows, sheepskins or an occasional rug on the built-in benches of ground-floor rooms, perhaps coverlets for beds, have been completely lost to us. The tablets discuss cloth, though not in terms of size or function except for tunics which they say sometimes needed to be well boiled. The long rolls of cloth carried by Keftiu in Egyptian tomb paintings are almost surely gifts of dyed wool for court dress (Fig. 28). Whenever something soft was required to sleep or sit on, piled fleeces or cloaks or straw would do.

Furniture was minimal. The only piece which survived in the Pylos megaron was a low three-legged table of painted clay, the kind usually called a tripod hearth or portable altar with a hollowed top, not strictly furniture at all but ceremonial equipment and movable heat. A Pylos fresco shows votaries carrying taller three-legged wooden tables loaded with cakes or fruit. The Treasury of Atreus was rumored to have held one red, one white, and one green marble table, each carved with shells and spirals, when it was first explored. A table of dark-red *rosso antico* has been found in the megaron at Mycenae,[2] and Pylos produced a variegated marble table top inlaid with irregular circles of red stone. Chairs have not survived at all, footstools only to the extent of some ivory inlays which fell out of the rotted wood (cf. Pl. XXXIX D). There was a wooden throne at Pylos, perhaps gilded or painted; it burned with the palace, and only the mark on the floor remains. Chairs pictured on gems or modeled in terracotta have simple forms (Pl. XLI C; Fig. 36). They sometimes have tall curved backs, and sometimes are jointed camp stools like those we carry to excavations or the beach. The terracottas seem to exaggerate the chair in proportion to the person in it, little men swamped in valleys of comfort (Pl. XLI C). Footstools are low, with scrolls or handles on either side, and bring special comfort to the feet when one is drinking, or so Homer reports. Most people did without specialized furniture. The servants probably slept out back on any convenient floor, squatted or knelt to their work, and hung their few personal possessions on a wooden peg or stuffed them into a chest.

Although light carpentry has not survived, there is a good deal of simple, built-in Mycenaean furniture. Clay benches are fairly common. One bench in a small waiting room off the megaron court at Pylos was whitewashed and then painted in front to imitate a wooden bench. The archives room had another under its storage shelves. The storerooms in the rear of the palace used benches as unshakable stands for the pithoi inserted in them. Another pithos stand held wine in the waiting room, anticipating the railroad buffet. Still another was cleverly placed in a corner of the bathroom, with two jars inside and many drinking cups to scoop out hot and cold water, or something more refreshing. The big Pylos bathtub is a more elaborate illustration of the same construction, a clay larnax set into a brick-and-clay container with a shallow step up to it, the rim of the tub painted in large polychrome spirals. The tub has three or four handles but seems fixed in its stand and has no drain, a detail which meant shallow baths and a lot of work for servants dipping out the used water and sponging the tub dry. The tablets describe such a tub specifically as "unpierced" (Tn 996). Not everyone rejoiced in the silver tubs of Agamemnon and Menelaos, but clay is fine enough. As far as we can tell the Mycenaeans usually made no provision for the other function of a modern bathroom. The queen's toilet had an awkward drainhole in one corner; most householders had a choice between their renowned ceramics and their beautiful scenery with overhanging cliffs.

The final evidence for this kind of minor physical environment comes from the celebrated thirteen Pylos Furniture tablets. Without these we should be poorly informed about a special class of palace furniture, so gaudy that even the king must have hesitated to use it daily, for it was apparently kept locked in a storeroom. These tablets have received more attention than any comparable set among the thousands of surviving clay fragments in Linear B because they offer so much continuous text and words of fairly transparent connection to later Greek words, although parts of the technical description are hard to translate. Even in those days the furniture must have been unusual because the scribe labors to explain exactly what each piece is like and has no ready ideogram in his repertory to set beside it. Similar sets of royal furniture as gifts or booty in campaigns are well known from Near Eastern and Egyptian records. A selection, without regard for minor puzzles of translation (words in italics are of doubtful meaning), will serve well enough here:

Ta 707.2–3

> tono kutesejo erepatejapi opikereminijapi seremokaraoi qeqinomena adirijateqe potipiqe
>
> taranu kuteso ajameno erepatejo *85-depi

> An ebony chair with ivory braces worked with *stags'* heads and men and little calves; an ebony footstool inlaid with ivory *butterflies*.

Ta 714

tono wea₂rejo ajameno kuwano parakuweqe kurusoqe opikereminija ajamena
kuruso adirijapi seremokaraoiqe kuruso [qoukaraoi] kurusoqe ponikipi ku-
wanijoqe ponikipi

taranu ajameno kuwano parakuweqe kurusoqe kurusapiqe kononipi

A *greenwood* chair inlaid with blue glass-paste and *electrum* and gold, the
braces inlaid with gold men and *stags'* heads, gold [bulls' heads], gold palm trees
and blue glass-paste palm trees; a footstool inlaid with blue glass-paste and *electrum*, with gold struts.[3]

These descriptions confirm our most wistful expectations of elegance in the
palace age; they demonstrate that many of the small inlays archaeologists used
to ascribe generally to decayed wooden boxes were more probably let in to the
whole surface of bigger articles of wood (Pl. XXXIX D). Usually the ivory inlays survive best, not the gold or glass. Real examples range from simple lozenges or volutes to shells, roses, dolphins, lions, columns, shields, and helmeted
heads. So far none of the whole vignettes with men and cattle, which the tablets
seem to describe, have been found. Perhaps the long gold cutout of palm trees,
lions, and a bull from the Shaft Graves (Fig. 19) came off some such wooden
article. The glass-paste inlays from the palace period contribute argonauts, lilies, spirals, and women in flounced skirts (cf. Pl. XLIV E). The total effect
must have been extremely nervous to live with. Furniture preserved from the
tombs of Tutankhamen and Midas has equally busy, contrasting surfaces; richness was all, and obviously the work cost a good deal, not only because it was
necessary to import the ivory and ebony, but also because of the weeks of labor
spent on finicky cabinet-making. It has been suggested that the Mycenaeans
valued their most prized objects as much for the labor put into them as for the
fineness of the design, whether it was 5,000 gold rods soldered into a sword
hilt or 40,000 colored beads sewn on a dress. It is fortunate, perhaps, that so little of this furniture was around to compete with the painted floors and walls,
the embroidered clothes, the small elaborate jewelry; and that the ornaments
have fallen out to become isolated treasures in museums.

Megaron and Workshops

The furniture, the painted walls, the textiles are only some of the minor crafts
which gave public and private rooms their physical aspect. One should add the

bronze and clay vases, the drinking cups and knives and spoons, wicker baskets, chests, mirrors, kitchen equipment, though not add them too densely. Other aspects of environment must be guessed at from the layout of various rooms. In almost all areas privacy was a hard thing to find—the Greeks have never felt much need for it at home, and could always walk away to find it outdoors. The megaron complex was the most public part of any palace with a constant stream of minor officials, tourists, servants, and craftsmen moving around it. We have seen how cleverly arrangements at Pylos were made to deflect some of this traffic: the sentry and guard posts at the main gate to screen visitors, the archives room set handily forward to keep routine transactions out of the main building, the courtyard drawing some people off into its secluded waiting room with the bench and the wine stand, offering shade to others under the balcony opposite, the corridors leading past the megaron entrance to the working parts of the building. Yet, in spite of this protection, the megaron was by situation and by desire a focal point for business requiring the king's voice, for reception of guests, and for large evening gatherings.

The megaron at Pylos has the classic form with nearly half its floor space taken up by the huge hearth (4.0 m. across) and four columns rising to the clerestory roof (Pls. XXII A, XXV). The king faced it from his throne on the long right wall and his position was accented by the painted octopus on the floor in front of him. The walls behind were frescoed with reclining griffins and lions; other scenes in the same room included a poet, a bird, a deer, a procession, and two ladies talking at a table (p. 197). On the floor at the throne's right runs a curious carved channel with round holes at either end which is variously interpreted as a libation channel for offerings to the gods or the installation for the queen's loom, assuming she was as usefully busy as queens in Homer (p. 284). No other palace has a cutting like this, but in other respects the throne room at Pylos matches official apartments across the rest of Greece. The hearth had ceremonial as well as practical functions, and efforts were made to keep it clean and handsome with constantly renewed coats of painted plaster in appropriate patterns of smoke-spirals and flames. The room is so large (12.90 × 11.20 m.; 42 × 37 feet) that the difficulty of roofing and lighting such a megaron in any palace has been recognized in hot arguments for several generations. At Pylos, at least, the ceiling seems to have been flat. The central part of the megaron, over the hearth, was two stories high, culminating thirty feet above the floor in a lantern which projected higher than the flat roof over the rest of the palace. Within the lantern the architects set a painted chimney box with tapering clay pipes inside it to draw off the smoke. The four columns around the hearth supported a balcony at the height of the second floor, to which people in upstairs apartments could come to look down upon the megaron. During the day, light entered the megaron only as it filtered through this balcony-opening from windows upstairs, and through the main door; at night, extra light came from the fire on the hearth, but the smoke must have drifted around before rising through the chimney. Homer always calls it "the shadowy megaron" in a phrase as old as this kind of architecture. For the formal side of ceremonies touching palace social life it replaced, to an important degree, the "theatral areas" and separate shrines of other civilizations.

The economic support for this social and ceremonial life came largely from the craftsmen quartered in the palace, who worked with materials grown on palace lands or imported to palace depots from abroad. It took a tremendous amount of staff work to run such a household, since practically nothing could be bought ready-made except trinkets and luxuries. All the architecture, decoration, furniture, clothes, and utensils from lamps to nails, from storage jars to boots, had to be made on the spot according to some pattern. The makers were local boys trained as well they could be on Pylos territory where they were not often in contact with their counterparts at Mycenae or Thebes or Iolkos. In spite of this, there is an astonishing degree of conformity and conservatism in what they created. Traditional patterns persisted.

Although Greek palaces were small compared to those of Crete, the Near East, and Egypt, they still required the same kinds of specialists to keep them functioning as richer civilizations did. Specialties which no one could have predicted from the remains are now found in the Linear B tablets; however, one must keep the unhappy truth in mind, that we cannot read Linear B as well as we think we do, and that many of the deciphered words are guesses from context or etymological gambles (p. 245). The staff was generally what one would expect: carpenters, metalsmiths, potters, tailors, armorers, masons, woodcutters, shepherds; they either had quarters inside the palace or their work can be identified from remains there. In addition, there were the women who wove and cooked, prepared the grain, meat, oil, and cleaned up after the others; peasants who lived out in the villages to farm allotted land, or watched the flocks on less arable ground; religious personnel, and soldiers. There was little room in the palace center for the odd-job man of a Middle Helladic town. The armorer does not seem to double as a mason or potter in his empty hours though he might help out with jewelry, chariots, or mending copper vessels.

He might have his own plot of land and do military service, but would not be trained specifically in more than one craft. Among surprising omissions from the tablets are two professions whose work we value highly, the painters and the writers. Perhaps they were called by Minoan craft names not yet recognized.

Many parts of the palace were used as general stores and workrooms, but the particular industrial quarter in the east block occupied a series of long work-rooms with stamped clay floors and crude brick walls (p. 166). One tablet found here in 1957 gives a lively illustration of the kind of work and materials handled.

Sb 1315

> rapte] riwoja anija teukepi 5 dipteras erutara 15 [+
> rousijewija 6 rapterija anija 3
> newa anija anapuke 5 'dwo' 2 apuke 9 anija eeropajoqewo 2
> apenewo 4 apuke apenewo 1 newa poqewija PAIRS 11

> 5 sets of reins all sewn up *fitted with metal parts* 15 + scarlet hides
> 6 russet hides 3 sets of reins all sewn up
> 5 new sets of reins without bridles 9 bridles (2 'doubles') 2 sets of reins
>   *studded with nailheads*
> 4 sets of carriage-reins 1 carriage bridle 11 pairs of new *halters*

Even taking into account the doubtful translation, this tablet illustrates several basic industries—butchery, tanning, harness-making, bronze-smithing for horse-harness accessories—and suggests the further obvious skills of carriage-making, horse-training, and chariot-driving. Other tablets from the same area seem to mention men who work in bronze and deerskin and goatskin, make undercarriages, axes, and shoes.[4] The noise and smell must have been terrific on a working day; the architect did well to isolate the block.

Clothes and Food

No survey of the palace and the people in it would be complete without at least a brief exploration of what the Mycenaeans wore and what they ate. Most men wore a simple tunic of wool, or linen in hot weather, with short sleeves and a skirt flaring out over their thighs (Pls. XXIX, XXXV; Fig. 34). The main colors are white, yellow, or blue, with a contrasting band of color at the neck, around the sleeves, and along the lower hem. A leather or embroidered wool belt cinched in an essentially loose-fitting garment. Certain frescoes and gems illustrate a more Minoan costume, inherited from the Shaft Grave period: a pair of short trunks or kilts, the chest and arms naked. It was not the regular costume of the palace age, but survived particularly in mythological or cere- monial scenes (cf. Fig. 44; Pl. XLIII E–F). Terracotta men wear striped trou- sers (Pl. XLI C). For hunting and war legs were protected by linen or metal greaves tied at the knee and ankle (Pl. XXIX A–C; Fig. 34). Some warriors preferred to fight barefoot, some wore leather sandals, some a high leather boot (Fig. 20 *b*). Painters never bother to show the cloaks which must have been worn camping out, or around the palace in winter, because men in frescoes are usually stripped for action, but heavy gold or bone pins survive for fastening cloaks at the shoulder and the tablets mention *pa-we-a* (φάρϝεα), large woolen cloths probably for making into cloaks as well as tunics. At Knossos where the textile industry was so good we hear of "double-cloaks" in natural white, or dyed red with murex juice (Knossos L 471, 474). A few special professional men wear long embroidered robes like women: these include priests, poets, charioteers, and, sometimes members of ceremonial processions (Pls. XXX A, XXXII). In rare scenes animal skins (lion or leopard) were tied around the ensemble—though no one should take the skin-suited daimons (Fig. 25) as a fashion guide. Pretty-boys and officers wear their hair long; some older men affect a jutting beard but practically never the moustache of the Shaft Grave era; ordinary soldiers and servants tend to have their hair cropped short.

Curiously, we know very little about women's clothes; although the pictures seem to tell so much, they are deceptive. Most scenes involving women are ceremonial: they appear in procession frescoes or as votaries on gems. These ceremonies generally reproduce the traditional palace modes of sixteenth- and fifteenth-century Knossos; we have no way of knowing how far Knossos court dress is a convention of art and how far it was actually worn in later Greece. It is a practical and pretty costume, with its short-sleeved jacket and ankle-length skirt and thin embroidered strips sewn on for flounces, yet one doubts that styles changed so little in three hundred years, women being what they are (Pls. XXVII–XXVIII, XXXVIII, XXXIX A). Sometimes a modification of the Knossos jacket also appears in Greece: instead of leaving it open over their breasts the ladies wear a white blouse or dickey beneath it (Pl. XXVIII C), and so do their work without embarrassing themselves or their servants. The Knossos style at its most articulate is seen in the famous ivory triad from My- cenae (Pl. XXXVIII), but there the little boy is wearing a garment much closer to what most Mycenaean women actually wore: a long belted robe which is simply a fuller version of the men's tunic. This robe appears on women in a few scenes in art. The ladies at Tiryns who drive out in their chariot to watch the hunt wear straight wool tunics like men (Fig. 33 c); so does the woman on the Warrior Vase, and the mourning women on late Mycenaean larnakes (Pls. XXXIII–XXXIV). Color is supplied by contrasting borders or inserts. The Cretan costume calls for more jeweled accessories and ribbons in the hair (Pl. XXVII); in the other working or daily costume we see the simpler toilette of an Elektra against the Phaidras and Aeropes of the Argive courts.

Language, housing, clothing, and art distinguish the Mycenaeans from their Aegean neighbors far more significantly than food, which was like any Mediterranean food, probably boiled to death in oil. The main dishes of the Mycenaean household were meat from sheep or goats or pigs (cattle are rare), wheat and barley gruels and breads, cheese, milk, beans, figs, grapes, pears, honey. A list of the known animals and plants of the Mycenaean world with a comparison to Homer is offered in Appendix I; it was a rich world for gourmets and for medical specialists. A great range of kitchen pots and implements (Figs. 38, 51) suggests that cooks were more sophisticated than even in Early Helladic times, and proliferation in ceramic shapes partly implies a correspondingly nice etiquette in palace society. Excavated houses offer an abundance of storage jars, stirrup jars for oil (Pl. XLV B–C), krater-bowls for mixing liquids (Pl. XXXIII), jugs and ewers for pouring wine and milk and water (Fig. 44), mugs, beakers, teacups, stemmed kylikes (Fig. 51) and handled saucers for drinking, small double or triple vases that look like cruets, tripods and braziers and grilling-stands and fire-rakers for the cooking, a few strainers which, if not used for Anatolian beer, might have been for honey or whey or yoghurt. There are practically no plates except in the eastern islands. Slabs of bread may have been adequate substitutes, or simply a knife to slice off meat from the common roast and a ladle for soup or porridge. Forks were unheard of. Other curious omissions are salt, which is so easy for Greeks to collect by the sea but which the tablets never mention, and onions. Rarer condiments and spices were well known both for cooking and for making aromatic oils and perfumes. Entire buildings devoted to the preparation of these existed at both Mycenae and at Pylos. Mycenae's House of the Oil Merchant (p. 181; Pl. XXIV B) functioned partly as an industrial shop outside the citadel where jars of special oils were dosed with plant products, some imported from the Levant and some home-grown, then poured in jars and heated and readied for export. Next door in the House of the Sphinxes a half-dozen valuable tablets were discovered from a series dealing almost entirely with spices whose names can all be recognized.

At Pylos oils are classified in six or more different ways, including scent, age, provenience, and intended use; it even comes flavored with rose or sage. One must assume that a certain amount of expert botanical knowledge was also turned to medical advantage whether the Mycenaeans had professional doctors or not. At least they knew about using opium extracted from poppies as a sedative.[5] As the poetic tradition looks back upon the Mycenaean landscape, it highlights districts and towns with special, fertile favors from nature: the grassy and sunny places, the places good for horses or cattle, for doves or grapevines, the places with deep clods of soil and springs of running water, the places where a man could live without fear of starvation.

PRIVATE HOUSES AND PROVINCIAL TOWNS

A group of four substantial houses, excavated outside the walls of Mycenae during the past ten years, offers a good view of the private dwelling in the palace age. The houses have been named West, Oil Merchant, Sphinxes, and Shields (Pl. XXIV B). West House is the oldest in the group; the others are designed in relation to it, perhaps by younger members of the same rich clan of nobles. It has a megaron opening off a small flagstone court, a kitchen section, and storerooms on the ground floor; the form of the upstairs apartments is not preserved. Interesting fresco fragments from a passage include a chariot scene and a frieze of blown lilies. The House of the Oil Merchant is more filled with evidence of industry and commerce. The eastern basement consists of eight storerooms opening off a long straight corridor; here large pithoi of oil were stored, with a heating arrangement for preventing the oil from congealing in cold weather, and perhaps for scenting it with added herbs. Thirty large stirrup jars were waiting in the corridor to be shipped away, all filled with oil, sealed, and stamped with a signet. Whoever burned the house shortly before 1200 B.C. knocked the spouts off these jars and set fire to their oil as it ran through the corridor. The houses of the Sphinxes and of Shields were named from the best of the ivory furniture inlays found in their debris (Pls. XXXVII B, XXXIX D). They too were filled with storage vessels and painted jars of high quality. The houses are the source for most of the Mycenae Linear B tablets, which record lists of personnel and rations, and spices apparently used for oil processing.

These houses do not attempt to imitate palace architecture on a smaller scale, but string their rooms along a main corridor in topographically convenient strips. Although only the basements are well preserved, one can see the remains of stairs to the upper floors which must have been arranged in the same long lines, perhaps with setbacks and balconies looking over the terraces on which all the houses are placed. Rich private houses inside the citadel walls also show this indifference to the formal megaron unit and are designed to suit available space, sometimes in a loose arrangement of square columned rooms and plastered ramps or stairs (p. 284). All are self-sufficient units provided with spacious basements; they have their own kitchens, altars, and hearths, and were independent of the palace for carrying out the daily routine of living.

At first the concentration of tablets in the houses at Mycenae suggested that they were in fact annexes to the palace, responsible for particular segments of industry such as shipping luxury oil or carved ivories abroad. Yet it is certain that they are more domestic than industrial in character, and that rich merchants lived upstairs in very pleasant surroundings. The frescoes which adorned the upper walls were of exactly the same type as those in palaces (p. 197): women in elaborate clothes, buildings with detailed façades as at Pylos and Orchomenos (cf. Fig. 32), soldiers and servants in white linen gaiters (Pl. XXIX C), great horses, charging bulls, and rosettes. The houses were rich in ivory and faïence which were lived with, not just stored there; most of the inlays were inset into furniture and chests of an elegant quality. The tablets affirm the existence of workers in kyanos or blue glass-paste, of fullers preparing cloth, and of women who form a domestic staff of mixed Hellene and barbarian origin. It is probable that a family or group of nobles owned this land outside the walls as private property and carried on the same kind of activities as the palace did, in much the same surroundings on a smaller scale. Perhaps most large cities were organized in this loose manner, as independent hamlets circling around a central fortification, each group owing feudal service and taxes to the ruler, but self-reliant for maintenance and ventures in trade. The proliferation of place names on the tablets certainly suggests that each such cluster of dwellings had a name of its own, just as every hilltop and vineyard has a special name in Greece today.

At greater distance from the main cities it is possible to catch at least a glimpse of independent country towns and how they functioned. Mouriatada on the west coast provides an example. This isolated place lay on a high inland hill north of Pylos and south of Kakovatos, and thus it was primarily agricultural rather than seafaring (Fig. 30). Here a local baron built himself a true megaron on a hilltop, oriented to catch a distant view of the sea (Fig. 52 f). Private houses surrounded him on the lower slopes of the hill, straggling down to a tall circuit wall. The town was new in the thirteenth century, like the palace at Pylos or the houses at Mycenae, and needed a high wall for defense in that dangerous though prosperous age, especially since it could not have maintained a professional army. Mouriatada was strategically situated, and economically sturdy if not affluent. The town possessed some of the extras of greater palaces: a gate with columns, a respectable tholos tomb, even bathtubs in the private houses. The megaron was painted simply with red and blue bands and had good plaster floors. It contrasts with palace structures in having a poorer quality of masonry and less spacious rooms, but shows how isolated provinces responded to the challenging and architecturally expressive age of the empire.

A brief survey of other private houses shows that life was carried on in similar environments all over the Mycenaean world until the troubles of the late thirteenth century which destroyed the palaces and initiated a bizarre, adventurous life with more marked local differences. At Tiryns the private houses lay lower than the palace, on a spur of the plateau protected inside a ring-wall, and even spilled over with confidence onto the plain below the city, unfrightened by the nearness of the sea. At Athens the houses were built both up on the Acropolis around the palace, and down on the slopes at the foot of the city stairs, or where wells assured a decent water supply (p. 267; Pl. XXIII A). This changed, of course, with the general savage attacks on Mycenaean towns shortly before 1200 B.C.; every surviving householder withdrew inside the walls in dwellings so flimsy and makeshift that almost no trace of them survives. At places like Amyklai in Lakonia the rectangular rubble houses had been undefended by any wall, and the town seems not to have been formally rebuilt in the twelfth century. At Miletos, overseas in Anatolia, the commoners were better protected by a thick fortification wall with regularly spaced bastions (p. 264), and the town continued its Mycenaean architectural traditions through the Dark Ages. Before these disasters the private houses and provincial towns of the Mycenaean empire offer a nice perspective on the concentrated color and art of the palaces themselves, and were in a real sense the source of palace wealth and power.

Chapter VII

The strong colors inside the rooms of mainland palaces were originally drawn together into harmonious designs, both figured and geometric. It is a depressing truth that these designs can almost never be reconstructed from the mass of smashed plaster an excavator finds. Except weaponry, fresco painting is perhaps the best of all Mycenaean arts, their most enlightening and most spirited expression. It is also the most difficult, technically, for the archaeologist. If a palace room had paintings on all four walls, on the floor and doorway, perhaps on the beams and ceiling, and if there were similar paintings in adjoining rooms or rooms above it, when the building collapses the fragments from all these scenes subside in a mingled heap of debris, and it is nearly impossible to be sure where a particular piece came from. There will be a few pieces with outlines of faces, feet, or garments; there will be many more pieces in solid color without indicative drawing, and geometric patterns from the borders and frames. The edges

Art
in the Palaces

of broken plaster fragments are too rough for exact joins, and very few people have the gifted eye to re-create the original composition with probable accuracy and fine imagination.

In our own time we have the advantage of experience, seeing bombed or torn-down buildings with inner walls still standing perhaps three floors high. The remains of wallpaper or paint, and the fixtures, inform us quite nakedly of the original "feel" of the room, and we make allowances for the harsh light by which such tones were never meant to be seen, for the diluting effect which rugs, lamps, and furniture once supplied. With Mycenaean houses, however, practically nothing is ever in place on the wall, and we have no direct experience of the light or furniture except that both were less than we are accustomed to.

Rooms like the main courtyard or megaron at Pylos had such simple outlines that their colors and scenes must have stayed in people's memory even more than their architectural plan. Most people are structurally unobservant but figuratively receptive. Since most Mycenaeans were illiterate and had much less large-scale art to look at than we do, they probably remembered what they saw in even greater detail. This may be a partial explanation for the likenesses among scenes from widely distant mainland palaces: the stock motifs of women in procession, the architectural façades, the hunting scenes, marine figures, and elaborate geometries. There is also a formulaic quality in every field of Mycenaean art, which is a conservative influence, just as formulas in Greek epic poetry are repeated unchangingly so long as they are pleasing and partly honest.

We tend to underestimate the pleasure brought by formal patterns in the ancient world, and overestimate figured scenes for their illumination of ancient life. There is more experiment by Mycenaean artists in their abstractions, however, than in their human figures, and in many cases a greater skill of hand. Painted ornament reflects centuries of workshop experience in designing pottery or metal plates or stone friezes, and the motifs are easily transferred from one field to the other. By comparison, the figure drawing is limited in type and rather childish (see Fig. 34). Apart from strong memory-impressions which would help persuade the artist to reproduce rather than invent, two other factors operate: an inherent conservatism of painting tradition, whose strength is often not recognized by us in our desire to make dates out of subtle differences, and a general lack of large-scale media like sculpture in which experimental figure composition could have been practiced. The lapse into amateurism is particularly clear when the frescoes and palaces stop, in the pictorial and illustrated vases which succeed them (p. 203). No one would dare put the Warrior Vase scene on the wall of a palace and expect to be paid for it (Pl. XXXIII B). The fresco painters were better than this, probably a small group of masters who stubbornly repeated the themes of their teachers as poets did.

Formulas were partly supplied by Minoan frescoes in their later phases, and recast to suit mainland interests. Parts of figured cycles survive from five principal sources in Greece: Thebes and Orchomenos, Tiryns and Mycenae, and Pylos. A few fragments from contemporary buildings abroad supplement these major cycles: the fourteenth-century processions and hunts at Hagia Triada (Fig. 33 b), the late floral decorations at Phylakopi and Trianda in the islands (cf. Fig. 23); there are scanty remains at other mainland sites like Gla. Sometimes expensive tomb gifts seem to reflect large animal and decorative themes from wall painting, transferred onto ivory boxes, silver cups, or gems. The revival of the pictorial style in vase painting after the fall of the palaces also fosters a re-creation of older compositions.

These sources show, first, that there are practically no local experimental schools in Greece, but common developments of transmitted themes; and, second, that Knossos supplied the prototypes for processions, for architectural façades and shrines, for court figures in conversation, for soldiers on parade, for marine and plant friezes. Mixed with these subjects are more purely mainland scenes, like hunting in chariots for boar and stag, sieges (Pl. XXXI) and violent duels, giant animals lolling heraldically in unnatural colors (Pl. XXX C), an emphasis on weapons and local costume, and on props to identify individual roles. When both the model and the Mycenaean development of it survive, as in the procession frescoes at Knossos and those at Thebes, Mycenae, Tiryns, and Pylos, there are signs of mainland differences.

Outlines are strong in Mycenaean painting, especially after 1300 B.C. Interior modeling and shading are minimal. Backgrounds are blank but treated in abruptly shifting colors, or unrealistically broken by waving bands of contrasting color (Pls. XXVII, XXIX B). Landscape motifs are used stiffly, to make a decorative pattern behind the figures or to divide them into paneled groups (Fig. 33 c). The motions of wild nature are usually ignored. There are tendencies toward starkness and repeated groups. Figures are hieratically self-conscious and are almost always shown in fixed profile, as in vase painting, colored silhouettes (Fig. 34). They are often arranged in registers, even of the loose kind in which the heads of one row overlap the feet of the one above it without dividing lines. They are generally involved in a story of simultaneous scenes. Color is bold. Blue and red predominate, with orange, pink, yellow, brown, white, and black for details and accents; green is rare. Line is harsher than in Crete, action more generous and recognizable. In many of these qualities we sense again the influence of the pot-painter or the gem-carver, working in reduced fields where meaning was to be quickly presented through doing, and where narrative impression counted far more than delicate detail. The quick-drying plaster on the walls also contributed to hasty execution. In several paintings it is possible to see the artist's mistakes which he could not correct because the surface had dried—a notorious example at Tiryns is a bull with two tails.

GREECE IN THE BRONZE AGE

The Cretan Background

Some of these Mycenaean distinctions had already tentatively started to develop in the later phases of Minoan fresco work. One of the most interesting problems in the field of Aegean painting is how to relate Mycenaean to Minoan frescoes historically and pictorially. The two rich periods of Minoan painting both fall in the later palace age, before and after the slight shock of the fifteenth century which may have been the time of Greek arrival (p. 140). The earlier period was more whole-sighted in its representation of human and animal behavior than the later period, or than mainland work. It was the period of the cat, pheasant, and roebuck scene at Hagia Triada, or the wonderful kneeling woman who plucks flowers in a meadow before a palace. At Knossos it was the period of high naturalism with playing monkeys, soaring birds and diving fish, or blown sprays of olive, lily, and iris.

There were many painters working at Knossos when the Greeks arrived, in several different styles, so that variety of theme and conception was from the beginning built into the mainlanders' impression of how a proper palace should be decorated. Naturalism was a strong component, and the earlier frescoes almost entirely succeeded in avoiding human subjects. Egypt excelled Crete in true naturalism, in skill at detailed, moving, and understandable drawing of animals, shrubs, flowers, and pools. The Cretans, even at their most fluent, disguised strained drawing with psychological beauty, with a wild, subtly colored but unreal distribution of flowers and rocks in rising swoops and hollows. Design was always poetically imposed upon reality, and as time passed the painters increased their tendency toward abstraction at the expense of what they really saw. Human figures gradually came on stage, and their behavior was tidied up by being confined within emphatic architectural frames as they walked on base lines instead of in loose grass (see Fig. 33 *b*). In the final phase Crete developed as Egypt was also developing, with a combined looseness of line and stylization of theme, an increase in the scale of figures and a disinterest in background scenery. More definite limits were made around each scene, more co-ordination with real architectural features such as timber framework and dadoes. Even landscapes or bird scenes like the Partridge frieze in the Caravanserai were held inside narrow frames, a bright strip at the top of a high black wall.

This formal development apparently seemed more congenial to the Mycenaeans than the fluid poetry of the earlier naturalism, and later it controls almost every development upon the mainland. The tremendously long painting from the Procession Corridor is repeated in Greece in varying scales, life-sized figures marching to offer ornate presents within the palace. The Dolphin fresco, high on the wall of the Queen's Megaron, where the fish are so carefully patterned in bright colors and given only blank plaster to swim on, affected Mycenaean conceptions of animal scenes, such as the pink and blue hounds in the Tiryns boar hunt. The heraldic organization of the Campstool frescoes, where court figures sit knee to knee in stiff sprays of garment, was adopted for genre scenes at Pylos. The theme of the griffins in the Throne Room, solemn symbols with bristly shading, was considered suitable for several public apartments at Pylos. The Toreador scenes at Knossos had lost the rich swing of the Vapheio Cups, and their high degree of stylized gesture and skinny figure is seen again in bull-jumping scenes at Mycenae and Tiryns. Beneath their differences in style, these late Knossos paintings share a pervading artificial carefulness, wooden brilliance, and divorce from natural setting. The abstraction that was thus already tentatively present in fifteenth-century Minoan painting must have appealed to the isolating streak firmly established in the Mycenaean artistic temperament. The earliest mainland pictorial scenes, the stelai of the Shaft Graves, have a similar linear, shallow clarity of figures defined within a frame and presented against a blank field as stereotyped expressions of activity. This preference persists, enormously enriched by Minoan color and quality in drawing, to form the substratum of the earliest Mycenaean frescoes in Thebes and Tiryns.

The Procession at Thebes

The oldest frescoes in Greece are generally agreed to be those in the House of Kadmos at Thebes (Pl. XXVII) and fragments from the earlier palace at Tiryns. It is not known exactly how old they are: after 1400 B.C., probably, about the time of the fall of Knossos. Thebes is a complicated, rich site only partially excavated because of its location under the modern town. Recent building operations have probed the Bronze Age palace remains and turned up a hoard of Oriental cylinder seals, matching the Greek legend that Kadmos the son of Agenor came from Phoenicia to found the city, bringing the art of letters with him. According to erratic Greek chronology this interesting event happened in 1518 B.C., during the archaeological period of the later Shaft Graves with its new princes and its first signs in the Minoan script, though the palace itself is several generations later. The tombs outside Thebes contain fine early pottery including specimens of the Palace style. In tradition, the palace at Thebes was destroyed before the other mainland palaces, two or three generations before the Trojan War. Two famous military démarches were staged there, the war about Oidipos' Sheep and the war of the Seven against Thebes. Mythical genealogy places these shortly before and shortly after 1300 B.C., in the same period of upheaval that brought Neleus to Pylos. A ceramic date for the destruction of Thebes is tentatively offered by the vases in the debris, particularly the inscribed stirrup jars from the oil stores (cf. Fig. 42), but these standard vessels are not easy to date within decades; some say III A:1, some III B.[1] Whenever the burning took place historically, the procession frescoes were still on the walls. They had been recently slightly retouched, and were probably designed in the early fourteenth century.

Other procession cycles also seem to belong to the earlier development of Mycenaean painting, but they are so conservative that the differences over one hundred and fifty years are primarily in a stiffening and more emphatic outlining, not in conception or composition. The Thebes and Tiryns sets offer such a contrast. The Tiryns frieze (Pl. XXVIII A) is assigned to the later phases of the palace, to its remodeling after 1300 B.C., although its fragments were found tossed over the west edge of the acropolis by the back stairs in conjunction with earlier pieces, the same kind of rubbish dump as yielded the procession fragments at Pylos (Pl. XXVIII B, C), and associated with the same kind of inscribed stirrup jars as at Thebes (Fig. 42).[2] Probably in every remodeling copies were made of the displaced subjects; this happened at least to the older and younger Tiryns hunts. In all the processional groups the influence of the Procession Corridor at Knossos is palpable, and if the fall of Knossos happened in the early fourteenth century as suggested there is no important gap of time between the Cretan and mainland versions. Once the composition is fixed and transmitted, the challenge to the painter resides especially in the rich embroidery of the costumes; the figures themselves could not have given him much trouble, because they all walk in the same conforming way, feet bare, breasts gorgeous in profile as tholos tombs, plump white faces demurely lowered toward the standard gifts (pyxis, vase, bouquet) they are offering the goddess.[3] Knossos and Pylos again show special links by including men in their processions; Thebes and Tiryns have only women.

Although it is pitifully fragmentary, the Thebes Procession has been restored after much hard work (Pl. XXVII). It has a more flowery, swinging style than the others and so is usually dated earlier as more "Minoan" in execution. It occupied the entire wall space of Room N, a small dark room off a corridor flanking the megaron, a room which probably had no outside windows so that the only light fell through the door from the corridor and perhaps from the adjoining cell. There are fragments of from nine to twelve women, just over life size (1.59 m.), most of them moving right but two moving left toward an off-center focus on the right-hand wall as you entered. This focal spot might have been occupied by a seated goddess, altar, or some other typical objective of ceremonial worship. At Pylos there are two fragments of a queenly figure in a feather crown which may give an idea of how goddesses appeared in such scenes (Fig. 33 *a*). The frieze at Thebes filled 13.90 m. of wall space (nearly 40 feet), framed above and below by timber wallbeams which were left exposed, with a painted stone dado below. The scene was thus lifted about one meter above the floor on a "stage-platform."

The women are richly dressed in Minoan court costume: a short-sleeved jacket with embroidered borders opening over the breasts and closed at the waist, hugging the hips over a tubular flaring skirt with rows of flounces stitched on at the knee and hem. They walk barefoot and have identical elaborate hair-dos: long black locks in a chignon constrained by red ribbons, careful spit-curls at temple and brow, four clubbed plaits tied with white ribbons which spray out at shoulder and waist. It must have taken all day to prepare; one is astonished that Linear B has yielded no word for hairdresser. The colors are flat and bright. The faces, with large slanting eyes and incipient double chins, have no contour lines as in later painting, but ears, lips, breasts, and hands are accented in red. Jackets rhythmically alternate between light blue and pink; skirts are light blue with dark blue, pink, yellow, and red flounces slashed with black. The bracelets and necklaces have pink and black strands of beads. The shape and color of the gifts these women hold are carefully alternated: a red (porphyry or bronze?) pyxis, red and white poppies or roses, blue and yellow feathered papyrus, a bottle obliquely striped yellow, pink, and white (gold, copper, and silver), a white pyxis (ivory or alabaster). A Minoan tradition is followed by breaking the ground into waving horizontal registers of contrasting colors: blue, yellow, white, and blue each outlined in black. These pale tones are normal for indoor or ceremonial scenes in Mycenaean painting; it will not be necessary to describe them in such detail again. Outdoor scenes have more red and brown in them from the weather-beaten skins of the male actors. From this fresco we see a Mycenaean talent for rhythmical variations, not regular but subtly counterpointed, as the women move across the rippling ground

191

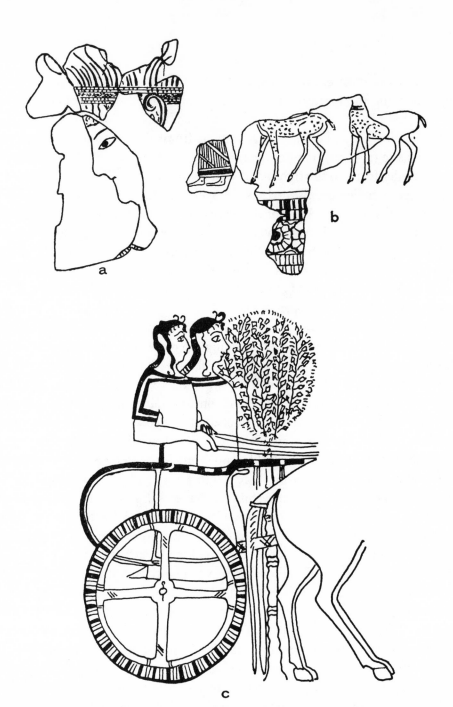

Fig. 33.—Details from frescoes: (*a*) woman in a feather crown, Pylos (after Blegen, *AJA* 1962, Pl. 40, drawing by P. de Jong); (*b*) robed figure and antelopes on an architectural stage, Hagia Triada (after Pernier and Banti, *Guida degli Scavi,* Fig. 21); (*c*) ladies driving a two-horse chariot in the country, Tiryns (after Swindler, *Ancient Painting,* Fig. 175).

in different poses meant to break monotony by undertones without disrupting the regularity essential to the procession scheme. But there is something mechanical about it in spite of its finesse.

Processional painting seems thoroughly at home in mainland palaces. It was transplanted from Crete but flourished in its new setting. Its popularity in Greece suggests that it illustrated a real performance which was enacted, perhaps yearly or on high festival days, at every major center. The Pylos texts tell of exactly such processions, with gifts to divinities (oil and metal vases), though they do not bother to list ephemeral roses and papyrus blooms. Rarely do palace records and palace art converge with information to this extent, supplying color and motion from one side, hard facts about gods and their possessions from the other (p. 295). The formal outdoor march of offering to honor a god is surely much older than any painted image of it in the Aegean, for even Crete and Hagia Triada do not develop the theme before the middle of the fifteenth century B.C. and then they betray direct indebtedness to Eighteenth Dynasty painting in Egypt, only transferring the imagery from a royal or funerary context to one of vivid native ceremony. The Mycenaeans continue this borrowed likeness, and perhaps their outward ceremonial forms were not very different from Cretan ones although many gods were new. Stone reliefs in the Near East and Anatolia exhibit the same features; many nations moved simultaneously toward the registered, the monumental, the dull stately showpiece of embroidery and handsome gifts, where individuals were distinguished by their props and not by expression or internal quality. This spirit, so congenial to Mycenaean taste, often held Mycenaean artists back from exploring beyond surface arrangements.

Excerpts from the processional cycles at Tiryns and Pylos illustrate minor variations on the universal theme. The woman from Tiryns seems stiffer, more formulaic, than her counterparts at Thebes (Pl. XXVIII A). The pyxis she carries, made of silver or alabaster or ivory, is minutely carved with two friezes of moving animals. At Pylos a fragment shows a woman in an unruffled but colorfully embroidered skirt moving to the right among floral ornaments (Pl. XXVIII B); a more interesting excerpt shows a woman facing left, with the snub countenance and full breasts often seen in Pylos natives today but obviously inherited from a mixture of Cretan and Amarna portrayals (Pl. XXVIII C). Her graceful hands are empty of gifts; possibly this is a recipient turned to face her worshipers. There are several life-sized processional fragments at Pylos, some placed fittingly in vestibules and corridors; they include naked red men, men wearing elaborate robes, and ladies' hands carrying bunches of red flowers. The wonderful queen wearing a feather crown is among the best surviving fragments (Fig. 33 *a*); mostly the scenes are bright, large, and slightly dull. There are painters with great authority and the clarity of classical vase painters, there are bold compositions; yet one must admit of the typical Mycenaean fresco specialist that he often drew carelessly and was quite incapable of expressing feeling.

Nature and Genre Scenes

Occasionally one sees a reaction against monumental narrative in favor of themes from nature: birds, trees, flowers, the tense leaps of nursery-colored animals, delicate cross-stitched stags and great crested birds (Fig. 35), the glimpse of an unreal aquarium. Though quick observation of nature is not a mainland forte, the painters are often enormously sympathetic toward animals they knew well, horses and hunting hounds, or the boar and deer they hunted. Excerpts from a famous restoration of the hunting scene at Tiryns teach us well about these matters. This intricate narrative of sport in the country has never been put together or synchronized with conviction—it is too fragmentary. A pity that Rodenwaldt, whose sense and taste were so sure in these studies, from a delicate sense of uncertainty refused to suggest dogmatically how the various scenes and fragments fitted.

Two ladies drive out from the left in an elaborate chariot (Fig. 33 *c*); they are notoriously uninspiring, for the artist's main interest seems focused on details of their underpinnings: the striped tires, the yellow axle, the lynch-pin, the clumsy cross-gartered yoke, the horses paired red and white as in Egypt; his trees past which the ladies drive are conventional indications of setting which do not create true landscape. Flat, round like mulberries, they seem to spring from the front ground line, although supposed to lie in a rear plane. The yoke passes behind both horses; the far girl has no arms. Only Carpenter has done the scene justice: "a pair of rigid white-faced maidens who guide wooden horses through a grove of . . . upended ping-pong paddles."[4] These are palace aristocrats trained to male sports, the painted counterparts of Atalanta who thrust herself into the Kalydonian boar hunt, of Kyrene who wrestled lions with such suavity, of Phaidra who on her sickbed tamed imaginary Venetian race horses.

Other members of the hunt are windburned to an athletic, unbelievable red.

Grooms hold the dappled hounds of the palace on long leashes as the horsemen organize for the hunt (Pl. XXIX A). Huntsmen on foot march out to beat the woods and swamps for game; they wear yellow or spotted tunics against a blue ground, and carry light javelins (see Fig. 34). Although wild landscape with its distressing irregularities is avoided, the game is shown in its real habitat: two boar grin behind their tusks as they crash through rubber-stalked swampland with spears in their muzzles; splotched dogs in pink, blue, and black leap at them like rocking-horses in a parody of the flying gallop; great birds swoop from the upper air past tree branches. A long line of frightened stags and does is contorted, the quarry scampering off, looking back with open lips, or crashing their antlers on the ground (Fig. 35). Everything is lively and light, active and broadly colored, with a pleasure that comes more from Aristotelian imitation of action than from a personal urge to draw well.

The fragment illustrated from a similar scene at Pylos, a scene involving many figures of huntsmen, leashed hounds, and stags, shows a novel use of rippled color-breaks to liven the composition (Pl. XXIX B). The hunter with a spotted tunic and white gaiters moves from the left over a yellowish ground against a pink stag on a deep olive or dark ground. The man's arms and the stag's needle-sharp hooves thrust from each side into the vertically rippled white break between them. Although the narrative as a whole is constructed in registers, with files of men posed over one another's heads to suggest parallel motion in depth, there is no constriction about the way this is handled. It goes back to the scattered-field system of the Dendra silver hunting chalice (Fig. 21 *b*), in order to fill the whole tall surface of the wall without breaking up individual parts by harsh lines. At Mycenae part of a big scene seems to show similar loose deployment of figures, as a sedan-chair bearer moves left hefting his burden to some ruined destination (Pl. XXIX C). In genre scenes, which are usually smaller in scale than processions, the painters have apparently freed themselves more from harsh borders and stage-platforms to explore depth.

The new frescoes from Pylos, which will be published within a few years, will amaze us by their variety and rich coloring in contrast to other palaces. There are two main groups: the plaster fragments which crashed with the walls of the palace when it was burned at last, and those already discarded by the palace in the course of redecorating, which lay in a dump below the hill. These older fragments are still thirteenth century, like the palace itself, and it is not yet clear whether stylistic development is observable between the two groups. Among them are most of the processional figures discussed, marvelous blue

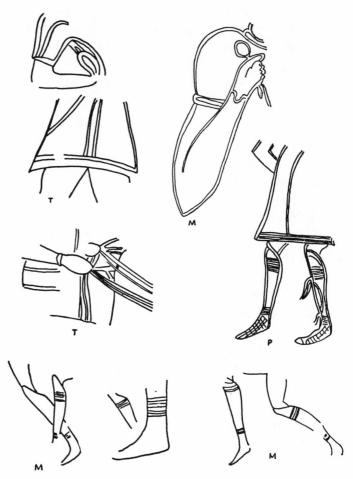

Fig. 34.—Types of human figures in Mycenaean frescoes; M = Mycenae, P = Pylos, T = Tiryns.

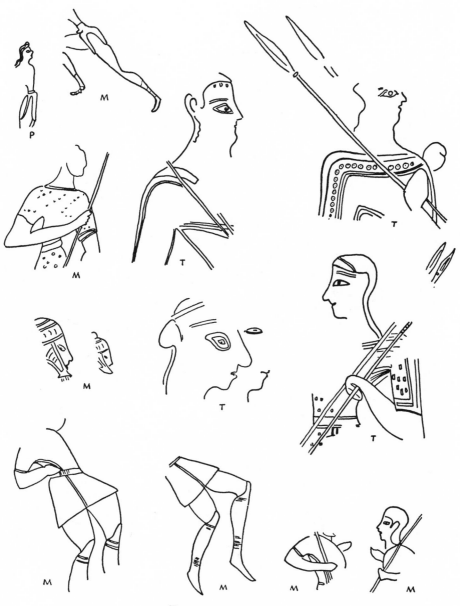

FIG. 34.—*Continued*

FIG. 35.—Types of animal figures in Mycenaean frescoes; M = Mycenae, P = Pylos, T = Tiryns

birds pecking a chain of red berries, slim borders of rockwork like tongues or candles, blue-green olive trees, pug-nosed and classically profiled red men, Negroes, men in loin cloths and animal skins, lions, and columns. In the palace interior a great mixture of themes brightened many rooms; in the narrow space of the vestibule, for example, there were fragments of a procession, architectural details, a bull's head, slender figures in embroidered kilts, and a man with a necklace. In other apartments there are dolphins and octopodes, argonauts (Pl. XXIX D) and sponges, lions, dogs, wild deer, horses (Pl. XXIX D), griffins and sphinxes (Pl. XXX B–C), soldiers on the march, warriors dueling, ladies chatting, men carrying tables with ceremonial cakes, and almost every kind of abstract ornament one knows in miniature on the vases of the fourteenth and thirteenth centuries. This range in figure style and subject reminds one of the many coexisting styles at Knossos; if the two palaces match in their richness, it is partly because the Pylos frescoes have been so carefully preserved, so tactfully restored, and partly because links between the two regions were early and strong.

Among the better reconstructed fragments are two very formal and curious scenes, both from the propylon. One shows a pair of white horses posed self-consciously on a stage-line or timber balk, while below them moves a frieze of stately argonauts with tentacles stiffly curled (Pl. XXIX D). The irrelevance of this decorative combination is charming. A more important piece from the propylon has already been discussed as an illustration of Mycenaean fondness for emphatic façades and entrances (p. 168). Two young sphinxes face each other heraldically with crossed paws on top of a masonry gate whose architecture is enriched by an elaborate column between antae (Pl. XXX C). This is a more imaginative and softer version of the Lion Gate (Pl. XVII B), with a neat slimness which also marks good ivories of the period (Pl. XXXVII B). It is certainly appropriate as a design for the main entrance of the palace, whether or not it reflects existing architecture.

The Pylos megaron sheds some light on how different fresco themes were put together in the same apartment. Into its competing ornaments were introduced four or five scenes, apparently unconnected. To the right of the door the famous lyre-player, nicknamed Thamyris (Pl. XXX A, p. 308), sat on his free-form rock striped orange, yellow, and blue. His pale garment flounced in buff sets off his dark skin and the scarlet sky; his five-stringed lyre with swanshead finials probably represents ivory. He pulls gently with an unmuscular hand to enchant the great crested white bird flying past. An unusual fullness in the bird and the rock contrasts with the primitive figure of the poet, feet in the air, body schematic, not leaning into his work at all. Beyond him on the same wall behind the throne come the monumental pairs of griffins and lions so reminiscent of Knossos, yet unlike. The ground changes to white behind them, the lions are tawny with dark accenting hairs, the griffins have rising bright plumes; they extend onto the wall at the king's right. Other Pylos griffins are pink (the Old Hall) or white with brown beaks and blue eyes (the Queen's Hall). The third scene was perhaps to the left of the door and so architecturally separated from the others. It presents two people in long spotted robes seated talking at a three-legged table. This is one of the rare times when a Mycenaean artist paints furniture from his daily milieu. A possible fourth thematic element for the megaron is represented by the haunch of a life-sized deer, from somewhere near the poet but not necessarily connected with him (it might come from a neighboring room), unless, like Orpheus, he draws all wild nature near to hear the music. A fifth scene is a procession of miniature red men opposite the throne. There seems to be no unity of subject in the megaron decoration. One guesses from other apartments with similar variety that the aim was to cover the walls with pleasant, often traditional motifs, but not to create a narrative or intellectual harmony. Only the heraldic animals by the throne seem symbolically fitted to their placement.

The last fresco there is space to discuss is the well-known siege scene from the megaron at Mycenae (Pl. XXXI). This megaron faces west instead of south, and the painted fragments were found along the west and north walls, that is, all on the left as one entered. Thirty times what survives would be needed to cover all the walls.[5] The fragments show, prominently placed on the north wall, a palace façade in the traditional architectural style: it rises three irregular stories high against a red mountain side, with grass and flowers below and a blue sky above. Its height is enlivened by details of checkerboards and disc friezes (cf. Fig. 32) and by the tapered Minoan columns in each window embrasure. A woman is seated at a window ledge on the right and looks out toward where the scene breaks off. Behind the palace is a frightful event in the Egyptian battle style: a huge horse and chariot race to the left over the body of a fallen enemy who, in the peculiar perspective of the age, is seen to hurtle head downward past the palace, though his accident must have happened on the hill behind. Below the palace two dim figures of women move unconcernedly in a landscape. Off to the left the officers of the chariot corps are giving orders to harness the horses and the young attendants stride quickly to obey. Two groups of men lead the horses toward the left; one chariot is still tilted up and waiting, two are all harnessed and setting off to the right, and there are running legs. In another part of the scene bodies are at falling angles or crouched as though to loose an arrow (Fig. 34). There are no joins between the different activities at the sides of the palace, and perhaps originally the effect was disjointed also. Figures are arranged in the loose kind of banked register noted in the Pylos hunt, and the ground breaks abruptly from muddy yellow to blue. The horses are red and white; the men wear blue-white or yellow tunics, their dark red skins contrasting with the white gaiters tied in black or red at knee and ankle. Such gaiters, probably linen, are worn in hunting scenes also, and the same spears are carried, but here we see no hounds, and two men at least wear boar's-tusk helmets. It is to all appearances a war for a city on a hill in a very old tradition like the Siege Rhyton (p. 100; Pl. XIV), but looser, more highly colored, and less intense. There is no panic among the women, the enemy is not shown.

Like the poetic parallel to this theme most familiar in Homer's view of besieged Troy, the fresco conceals history under a veneer of projected local formulas. In Homer, language, names, dress, architecture, and divinities are all supplied for the Trojans out of a generous Greek store. This seems to be a mainland habit. Egypt offers a contrast. Most Egyptian compositions of kings in chariots, besieged cities, and falling enemies are Ramesside stone reliefs charged with historical relevance by thirteenth-century campaigns against the Sea Peoples (p. 271), though the subject had been reviving periodically for nearly three hundred years in the reigns of pharaohs whose attacks were successful.[6] Egyptian sculptors are careful to indicate national differences in these international melees. Even when they confuse costumes and hair-dress among Hittites, Syrians, Philistines, or Libyans (cf. p. 148) their attempts manifest a historical interest which is the figured counterpart of Egyptian written records. Interpretations of the Mycenae megaron fresco must, on the other hand, be bland or diffuse. Either there is no special history involved, or none of the enemy happen to be preserved, or it is civil war (p. 269), or the artists could only paint what they had always painted without using experience directly. All the characters are typical Mycenaeans.

Two contradictory principles of Mycenaean art are illustrated here. First, it has stronger narrative and dramatic movement than in Crete. One may be tempted to recognize individual models in Minoan art, or realistic views of the palace, or the fashionable pet or garden of the moment, but these suggestions are suspended in a timeless, immobile world where vibrant fish swim energetically nowhere and princes march beautifully dressed through corridors empty of identity. Mycenaean art is self-consciously local. The painter usually insists on some scenic point of reference, however conventional—architecture, trees, hills. Through interlocking, often vigorous, action he seems to be suggesting some specific event, some famous hunt or raid already perhaps codified in poetry (p. 309). The figures are not drawn in the conviction of movement—Cretan figures are much more suggestive of energy and changing posture—but they are recognizable action stiffened into formula. One would expect in theory that such an emphasis on the story-line with indicative gesture would connect psychologically with a sense of history. But the history is entirely missing, from the Siege Rhyton to the burning of Mycenae, from the Linear B texts to the final Trojan epic. This is the second trend which seemingly negates the first. Even Cretans show more alertness to the *poikilia* this world offers us when they sketch black soldiers or bearded aliens (Fig. 20 *a*). In Greece everything alien is ignored,[7] the same visual world is repeated from palace to palace without differences of understanding, and all the excitement that comes from the meeting of different civilizations is blanked out.

This is a very insular turn of mind. It does not match the reality of trade, in which Mycenaeans sailed all over the Mediterranean to meet everyone of interest from Trojans to Sicilians (p. 254). The only exception they ever made to their exclusion of the outside world were the Cretans who mercifully impressed them at the very beginning of their artistic training. After the fall of Knossos they continued to be satisfied with what they had already learned to do, swerving only into local rebellions and experiments. The late palace frescoes show that inevitable stiffening of style which comes from working tamely in habitual fields. Like the poets, most painters prefer good formulas to inventions which might turn out poorly. Their art expresses a double inability: to conceive of a man as simply existing without being cast in a standard role, to conceive of him as existing at all in un-Mycenaean terms. This temperament was not uniquely Mycenaean in the Bronze Age, but mainlanders are far less tender toward the individual than the Egyptians or Minoans. They like action, familiar themes, bright colors, bland monsters. The visual world is filled with definitions and fantasies. The painted cycles of the palace age are memorable expressions of a temperament we do not yet really understand.

VASE PAINTING

Most Mycenaean vases are technically excellent but dull. They command admiration for their fine fabric, their clean authority of shape, their spare geometry of ornament. They were better in texture and paint than most ceramics of the second millennium, and contained quality produce, and were consequently exported to every major town in the islands and the Levant (Pls. XXXII, XLV A; Fig. 40).[8] This is especially true of the long period of empire pottery, from the middle fourteenth to the late thirteenth century; that is, from the consolidating years after the fall of Knossos to the eventual disruption of Aegean economy caused by the Sea Peoples. The thirteenth century, Late Helladic III B, is particularly an age of export pottery, some of it made in mainland centers and shipped abroad, some of it made in local workshops where Mycenaeans had founded permanent colonies (Rhodes, Miletos) or had established trading communities within the framework of a foreign civilization (Enkomi, Ugarit). The shapes are standard—stirrup jars for oil, feeding bottles, alabastra, three-handled jars, kylikes, pilgrim flasks (see Fig. 51); and the designs are standard except for the tremendous range they offer—flowers and marine life reduced to pot hooks, scales, spirals, rosettes, chevrons—all the inherited repertory of the earlier experimental period. This pottery fills rows of museum cases with red or chestnut glaze on pale ground, historical and economic documents of great value but too organized to ruffle the imagination as art. Only in certain rare classes does the painter attempt a figured scene and show that the field of representational painting was not limited to frescoes.

Pictorial Vases

The pictorial vases present some very curious compositions involving human figures, wild animals, plants, and fish. One extensive group is known as the chariot krater series from the main motif; other kraters, chalices, and jugs offer bulls or wild goats, fish and octopodes, flying birds and fleshy plants in an extremely ornamental manner, so authoritatively drawn that they can be attributed to individual workshops or artists in the empire period (Pl. XXXII). Paradoxically, after the end of the empire and the burning of the mainland palaces, there is a new impulse toward picture-making (Fig. 50). This impulse finds expression in the III C Pictorial style which is often quite close to fresco work, in the Close style of octopus and bird images, and in a very rare class of painted funerary monuments which includes a handful of painted sarcophagi and stelai. Pictorial vases operate at a far lower level than fresco painting because they were produced in greater quantities by simple craftsmen and were in some cases designed only for tombs, but they extend our knowledge of fresco motifs and add some special symbols in a streak of bizarre fantasy.

Two illustrations are representative of the best kind of unspecialized pictorial vases (Pl. XXXII): one shows heavy ornamental bulls with unreal dapplings and space-filling birds (C), and the other, a unique, quasi-historical naval scene (A; cf. Fig. 43). We see a cross-section of two Mycenaean ships about to sail, each one flanked by a pair of officers, one in a long robe and one nude, both with conical helmets. More officers stand stately on the decks in robes, their great swords still in the scabbard, made pharaonically enormous compared to the crew who are busy in the hold. The conventional stick figures and robe figures, the unnatural emphasis on eye, buttock, and calf (the important parts of an athlete's anatomy), the thorough stylization, and the suggestion of humor and narrative interest are typical of the drawing on most pictorial vases (cf. Fig. 50). Symmetry and ornament are far more important than in fresco work; there is an obvious departure away from accurate representation and toward abstract design.

Both these vases come from Enkomi, the port on the east coast of Cyprus facing the Levant where Mycenaeans first began to settle in small groups after the fall of Knossos. Pictorial vases are much more common here than on the mainland. But the mainland also made them (sherds were found connected with a potter's kiln at Berbati near Dendra and fine specimens are known from Mycenae, Tiryns, Argos, Corinth) and connoisseurs can guess which are exports to the east from the older factories at home or which were made directly in Levantine ateliers. At Koukounara near Pylos a variation with exotic birds and plants makes its appearance shortly after 1400 B.C. (Fig. 50 a), perhaps under the influence of the Cretan bird-and-foliage vases known in the Warrior Graves (Pl. XVIII I; Fig. 26 e). One of these may represent the first egg-laying chicken in Greece. Tuthmosis III met this bird for the first time in his Eastern campaigns—"the bird that gives birth every day"; it would be exactly like the Mycenaeans to draw it instead of domesticating it.

The special kraters with chariot scenes are large open bowls, on a high foot or stem, which may have been made particularly for tombs. A typical vase shows two people driving a chariot and team, usually to the right, through a landscape suggested by plant motifs, birds, waves, or fish. There are often subsidiary figures: a pair of youths belt-wrestling, a soldier with a spear, attendants walking behind, extra figures riding in the chariot (Pl. XXXII B, D). While no two are exactly alike, they are swiftly recognizable as a class, and this very standardization of theme suggests that they had a standard use for which the story did not need to be made carefully explicit every time. At first the drawing is very good—a krater with galloping horses from Mycenae ranks with frescoes for its large-scale liveliness—but during the thirteenth century (III B) the men grow spindly, the horses' bodies are joined for economy with only two muzzles and eight legs to distinguish them, their legs poke through the framing bands, and the chariot is so curtailed that the driver seems perched on the horses' rumps.

It is sometimes suggested that the chariot motif conveyed a specifically funerary message.[9] Chariot compositions occur in three contexts in Mycenaean art: hunt, war, and funeral games. Since the kraters were developed to attract a wide market, and are generally though not always found in tombs, it is plausible to imagine that they satisfied a demand for funerary symbolism rather than appealing to retired soldiers as a memento of past exploits. The connection of chariot scenes with burial had been exploited by Mycenaean artists already on the Shaft Grave stelai (Fig. 17; p. 91); the empire version looks more like a processional cortege to the tomb than a contest at the funeral games. The prototype for such symbolism in painting is on the Hagia Triada sarcophagus from south Crete, whose long scenes of funeral cult are flanked by short panels of women driving chariots drawn by a pair of griffins and a pair of wild goats. Fortunately the interpretation of that enigmatic monument is not our problem here, although its style is directly connected to the earliest vases in the series of chariot kraters, both being manufactured around 1400 B.C. The way the artist divided his scene into registers and panels, using bright primary colors and ornamental motifs like rosettes, breaking the background color abruptly from yellow to blue, also emphasizes the connection of the sarcophagus to frescoes at Hagia Triada (Fig. 33 *b*) and on the mainland. It seems to express the mixed traditions of the Greek period at Knossos, for the costume of its figures is more Mycenaean than Minoan, and its dead man wears the same long robe without armholes that many figures on chariot kraters wear, with their atrophied hands poking out in front like little claws to grasp the reins.

Perhaps, in certain eastern regions, the kraters substituted for sarcophagi, which are always rare and expensive in the Aegean. There are two or three other sarcophagi on Crete and the mainland which employ the same theme, most recently one with a riot of marine and hunting scenes, priests and bulls, around the chariot.[10] On most vases the long robes would indicate the deceased or priests, the vases shown as filling ornaments in the air (Pl. XXXII D) would represent gifts to be placed in the grave, the attendants and belt-wrestlers would be participants in the funeral ceremonies. Other vases of the same shape have even more unusual outbreaks of imagery. A small goddess sits hunched on a throne, receiving a file of soldiers with spears and swords (Fig. 36). A chariot may be drawn by griffins or sphinxes, or the main scene may be an altar topped by horns of consecration.[11] These are painted versions of themes which are excerpted also for gems (see Pl. XLIII F), reflecting a whole lost range of monster-and-cult symbolism in Aegean thought, which is never satisfactorily interpreted because it is mute and condensed from a set of codified emblems never discussed in the documents. It is very doubtful indeed that these or any

FIG. 36.—Homage krater, Musée du Louvre. (After Karageorghis, *AJA* 1958, Pl. 99.)

pictorial Mycenaean vases are illustrations of lost epics, but if any group merits attention as a possible reflection of religious custom it is the chariot kraters, a standard tomb gift in regions where Levantine custom encouraged it. Their gleeful shorthand of reference terms confuses our interpretations and not all of them need to be loaded with messages from beyond the grave. Skilled painters of the empire turned out the same variety of themes that gem-cutters did, and if they had a steady market of bereaved families for one class of picture they also amused themselves with other scenes, the animals and plants and fish of the palace decorators.

Painting after the Palaces

The paradox of a revival in painting toward the end of the thirteenth century when the political situation had become desperate for the Mycenaeans (and everyone else in the Aegean) may be explained in two ways. One is economic, one demands a perspective on international relations. The simple export pottery of the thirteenth century turned up in quantities along all the eastern littoral from Anatolia to Palestine (Fig. 40). It is dated by the Late Bronze destruction levels of Tarsus, Enkomi, Ugarit, Alalakh, Hazor, and Megiddo. It connects the Mycenaean commercial world with quite an accurate chronology to the invasions of the Sea Peoples, and to the last power struggle between the Egyptians and the Hittites which ended in mutual exhaustion at great battles off the Delta in 1187 B.C. and off the coasts of Cyprus shortly afterward (p. 273).

In the final moments of this empire style of vase painting two new trends appeared. One was an even further simplification, or discouragement, of routine abstract ornament. This is called the Granary style because it was first recognized in the Granary at Mycenae, a building erected to help supply the citadel in case of attack. Typical Granary vases are deep bowls and water jars with plain black bands or wavy lines on a buff ground, and this fabric is found in a majority of destruction levels in Greece (Fig. 51). It occurs on the floors of the palace at Pylos just before the burning, in the burned houses outside the citadel at Mycenae (Pl. XXIV B), on the Acropolis at Athens as she withdrew behind her walls and protected her water supply (p. 268); overseas it turns up at Troy and Tarsus.

The second trend was a rebellion against simplicity known as the Close style from its love of covering the whole surface with close complications of older motifs. It took two forms. Mycenae made the best mainland version—sober, miniature, and dense. The island schools preferred splashy octopodes, birds, and fishes (Pl. XLV C; Fig. 51) in fantastic arrangements. The Close style overlapped the later phase of simple empire vases, and has been found especially in eastern coastal sites; Perati in Attica (p. 302), Hagios Ioannis near Monemvasia, or the Cycladic islands. Crete, Rhodes, Cyprus, and Naxos were particular centers. After its first fashionable success it was perpetuated in places where refugees from the burned palaces congregated; pried loose from home comforts, they had very little other art except their weapons to admire.

This revival reverses the thirteenth-century phase of physical security and dull pots. While the Mycenaean centers were at their most protective and active there had been a kind of population explosion, or so one judges by the tombs which hold three or four times as many skeletons from the period 1350–1220 as from any other. Most of these Mycenaeans seem to have been middle-class artisans, farmers, and merchants able to afford the minor arts that had earlier been limited to princely families. A stereotyped artistic production grew out of their increasing demand for possessions. Identical glass-paste beads, knives, vases, and figurines were hastily turned out in quantity, and after even a generation of this mass production the standards in each workshop had probably slipped. The thousands of unpainted pots in the Pylos palace speak eloquently of mercantile prosperity accompanied by loss in individual taste. But after the Sea Peoples broke Aegean communications and upset trade, the humble household or tomb vase seems to acquire new importance in the absence of other minor arts, and there was a distinction again between good and bad, local styles instead of international conformity. This explains the contradiction between the newly florid and representational III C Palace style and the lack of palaces for it to flourish in.

The Close style is less important for the history of Mycenaean painting than the new scenes with human figures, but it merits a brief description for its charm and its influence on later traditions. The characteristic vase is the stirrup jar, whose belly is painted with stylized octopodes and birds (Pl. XLV C). Subsidiary motifs are geometric and ornamental; the paint shifts to lustrous black. The octopus hangs sac downward, elongated to a melancholy point, with large staring eyes formed from spirals or circles; between its symmetrical tentacles fish leap, birds fly in and out as though through branches of a tree. One famous vase from Kalymnos near Rhodes includes crabs, lobsters, a hedgehog, wild goats, and a mountain. This is a revival of the old Marine and Palace styles in a newly cluttered, unconsciously humorous way (see Fig. 50). When this style degenerates it goes two paths: toward a monumental geometry with an abstraction of figures and careful ornaments, or toward a paneling of impressionistic birds and fish. The former, controlled, eventually produces Protogeometric in Greece; the latter has as offshoots the Philistine and Cypriote figured pots of the Dark Ages.

Vases of the III C pictorial style on the mainland are rare but important. Some try for monumentality, some are sketches of animals by hands that have almost totally lost their skill (Fig. 50). The most famous is the Warrior Vase, found in a house at Mycenae in a context of the early twelfth century. It is illustrated here (Pl. XXXIII B) with another unusual vase of the chariot class, the Window Krater from Cyprus (Pl. XXXIII A).[12] Both show stronger links with fresco work than normal. The Warrior Vase in a sense continues the themes of chariot kraters, without the chariot. Six men march out in single file on one side, five on the other, carrying shields on their left arms and spears with bags tied to them in their right hands. A lady in a long two-colored robe lifts her hands over her head as though to say farewell or mourn them. The drawing is much more solid and detailed than in the earlier chariot kraters; it is more like a fresco procession on a smaller surface. Male costume has changed since the later frescoes of Mycenae and Tiryns; the short fringed tunics, small shields which can be managed with one steering hand, skin helmets (on one side with horn, crest, and plume, on the other with spines as though made of hedgehog skin) suggest that the warriors have been in touch with some of the new armament developments brought into the Mediterranean by the Sea Peoples. By including such novelties the painter shows he can use his own observations as well as draw on older fresco traditions.

The scene does not explain itself. Some consider it a battle between two squads in different helmets, some a continuation of fresco hunt scenes where the javelin is more useful than the sword, some a scene of mourning comparable to funerary processions on Geometric kraters. This last view has a good deal to recommend it. The woman with raised hands is placed like the woman holding a flower on the earlier Window Krater as she looks out of her architectural frame toward a departing chariot with two drivers. She, and her six sisters in the other windows, may be saying a final good-by with raised bouquets. On the later vase, when chariots have almost disappeared from painting and terracottas because they were too expensive to maintain, the warriors go out on foot to take part in the funeral games. Parallels for these rare vases are entirely in the realm of funerary monuments. A painted grave stele from Mycenae is so close in date and style to the Warrior Vase that it has been attributed to the same painter's hand (Fig. 47 *a*); it is genuine fresco work on stucco over an old carved stone. In the upper register five twins to the Warriors march out with raised javelins, small shields, fringed tunics, and gaiters; in the lower register appear a hedgehog, three stags, and a doe—reminiscences of the Tiryns or Pylos hunt scenes. Such a scene on a grave stone ought to have funerary meaning (p. 302).

The pictorial style includes many genre scenes too (Fig. 50). It may be unfair to call the selections here the Wild style, but many of them are so far from the refined conventions of frescoes and the stereotyped chariot kraters that they strike the eye as barbaric or deliberately funny. Comically helpless drawing begins already in the early fourteenth century with such compositions as the Circus Pot from Mycenae (Fig. 50 *c*, *f*); it can be excused because the artist found no prototypes in the major arts for what he wanted to draw. If the Minoans had not supplied the Mycenaeans with a set of forms for painting, this childishness might have lingered longer. Even by the end of the thirteenth century a latent caricature element persists for drawings of men in action. The bull-jumpers and boxers make impossible leaps with missing muscles. Faces sprout whiskers, chins droop slackly. Men marching with spears in ceremony are quite a common subject in the latest period, but none of them possess the solid energy of the Warrior Vase. Animals and birds, running or dancing, are favorites (Fig. 50 *b, d, e, i*). They keep the lively naïveté of the frescoes and indeed are even more charming for being freed of human interference. These excerpts from nature increase after the ruin of the palaces, being especially characteristic of early III C pottery, and make a refreshing close to the long tradition of Mycenaean art.

Painted Larnakes

A final group of monuments is so newly known and so reluctantly published that any discussion must be painfully tentative. It is a series of terracotta larnakes or sarcophagi from central Greece, painted with odd scenes of mourning or marching figures (Pls. XXXIV–XXXV; Fig. 37).[13] The larnax is a stone or clay box which is made in two standard shapes, the bathtub and the chest. Mycenaeans used the former as a real bathtub in their palaces and private houses, but the chest form, elevated on four square legs with a gable roof, has been almost completely a stranger in Greece until the last few years. Both types were invented in Crete and used for burials throughout the fourteenth and thirteenth centuries; there are clay examples as old as Middle Minoan, but it is only after the destruction of the Cretan palaces that the larnax becomes widely popular.

The new group of chest larnakes in Greece is startling because the mainlanders almost never used coffins for burial, except very rarely for a child (p. 301). It now seems that an unknown community near the site of classical Tanagra in Boiotia was using the chest larnax as a matter of course in the years near 1200 B.C., and ornamenting it in an idiosyncratic local style. The influence of Crete is perceptible in this novelty, but the painting is not Minoan; indeed, on Crete, figured scenes of this sort are of the utmost rarity among the hundreds of known specimens. The style on these larnakes is indebted to mainland fresco work and to the subjects on late chariot kraters; it is mixed with traits of the Close style and is expressed in a peculiarly elongated and sketchy manner. Sometimes the bathtub larnakes of the palace age had been painted with spirals, or even a chariot, but their style is far more predictable.

The larnakes seem to reflect the mixed and absorbing character of the period when the palaces were destroyed and movements of people on a fairly large scale among Greece, Crete, and Cyprus helped spread all kinds of novelties. Greece at that time began to know new sword and spear forms, Hittite bronzes, Syrian seals (cf. Pl. XLVIII), European axes and pins, and the eastern habit of cremation burial (p. 301). Larnax burial in particular villages on the mainland is not too surprising in this medley of migration and borrowed habits.

The group of painted larnakes includes fourteen complete examples and fragments of two or three more. The coffins are made for both adults and children and range in size from about 0.40 m. to 1.05 m. A curious feature is the presence of small bored holes in the bottom as though to ensure air circulation when firing the thick clay, or drainage. Nothing is known about how they were used, since none of them has been found in regular excavations. In Crete they would have been placed inside regular chamber tombs and would have held a pot or two, and trinkets like knives or beads, along with the dead person. It is a pity no pots were kept from the Greek group; on stylistic grounds they should be dated about 1200 B.C., to the early III C period, using motifs from older vases and palace frescoes. The clay is coarse, the ground is buff, and black and red paint is applied directly over it without any preparatory slip. An example in mint condition from the Agora at Athens preserves a bright scarlet tone the best (Fig. 37), and an example now in Kassel has a particularly effective interwoven contrast of the two colors. One is polychrome: red, white, and blue.

The German larnax (Pl. XXXIV) expresses the style of the group at its best. It demonstrates how the painter almost automatically divides his field into narrow panels in preference to creating a connected scene. Each panel (except one blank end) shows a mourning woman with her hands raised toward her head. Curiously, the women are all in different costumes. Their dresses are red, white, parti-colored, or obliquely rippled. Two have skinny stick-arms, short dark hair, and staring eyes; two have a fleshier anatomy outlined with interior details instead of being silhouetted. The one on the end seems not a mortal woman at all, since her "arms" ruffle into wings and on her head a flamelike plume grows out of a little crown. They all have the same kind of "tails" spreading below their hips which are more elaborately seen on the Hagia Triada sarcophagus. There are careless plants in the field, and overhead and underfoot a row of disc beam-ends derived from architectural façades in frescoes (cf. Fig. 32). Seen with the checkerboard panels these produce an impression of deliberate architectural framework as on the Window Krater (Pl. XXXIII A).

The gesture of mourning obviously connects them to the lady on the Warrior Vase; they may be nearly contemporary.

The motif is much the same on all the others, though different artists handle it in different ways. An example in France uses a fuller, more solid style in the tradition of the Hagia Triada sarcophagus (Pl. XXXV A). The women wear a piece of cloth across their breasts in mainland decency while otherwise preserving the ceremonial Minoan costume of jacket and flounced skirt. They have the ski-jump noses and receding chins of the men on the Warrior Vase, and their costume and stance recall the mourning woman there. They touch their fingertips to their heads, which are crowned by flat caps with long plumes floating down behind their backs. An arcaded pattern frames each woman above, and an ivy-leaf filling ornament separates their bodies. The women move toward the right on the front of the sarcophagus and toward the left on the back, that is, both files are in tuned step toward the same goal. The vase originally illustrated with this larnax does not belong to the same burial, it seems.

A very similar fragment in New York, perhaps by the same artist, is the same kind of procession. It preserves two somber figures and part of a third. One turns back with a swish of skirt. The mourning women face each other in stylized disbelief (Fig. 37). The fragment reminds us that only in the late period of Mycenaean art does the artist consciously attempt to provide a facial expression which will indicate sharp emotion. How much charm the effect can have is shown by the end panel of the well preserved larnax now in Athens, which stations a caricature mourner with thin looping arms between a pair of upright pillars from which grow lines like flames or locks of hair cut off in despair (Fig. 37). This is the most discouraged Mycenaean to last beyond the Bronze Age. The other end of the larnax is decorated with monumental horns of consecration, emphasizing the religious aura of the occasion. Another larnax in Athens introduces royally clad male mourners with hats and swords, like princes weeping for a lost successor. Another child's larnax separates the mourning figures by a solid strip of checkerboard ornament, each locked in a separate panel like the women on the Window Krater.

The last example there is space to discuss introduces a new element (Pl. XXXV B). Half the long side (it was sawed apart for export and the back is missing) is occupied by a mammoth bird. He is painted in the reserve outline and ornate style first seen on chariot kraters, later on Close style stirrup jars. He walks through a landscape indicated by large flowers of a typical Mycenaean botany, and wears two collars. In front of him, divided from each other and from their animal guest by streaming lines, two men march in single file. They seem to be soldiers, although unarmed. They wear short embroidered tunics and gaiters or leggings tied at knee and ankle. The one on the left has cropped hair and a curly beard; the one on the right has longer floating hair and a beaked nose. The paint has flaked away from many of the original lines, but the artist's familiarity with a previous world of chariot kraters or of frescoes is implicit in the large, conventional design. This seems to be the only larnax with no overtones of mourning. The whole panel is again framed by discs representing beam-ends above and by a row of vertical spirals on the side; the design is

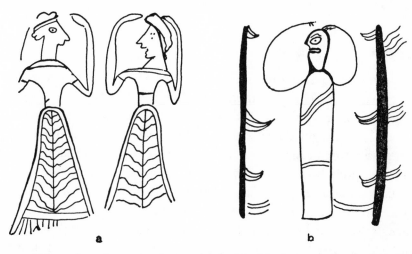

FIG. 37.—Figures from late painted sarcophagi: (*a*) side fragment (courtesy L. Pomerance); (*b*) narrow end of sarcophagus in Athens (courtesy the late J. Threpsiades).

known from the fragments with marching soldiers from Orchomenos. The short side panels, badly preserved, have palm trees and multiple horns of consecration stacked in tiers.

These larnakes will be collected and more fully analyzed soon, one hopes. Their presence on the Greek mainland may be surprising, and yet taking the long view one wonders why this should be so, considering the number of Cretan larnakes and the revived connections between Crete and Greece in the latest period of the Bronze Age. They are not forgeries, although some have been tempted to call them so when puzzled by their iconographical queerness. They make us understand why Greek myth should later have elaborated on the theme of the king who died in the bathtub, like Agamemnon in his palace at Mycenae, for the bathtub and the coffin were originally the same article and

213

called by the same name, and although Agamemnon was murdered in a silver one, we hear, and these are common painted clay, the change is only poetry working on a seed of truth with elegant distortion. They are the last survivors of the monumental funeral paintings begun by the Hagia Triada sarcophagus. They are exactly what one would expect on other grounds in painting after the palaces fell. They preserve elements of the fresco tradition in a world where frescoes were no longer being done. They modify it for their special purpose, include the new motifs made popular by the Close style, and show that double trend of hasty execution and pictorial liveliness which is the final expression of major Mycenaean art.

SCULPTURE

Monumental stone sculpture is almost missing in Greece, except for the Lion Gate at Mycenae. The Mycenaeans are like the Minoans in satisfying their glyptic instinct on a miniature scale: ivories, terracottas, carved gems. It seems odd that these two gifted civilizations should have ignored the progress of monumental sculpture in Egypt or Anatolia, where free-standing statues and carved reliefs had surely been noticed by Aegean travelers. In Greece the absence of a sculptural tradition is particularly odd because good stone was quarried and used in monumental architecture, and masons were highly trained. Some experiments were made toward the end of the palace age and afterward—the Lion Gate and the Mycenae plaster head represent two types of achievement, in relief and in modeled stucco—but the historical moment was too late to permit fruition. It was the lack of Minoan prototypes which probably delayed this branch of art so long, because sculptural instinct was already present in the Shaft Grave stelai (Figs. 17–18, p. 90).

Crete had made some progress in sculptural technique during the fifteenth century, modeling and painting life-sized stucco reliefs like the charging bull or Priest-King of Knossos. These attempts were raised painting rather than a genuine three-dimensional creation, and were never really passed on to the Mycenaean world although the Greeks had been familiar with them at Knossos. Neither did the Mycenaeans ever fully associate the arts of narrative representation and public writing with the large architecture of which they were fully masters. There are no narrative stone reliefs in tombs or palaces. One must recognize and respect in Crete and Greece this lack of the commemorative and documentary spirit which helped develop gigantic ruler-statues, portraiture, and historical reliefs abroad. As in painting, Aegean talent is for decorative ornament and minor genre scenes.

Circumstances now make the Lion Gate at Mycenae seem unique, probably falsely (Pl. XVII B). It is high relief on the veneer of the relieving triangle over the city gate, and survives because the walls framing the gate were never dismantled below the lintel level. Counterpart slabs must have once ornamented the ruined gates of Tiryns and Athens, and perhaps the façades of major tholos tombs; the parallel in painting is supplied by the Sphinx Gate from Pylos (Pl. XXX C). The design is not original; it was projected into large-scale relief from a familiar composition on gems and ivories (Pls. XXXVII B, XLIII B). The motif of heraldic animals posed on either side of a column is older in Greece than the Lion Gate by at least 250 years, if that monument was created in the great rebuilding of Mycenae around 1250 B.C. (p. 269). The versions in the minor arts preserve variations on the scheme and suggest restorations for the lions' missing heads: dead symmetrical, in any case, and probably staring parallel down the entrance chute to strengthen the architectural focus of the narrow approach; the dowel holes agree.[14]

The theme of the gate seems both religious and "canting": the royal lions standing on divine authority (represented by the two altars under the plinth) guarding the megaron of Mycenae (the column with the discs above standing for the abbreviated entablature). They are decorative symbols of the king's double religious and political authority. But religion is so often used casually in Mycenaean ornament that the slab should not be interpreted too significantly. It is hard to judge its value either as art or as a typical piece of Mycenaean sculpture. Even in its weathered condition the modeling is clear (it had to be, at that distance and height), the powerful paws and haunches as clean as though carved in ivory. It does not suggest that other lost reliefs on the same scale differed importantly from reliefs in the minor arts.

In the same way purely decorative stone sculpture like the rosette-and-triglyph friezes from the palaces at Mycenae and Tiryns, or on the façade of the Treasury of Atreus, share their motifs with painting and with ivory carving (Pl. XXVI). The scrolled schist ceiling of the side chamber in the Orchomenos tholos tomb (p. 121) makes monumental a design even more familiar in painting, used earlier on the door of an Early Mycenaean chamber tomb at Argos done in four colors (Fig. 45), or on the Spiral frescoes of the palace repertories. The carved marble ceiling or dado fragment from the Kadmeion at Thebes (Fig. 31) illustrates this aggrandizement of jeweler's patterns, for the scale-net was first seen on the Silver Siege Rhyton (Pl. XIV) and is a commonplace on bronze, ivory, gems, vases, and painted walls or floors. It is an interesting piece in spite of its battered surface because it projects formal miniature patterns onto a grand scale in expensive material. One would guess, therefore, that sculpture was not felt to be a distinct artistic field in the Mycenaean world. Ornament is primary, and the special laws or potentialities of the material in hand are secondary. Stone is used particularly on buildings where the creators desired to make an uncommon impression of expense and majesty.

The façade of the Treasury of Atreus is the most conspicuous of these buildings (Pl. XXVI). The whole entrance system was overwhelming in size (p. 122), gaudy in color, of highest quality in carved detail. Not one element of design was invented for this building; there is only a subtle combination of commonplaces. The lower greenstone half-columns with chevrons, spirals, and petaled collars flanked double bronze doors; the slender upper half-columns contrasted with two tones of red stone in the façade where spirals and split-rosettes ran across the triangle to join the diagonal spiral bands on the shafts. Whether the Elgin gypsum slabs showing parts of charging bulls in a treescape actually once flanked the triangle at the summit, or whether the whole design was richly abstract, the physical evidence no longer tells us. Aesthetically the bull slabs seem the wrong shape and diffuse the power of the arrangement by breaking outward. Although its parts are smashed and scattered through many museums, the Atreus façade illustrates more persuasively than any other Mycenaean monument the painterly quality of palatial sculpture.[15]

Even on a small scale Mycenaeans apparently preferred color, and media which they could paint, such as terracottas. There is very little figurative stonework. The fragment of a steatite rhyton from Epidauros (Fig. 20 b) is a tantalizing excerpt from a narrative scene. The tradition of such rhyta is Minoan, of course, but the military theme of men marching over mountains, armed warriors, a ship and a sportive dolphin, continues the subject matter of the Silver Siege Rhyton; again, stone or metal makes little difference to artistic execution. Occasionally a primitive limestone head is found in Greece which is guessed to be Mycenaean because it suits no other period. Expensive stones are sometimes carved into household objects, such as alabaster toilet boxes, fluted marble bowls, or pedestaled marble lamps ornamented with spirals; rarely one finds a carved steatite knife handle, or a little amulet in animal form. In general, however, Mycenaean sculpture is plastic rather than glyptic, and for masterpieces of carving one must look to other media, ivories, and gems.

Plastic modeling on a large scale is extraordinarily rare, considering the experience of mainlanders in modeling terracottas and throwing vases, and the commanding size of many buildings. The best known mainland piece is a painted plaster head from Mycenae, life-sized and freshly preserved (Pl. XL C). It illuminates an otherwise lost art of mixed fresco and sculpture. The hair and eyes are dark blue, like the brows and hair of divinities in Homer. The hair is bound with a red fillet and covered by a pale blue striped cap rather like the headgear that sphinxes and mourning women wear (Pls. XXX C, XXXIV–XXXV, XXXVII B). The dead-white countenance is brightened with beauty spots of dotted red rosettes, the ironic gash of the mouth is fashionable in scarlet. The slanted eyes recall frescoes, the high cheekbones and large ears and drooping mouth have a quality in common with the Shaft Grave masks or portrait gem (Pl. XI A, C). The context of this head did not reveal how it was set up at Mycenae; it may have been a sphinx in public position like those of the Pylos fresco (Pl. XXX C), or perhaps a goddess like those from the Keos shrine.

The Keos goddesses (Pl. XL A–B) are not strictly mainland art at all, and it is not yet certain to which epoch they should be assigned. This extraordinary group is one of the most valuable recent finds of Aegean archaeology. There are at least fifteen female figures, discovered in a clearly religious context in a shrine at the town of Hagia Eirene on Keos (pp. 118, 285). The shrine flourished at the very end of the palace age and into the twelfth century, but the great statues may have been initiated as a series in the earlier flowering days of the town, in the fifteenth century. Some are nearly life size, some are about one meter tall; they are thus larger than figures from late Cretan shrines, the brilliant series of clay goddesses crowned with doves or horns raising their arms into the air. The Kean sculptors made their figures of rough brick-red terracotta, firing them in sections over wooden armatures and joining the parts together, then coating the surface with a finer slip. The figures face out frontally, supported on the broad bases of their flaring skirts, with their hands resting lightly on their hips. Most wear a Minoan type of short-sleeved jacket, which is drawn apart to frame their naked bosoms. Some are entirely naked in the upper body; one of these illustrated here (Pl. XL A) shows an almost grotesque disparity between the full drooping breasts and the narrow lissome waist. Some wear a thick collar of office, some a simple garland. Their hair is usually long and falls in a thick twist to the waist behind; it is bound over the brow by a rolled fillet or a cap. Their faces are individual but conform to a general model: a long oval head with prominent high cheek bones and jutting chin, arched brows over small, wide-open eyes, sharp noses with fleshy nostrils; their pleased countenances show the genuine archaic smile of first attempts. Their appearance must have been overwhelming as they stood in the shrine (p. 286), but for the moment they remain a curious experiment, an eddy, in the development of Bronze Age sculpture which has no real counterpart on the mainland. Perhaps Mycenaeans had not the religious intensity to inspire such monumental figures, which are unique even among the imaginative men of the Cyclades.

CARVED IVORY

Ivory carving is one of the most sophisticated and beautiful arts the Mycenaeans practiced. Like fresco work, it deserves much more exploration than scholars have given it. Since most raw ivory came to Greece through Syrian harbors,[16] there is a more accented orientalism of style than in other media, and a trail of rich ivory deposits leads from Mycenae through the islands of Delos and Cyprus to the Levantine centers of Ugarit and Megiddo. Influence was active in both directions along this route. Angular animal combats and the flying gallop and the goddess in flounced skirt traveled east, plant design and heraldry worked their way more tentatively west. In contrast to the later Orientalizing period of Greek art (700–600 B.C.) the source of artistic power seems to come from the mainland, and the East is content to admire, import, imitate. At first the Minoans had taught the mainlanders the necessary techniques, and yet Minoan styles are not crucial to mainland styles. The reason is probably simple. Minoan ivories of the best class are little statues in the round—a bull-leaper, a playing boy—but Mycenaean ivories of the best class are relief plaques. Whole figurines are extremely rare and make a particularly Minoan impression, like the splendid triad of two women and a boy from the Mycenae acropolis (Pl. XXXVIII), probably mid-fourteenth century. Ninety-five per cent of Mycenaean ivories are unlike this. They are furniture inlays (Pl. XXXIX D), plaques from boxes or tables or footstools, toilet pyxides (Pl. XXXVI), mirror handles. Special, un-Minoan styles were developed for them to create flat, powerful forms in a small framework.

Ivory carving waits for its full development until the expanded palace period when demand for such inlaid expensive objects was strongest. Before 1350 B.C. there is very little. The oldest piece is a hybrid casket from the Fifth Shaft

Grave (Pl. XXXVI A), of imported(?) sycamore wood with ivory architectural inlays on which little dogs crouch as though guarding a house. Otherwise the early period limits its use of ivory to small things like sword pommels which needed a light balance and a princely gloss (Pl. XIII A). The magnificent phase begins in richer burials after the fall of Knossos, and is most brilliantly illustrated by the great ivory pyxis from a princess' grave on the slope of the Athenian Acropolis (Pl. XXXVI B–C).[17] A violent battle between winged griffins and stags takes place in an angular, woody style which contrasts with the contemporary Dendra hunting cup (Fig. 21 *b*) although both use the double perspective of the world of frescoes. Here it is appropriate because the griffins are flying down from the sky to attack the herd on the ground. No other Mycenaean ivory matches this in its controlled organization of savagery and agony, the simple power of the bodies, the subtle use of landscape like the tree overblown in the rush of the griffins' leap. The box is carved from a section of tusk a little over six inches tall and four inches across, and into this compass it crowds two griffin, four deer, two fawns, and two lions without sacrificing grandeur of conception or sympathetic detail, like the young deer leaping over a stone pile to get away, with its tongue out in terror.

Mycenae was a major center for ivory carving from the middle fourteenth century onward.[18] Her chamber tombs are rich in good examples; the citadel and outer houses have also yielded one or two royal pieces and a number of simple furniture inlays (p. 182; Pls. XXXVII A–B, XXXVIII, XXXIX C–D). The city imported raw tusks and finished articles from Syria and Canaan, just as she imported wine and copper; and just as she manufactured and shipped out her own wine and tools, her craftsmen made local ivories sometimes copying foreign styles and sometimes inventing new designs in the mainland idiom.

One unique tusk section represents the kind of finished import which helped to disseminate Levantine techniques and motifs (Pl. XXXIX C). Most Mycenaean ivories are sawed into shapes which do not reflect the original form of the tusk, but this one was used as a hollow holder for something precious, perhaps once terminating in a hand and spoon like the libation vessels used in eastern sanctuaries. It is badly damaged, yet one can still see the design of a tall columnar plant in a field of lotus blossoms, fluted with zigzags on its stem like the façade columns of the Treasury of Atreus (Pl. XXVI B), the blossom spreading to a lusher version of the Aeolic capital in the Sphinx Gate fresco at Pylos (Pl. XXX C). On either side a reclining wild goat with curved horns faces out; at the left a human figure attends (only the feet are preserved);

above a predatory bird soars vertically, shadowing the scene with his wings and tail.

Among Mycenae's own heraldic and mythological scenes two artistic veins are prominent: the pastoral, and the formally symbolic. On a small plaque for inlay a griffin reclines at peace under a papyrus thicket, a dreaming piece compared to the wild strength of the Athens pyxis (Pl. XXXVII A). A later plaque which christened the House of the Sphinxes illustrates the neat, metallic richness which seems characteristic of the best thirteenth-century work (Pl. XXXVII B). The sphinxes are formally set in the Lion Gate convention, paws on a column flanked by horns of consecration, their muscular posture enriched by deep chiseling for the triangular feathers of the lifting wings. Under plumed caps they gaze at each other with the wonderful oriental smiles of pleased women.

The palace at Mycenae seems to have kept its ivory divine triad on display until the latest period of its power, stored in a strongroom with other valuables in faïence and terracotta. This extraordinary composition of two women and a child, probably two goddesses and a young divinity or hero, must be an heirloom from an earlier age and is obviously a masterpiece in any century (Pl. XXXVIII). The balanced and curved volumes, the smooth, thoughtful, psychologically suggestive faces, the brilliant details of embroidery and jewelry which do not blur the figures but emphasize their unity and majesty—these have no match in other mainland creations. It may be fourteenth century, sprung from the sensitive Minoan tradition; perhaps Aerope brought it with her when she came from Crete to make mischief in the House of Atreus. By contrast, when Mycenaeans try to re-create three-dimensional ceremonial figures the effect can be whimsical (Pl. XXXIX A). A little lady from Prosymna is created from an anthology of Minoan mannerisms—the jeweled collar, the full gracious breasts, the open bodice and richly embroidered skirt—but the mysterious smile of the Mycenae goddess has become a self-conscious grimace, and the proportions are so short and awkward one is not certain whether she is standing or sitting. She sags.

After 1300 B.C. more local schools and styles spring up all over the mainland. Motifs become progressively stiffer and more symmetrical, as in vase painting. Monsters are increasingly popular, human figures and plants fade away. Some reliefs are extremely flat, with careless broad-planed animal bodies as on a famous plaque from Attic Spata. Others employ deep incision without any modeling, in a fusion of carving and engraving techniques. This style is beautifully illustrated by a cutout plaque from the hoard of ivories discovered in 1947 as a foundation offering under the shrine of Artemis on Delos (p. 287; Pl. XXXVII C). This is an angular and difficult composition, powerfully immobile, drawing its strength from two sources. One is the conservative display of the old conventions for speed and locked struggle such as the flying gallop, the tensed limbs, the griffin's turned head and hissing beak. The other is the precision with which the craftsman translated internal details like muscles and manes from relief to flat drawing. Every detail of the griffin can be matched on the magnificent plaque from another hoard at Megiddo in Palestine (Pl. XXXVII D). Only, the Megiddo griffin is more heavily enriched with triple triangular breast feathers; his great muscles are naturally more rounded, being in high relief, and his pose more quietly royal. This plaque is surely pure Mycenaean in design and idea, a document of Mycenaean trade with Palestine to match the Syrian tusk at Mycenae. Each illustrates the countermovement of styles between mainland and Orient, without being contaminated by the mixture so striking in ivories at halfway colonial stations like Enkomi in Cyprus.

Another plaque from the Delos hoard is carved in a fuller style which makes it seem earlier than its context at the end of the palace age (Pl. XXXIX B). The warrior with his figure-of-eight shield, plumed boar's-tusk helmet, and giant spear illustrates Aegean military issue; the loving attention to weaponry and the slightly comic stocky energy seem Mycenaean, but Crete must have contributed the swelling planes, the full-cheeked fleshy-nosed face, the slender waist encircled by belt and codpiece. This is practically the only surviving figure of a man in Aegean ivory, in contrast to symbolic monsters and courtly females. Ivory carving carried its own set of subjects, which do not reflect the chief themes of palace painters whose larger surfaces encouraged multiple figured narration, but which relate quite precisely to subject matter in the finer sculptures, gems, and metalwork.

TERRACOTTAS AND PLASTIC VASES

The plastic instinct expressed itself in a purely Mycenaean set of small figurines which have no counterpart until very late Crete. How much the lack of Minoan prototypes contributed to their sketchy clumsiness is obvious (Pl. XLI A–D); these are original mainland creations into which the mainland ateliers seldom put any hard work. They are in ordinary pottery fabric, buff with stripes of reddish-brown paint. Whether the potters made them as an amusing sideline or women in the villages made them at home, they are fairly standard. The most common types are the little females with arms bent at their sides or up-raised into the air, the so-called Φ and Ψ types named after letters of the Greek alphabet (Pl. XLI A–B). Their dress is long and flares slightly at the feet; their hair is often worn in a long plait loose down the back. This is the plain Mycenaean costume and a far cry from the elaborations of frescoes and ivories where prototypes existed. They are especially common in the III B em-pire, although it is not clear whether their dates should be strictly limited to the thirteenth century.

These women are found in tombs and in house deposits equally. It is inter-esting that they should be included among tomb gifts so regularly, like the Cycladic idols of the preceding millennium, but since they occur in several other contexts as well, their religious importance must be modest (p. 291). Oc-casionally there are more dramatic renditions: a woman in a throne, two women joined with a child at their breasts or on their shoulders, little figures with arms raised over their heads in mourning (Pls. XLI E, XLII F), a goddess riding sidesaddle on her beast (Pl. XLI F). In these there is some attempt to imitate more expensive models known on gems and in ivories, the common figurine taking on new life because it reaches beyond the conventional limits of the craft.

Women are by no means the only theme. Especially toward the end of the palace age there seems to breathe a new spirit of fantasy and of interest in genre studies. A similar energy of experiment inspires a series of quick clay sketches in late Crete as well: in both regions, perhaps, an expression of the same restless-ness with standard empire products that causes animal protomes to be slapped on vases or livens the pictorial exuberance of the Close style (Pls. XLII D, XLV C). In Greece the terracotta makers turn out figurines of little men lolling in three-legged chairs (Pl. XLI C), of athletes practicing the bull-jump or at least clinging to their quarry's horns, of the breadmaker bending over her dough, the open-mouthed cow (Fig. 49 *b*), the pack-horse with pilgrim flasks tied to his saddle ready for a journey (Pl. XLII A), streamlined and sketchy chariot horses racing with the driver perched on so abbreviated a vehicle he seems glued to their rumps (Pl. XLI D); there is the sedan chair, the empty chair, the three-footed monkey toy, or the boot with curled toe in an Anatolian tradition of six hundred years' standing.

An art hybrid of modeling and potting created a delightful series of plastic vases, which increase in numbers as the Mycenaean world draws toward its death (Pl. XLII). The first attempts were apparently to make ritual or libation vessels, like the pitcher from a cave on Mount Hymettos in Attica, which has little pitchers riding its shoulders, all pierced for liquid to flow from small to large (Fig. 51). In the III C period the developed kernos becomes better known: usually a hollow ring-vase with little receptacles mounted around its circumference. A good example from one of the islands has a bull's head pro-tome, four (once five) miniature vases of different shapes, and a twisted basket handle on which a pair of small doves perch (Pl. XLII D). Many animal vases have considerable charm, like the pack-horse or tuneful cow mentioned above, the scaly head of a predatory fish from Tiryns (Pl. XLII E), or a flat-footed duck with eyebrows from Achaia (Pl. XLII B). These provide the same inno-cent pleasure as the cow-creamers of the childhood breakfast table, though they may be awkward sculpture. A large bull's head from Karpathos brings the aristo-cratic drinking rhyton of the Early Mycenaean Age, then a cup for princes in silver or in stone, down to the price level where any successful man could buy it (Pl. XLII C; cf. Figs. 28, 41 *d*).

Gems, Jewelry, Metalwork

Minor arts in the Bronze Age are specially designed for personal ornament and interior decoration. Only gems are invested with an extra authority, from their religious significance and their use to seal up treasures and export goods. Like other classes of art, gems become relatively more common and less beau-tiful after 1350; the gold ring is worn only by a few exceptional people, and sard, chalcedony, carnelian, or steatite tend to replace the harder amethyst and crystal of the early tradition. It should be remembered that all gem-stones and rings are worn on cords in the Aegean world, the gem-face turned in against the inner side of the wrist for protection or strung on a necklace with plain beads; the hoop of a gold ring is used as a handle to make impressions on clay.

Themes popular on the oldest gems, the brilliant series from the tholos tombs and the early fourteenth century (Pls. XIX, XLIII) continue their appeal, but often with knobby accents from the drill and wheel marks which make them look dislocated (Pl. XIX E). This emphatic, ridged style is already incipient in the splendid sard lentoid of two lions attacking a stag which is contemporary with the ivory griffin pyxis from Athens and shares its majestic, controlled vio-lence (Pl. XLIII B). Later, technique often runs out of control at the expense of naturalism, and creates the sketchy heraldic styles of the griffins on the altar endorsed with the Linear B sign for *wheat* (Pl. XIX L). This thirteenth-century official combination of scenes and writing is particularly active in the store quarters of Mycenae and Pylos, where sealings from gems may be written across or on the back as an extra guarantee of inspection. Seven such sealings were found in the doorway of the House of the Sphinxes at Mycenae, all impressed from a single seal with the design of a man between two rampant goats, and then set hard over knots of string which tied containers or locks on cupboards. The words on these sealings are names of pots which were perhaps being readied for export overseas, and the fingerprints of the inspector are still as clear as on a prison record.[19]

The few gold rings known from the late period preserve ancient Minoan cult symbols but often re-create them in the newer disjointed style: scenes of adoration, altars and trees, the goddess receiving daimons or princes (Pl. XLIII F). They are jewels in themselves, for priestesses and the guardians of various sanctuaries, and suggest as well as any medium of art the strongly conservative tendency of Mycenaean iconography. They contrast with the signs of religious innovations which the Pylos tablets suggest to be increasing in the thirteenth century (p. 294). Most gems of this phase must have been made in Greece itself and stylistic reinforcement from Minoan imports fades away. So far, the only find on the mainland which is comparable to the Lapidaries' Workshop at Knossos is an extensive hoard of cut and uncut agates and crystal from the palace of Kadmos at Thebes. Unfortunately these stones are simply in the polishing stage, not yet engraved, so that we cannot watch the precise steps the Greeks took in re-creating gem designs from older models.[20] The new, accidental discovery of thirty Near Eastern cylinder seals at Thebes may at last provide evidence for the source of many seemingly oriental compositions on Greek gems, since the imports and the new stones ready for cutting are documented in the same vicinity.

There is not exactly a failure to create a genuine mainland style, but more an apathetic satisfaction with hasty versions of old designs, and some gems from III B chamber tombs may be very crude indeed. The same alleviating streak of fantasy which characterizes terracottas and painted vases is seen in some religious gems, particularly those with daimons and dances. One flattened cylinder from thirteenth-century Naxos (Fig. 44) is an extraordinary sketch from a religious ceremony, a warrior making offerings before a palm tree (cf. p. 290). As on ivories, monsters are the most popular images, especially griffins and sphinxes (Pl. XIX L). The few genuine cylinder seals imported in the latest period (Pl. XLVIII; cf. Fig. 29), in stone or faïence, come too late to have a real effect on mainland style.

Our impressions of metalwork in the late fourteenth and thirteenth centuries are a bit distorted, because the accidents of survival favor tomb gifts over household or professional objects. Some of the best craftsmanship goes into weapons, which we have in quantity: the daggers, knives, spear and javelin points, arrowheads, and razor-cleavers familiar in any cemetery (Fig. 39). In this respect tradition has not altered from the Shaft Grave period, except that the middle-class expansion already spoken of makes a mass-produced weaponry which is perfectly efficient (it had to be in that age of raids and mercenaries) but less ornamental or involved with precious material than before. A few dagger blades are still inlaid with niello figures of dolphins or flying birds (Pl. XIII D), and hilts quite often have gold rivets, but on the whole aristocratic elaboration is finished.

When exceptional finds are made in III B tombs, like silver cups or gold wires, they may well be heirlooms from a century earlier. The fourteenth century continued the aristocratic tastes of the Early Mycenaean Age, with gold collars and drinking cups or elaborately wrought necklaces. An example from Mycenae is full of stylization and richness, linked gold beads each made up of a pair of argonauts swimming belly to belly (Pl. XLIV A). Firm granulation and traces of enamel enrich a design perfectly familiar in fresco and vase painting (cf. Pl. XXIX D). But already about 1400 a curious cheapness in funeral gifts began. Princes' graves had always been graced with thin gold foil objects which imitated the sturdier jewelry of real life; sometimes these were fastened to funeral dress or perhaps entwined in the hair, and they are terribly frail, like the gold flowers and flying wasps of Peristeria (Pl. XLIV B–C). After the standardization of economy began, deliberately inexpensive copies of precious objects were made; this was noticed by Mrs. Immerwahr in clay goblets and small dishes from Athens, Dendra, and Ialysos, whose visible surfaces were coated thinly in tin to resemble genuine silverware at less expense (cf. Pl. XX B). After the period of the Dendra cemetery metal vases of any type are rare (Fig. 38), although a certain number of royal pieces were used in palace circles until their destruction. Personal ornaments in gold or silver are made flimsily in rather conventional forms from molds (Pl. XLIV E). One extraordinary royal sceptre from Kourion in Cyprus must have been treasured for a good many generations, representing a lost series of rich insignia enduring into the twelfth or even eleventh century among Mycenaean colonists. It has a pair of

FIG. 38.—Types of Mycenaean metal vessels (bronze except as noted). Left column: Mycenae, Mycenae (gold); center column: Amorgos (silver), Vapheio, Mycenae, Mycenae; right column: Vapheio, Vapheio, Athens, Mycenae, Mycenae.

eagles or hawks in gold with cloisonné insets for colored enamel on their wings; they are mounted on a ball covered with cloisonné cells inlaid with blue and white enamel, the whole set on a slender gold shaft (Pl. XLIV D).[21] This is the last survival of the elaborate traditions in public jewelry inaugurated by the Shaft Grave princes.

Most empire jewelry is lovely when restrung, but standard and not of high quality. Designs are reproduced en masse from molds made to identical patterns in all parts of the country. A basalt mold from Mycenae has places for several trinkets: voluted flowers for necklace beads, an octopus and a nautilus on plain flat plaques, and simple abstract designs (Pl. XLIV E). These designs are no different from their counterparts in other fields of palace art such as fresco or ivory; they are not specifically jewel motifs. Often blue glass-paste substituted for gold, using the same patterns; it is a favorite material in later thirteenth-century tombs, and can be charming. Faïence was equally used for inexpensive costume jewelry. Gold necklaces and bracelets give way to a profusion of colored stone or glass-paste beads, such as the pink and black ones the painted women at Thebes wear (Pl. XXVII). This relish for parti-colored strands became evident first in tholos tombs, where the corpse may be literally draped from neck to waist in long loops of round beads in frit and soft stones. Empire work favored carnelian, malachite, agate, and dull black steatite in place of the amethyst and amber so conspicuous in the Early Mycenaean Age. The beads come in many shapes: ribbed, fenestrated, gadrooned, imitating wheat grains or double cones. A single bead sometimes combines two colors of glass, or is capped with a contrasting metal, gold on malachite or crystal. Men as well as women wore these ornaments. The clothes of both sexes were enriched with bronze pins, and stone or terracotta conical buttons. The only kind of modern jewelry which the Mycenaeans did not particularly care for was the earring. They seem to have gone out of fashion with the Shaft Graves. Even the best dressed women in frescoes appear without them.

Rare metals still circulate in the palace age, but mostly in utilitarian forms. Lead appears as weights for fishing nets, or in strings and sheets in graves (p. 303); there is an occasional tin amulet, a gold foil trinket for a child, an iron ring or dagger or even a key. Silver remains extremely scarce; bronze is the rule, in practical shapes.

The source of all the bronze being forged in Greece during the palace age is not quite clear. A lot of it came in rude ingot form from the Cyprus mines or from Ugarit in Canaan. Some smaller quantities may have been mined and cast on the mainland, for Bronze Age crucibles have been found at several sites. Tin was once reported near Kirrha in Phokis; the mine was not found. Tin is not frequent in limestone although bauxite is. Copper in the hills behind Mycenae may have helped her to power, though its Bronze Age extraction cannot be proved. But copper and tin were basic, vital Mycenaean imports from abroad, exchanged against pottery, oil, wine, and timber. The handiest source for tin was probably Asia Minor, though again the precise places are not known; it may have been brought by caravan to Anatolian seaports from as far away as the Caucasus. Canny merchants set their strongest outposts in just these caravan terminus regions: Miletos, Rhodes, Enkomi, Ugarit.

The West was a secondary source for metals, and Mycenaean trade is evident from at least 1500 B.C. onward, along the routes toward, and at the commercial outlets from, the Tuscan ores which later made the Etruscans rich. Tin may also have trickled through from farther off: Spain, or through France from Cornwall, or from central Europe over the Alps down the Adriatic, or down the Vardar valley into the north Aegean. Here the Mycenaeans were in touch with at least one iron-smelting town of Balkan culture, Vardaroftsa on the Vardar. However, the quantity from these sources could not have been significant. Along these outer trade routes came innovations in weapons and tools for both parties: an Italian mold for a winged ax at Mycenae, many new cut-and-thrust swords which are a feature of the new tactics introduced during the epoch of the Sea Peoples' invasions. Such exchanges of technology do not concern us here as art, although they were enormously important for military history (p. 273).[22]

The common bronzes forged on the mainland were technically excellent. They include toilet articles like mirrors and tweezers, tools like saws and chisels and awls, bronze scale pans, lamps and basins (Figs. 38–39). Against these limited offerings we can set valuable information from palace workshops, the tablets, and the Cape Gelidonya wreck to illustrate the activities of blacksmiths for all the metal objects demanded by palace economy. The smith's house at Malthi and the bronzeworkers' quarters at Pylos have already been mentioned (pp. 75, 166). A most important series of Pylos tablets describes how bronze is allotted from central holdings (presumably inside the palace) to smiths in scattered villages so that it can be forged into swords, spearpoints, arrowheads, even ship fittings. A sophisticated system of weights and fractions has been developed. It has been calculated that the amounts involved are enough to make 534,000 arrowheads or 1,000 bronze helmets out of over a ton of crude bronze—

and this from only the surviving fraction of the relevant tablets at not the richest of the Mycenaean centers.[23] Such statistics correct our narrowly focused view on gleanings from tombs.

The Bronze Age shipwreck off Cape Gelidonya (a promontory on the southern coast of Anatolia which endangered many ships sailing from Syria to Rhodes; see Fig. 40) has done more to illuminate the practicalities of Aegean

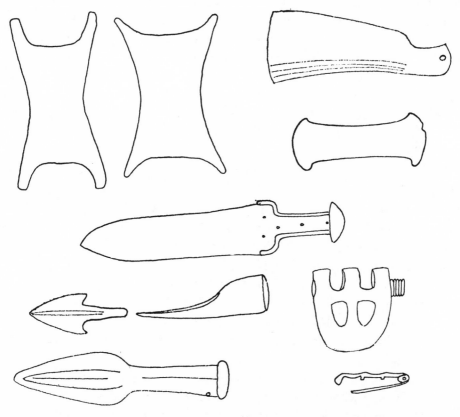

Fig. 39.—Types of Mycenaean weapons, tools, pins, and ingots

metal trade than any other discovery of the decade. An independent tinker's ship foundered there with its entire cargo of copper ingots and bronze tools. It was on its way west from Cyprus or the Levant near 1200 B.C. in the years preceding the Sea Peoples' battles at the Delta or off Cyprus (p. 273). Since both the raw and the finished metal were on board together, one may assume that the captain and crew stopped off to forge whatever was wanted in local harbors; they had an anvil and a set of hematite weights for doing the work and

229

setting the correct price. These weights were calculated in the Egyptian-Syrian-Cypriote system in multiples of 9 from a unit of 9.3 grams, so presumably it was not a Mycenaean ship, but most of the tools and ingots are like those of the mainland. The ship was only between 8 and 9 meters long, and most of her cargo rode on deck in baskets, surrounded by brushwood bulwarks. The dangers of such a floating smithy are obvious, and if she had not sunk she would have burned sooner or later. The ingots (Fig. 39) dispose of one beloved Aegean fiction: they seem not weight or currency units at all, but unsubtly cast in a form easy to carry, with projecting stubs at the corners (the "ox-hide" shape). They had foundry marks stamped on while the metal was still soft. The tools on board included axes and adzes, hoes or plowshares, a socketed spade, a spit for grilling meat, and, more elegantly, a rod-tripod, and a mirror to help the captain tend his mercantile façade. One would have expected also the razors so many Mycenaean men are buried with, but perhaps the crew were bushy Asiatics or did not bother to shave at sea.

From the Gelidonya wreck it becomes vividly clear that copper export was big business, that mines and foundries in places like Soloi and Enkomi on Cyprus discharged their product in ingot form to independent traders (probably through harbor clearinghouses at a standard price), and that the raw material could either go straight to its destination at industrial centers abroad or be worked to order in small quantities at intermediate harbors. The Gelidonya ship carried tin-oxide in cake form (powdered by the sea) along with the ingots, for tempering the bronze. The tinkers' anvil was always with them, and they could make molds for the tools in beach sand, or carry standard gypsum molds which did not survive sea water. Some of the tools were broken before the ship sank, indicating a trade in scrap metal and junk as well as finished products. In larger-scale enterprises the ingots would go directly to, say, Mycenae or Pylos; a whole ingot and pieces broken off for small objects are known from Mycenae, and the ox-hide ingot ideogram in both bronze and silver appears on the Pylos tablets.

Distributed from the palace to the local smiths, returned for military and household use, calculated by weight before and after forging, this bronze was essential to all aspects of Mycenaean economy. It was the first thing to be looted or melted when the palaces fell. Sometimes weapons were stuffed in crevices for concealment during a crisis, and never reclaimed. The famous robber's hoard of Tiryns was also ultimately lost to its own greedy owner. It was found in the ruins of a house in the lower town, and contained objects made in several periods, from perhaps the Shaft Grave epoch to the early Dark Ages. Among them were the great gold ring depicting a goddess receiving daimons, many other rings and jewels, bronze vases and cauldrons, huge swords, iron sickles, a rod-tripod of Cypriote manufacture, a Near Eastern cylinder seal (Pl. XLVIII), amber from Europe—the man must have broken in on the eternal repose of everyone available, from the old princes of Tiryns to his own wealthier contemporaries. A Dark Age attack on Tiryns fittingly destroyed him and his house, leaving his treasure intact to give us a glimpse of how fiercely men desired precious metals as the Mycenaean world collapsed.

Chapter VIII

Physical aspects of Mycenaean life have been explored in the palace setting (chap. vi) and the arts of the palace age (chap. vii). It is more tenuous to reconstruct the relations of the palaces to society at large, to one another, and to the outer world. The character of such relations is uncertain, as most Aegean history is uncertain when considered in terms broader than chronology and craftsmanship. There are three principal sources of evidence for Mycenaean history and society in the "empire" period of the palaces: the Linear B documents, foreign records and foreign exchanges of goods, and Greek tradition. These help to highlight though not fully illuminate the structure of society at home, the activities of the Mycenaeans abroad, and the chief actors whom the Greeks partly remembered.

The palaces each controlled territory and trade across quite wide regions of Greece (Fig. 30). The Argolid, Attica, and Messenia have been more thoroughly mapped than other districts. Groupings of sites show that there was space for several walled towns in each county, but probably room for no more

232

Society and History
in the Mycenaean World

than one major system of political relationships. It is not yet clear how Mycenae, Tiryns, Argos, Midea, Berbati, Nauplion, Iria, Asine, Epidauros, and Lerna managed to coexist harmoniously in the relatively small Argolid, but archaeology shows they did, by alliance or by domination from Mycenae. Thebes, Orchomenos, and Gla faced a similar problem in Boiotia. In Attica, Athens and Eleusis, Marathon, Menidi, Thorikos, Spata, and Perati must have coordinated their power in some way, perhaps in an amphiktyonic league or in an inherited feudal hierarchy.

Each substantial town would have been controlled by a prince or baron who had immediate control over the peasants on his estates and over the free people, or *demos,* who also owned land in his district. Such smaller towns and villages supported the palace economically, carrying out a more or less independent routine from day to day but liable to sudden inspections and imposts

FIG. 40.—Aegean sites with Mycenaean trade pro

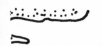

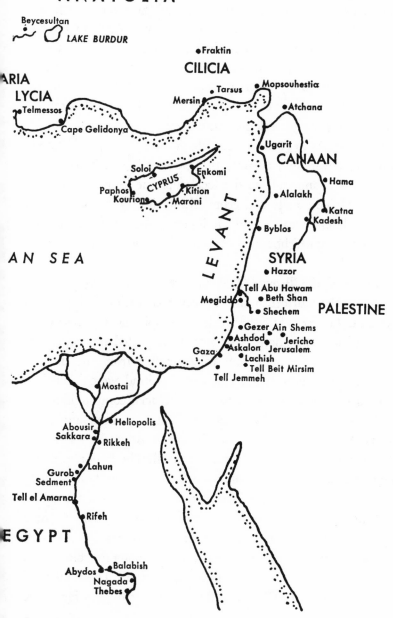

Boğazköy
(Hattušaš)

ANATOLIA

Beycesultan
LAKE BURDUR

•Fraktin
CILICIA
Mopsouhestia
ARIA   •Tarsus
LYCIA   Mersin   •Atchana
•Telmessos
Cape Gelidonya   Ugarit   CANAAN
                                  •Hama
        Soloi   Enkomi
              CYPRUS Kition   •Alalakh
Paphos•   Kourion Maroni   •Katna
                              Kadesh
                      •Byblos
AN SEA   SYRIA
        LEVANT   •Hazor
                      Tell Abu Hawam
                   Megiddo •Beth Shan   PALESTINE
                      •Shechem
                   •Gezer Ain Shems
                   •Ashdod   •Jericho
        Gaza   Askalon Jerusalem
                   •Lachish
              •Tell Beit Mirsim
        Tell Jemmeh

        •Mostai

Abousir •Heliopolis
Sakkara •Rikkeh

Gurob• •Lahun
Sedment
Tell el Amarna

•Rifeh
EGYPT

        •Balabish
Abydos•
Nagada
Thebes

cts or colonies, fourteenth to twelfth centuries B.C.

by officers of the central palace. Links to the center may have developed spontaneously in a half-conscious search for security and trade advantage, or may have depended more chancily on the character of the ruler in the central palace and the ambitions of the countryside barons.

The palace itself, as a physical structure, could not have been built unless the district had been organized successfully to enrich the town which was emerging as the central political force. There are so few palaces in Greece, and so many towns, and the palaces reached their height so late in the history of Bronze Age Greece, that the pattern of control which finally became established must have been fixed by a series of accidents. These accidents include: the natural advantages of the chosen palace site, such as good defensive position and good harbors; the genealogical and mental endowments of successive rulers; external threats to each district which forced internal harmony for the sake of military advantage; possibly the use of religious office to ensure the allegiance of the countryside to the local supreme king. The district would have been unstable politically and economically unless the palace kept a clear superiority in soldiers, wealth, and intelligent policy. Later myths record many skirmishes among neighbors which range from adventure to bloody catastrophe.

As in earlier periods of the Bronze Age, Greece was still composed of independent countries in the fourteenth and thirteenth centuries. It is doubtful whether late Mycenaean Greece was either really an empire, as we loosely use the term, or a string of local kingdoms who neither respected nor supported one another. While it would be dangerous to generalize from the difficult tablets at Pylos, at least they show that records of this kind were limited to a single thickly-settled territorial unit and to certain crucial commodities like land, metal, and flocks. So far the Pylos tablets do not mention any town beyond Messenia—no Mycenae or Tiryns, no Thebes or Athens; they do not seem to discuss Pylos' relations with other palaces at all. The major evidence for political homogeneity across Greece comes, in fact, from the homogeneity of Mycenaean art, and that can be explained in terms of common traditions, conservatism, traveling craftsmen, and motifs borrowed from field to field without needing any models from an artistic center like Mycenae. The richest town with the best work would naturally influence styles among neighbors, and across geographical barriers, as objects were diffused by trade. The pottery of Mycenae, which is by far the best in Greece, affected local potters as far as the west coast or Thessaly, but this is not to be confused with political sovereignty. It only means communications were open.

There are few persuasive arguments either for or against the empire concept: *for,* the stretches of built road uniting provincial towns, if not one province with another, and the legend that Agamemnon could collect all major cities under his authority to fight at Troy; *against,* the variety of protective walls, the fact that almost all palaces were burned without a sign of a foreigner in the land, and the poetic records of raids and full-scale wars, Greek against Greek (p. 269). It is likely that any general organization of Mycenaean power had no more stability than a classical alliance among city-states, that politics were personal and affected by bloodlines and trade convenience, and that it would be quite wrong to think of Greece as a political unity like the Hittite or Canaanite realms.

Since the Pylos records do not cover political or foreign events, their evidence for the history of the period is restricted. In combination with records of the Hittites and Egyptians, and with what may be deduced about trade and military skills in the Mycenaean world, they do supply some data for a tentative reconstruction of empire history.

Linear B and the Mycenaean Records

Writing in any civilization is important; for students of the highly verbal Greeks it was overwhelming to realize in 1953 that even their Bronze Age script could be read. In order to understand Linear B and make reasonable use of it for history it is necessary, however, to understand the limitations of its use in the Mycenaean world, and the limitations of what we can expect to extract from it.

Use was limited because the Mycenaeans learned as a people to write rather late in their historical life though individuals could perhaps write earlier. The script they used was not their own invention but an adaptation of a Cretan syllabic system that was awkward to compose and to remember and relied heavily on ideograms for intelligibility. The necessity for using it was felt strongest in the palaces whose needs a few trained persons could supply, so that while the new invention was extremely significant within the palace context it did not percolate very far among ordinary people. The situation was perhaps parallel to that in modern Africa, where a low 5 per cent literacy rate does not cripple internal power so much as relations abroad, and leaves most people locked inside a set of traditional social forms where myths and personal leadership are influential. Such forms are most easily broken from outside by political urgency or oral persuasion. In Greece, by a paradox, they were altered by the dissolution of the palace system which brought a complete loss of written legacy, but bred strong epic poetry which persuaded toward literacy later and preserved the memories if not the practices of the traditions. Before that happened, the Mycenaeans like the Minoans seem to have understood education in terms which had little to do with literacy and, more than their Mediterranean contemporaries, to have felt free from any need for a codified body of cult, law, or past history.[1]

Within this limited framework, Linear B helped the palace literates to handle a good range of commercial and social records. The decipherment, which was young Michael Ventris' extraordinary contribution to Greek studies, brought light to many archaeological specialties, but since his death it has been handled less lucidly and in conflicting styles by archaeologists and philologists. The results have been exciting and a little dangerous. A demonstration of how the decipherment works on specific tablets will be given below so that each reader may judge how much confidence he wishes to put in the evidence of the tablets. One is often tempted to trust this evidence too far, and yet no history of the palace age can be reconstructed without relying on some of it.

When the Greeks first realized that the Cretans could write, the Cretans had already developed Linear A, their second script but the first one to be widely used. Linear A and its reflections traveled to Greece first on the inscribed bronze cauldron of Shaft Grave IV (Fig. 6 *t*), then as an influence on the masons' marks of the Peristeria tholos façade (Pl. XVI B; Fig. 6 *v*). Neither of these examples is writing in any real sense, but simple marks analogous to those which had been scratched on pots in Greece since Neolithic times and which were used fluently on the sherds from the Lerna Shaft Graves (Fig. 6 *o–s*). The Cyclades and Cyprus also felt a fresh impulse toward making them during the sixteenth century. Pot marks, masons' marks, and isolated sign forms were thus minor by-products of Cretan influence abroad in the Early Mycenaean Age, and from this period dates the mainlanders' awareness of a gift which other civilizations had and they did not. They seemed not to grasp the implications until they were forced to supervise the administration of the wealth of Knossos in the fifteenth century, and not to transfer their knowledge to the mainland until they themselves passed into a phase of centralized palace economy after 1400 or 1300 B.C.

In the Early Mycenaean Age, Greek tradition says, Kadmos the Phoenician brought writing to Greece. Whatever truth lies behind this legend is lost to us now; it is not clear whether Linear A is meant, or Linear B, or some genuinely Near Eastern script, or whether priests in the sanctuaries at Thebes made up the story in the archaic period to glorify the antiquity and intellectual attainments of their city. Yet the House of Kadmos is so linked in history and myth to Bronze Age Canaan that one cannot dismiss the tradition thoughtlessly or ascribe it wholly to a later era. The inscribed cauldron from the Shaft Graves makes the famous cauldrons inscribed in Kadmeian letters at Thebes seem less impossible, although the ones Herodotos saw in the temple of Apollo were surely archaic reproductions and forgeries. The newly discovered Oriental cylinder seals in the palace at Thebes are another strong link with the literate East. The presence of certain Semitic words and names in the Pylos and Mycenae archives might have been reinforced through the presence of Easterners in central Greece as well as through direct trade with the Levant. Several myths about heroes who lived before the Trojan War use the theme of writing to assist their plots, and the range of materials (papyrus, bronze, wood, apples) may reflect the similar range abroad.[2] The palace at Thebes surely still holds tablets, perhaps even bilinguals, as well as the twenty-eight inscribed stirrup jars found in its storerooms (see Fig. 42 *d*); the wine jars that came from Canaan to Greece were also inscribed occasionally (Fig. 6 *u*), and there is no external reason to deny the possibility of mixed scripts and languages in Mycenaean towns. But as far as archaeology informs us, the frequent contacts of Greeks with merchants of Egypt and the Levant from 1500 on never convinced them of the value of a bill of lading or written receipt. There is no cuneiform in Greece, and hieroglyphs only on two or three souvenirs from foreign ports (Fig. 29 *f–g*). Unless their international business was transacted on papyrus, the Mycenaeans seem to have been stubbornly anti-script.

The circumstances surrounding the development of Linear B at Knossos in the fifteenth century have been briefly explored (p. 146). Oddly, Knossos shows no trace of bilinguals or practice texts. The script appears fully matured. Of course, tablets were not kept long, because their contents had no lasting significance, and the first efforts to develop Linear B from Linear A may easily have been discarded. It is also barely possible that the "invention" took place in some other town where Greeks and Minoans lived together, and was transferred to Knossos as a developed instrument. At least the few Greeks at Knossos understood what an advantage a script gave them in managing complex economic routines and dealing with other literate palace centers in the island. Per-haps they never used Linear A because, as empire-builders in the British style, they were incapable of learning any foreign language. Probably a fair number of invaders understood the tongue of Knossos, but the political realities must have been such as to make the foreign mainland language the master one, not the local language which could already be written. The staff of the palace would have needed both languages, since Linear A apparently continued to be used at other sites.

Linear B was used more intensively at Knossos than Linear A at any other site. The survivals may well be deceptive, yet Knossos has twenty times more Linear B than Hagia Triada has Linear A. It is limited in its uses, however, to tablets, labels, and sealings, and later on the mainland to a few inscriptions on oil jars, personal vases, and an occasional ring (Figs. 42, 46). Linear A, by contrast, is set on stuccoed walls with frescoes, drawn in ink on cups, used for storage and wine jars, statuettes, offerings in sanctuaries, rings, and articles of furniture or inlays. Linear B seems thus the product of a narrower literary impulse. One should probably not expect extensive unpragmatic texts in it; one should expect the texts to be more or less "contaminated" by Minoan names and technical language.

Linear A offers several problems in relation to Linear B beyond its present undeciphered state. It is not entirely consistent within itself as a script; north-ern Crete including Knossos seems to have favored slightly different forms of signs from southern Crete, where most of the documents survive. Comparing the Hagia Triada Linear A tablets to the Knossos Linear B tablets one sees that nearly half the Linear A signs have been discarded and replaced by new forms in the younger script; the change at Knossos itself might not have been quite so profound. Apparently the change does not simply mean that Greeks could not pronounce certain Cretan sounds, for the new signs are spread up and down the syllabic grid. One simple explanation might be that whoever invented Linear B did so outside of Crete, working from some limited quantity of Linear A, say a diplomatic letter or an invoice for one shipment, or even a song. This bilingual genius could then have used all the Linear A signs he had for the closest sound in Greek, and made up new signs for the sounds not represented in his text. But the actual process of creating the Linear B script will remain a mystery until the discovery of a text earlier than any now preserved. Another problem not yet solved is the chronological relation of the two scripts, that is, how long Linear A continued in use on Crete after the introduction of Linear B.

Linear A was quite new in the second age of palaces in Crete, after about 1600 B.C., and became most common following the widespread destructions by earthquake in the sixteenth century (p. 140). In contrast to the sparse but beautifully drawn hieroglyphs of the earlier palaces it is messy but efficient and records really large quantities of cattle, grain, vessels, and other items appropriate to a prosperous agricultural economy (Fig. 41 *a*). It is oldest and most abundant in the south, where one can watch it being developed from the hieroglyphic system at Phaistos, well before the earthquake horizon, in conjunction with sealings from farm produce delivered by neighboring landowners. Each palace center using it writes it in a slightly different style, yet it is uniform enough to picture a very homogeneous Crete in the rich phase Middle Minoan III B–LM I A. According to the excavators of several sites at which it occurs, the Cretans continue to use Linear A through most of the period in which Knossos shifted to Linear B, and in some cases it is possible to note an influence from Linear B upon it. If the suggested chronological revision for Knossos put forward above has any truth in it (p. 145), the bustling image of island economy reflected in the Knossos tablets need not be at odds with other palaces also controlling their daily bread in their own language. When they do business with Knossos, no Linear B receipts are sent to them, and conversely Linear A is not stored in the Knossos archives. However, this is no proof that the scripts are successive rather than overlapping. Quantities of goods enter Linear B Knossos from known Linear A sites:

KN C 59.3b

| TURISO | wekata | BULL | 6 | KUDONIJA | wekata | BULL | 50 |
| Tylissos | working | oxen | 6 | Kydonia | working | oxen | 50 |

Since records of this sort would not be kept on file indefinitely one must either imagine that Linear A Tylissos still existed shortly before Knossos fell (cf. Fig. 41 *a*), or that all the place names in the Knossos tablets refer to farm regions whose traditional centers lay in ruins. The first alternative seems more sensible.

The Linear B tablets at Knossos are written in sketchy archaic Greek with few stretches of continuous sentences. There are many names of people who are not Greek and some who are, many names of towns and villages in the island of which a relatively small proportion can be identified, and peculiar adjectives which may derive from Minoan technical vocabulary. They seem generally more formulaic and terse than the Pylos tablets, though some tablets are wordy, and they are less quoted than mainland tablets, except for the chariot and

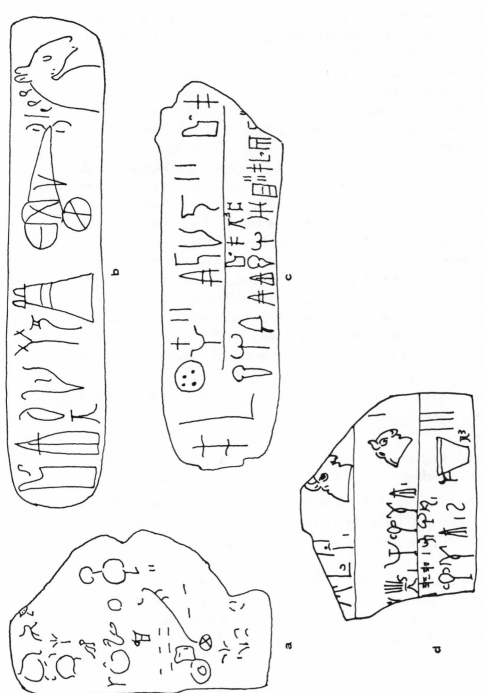

FIG. 41.—Tablets from Crete: (a) Linear A tablet, Tylissos, showing a four-wheeled wagon (after Evans, *PM* IV, Fig. 769); (b) Linear B tablet, Knossos Sc 230, recording the issue of a cuirass, chariot, and horses (after Evans, *PM* IV, Fig. 763 *a*); (c) Linear B tablet, Knossos S 8100, recording the issue of a set of armor (after Chadwick, *BSA* 1957, 147 and Pl. 27); (d) Linear B tablet, Knossos K 872, listing gold cups and bull's-head rhyta (after Evans, *PM* II, Fig. 336, slightly altered).

weapon texts (Fig. 41). When ideograms and numbers explain the meaning, they give a rich impression:

Co 903

> WATO akoraja RAM 60 EWE 270 HE-GOAT 49
> SHE-GOAT 130 BOAR 17 SOW 41 BULL 2 COW 4

Wato is an unidentified place. *Akoraja* represents Greek *agoraios*, "belonging to the herd"; the rest luckily elucidates itself. In other cases even a combination of Greek vocabulary and self-evident ideograms cannot enlighten us much, as in a text about treasures in the palace storeroom (Fig. 41 *d*):

KN K 872

>]keraa   BULL PROTOME
>]meno neqasapi   BULL PROTOME 1
>]pitete kuruso
> ne?]qasapi   WE DRINKING CUP + WO 3

This is clearly part of a list of luxury objects stored in the palace, the kind of golden cups and bull's-head rhyta most familiar from fifteenth-century Knossos and the pictured Keftiu of Tuthmosis III frescoes (p. 148; Figs. 28–29) and still available to Greek connoisseurs. *Keraa* are horns, *kuruso* is gold (κέρας, χρυσός), but the other words and the abbreviations remain mysterious: technical terms for how these precious objects were made or decorated.

It cannot be accident that the most "Greek" stretches of the Knossos tablets concern things the Greeks brought to Knossos or exploited there: chariots and horses, weapons and armor, divinities fitted into a Minoan framework of ceremony (p. 293). One receives the impression that the Greek community used its power well to control the flow of business, but did not interfere deeply in the daily life of Knossos or try to change it much: rather, Minoan traditions affected the Greeks in every field but warfare and language. A most interesting tablet, probably from the Little Palace where the Greek military administration at Knossos may have centered, records the issue of bronze armor like that so happily discovered in the contemporary warrior's grave at Dendra (Pl. XXI A–B; p. 135). It reads (Fig. 41 *c*):

KN S 8100

> qero$_2$ 2 epomijo 2 opa[wota ×
> PARA
> koru HELMET   o[pawo]ta
>   epikoru[si]ja   4 parawa[jo 2

(Issued to) Para (Pallans?) 2 *guala* (= 1 cuirass), 2 shoulder guards, *metal plates* (no number preserved), 1 helmet, 4 metal plates for the helmet, 2 cheekpieces.

Guala, as we have seen, are the front and back sections of a cuirass thonged at the sides, with shoulder guards attached at a vulnerable point: an archaic kind of armor which survived in epic poetry as an heirloom (p. 136). A bronze helmet was found in the Warrior Graves near Knossos; Para is being fitted out with the best and most modern war gear. Another tablet (Fig. 41 *b*) records the issue of a cuirass, a chariot, and a pair of horses (the number is broken away), equipment which apparently belonged to the palace rather than to individuals and was given out for special war maneuvers. The tablets supplement enormously the kind of knowledge provided by straight excavation, and in spite of their difficulties create a picture of an extensive warrior aristocracy settled prosperously in an old Cretan royal town, defending its interests, drawing on the agricultural wealth of the whole island, encouraging the manufacture of oil and textiles for export, and enjoying Minoan luxuries of craftsmanship and culture.

In the Pylos texts of the late thirteenth century the proportion of intelligible Greek seems to increase. Many words and personal names still cannot be turned to Greek, partly because of our imperfect understanding and the archaic nature of the dialect, partly because they were un-Greek in origin, borrowed vocabulary and local native dialects or personnel. The tablets do provide a more organic view of palace operations than at Knossos. There are four steps in extracting sense from them: reading the signs accurately (not always easy; see Pl. XLVI); equating them with the agreed-on syllabic sounds; translating the sounds into Greek; and translating the Greek to a reasonable meaning in any other language. The first and third steps are hardest, for Ventris did the second, and the fourth is primarily a convenience.

Two Tablets from Pylos

A closer look at two connected Pylos tablets shows how the system works, and how simultaneously illuminating and frustrating it can be (Pl. XLVI).[3] The scribe wrote these two "page" tablets shortly before the palace was destroyed. With the logic of Holmes, Professor Bennett has traced how, when the scribe faced the job of describing a distribution of land(?) to certain important army officers and others, he ruled twenty lines on his first tablet and mentally cast his text into four distinct paragraphs. After the first two lines he realized his nineteen spaces were not enough, erased and reruled the bottom of his tablet for three extra, still could not fit everything in, started a second tablet with more confidence, miscounted only once and squeezed in an extra space, finished the text, dried the tablets in the sun, clapped the faces together, tied them with string, scribbled on the back of the top one what it was all about, and put them on the right-hand end of the lower shelf above the clay bench on the short wall of the archives room (Pl. XXII A, lower left). When the palace was burned and looted these shelves fell, or were pulled, outward, the two tablets slid onto the bench below, and were smashed by a wicker basket full of ration tablets falling from the shelf above. Shelf, string, and scribe disappeared at about the same time, but the tablets have been put back nearly completely from more than twenty fragments, understandably mutilated, but of great interest.

This pair of tablets is representative of most Pylos texts. It is highly formulaic and repetitive. A large proportion of the text is made up of personal names and place names which can sometimes be wrenched into Greek, sometimes not. Almost all the other words have been challenged as meaningless or linguistically feeble. It is hard to extract neat sense from the whole, and in this it is also typical, for most Pylos texts are no easier, no more certain. It took several years even to realize that the two belonged together, for the ideogram on Sn 64 was ZE, usually short for *zeugos,* a pair or yoke of animals, and the ideogram on An 218 was first MAN, then ZE.[4] Only when the handwriting, shape, and breaks of the two were observed to match, could Bennett piece together their history, and Ruipérez outline the translation presented here. Even so it is not clear whether the subject is really a charter of land or a list of priests and soldiers in some other context.

A land charter has seemed likely because the ZE is often followed by a fraction—three, six, or twelve—which would make one uneasy if the subject were yokes of animals. The yoke in this case may be equivalent to Latin *iugerum* and of similar derivation: the quantity of land a yoke of oxen could plow in a day. This may be roughly equivalent to a classical *plethron,* or about ten thousand square feet. The average size of a farmstead near Pylos would be about the same, though settled and cultivated land is usually measured in terms of wheat, 82 to 108 litres the lot.

The text does not say where the land is, nor why it should be allotted this way. One supposes it is new land for Pylos, since responsible officials are to draw the boundary lines. It may have lain in the hilly frontier border east of the Messenian Gulf toward Lakonia. The label on the two tablets speaks of

], [—], letters missing; { }, extra word written by scribe; p̣i̤, dots indicate uncertain reading; *man,* italic type indicates uncertain meaning; ( ), supplement to translation, guesswork; *, restored form, not known in classical Greek.

An 218

𐀆 𐀴 𐀡 𐀐 𐀍 𐀐 𐀀 𐀆 𐀦 𐀵𐀄 [

odaa₂ anakee operote

ὡς δ' ἀρ ἀναγέεν ὀφέιλοντες

Now: *to draw boundary lines,* those responsible

𐀭 𐀪 𐀨 𐀐 𐀍 𐀄 𐀲.[𐀠𐀠] 𐀕 1

risowa ijereu [pịja?   MAN 1

'Ρισοϝας ἱερεὺς [Φιας

Risowa priest [from. *Phia?*   MAN 1

𐀺 𐀨 𐀦 𐀵. 𐀐 𐀍 [𐀄]𐀴. 𐀴 𐀐 𐀔 𐀐 𐀐 𐀨   𐀕 1

newokito ije[re]u daijakereu   MAN 1

Νεϝοχιτων ⎱ ἱερεὺς δαϊαγρεύς
Νεϝοκιστος ⎰

Neochiton ⎱ priest *land-divider?* ⎱   MAN 1
Neokistos ⎰ (from) *Daiakereus?* ⎰

𐀴] 𐀨 𐀦 𐀪 𐀄 𐀐 𐀔 𐀐 𐀵. 𐀔𐀦 [𐀦   𐀕 1

ro]uko kusamenijo metapa   MAN 1

Λο]υκος Κυσαμενιος Μεταπας

Lo]ukos Kysamenios (from) Metapa   MAN 1

𐀴 𐀀 𐀭 𐀫 𐀦 [———] 𐀆 𐀞 𐀵 𐀼   𐀕 1

aeriqota [—] owitono   MAN 1

Ἀέριφοιτας [——] Οϝιτονου

Aeriphoitas [—] (from) Owitono   MAN 1

246

⊼ ⵀ[ꞁ ꜱ ꞁ ꞁꞁ [- - - -]   ⵖ ˙

aikota adara [MAN 1

(*Greek uncertain*)

Aikota adara   MAN 1

vacant 2

ⵀ ꞁ ⵜ ꞁ A ⵂ ꜱ ꞁ ⵜ ⵖ ꞁ ⵥ₂

odaa₂ ekejoto akotono

ὡς δ' ἀρ ἐγκείοντοι ἄκτοινοι

Now: settling on (the land) without owning land-portions

⵼ ⵀ ꞁ ⵂ A ꜱ   ꞁ ˙

pakuro₂ dewijo   ZE 1

Παχυλος ΔεϜιο

Pachylos Dewios' (*man*)   LAND 1

] ⊕ Ψ Ϝ ꞁ A ⵖ ⵜ ⵜ [ⵀ ꞁ ⌀ ⵗ   ꞁ ˙

]kareu ekomenatao *34*-te   ZE 1

]καρευς 'Ερχομεναταο (or-ταων)

]kareus *Erchomenates' 34*-te   ⎱ LAND 1
    the *34*-te of (the men from) *Orchomenos* ⎰

] ⵂ ⵖ ꜱ   ꞁ ˙

]no kekijo   ZE 1

(*Greek uncertain*)

]no *Kekijo's* (*man*)   LAND 1

]meta porudasijo   ZE 1

(*Greek uncertain*)

]meta *Porudasijo's* (*man*)   LAND 1

]menua₂   ZE 1

]Μεννας

]*Menyas'* (*man*)   LAND 1

marateu apuka   ZE 1

μαραθευς ———

(the) *maratheus' apuka* }
Maratheus (from) *apuka* }   LAND 1

]qotewo i*ju*   ZE 1

]ποτηος υιυς

]*poteus' son* , LAND 1

Sn 64

qasi]rewijote

Βασι]λεύοντες

in their capacity as military chiefs

248

]ja moroqa toto weto oakerese   ZE 1 *fraction* 3

——— *μοιροκκ^was τοῦτο Ϝέτος ὁ ἀγρήσει

]a the portion-holder this year *what he may choose*   LAND 1 *fraction* 3

kadowo moroqa ouqe akerese   ZE 1

——— *μοιροκκ^was οὔτε ἀγρήσει

Kadowos the portion-holder *but he may not choose*   LAND 1

ruro moroqa ouqe akerese   ZE 1

Λυρος μοιροκκ^was οὔτε ἀγρήσει

Lyros the portion-holder *but he may not choose*   LAND 1

kurumeno moroqa iterewa korete toto weto [o]akerese   *fraction* 6

Κλύμενος *μοιροκκ^was ΙτερεϜas *κοιρητηρ τοῦτο Ϝέτος ὁ ἀγρήσει

Klymenos the portion-holder the *marshal* at Iterewa this year *what he may
  choose*   *fraction* 6

perimo timitija korete toto weto [o]akerese   ZE 1 *fraction* 3

Φεριμος Θεμιστιας *κοιρητηρ τοῦτο Ϝέτος ὁ ἀγρήσει

Pherimos the *marshal* at *Themistia* this year *what he may choose*
                                        LAND 1 *fraction* 3

perimedeo i*ju* posorijono teranija {akerese} toto weto oakerese   *fraction* 12

Περιμηδηος υἱύς ——— ——— {ἀγρήσει} τοῦτο Ϝέτος ὁ ἀγρήσει

Perimedes' *son teranija at Posorijono* { *may choose* } this year *what he may choose*
                                                                        fraction 12

pokiroqo eqeo atomo   ZE 1

Ποικιλοψς ——— ———

Poikilops *eqeo atomo*   LAND 1

                                                        vacant 3

odaa₂ kotona ekote

ὡς δ'ἀρ κτοίνανς ἔχοντες

Now: land-portions possessing

etawoneu totoweto oakerese   ZE 1   *fraction* 6

Εταϝονευς τοῦτο Ϝέτος ὁ ἀγρήσει

Etaoneus this year *what he may choose*   LAND 1   *fraction* 6

250

〚symbols〛

aqizowe {toto} totoweto oakerese   ZE 1

——— {τοῦτο} τοῦτο Ϝέτος ὁ ἀγρήσει

Aqizoes {this} this year *what he may choose*   LAND 1 [

〚symbols〛

neqeu etewokereweijo totoweto oakerese   ZE 1 [

Νεφευς ἘτεϜοκλεϜειος τοῦτο Ϝέτος ὁ ἀγρήσει

Nepheus Eteokles' (*man*) this year *what he may choose*   LAND 1 [

〚symbols〛

mewi erutara metapa kiewo totoweto oakerese   ZE 1 [

ΜεϜις(?) Ἐρύθρας-Μεταπα Κιεως τοῦτο Ϝέτος ὁ ἀγρήσει

Mewi (from) *Erythras-near-Metapa Kieus'* (*man*) this year *what he may*
    choose   LAND 1 [

vacant 3

Label

〚symbols〛

diwesipou timitoqe[ro

——— θεμιστοπό [λοι

diwesipou boundary judges

251

boundary-drawers as *themistopoloi*, or agents of *themistes;* eventually Greek *themis*, *themistes*, came to mean justice or a traditional code of right practice, but it apparently originated in the notion of a mark or line fixing the proper limits of something.

At least two towns in the dominion of Pylos take their names from this root: *Themistia*, where Pherimos is marshal (6), and *Timito-akee*, the most distant town and naval station in the farther or eastern district of Pylos. The name might be translated "the mountain glen (*ankos*) on the border," some harbor backed by hills where the western spurs of Mount Taÿgetos run down to the Messenian Gulf. Perhaps the transaction takes place near here, in an encroachment on land more properly Lakonia's, one of many skirmishes in the late thirteenth century within the limits of the Mycenaean empire as well as abroad against foreigners.

Two priests and three military men are to see that the lines are fairly drawn. The three soldiers are known from other tablets as *hepetai*, or military attachés of important rank stationed in country districts of the dominion. The receivers of the land are then divided into several categories. Seven men get one ZE of land each but may not own it; they have no titles except of dependency, and perhaps a common sound may be detected in their names, such as Pachylos, "little fat boy." On the next tablet (or perhaps leading off the whole transaction if Sn 64 comes first) comes a more important group whose description is badly mutilated but restored by Bennett and Ruipérez as *basileuontes*, being *basileis*. *Basileis* are ostensibly kings in Homer, usually in a military context as the leaders of territorial units of soldiers; so Achilleus is *basileus* of the Myrmidons, and Odysseus of the men from the western islands. In the thirteenth century the title was scarcely royal, but applied to men who served as regimental officers, oversaw certain kinds of craftsmen, and had to deliver varying amounts of gold to the palace. The seven men in this group have other titles as well: four are possessors of *moirai*, or "allotments, portions," whether of land or honor; two are marshals of the army (*korete* seems an earlier variant of *koiranos*, a military lord in Homer); two have titles which so far defy translation (*eqeo atomo* and *teranija posorijono*). Their allotments are complex for no clear reason.

The last group consists of four men of middling importance who already own some land elsewhere. *Neqeu* stands in a familiar or feudal relationship to a very high ranking personage, Eteokles; the others had a more restricted acquaintance with the palace archivists.

The tablets are set forth here as they have been worked out by several eminent scholars. What kind of sense they make is a matter for personal evalua-
tion. Much depends on the verbs. Forms of six verbs appear in the two texts,
which is a high proportion and most welcome. But *basileuontes* is broken off
and tentative. *Akerese* is sometimes prefixed by *o,* sometimes not, and this
separable prefix causes a good deal of trouble; it may stand for an object, as
presented here, or an introductory "thus" (ὡς), or an exclamation, or "in
addition to." It has no counterpart in this position in classical Greek. The verb
itself should be a future third person singular of ἀγρέω "to take or seize," or
in the middle voice "to take for oneself, choose." But why are two men *not* to
choose, when their allotments have already been made? does the verb mean
something else? or is the plausible equation of *ouqe* with the familiar negative
οὔτε a wrong one? Three verb-forms of reasonable type can be caught in passing: *ekote* for ἔχοντες, "having"; *operote* for ὀφείλοντες, "owing or being responsible"; *ekejoto* for ἐγκείοντοι, "lying in or on," is impure in form though
plausible in meaning. *Anakee* for ἀνάγεεν, the infinitive of a verb which in an
extremely rare meaning in Aristotle is "to draw a line" as for a boundary, more
normally means to bring up (soldiers? tribute?), or to launch a ship or carry
freight by sea or several other normal actions which are only awkward here
because of the ZE with its fractions.

Of the nouns, some are untranslatable titles which did not survive the Dark
Ages; some are difficult because they contain rare signs, like *i-65* (*iju,* υἱὺς,
son?) or *34-te;* even the apparently simple phrase *toto weto,* "this year," has
phonological awkwardnesses according to those who know best. The names
are problematic too; *Aqizoe* and *Aikota* are hard to make Greek, and by later
rules *Mewi* might be a lady.

The details of these tablets have been set out with more fullness than might
seem appropriate for a survey of this kind, in the hopes that the dangers as well
as the fascinations of Linear B may become apparent to readers who have no
personal experience of it as a discipline. On the one side, a roster of social classes
with eminent and deserving men known by name, the priests charged to over-
see the proprieties and technical details, the accented role of the military leaders
and the beneficent despotism of the palace center, the glimpses into landholding and land-measuring systems, the historical interest of new land being acquired by Pylos in the year before she fell; on the other side, thoroughly deceptive ideograms, a series of difficult verbs, untranslatable titles, names which

253

cannot be pressed into Greek, underlying peculiarities of both the allotments and of the terms on which they are made. It is scarcely surprising that popular accounts of Linear B make the most of the former set, and technical journals explore the latter. The social history in the tablets cannot be taken at face value without the philological scrutiny of many experts and their partial agreement, which is not yet available for the bulk of the tablets. One is tempted to state flatly that Linear B ought not to be popularized just now. From many points of view the student who knows nothing specific is better off than the one who speaks too glibly of Aigeus the Cretan or the Rowers going to Pleuron, and from these shadowy characters constructs massive pictures of trade with Crete and of the Dorian invasion. In a real sense Linear B is less well known than Etruscan which nobody claims to translate confidently.

Merchants, Soldiers, Kings

From the palaces and the tablets many figures have emerged in special roles, dragging titles after them like last names. There have been kings, craftsmen, priests, army officers, local officials, landholders, ladies, huntsmen, servants, and peasants. Of all these roles one would single out as basically important to the Mycenaean empire those of the people who trade abroad, the people who fight, and the political leaders who direct them. Traders are especially vivid abroad (Fig. 40), since it is hard to be sure about trade between similar Mycenaean cities at home from similar remains. Soldiers had been the core of Mycenaean power from the Shaft Graves onward, at first represented by individual aristocrats, then apparently by an elite corps at the time of the fall of Knossos, and now in the thirteenth century organized into units of common men trained to fight on foot with horse-taming officers to lead them. Kings we know practically nothing about except as the tablets record their privileges and Greek poetry records their names.

Mycenaean ship captains and merchants overseas have appeared several times in this survey already. In the Early Mycenaean Age they sailed to Lipari and southern Italy in the west, to Troy and Syria in the east, to Egypt and Palestine in the south (cf. Fig. 22). These trade connections were strengthened during the Greek period in Crete, and accelerated with the Mycenaean acquisition of many former Minoan colonies or trading harbors near the time of the fall of Knossos (p. 152). Most of the Mycenaean pottery found in foreign cities belongs to the full empire period, the III B pottery of the thirteenth century.

The map (Fig. 40) shows the major sites where such evidence for Mycenaean trade is preserved, and makes it clear that Greek contacts were limited to coastal emporia and a few major river routes. It is rare to find a Mycenaean object far inland; where this happens, as at Fraktin or the Lake Burdur region in Anatolia, the vase is usually a stirrup jar or oil container which may have passed up the caravan routes through several hands, valued both for the fine oil and for the ingenious container. Even where colonies of Mycenaeans were more or less permanently settled in the east, as on Cyprus or Rhodes, at Miletos or Ugarit, their trade does not generally seem to penetrate more than a decent distance beyond Levantine and Anatolian beachheads.

Some of the materials the Mycenaeans desired as a return on their exports were brought to the shore from considerable distances; important items of this kind would be Anatolian or Caucasian tin and Syrian ivory, exchanged in harbor colonies like the rich one at Ugarit. Here in the capital city of Canaan the records cast light on the activities of a mixed colony of merchants speaking many languages. There were men from the Didyma-Miletos region of Asia Minor, Ionians from Caria, Cypriotes from Alasia, and Cretans or Mycenaeans in the days of the fall of Knossos. Ugaritic merchants ask permission to import manufactures from Crete duty free, and great jars of Canaanite wine begin to turn up at many sites in Greece (cf. Fig. 6 *u*). Other foreign stations must have been equally bustling and mixed. The ship that foundered off Cape Gelidonya (p. 229) is a mute witness to the profits and the dangers of trade in days when coastal waters must have been crowded with rival craft. It also suggests that most of the cargoes were raw material for manufacture back on the mainland, and indeed the palace age in Greece exhibits a striking imbalance between Mycenaean exports and visible imports.

Outgoing cargoes were primarily the technically excellent Mycenaean pots, mostly storage jars or stirrup jars for exporting oil. Enclaves of Mycenaeans who had settled overseas could turn out more fragile shapes like drinking cups or flasks for local trade, and shippers might also pack painted kraters or cups for the luxury market. Other regular exports included forged bronze weapons, especially swords and daggers, and sometimes live smiths to make them abroad. Although the civilizations of the east and south had their own long-standing traditions in weaponry, the Mycenaeans had reached a high enough standard of technology to make their work appreciated by overseas connoisseurs. Other exports are archaeologically untraceable but probable: Greek wine, textiles, timber, and perhaps mercenary soldiers. In return there came bronze, tin, and

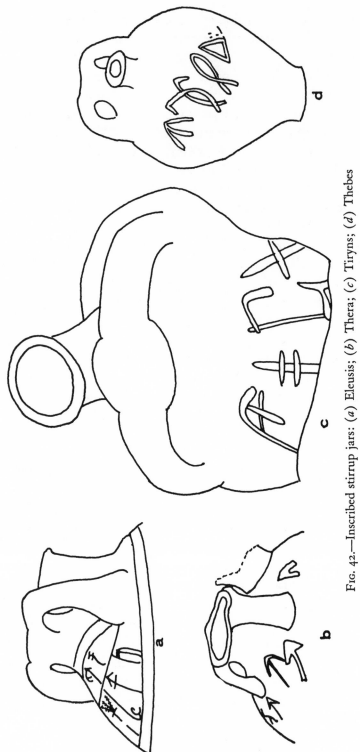

Fig. 42.—Inscribed stirrup jars: (*a*) Eleusis; (*b*) Thera; (*c*) Tiryns; (*d*) Thebes

wine from Canaan; women, bronze from the Cypriote mines; silver and perhaps horses and textiles from Troy; ivory, spices, and murex-dyed cloth from the Canaan-Palestine coast; a little faïence, alabaster, and gold either directly from Egypt (where Greeks were living at Tell el Amarna and Gurob) or from Egypt's Levantine outlets. Trade toward the west was more abundant than in the fifteenth century, as the pottery remains suggest, but the ships brought back much less amber and only a little liparite. Tuscan metals may have played some attractive role but less than metals from the east.

Apart from metal, these foreign imports are luxuries destined for royal or temple treasures, according to the tablets, or for the graves of the wealthy. They are not the kind of thing an economy lives on. It is not easy to assess how vital merchant traffic was to the Mycenaean standard of living, but the quantity of vases abroad and the lack of finished imports at home is guarantee enough of ships constantly passing across the Aegean. One wonders whether the main import was not in fact some perishable kind of produce like grain.

The population of Greece was more dense during the thirteenth century than it would be again until the fifth. Recorded settlements exceed thirty in Attica, sixty in Lakonia, ninety in Messenia-Triphylia; almost every rise of ground in the Argolid was occupied. The Pylos texts indicate such a heavy proportion of skilled labor not engaged in farming, plentiful meat and oil but fewer cereal staples than one would expect, that one wonders how major palace areas could have been fed without supplies being brought in from elsewhere. Land was rich enough in districts around Mycenae, Thebes, and Pylos, and farm tools like spades and adzes are well attested, but not plows or yokes of draft oxen. Whenever Greece is overpopulated it reacts in two ways: emigration rises, and food is imported. Mycenaean emigration is proven for the palace age, in several waves to places like Enkomi, and increases in the "refugee" period after the Sea Peoples' destructions of the late thirteenth century (p. 270), and it is possible that the shrinking within itself experienced by Greece after the burning of the palaces could have been partly because overseas grain markets were cut off in the general disruption, and a double threat of conquest and starvation crippled enterprise. If this is true, the Mycenaean merchants kept the mainland alive as well as in touch with other civilizations.[5] They are an anonymous, adventurous, essential element in empire society, whose lives will not be completely illuminated until some Mycenaean harbor installation is discovered and excavated.

A little can be learned about the merchants from remains of wrecks (p. 229) and from representations of their ships. The ships of the Mycenaean world are almost as various in design as weapons, and every representation of them by Greeks has elements of fantasy or clumsiness. In contrast to their Cycladic predecessors most Late Bronze ships are equipped with sails and mast, and have a capacious storage deck (Fig. 43; Pl. XXXII A). They are primarily cargo ships, not warships. Oars and rudder are regularly pictured but the sailing crew usually ignored, although there are hints in the Pylos texts that rowing was an established profession. A stirrup jar from the island of Skyros (Fig. 43 *f*) illustrates late Mycenaean craft well, though this one is unique for its bird figurehead, which matches some Philistine ships in the Sea Peoples' era. Curiously, most shipping pictures were painted in the latest historical period, after the fall of the palaces, and assure us that the Mycenaean sailors still traveled and traded with courage in spite of the Sea Peoples' disturbance (p. 273). They helped create the paradoxically lively existence of Late Helladic III C which is so marked by the exchange of foreign souvenirs in the Levant and Greek coastal towns like Perati, Tiryns, Tragana, or Asine (cf. Pl. XLVIII). Wine from Canaan, seals from north Syria, iron from the Hittite caravans, terracottas from Crete, ivory and faïence and gold are still brought back to Greece in the early twelfth century to counteract a lower standard of architecture. When such souvenirs are found in graves, as at Perati or Ialysos (p. 302), they may be personal possessions of dead sailors. Often enough the sailors were drowned or lost their ships, as in the Cape Gelidonya wreck, and once or twice a stone stele was set up with a crude doodle of a ship, one of which has been considered the memorial for a sailor who never came home (Fig. 43 *c*).[6]

The Mycenaean soldier is a more vivid figure. From the end of the Middle Bronze Age, militarism was so congenial to the mainland temperament that both its aesthetics and its technology focused on the trained soldier with his equipment, and this is also the aspect of the Mycenaean world most striking to outsiders in their rare comments about Achaians. Little more need be said about a soldier's outfit at the beginning of the empire period than the Dendra Cuirass Tomb has already taught (Pl. XXI A), except that there was less uniformity about helmets and attack weapons than in comparable cultures like the Hittite or the Egyptian. Mycenaeans absorbed very readily any improvements in armaments that they noticed abroad; odd daggers from Sicily or swords from Canaan caught their fancy and they continued to fight and to be buried with pieces they captured. This variety is to a certain extent ironed out in the traditions of

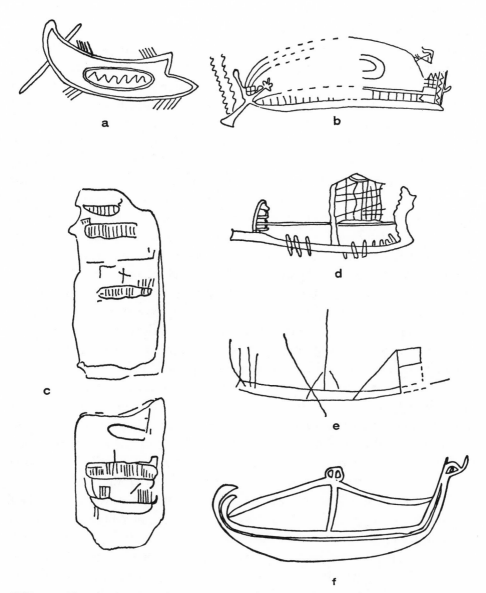

FIG. 43.—Ships in the Aegean: (*a*) Middle Helladic, on a sherd, Iolkos (after Theochares, *Archaeology* 1958, 15); (*b*) Late Helladic III C, on a sherd, Tragana tholos (after Kourouniotes, *Ephemeris* 1914, 108); (*c*) Late Helladic I(?), on a stone stele, Hyria (Dramesi) (after Blegen, *Hesperia* Supplement 8, Pl. 7); (*d*) Late Helladic III C, on a stirrup jar, Asine (after Kirk, *BSA* 1949, 117, Fig. 5); (*e*) Late Cypriote III, on a stone stele, Enkomi (after Schaeffer, *Enkomi-Alasia,* Pl. 10); (*f*) Late Helladic III C, on a stirrup jar, Skyros (courtesy the late H. Hansen).

frescoes and vase painting but is clear enough in tombs, particularly from the time of the fall of Knossos onward.[7]

There were several categories of soldiering in the empire period. At home, ordinary infantrymen were organized in squads assigned to a high-born officer, equipped with rations for special marches and assigned to certain strongpoints along the roads. This information comes from the so-called Home-Guard (An) tablets at Pylos which cannot really be read since they are mostly names of men and places, but they harmonize with the evidence from roads and fortified outposts. Such men wore padded linen cuirasses and leggings, probably leather helmets strengthened with metal strips, and fought with the sword, the battle knife, and the spear (cf. Fig. 34). Certain groups were trained in archery; others may have continued the barbaric art of the antique sling which later Greeks knew as a specialty among Cretans and the Lokrian tribes north of the Corinthian Gulf. Officers wore more elaborate versions of the same armor, including the boar's-tusk or bronze helmet with horns and plumes (Pls. XXXIX B, XXXII A, XXXIII B), cuirasses of bronze plates, occasionally bronze greaves and ankle guards (Pl. XXI C). Their defensive armor continued to be the figure-of-eight shield and their attack was particularly with the long sword and the *paraxiphis* or medium dagger, one in each hand, and the long spear used also against stag and boar. Concessions to modernism almost escape the artists, who showed these warriors in traditional costume, but on a few pieces a new high boot in the Hittite style appears, and in the Pylos tablets the armor actually issued is more advanced than in the pictures. Officers are given corselets with several bronze plates and helmets with cheek pieces; swords, spear and arrowheads, and possibly axes are all listed, some made locally in the palace armory.[8] Battle rations were grain (wheat, barley, linseed), figs, and wine.

We cannot be sure how "professional" the army was; that depended on local circumstances. Aggressive kings overseas, like the king of Aḫḫiyawa who gave the Hittites such irritation in the late thirteenth century (p. 272), undoubtedly commanded a quite professional division of paid soldiers whose métier was campaigning in the exposed territories of the dissolving eastern empires. At home surely most soldiers were farmers and craftsmen in everyday life, called up in emergencies and made confident by the early training in familiar weapons which any Mycenaean boy would have received. Men who had no niche in palace society free-lanced for any convenient paymaster; this category would include escaped captives, natural rebels, murderers—those with a lust for cash rather than security. Many of these mercenaries took service with Hittites,

Libyans or Egyptians in the encouraging thirteenth-century conditions of the Sea Peoples' raids—both as individuals and as organized corps—and contributed to the diffusion of foreign trinkets and words which marks the latter years of the empire (p. 302; Pl. XLVIII).

At home supreme authority over the fighting forces was naturally vested in the *wanaka* or ϝάναξ, "the king," and in his military deputy, the *lawakete* or "leader of the (fighting) people." The regiment commanders and the *basileis* of provincial estates, who were given new land in the Pylos tablets just discussed, operated below them. Only the upper ranks of these men were trained to fight in chariots. Since the use of the horse and the expensive chariot squadron is particularly associated with aristocratic militarism in the Bronze Age—the power of the Mycenaean war machine is often felt to derive from Greek skill in the art—empire horsemanship deserves a closer look.

The chariots carved on the Shaft Grave stelai (Fig. 17) are almost the earliest Mediterranean representations of the new weapon.[9] Obviously the horse comes before the chariot, and he comes slowly from the north and east after 2000 B.C. Horse bones appear in Troy about 1800 B.C. and as far south as Buhen in the Sudan before 1675 B.C., preceding the high Hyksos period. The Hyksos bury their dead with horses as tribes in south Russia had even earlier; the Shaft Grave stelai connect horses with Mycenaean funerary rite too (p. 92). There are no Middle Helladic horses yet known in Greece (except one dubious mule), another argument for seeing the Shaft Grave era as the moment for fundamental innovations. The Hittites and Mitanni became experts about the same time. A few horses were probably taken to Crete by ship in the fifteenth century and there, with good grazing land, multiplied so well that the records at Knossos vastly exceed those at Pylos. Tylissos knew a four-wheeled wagon (Fig. 41 *a*). Cyprus had a few horses, and even a camel, by 1400 B.C. Once the animal was widely bred, the chariot also became standardized and was basically the same in all Aegean regions (Figs. 33 *c*; 41 *b*; Pl. XXXII). It was a light two-horse affair with a shallow leather or wicker body stretched over a bentwood frame, two large wheels, a flexible pole, and a simple inefficient yoke system attached over the horses' withers. This lightweight racing or fighting chariot was not sturdy enough to survive except in certain protected royal burials of Egypt, but the many pictures and models are valuable documents; Linear B and Homer add details.

After 1400 B.C., when the painted chariot kraters begin, the Mycenaean chariot grows large enough for three or four people although two is the normal complement (Pl. XXXII D; Hittites use three and outweigh Egyptians with only two. They are made at home in chariot workshops like the one in the east wing at Pylos, of hides with the hair still on them or of wicker plaits; these materials are reflected in the spotted or cross-stitched versions on vases. Knossos and Pylos do not need to import hardwoods for the frames as Egypt was forced to; we hear of nothing so exotic as the "wood . . . brought from the god's land of the highlands of Naharain" that Ken Amun records. The frame itself is of ash or elm or birch, the wheels of elm or willow or cypress bound in some harder material, thick leather or bronze or silver. A detachable tailpiece is added, perhaps to close up behind the riders, to give more foot space, or to carry a dead stag or enemy armor home after a lucky foray. All the wooden parts might be inlaid with ivory or painted crimson; the ladies from Tiryns drive out in a crimson one with white trim, yellow wheels (bronze?) with blue tires (silver?), a white pole wrapped round with black thongs, and red leather reins (Fig. 33 c). These colors turned up in the harness tablet already tentatively translated (p. 178); the famous Knossos chariot tablets had the same scheme:

KN Sd 0413

      IQI]JA paito araromotemena dowejo iqoeqe poniki[CHARIOT
      araru]-ja anijapi wirinijo opoqo kerajapi opiijapi

    A chariot from Phaistos, all put together, with a wooden pole, painted crimson, outfitted with harness, leather cheek pieces, bits made of horn.

The gaiety persists in epic poetry where chariots are inlaid with bronze, gold, and tin, even (for the gods) made of "wicker" in gold and silver, the reins of crimson leather, ivory ornaments on the bridle. At Pylos the horses and chariots themselves are very rare, though it is horsy country now. Probably this lack is accidental, since the wheels for transport are recorded in number, even old thin pairs worn out by the road surfaces, bumpy then and excruciating now. Counting the surviving tablets one reaches a total of 25 ready and 200 incomplete chariots at Knossos, no chariots but 146 pairs of wheels and (2?) horses at Pylos.

    Chariot-makers were nervous enough about the harness rig (there is no gear to keep the team close up to the pole and they could sidle away at will) to provide a double pole. The main one sprang from the axle, a pole-support from the front rim, meeting at the yoke. The strain on the horse is mainly taken by a collar across his windpipe with sometimes a chest girth to distribute the pressure. It is not clear how well the bridle controlled the team: it is made like a halter with a nose band to pinch and guide. Curiously, only one metal horse bit has ever been found in Greece, at Mycenae itself (and two overseas at Miletos where Greeks learned some horsemanship from the Hittites); most bits must have been thong or horn, or else they were not much used. The Mycenae bit has spikes inside the cheek pieces to press sharply on the sensitive lips if the horse got fractious.[10]

Once the machine became mass produced the great Eastern chariot-nations developed techniques for using it in formation, difficult but formidable when it worked, and demanding a whole background of horse trainers, stables and paddocks, constant practice, good roads or level open country, and the kind of light armor and throwing or shooting weapons which would give the driver maximum maneuverability and protection. Greece never got quite so good as plains countries like Anatolia, Syria, or Egypt; the ground simply is not clear enough for formation driving.

To a certain extent this limitation was offset in the empire period by a network of fairly decent roads. The roads from Mycenae toward Tiryns and Asine, and north toward Corinth, have been traced and studied; the Pylos-Messenia roads are now under scrutiny, and there are other good systems in Boiotia and southern Thessaly. They average under 2.0 m. wide but some are as broad as 3.50 m. so that two chariots or wagons could pass without Oidipos' complications. The surfaces are usually dirt, packed hard, and retained by lines of boulders; they are even stone-paved close to cities so that one can still trace the wheel ruts through the Lion Gate or see the place outside Athens' gates where the animals had to be stationed. There are bridges and stone culverts to keep the roads open during flood times; on the whole Greece would not have such a good system again until the Hellenistic Age. Yet even on the roads the jouncing must have taken great practice to counteract, especially since one rode only 0.50 meters (twenty inches) off the ground on a platform of leather straps, and anyone leaving the road for the rock and thorn hills would have been liable for a spill within ten yards. The idea of fighting five or ten chariots abreast as a regular practice on the mainland seems like military daydreaming. This may account for the rather independent behavior of charioteers when the epic watches them at Troy. Riding was scarcely practiced as a military art at all, except to carry messages between units or get teams whose chariots had cracked up away to safety. Two or three times the artists draw or model men on horseback whose seat seems unpracticed and precarious.

Walls and Politics

With such military forces to dispose of, and a fleet of ships partly mercantile and partly military, kings of mainland sites could protect themselves, raid neighbors, or occasionally join in larger expeditions like the Seven against Thebes or the War at Troy. At most east coast sites the thought of protection seems uppermost. It is difficult now to imagine what dangers so threatened Greece during the empire that she created the massive Cyclopean defense walls which later Greeks imagined must have been built by giants. Mycenae, Tiryns, and Athens offer a three-faceted image of a defensive posture so monumental one would believe the whole mainland in a state of siege; yet while the walls were being built, ships were trading perfectly peacefully overseas, and Mycenaeans were mixing with foreigners or living among them free from apparent strain.

The major Cyclopean walls of the Mycenaean mainland are late. Some of them are built along the lines of older walls marking the citadel limits, or increase the territory on which the city core was built. The prime examples are Mycenae (Pl. XXIV A) and Tiryns, whose walls grow more massive and sophisticated with each later design, and are swung far outside the original palace plateau to protect outlying houses of commoners after 1250 B.C. Their deep guarded entries, posterns, and arched hollows or galleries in the thickness of the stone or against the inner face of a boulder wall are illustrations of experienced military architecture. Some features, like gate and tower construction, were thinly foreshadowed by the old walls of the third millennium, but others, like secret sally ports or battered inclines or rock-dug cisterns, seem to be borrowed from traveler's reports of such great Anatolian fortresses as Boğazköy. A simpler effort is represented by the wall at the Isthmos of Corinth which runs north–south behind the eastern harbor, apparently defending farmland from sea raiders. Like the contemporary III B city wall at Miletos it is built thick but not massive, with a double cutstone face, a rubble core, and towers protruding at intervals (at Miletos the towers are spaced every 14 m., roughly 46 ft.; at Tiryns, Mycenae, and Troy about 12 m. or 38 ft.). Other towns whose walls are first built or definitely strengthened in the thirteenth century include Athens, Hagios Kosmas, Gla, Eutresis, Iolkos (?) in the vulnerable eastern mainland, and Mouriatada in the west.

These walls have always puzzled believers in a united mainland empire, for they are obviously at odds with any sense of political safety. Whether they defend inhabitants or hold treasure away from neighborly raids does not matter much; they are too expensive to be mere gestures of monumentality, and underline the lively feelings of danger which most Mycenaean towns experienced in this period. The danger is certainly homebred (p. 269), and natural when polis organization is the rule.

As each regional capital seems to regard itself as an independent power cautious of its neighbors, so we should expect the signs of individual enterprise overseas. In fact, our knowledge of Mycenaean pottery is not yet subtle enough to assign foreign fragments to a particular center or workshop, although laboratory tests have made certain advances toward solving this difficulty. Pottery from Mycenae is high in quality; Rhodian pottery is distinctive enough, with its bright red paint and fine fabric; sometimes the products of Cyprus, Kos, Naxos, or Chalkis can be recognized by experts. But even koiné sherds are strong evidence for overseas adventure undoubtedly led or backed by individual kings, and their density or distribution in tombs helps to distinguish the droppings of casual trade from genuine settlements. Every year of excavation reveals more Mycenaean projects in both categories. Recent examples are the large thirteenth-century cemetery at Müskebi near Halikarnassos in southwest Anatolia, the hoard of Mycenaean vases under the Gate of Persecution at Ephesos, the first sherds at Jerusalem in Palestine and at Cyrene in North Africa. Island settlements which began in III B probably met no opposition from local inhabitants, who were thin on the ground; Anatolian or Levantine settlements like Miletos and Ugarit depended for their lives on either their commercial value to the natives or diplomatic tenders of allegiance. Each colony or trade expedition faced different local conditions: goods to be traded, languages to be learned, political structures to adapt to. The same fragmentation of Mycenaean power as on the mainland would be the inevitable outcome, with kings judged by their ability to serve local interests first, to avoid larger trouble unless it were personally profitable or inescapable because of family blood ties or sworn alliances. Obviously the Mediterranean political situation from about 1360 to 1190 B.C. was very flexible and included many shifts in power, many strong princes in the east, exciting and nervous events in Greece which archaeology cannot entirely reconstruct. The defense walls of Greece are one clue and documented history in the Levant is another.

Gla and Athens

These two cities represent the changing demands of the empire period as clearly as more familiar Tiryns or Mycenae. Athens has the longer history of the two, Gla is more isolated and romantic. The ancient name of Gla (Pl. XXII B) is not known but it may have been the Arne of rich grapevines which contributed men to the Trojan expedition. It rises as a low island out of the Kopaïs basin in central Boiotia which was then a lake and is now a fertile plain. Mycenaean engineers had already arranged dikes to drain the lake by 1300. Around the island rim runs a fortification wall nearly two miles long with great double gates on all four sides; the city could probably be reached by wheeled traffic at some seasons, and roads radiated out across the plain as they did from Mycenae. Within this complex is an architectural plan almost unique in the Aegean world: a long L-shaped palace hugging the north wall and a lower city in the form of a deep rectangular agora framed by compartmented buildings. The palace avoids the centralized megaron scheme of other palaces and reminds one of Crete, with its long corridors leading past the main megaron at the west entrance to a series of rectangular compartments around two sides of an open court. Its Mycenaean orthodoxy in decoration is assured by remains of frescoes with bands and plant motifs, and by a pair of horns of consecration which fell from a roof edge. The Agora is built similarly on stone foundations with mudbrick walls, impressive adjoining rooms with columns; here too are remains of frescoes, plaster floors, and abundant pottery of the later fourteenth and the thirteenth centuries. Gla should have been an impregnable city and yet it was abandoned about the time its neighbor Thebes fell, mid-III B at the latest. Since there is no sign of anything alien on the site—or indeed on any Mycenaean site which got in trouble in the thirteenth century—and Gla is too far inland to be bothered by sea raiders, one can only suppose that a normal function of defense walls was to protect one group of Greeks from another as in the classical period. Perhaps Thebes was laid waste by the Epigonoi avenging the Seven against Thebes, as legend says, but if survivors fled to Gla they did not survive there long. The simultaneity of city troubles in the late thirteenth century also had overtones of some larger disaster which cannot be separated from the Levantine raids of the Sea Peoples (Appendix III).

Athens is one of the very few royal citadels which never fell, and it was among her citizens' proudest traditions that the walls on the Acropolis protected not only the Mycenaeans of Attica but also the refugees from less lucky cities as far away as Pylos. Mycenaean Athens is hard to reconstruct in the imagination, yet the shape of the Acropolis now is that originally planned by Mycenaean architects and the traces of buildings there have been charted, most recently by Dr. Iakovides, from slight impressions on the rock, to the extent that a plan can be drawn (Pl. XXIII A). The walls and palace were built late in Athens' Bronze Age history. From Neolithic onward, the most flourishing settlements in Attica had been out in the country, exploiting sea wealth like Hagios Kosmas, or the fertility of the middle plain like walled Brauron. Kekrops, the first king of Athens, was traditionally supposed to have reached the Acropolis in 1581 B.C.; there are, at any rate, sherds of LH I–II on the site of the later palace, and a little house north of the Erechtheion, confirming some dynastic consolidation in the period of the early tholoi—though the tholoi are all out in the country estates of other kings, at Thorikos and Marathon and Menidi. There ought to be one under the Acropolis or on Philopappos hill; it has not been found. After the fall of Knossos new wealth concentrated around the foot of the Acropolis, illustrated by the royal grave with the ivory pyxis and many fine vases (Pls. XXXVI B–C, XVIII G). Some sailors had been to Knossos itself, with Theseus or alone, and brought back Knossian vases (Fig. 27). From then until 1200 came a high proportion of foreign imports, Egyptian faïence and scarabs, wine jars from Canaan, tin and liparite, and a close communion in vase painting with styles in Crete and Rhodes. An Attic vase has been tentatively identified in Troy VI. Athenian trade lines seem stronger overseas than with Peloponnesian sites.

The old entrance to the Acropolis was where it is now, just south of the Propylaia where two roads shrank to footpaths at the summit. The hill remained unfortified until late in the thirteenth century. Then the opening was guarded by a massive tower and double gate about the size of the Lion Gate at Mycenae and probably once topped with a similar sculptured relieving triangle; the total height of the fortification from below was a dizzying 150.0 meters. Beyond the gate was an open square with a guardhouse commanding the path to the palace (under the Erechtheion) whose megaron faced outward toward the gate, raised on a stepped platform and flanked by side terraces with living quarters and storerooms as at Pylos. Two column bases used to be attributed to the megaron porch but have now been classified as Geometric, perhaps from "the strong house of Erechtheus" Homer mentions. There were at least two well-guarded minor entrances to the citadel, one with steep stairs to the caves below the north cliffs where the massive Pelargikon formed an extra ring of defense, and a broader easier way down to the Agora from the north side of the palace—a route which later seemed so dangerously exposed that it was shut up completely with a crosswall. Small houses were then built along this route; but they were soon abandoned and new houses were built inside the wall and a guardhouse set in the southeast corner. The date of this defensive retreat is nearly the end of the thirteenth century, climaxing a nervousness that had been active for a generation or two before.

While the people on the slope outside were wondering whether to stay there, the Acropolis prepared for siege by the construction of the fountain house inside the thickness of the north wall. Here ingenious engineers dug a shaft 120 feet deep for a wooden counterpart of Mycenae's stone underground fountain or the massive water system at Tiryns, all made at the same time. Five flights of stone and wooden steps led down in a wooden framework to a platform over a catch basin far below sunlight. It was always steep—many women lost their water jars down it—and the dampness was so hard on the wood that it seems to have rotted through after only about twenty-five years of use. Then supplementary water was sought by digging wells on the slopes just outside the walls. There were even graves inside the Acropolis at this period, perhaps by the relaxation of some ancient rule, for the Agora down below was the traditional cemetery.

The whole plateau with its late buildings might have held a permanent population of two or three hundred including guards; in crises two thousand or more could have been protected inside temporarily. In peaceful times most people stayed down below toward the Areopagos, the Pnyx, and the Olympieion, with wells for each cluster of houses and sheds for the cattle who grazed in the plains toward Hymettos and drank from the Ilissos stream. It is extremely expressive of countrywide fear that the stubbornly agricultural and seafaring population abandoned its homesteads out in the country and came to the rock of Athens or, a little later, took refuge on the island of Salamis.

Trouble on the Mainland

Absolute dates are impossible to come by, especially since pottery styles are slightly different in different regions. Athens has little Close style or foreign imports from its later days, although the eastern shore cemetery of Perati is filled with them (p. 302). Broneer and Iakovides have suggested that the main part of Athens' walls, the gate and fountain, were built after 1250 B.C., that the north gate was closed off perhaps about 1220 B.C., the houses outside built and abandoned *ca.* 1200 B.C. when the fountain also collapsed, and that the prince continued to live up on the rock with a few subjects until the beginning of the Dark Ages. Kodros, the last king of Athens (a Neleid refugee from Pylos), died fighting the Peloponnesians in the twelfth century. Mylonas has outlined a similar history for Mycenae. The Lion Gate, Granary, and whole southwest perimeter were designed around 1250 B.C., the houses outside the wall and the palace were attacked and burned *ca.* 1220 B.C., the northeast ring and secret cistern were then built and the citadel inhabited until sometime in the twelfth century, when it was utterly sacked. Wace and his British successors on the site would raise the dates for the monumental architecture by a generation or so, but agree that the Gate and Granary are the first, the cistern the last, expressions of precaution lasting through three or four generations determined to protect the Argolid. According to Greek legend the various Mycenaean states were constantly attacking one another during the thirteenth century: Peloponnesians against Athenians, Athenians against Eleusinians, Thebans against Orchomenians, Athenians and Boiotians against Eleians, Eleians against Messenians, Arkadians against Lakonians, Kalydonians against Aitolians. The two concerted wars fought against Thebes, and the fierce citadel-based brigands who annoyed Herakles and Theseus, are only the most familiar episodes in an age of constant aggression and civil dynastic war. Mycenae itself was burned two or three times, surely by Mycenaeans. At the same time, the empire, if we can continue to call it so without overtones of political unity, was affected as a whole by the energetic series of crises in the Levant in which Mycenaeans played their role.

A tentative chart has been constructed (Appendix III) to suggest how widespread thirteenth-century defensive building was, and what happened to major cities at different times according to the archaeological record based on pottery. A picture emerges which is predictably different for different parts of Greece. Many sites acquired new wealth after the fall of Knossos and built their first walls and palaces then. Some, like Pylos, received new dynasts around 1300, and many began then to reconstruct their palaces (p. 163). By the middle of the century most towns which had been unwalled before build defensive circuits; those who had them already refurbish the towers and protect the food and water supplies.

In one or two generations comes the big time of trouble. Mycenae and Tiryns are attacked but survive to strengthen their siege defenses. West coast sites from Olympia southward are burned (Pylos) or abandoned (Mouriatada). Achaia, the Ionian Islands, and Attica receive an influx of refugees; the country towns build new walls, and Athens withdraws inside her citadel. Prominent cities in Boiotia are abandoned. The islands receive refugees, from Naxos to Crete. The Dodekanese are particularly active and apparently rich. Cyprus is caught up in the devastation that swept along the Anatolian and Levantine coasts; Enkomi, Ugarit, Atchana, Hazor, Megiddo, and Troy burn down.

After this general disaster comes a period of brief revival with foreign trade once more partly in the hands of Mycenaeans. The mainland cities pull themselves together, create a new vivid style in vase painting (p. 206), and acquire new kinds of weapons, iron, cremation burials, eastern pottery (p. 301). Certain refugee centers are even prosperous: Iolkos, Attica, Naxos, Crete. Bands of roving Mycenaeans settle overseas at Tarsus, Enkomi, and coastal sites in Crete. There are still a few people living where the old palaces had been burned, at Pylos and Thebes among others (cf. Fig. 43 b). Then a second attack afflicts places still worth attacking; Mycenae is finally taken. Sites by the sea are generally abandoned and there is a progressive withdrawal to safer hill-villages. People continue to bury each other at the old centers, but there is no architecture left to see how they lived after ca. 1150 B.C. Yet, continuity between twelfth-century wares and the Protogeometric wares of the Dark Age is affirmed at the following places: Mycenae, Tiryns, Argos, Amyklai, Pylos-Tragana, Kephallenia, Ithaka, Athens, Salamis, Thebes, Delphi, Iolkos, Keos, Delos, Samos, Naxos, Knossos, Phaistos, eastern Crete, Kos, Rhodes, Ephesos, Miletos, Halikarnassos, Tarsus, Enkomi. Whatever sufferings or changes of political systems these towns experienced, their people lasted out the Dark Ages on the spot. They lost even their III C standard of living but did not lose contact with their Mycenaean heritage. It should, perhaps, come as no surprise that these are precisely the towns to figure strongest in Homeric epic.

The kings of the empire age, then, lived through a period marked by constant aggression against one another, by involvement in the larger disasters of the Levant, by strong commercial trade and the deployment of well-trained fighting men. The two outside factors which contributed to their downfall are known from different sources: from history, the Sea Peoples, and from Greek legend, the Dorians.

THE MYCENAEANS IN THEIR MEDITERRANEAN SETTING

The Mycenaean world was not quite a cultural unit, nor was it ever a political unit complete in itself. Mycenaeans were constantly turning to other nations and overseas markets to support their economy. Their sea voyages and eastern colonies made them peculiarly vulnerable to disturbances in the eastern Aegean, and the greatest single disturbance to peaceful trade was the eruption of the Sea Peoples as fighting elements in eastern power politics. The Sea Peoples are one of the historical mysteries of the Late Bronze Age. They are not a single group, although the Egyptians sometimes spoke of them this way as they looked northward from the Delta to the disturbed islands and coasts of the central sea. The Sea Peoples are a phenomenon, not a race: tribes of coastal inhabitants who profited by the desire of the inland powers to have experienced sailors and mercenary infantry fighting for them. Between mass engagements, they seem to have free-lanced.

Occasionally, groups of Sea Peoples or coastal enemies are illustrated in Egyptian relief sculptures or described in Egyptian historical records. Some Sea Peoples can be identified with known geographical districts or towns, though many are still hard to pin down. The earliest, named in the fourteenth-century Amarna letters of the Egyptians, Hittites, and Cypriotes, are the *Denyen, Lukka, Shardana,* and *Shekelesh.* These four begin their activities soon after the fall of Knossos. The Denyen are often identified with the Danaans, either the Greek-speaking Mycenaeans whom Homer knows by this tribal name, or a related group living in Cilicia near Tarsus.[11] The Lukka live in Lycia, opposite Rhodes and Cyprus, where the deep mountain-circled harbors of southwest Anatolia offer perfect retreats for pirates, and where tradition said some Minoans had fled as colonists after the death of Minos at Knossos.[12] The other two have been identified tentatively as Sardinians and Sicilians, perhaps not operating from those great islands but moving toward them. These tribes seem to have been shaken loose from their provincial village lives into piratical or mercenary careers by the alteration in commercial and political patterns created at the time of the fall of Knossos. They trade with Mycenaeans in pottery and metal, and there can be no doubt that Mycenaean sailors knew them well.

About 1300 B.C., when the real Mycenaean empire begins, the roster of the Sea Peoples swells; they fight on both sides at the critical battle of Kadesh in the early years of Rameses II, *ca.* 1286 B.C. This was the moment when Mu-watallis, King of the Hittites, massed all the lands that could be brought against the Egyptians, with 2,500 chariots, three men to a chariot, covering the mountains and valleys. Mercenary troops including the Lycians, Dardana (Trojans?), and other Aegeans from the Levant fought for Muwatallis; the Shardana fought for Rameses. The Egyptians won at such great cost that they withdrew rapidly from Syria, and the real phase of Mycenaean III B expansion into Levantine ports took place.

The mainland defenses were strengthened after the accession of Muwatallis' grandson Tudhaliyas IV, *ca.* 1250, who campaigned against the cities of west-ern Asia Minor where Mycenaeans and their Anatolian contacts had been previously undisturbed. It is particularly in the reigns of Muwatallis and Tudhaliyas that Hittite correspondence mentions the Aegean kingdom of the Ahhiyawa who are behaving with irritating dash and independence off the Hittite southwest frontiers. The Lukka were behaving equally badly. The Ahhiyawa and the Lukka were both operating in southwest Asia Minor and on the islands immediately opposite, like Rhodes, Syme, Kos, and Kalymnos. They were pirates and traders with light settlements, forces to be seriously considered by the Hittites and the Alasiotes of Cyprus. The Ahhiyawa were certainly eastern Mycenaeans. Nearly thirty sites with Mycenaean pottery are known in Asia Minor; some of these are real colonies, like Miletos, Ephesos, and Müskebi, others are towns in touch with coastal Mycenaeans and enjoying their trade. At several points the Mycenaean settlements were within nominal Hittite territory, and it is no surprise to hear that the Hittites were annoyed by the independent war-leaders or kings who refused to become vassals and interfered with the allegiances of western Anatolian cities. The main center of the Ahhiyawa was probably on Rhodes; other settlements were perhaps organized in a loose federation under the king of Ahhiyawa. Ahhiyawa is the Hittite pronunciation of either Achaiwa, land of the Achaioi, or Argeiwa, land of the Argeiwoi. Achaians and Argives are almost interchangeable in Homer for the Greek tribes at Troy.

These Achaioi or Argeioi join with other Sea Peoples to confront the pharaoh Merneptah in his fifth year (1233); their allies are the Shardana, Shekelesh,

Meshwesh, Teresh (Tyrsenians from Lydia?), and Lycians. Merneptah also has to deal with the Libyan tribes of charioteers, some of whom were migrant Trojans according to Greek tradition. This is the moment when the eastern Mycenaeans are in closest touch with the mainland and bring it their special version of the Close style, which overlaps with the mainland late empire style of III B (Pl. XLV C; Fig. 51). Their ships bring not only the traditional cargoes of bronze and luxury items, but iron (formerly a monopoly of the Hittites), Mitanni seals and Hittite bronze statuettes, (Pl. XLVIII), the new cut-and-thrust swords, and the new fashion for cremation burial (p. 302). Such innovations are clearest at eastern coastal sites like Mycenae, Tiryns, or Perati in Attica, and particularly mark the period of revival after the first disasters, though they begin before them. The transitional period III B-C seems to ruin places as distant as Pylos, Mycenae, Ugarit, and Troy at roughly the same archaeological moment (Appendix III), because pots are less sensitive time markers than documents, but historically one hopes a more precise sequence may develop some day.

The career of the Sea Peoples culminates in two large-scale battles at the end of the Late Bronze Age: the famous sea fight off the western Delta won by the Egyptians in the eighth year of Rameses III (*ca.* 1187 B.C.), and a newly recorded triple sea fight between the Hittites and the Cypriotes off Cyprus near 1180 B.C. The first is brilliantly commemorated in the reliefs of Rameses' temple at Medinet Habu. Inscriptions tell us that the Danaans had been again fighting the Egyptians by the side of the *Peleset* (Philistines), the *Alasa* (Cypriotes), the *Shekelesh,* the *Zakaray,* the *Thekel,* and the *Weshesh.* Some of these tribes are distinguished by feather-rimmed headdresses, or bird-prows on the Philistine ships (cf. Fig. 43 *f*), but the Danaans and Cypriotes are unfortunately not identifiable by any peculiar style. The second battle, won by the Hittites under Suppiluliumas II against three waves of Sea Peoples' ships attacking from eastern Cyprus, is the last large-scale outbreak of organized hostilities with the Sea Peoples as allies of both sides.[13] In spite of victories, both Egyptians and Hittites are too disorganized to maintain their empires, and both great nations fade out into the real Dark Ages just when the Greek mainland does, by the middle of the twelfth century. Two centuries of raids and sieges weakened frontier stability everywhere, and there had been at the same time serious movements of land-traveling tribes from the north and east who spilled into the old imperial provinces of Asia Minor and the Mesopotamian uplands; the Egyptians note the threat of migrants in ox carts, as one symptom of the great shift in tribes which slowly overran the established civilizations of the Bronze Age. Within the next three centuries the Assyrians, Philistines, and Phrygians would build new political empires in the East, the Italians and Central Europeans would emerge into a bright technological period, and the age of migrations in Greece would redistribute the survivors of Mycenaean civilization and establish the Dorian newcomers. A generation after the Delta and Cyprus sea battles, Mycenae was destroyed for the last time, her citadel burned. Five generations later, by 1000 B.C., the new Greek cities of the Ionian coast are already initiating the next great phase of Greek civilization.

Troy and the Dorians

It remains to fit two momentous events of Greek tradition into this schematic outline of crises: the Trojan War and the Dorian invasion. We do not know enough yet to do this with much conviction; many chronologies and interpretations have been offered lately which complicate the historical picture and often cancel one another. The most convincing reconstruction will be one with simple patterns of movement which still allows for individual local histories.

To later Greeks, the Trojan War was the beginning of history, not the end. Their memory reached back only two or three generations before it. Relations had been established between Greeks and Trojans long before such memories were preserved in epic poetry, however, and Troy had been a recognized port of call for Mycenaean ships for several hundred years before Agamemnon's expedition (see Fig. 23 e–f). Troy is one of the two great stone-walled cities of Asia Minor which seem directly comparable to the palace-citadels of the mainland—the other is the huge Hittite capital of Boğazköy or Hattušaš—and there are a few uncanny similarities of architecture and fortification design which link the two areas. The Hittites, Trojans, and Greeks shared a common Indo-European heritage to some extent, and other likenesses would have been encouraged by travel and tourism. Yet, beyond architectural features like the masonry of walls or the design of underground galleries and tunnels, the cultures are sturdily independent and locally distinct in aspects like religion, language, political organization, manufacture, and costume. The Hittites do not concern Mycenaean history so much, because their contact with Mycenaeans was limited to casual coastal encounters. Troy, on the other hand, always was drawn toward the Aegean rather than the Anatolian world, cut off from the interior by the massive ranges of Mount Ida, and with a daily view across the north Aegean islands like Imbros, Samothrace, and Lemnos.

The great city of Troy VI was founded about 1900 B.C. by newcomers perhaps related to the Minyans of Greece (p. 67), and until its destruction about 1300 B.C. it was always more advanced architecturally than corresponding Mycenaean cities. But the Trojans never had the same brightening contact with Crete and the Levant that the Greeks did, and so never learned to write, or paint their own pottery. They were even curiously isolated from their Hittite neighbors, and their foreign contacts were primarily in the Aegean sphere. Imported vases from the Greek mainland first appear in Troy about the time of the Shaft Graves, and in the early tholos period there was quite a demand for Greek manufactures (Fig. 22 *e–f*); this commerce steadily increased after the fall of Knossos (p. 152), and the crest of imports seems to come in the early fourteenth century (Pl. XVIII H). As usual, it is hard to tell what the Mycenaeans took in return, for there are no recognizable Trojan objects in Mycenaean cities in Greece, but the trade may have focused on silver, purple dye and dyed textiles, possible the famous Trojan horses, and even grain from the broad fields of the north. Clearly the Greeks had shifted their attention seriously from Crete toward Asia Minor after 1400 B.C. Their involvement with Troy is like their renewed colonization and new settlements at town sites farther south; Ephesos, Miletos, Müskebi, Kos, Ialysos on Rhodes, and Enkomi on Cyprus (Fig. 40).

Around 1300 B.C., after a few pictorial vases from Mycenaean workshops in the Levant had reached the citadel along with a few empire vases from the mainland, Troy VI H suffered from some catastrophe which effectively damaged her walls. Blocks from the superstructure were tossed to the ground and the great houses on the acropolis fell in ruins. The early excavators, Schliemann and Dörpfeld, interpreted this catastrophe as the Trojan War itself, especially since the Sixth City matched the poetic image of the splendors of Troy; this theory has been revived in several quarters lately, but whatever happened to Troy then happened too early for any sound chronology of the Trojan War. Professor Blegen and the Cincinnati expedition understood it rather as a severe earthquake, especially since they saw no traces of fire, and the ultimate Greek victory is always imagined by the epic poets in a setting of crackling flame. But it cannot be accident that Greek tradition puts the first Trojan War just at this moment: a planned raid by mainland Greeks against the citadel of Troy which pulled the city apart in the time of King Laomedon. This raid was led by some very prominent heroes: Herakles, who had been cheated twice by the tricky

Anatolians, bringing the men of Tiryns and the princes Telamon and Iolaos as lieutenants. They went on to fight the Amazons of the interior—a fabulous race in later Greek myth, but attractively identified by some scholars with the Hittites in their fringed and feminine kilts. Whatever the historical core of these traditions may be—and they are certainly contaminated—Herakles was not doing anything extraordinary by raiding Anatolia then, nor was the hero Aiakos out of place in acting as consulting architect for the Trojan walls a generation earlier. Mycenaeans were in constant touch with the Anatolian coast, often aggressively.[14] Perhaps it was this trouble in Troy that inspired a few Trojans, the branch called Dardanians of Aeneas' stock, to take mercenary's pay with Muwatallis at the battle of Kadesh, as later some would move south to Libya. Trojan fame as charioteers would make them welcome.

A new city was created out of damaged Troy VI H, a direct continuation of it though labeled Troy VII A. It was smaller and more rubbly than before, but even with patched walls and towers was still an impressive citadel. Modest houses spring up against the walls, inside and outside, and boast a new feature which speaks of precautions about future raids: gigantic pithoi to store wine and oil and grain, sunk inside the houses with only their lips protruding above the dirt floors. This reconstruction is roughly contemporary with the renewed defenses of citadels on the Greek mainland. The volume of Mycenaean imports is reduced to a trickle, so that it is particularly difficult to relate the chronology of Troy VII A to mainland events, but the few distinctive pieces are from broken vases characteristic everywhere in the Mycenaean world just before the great destructions, from Pylos in the west to Ugarit in the east; they belong technically to the transitional ceramic period LH III B–C. This city comes to an end in flames, and in spite of its shoddy aspect is generally felt to be the city Homer sang about. Two doubtful skeletons and one arrowhead of a common Aegean type are all that survive as relics of the "great siege." Survivors clean up the city once more and live in it for a while, still importing a few Mycenaean vases of the same III B–C type. Eventually they accept among them a group of aliens whose prime archaeological creation was an ugly handmade pot with knobs on. In a little while the city is abandoned, after nearly two thousand years of habitation.

When one compares this real image of Troy with Homer's poetic image, the gap is great and disappointing, but one should never underestimate the healing powers of poetry. The Troy of Telamon's time may have shed some of its lustre on the Troy Achilles fought for in the next generation, finally overthrown by a generation younger still (Epeios, who made the Wooden Horse, was Telamon's great-nephew). Mycenaeans certainly knew Troy in the fourteenth century when it was still uninjured and splendid. The familiar epic epithets—steep, with high gates, fine walls, well-established, windy, holy, and grand—could easily have been coined for the great city before its walls were cracked or patched. Many details in the epic account of the siege at Troy are of course older than the Trojan War itself, part of an antique and traditional siege poem about the sack of a walled town by the sea. The theme had been reflected in different terms in the world of Mycenaean art since the Silver Siege Rhyton of the Shaft Graves (Pl. XIV); the siege scenes of Mycenae and Pylos were painted before the final episode at Troy (p. 200). The Trojan War became the ultimate version of this artistic theme because it was genuinely the last successful siege of a walled city in the old style. After its conquest the Mycenaean world became too fragmented to undertake another such allied expedition.

If there is any truth at all in epic tradition, we must see that some of the details in Homer's account harmonize extremely well with the general international situation in the thirteenth century. It is possible that Paris and his restless Trojans first came to the mainland in the guise of friends or allied Sea Peoples, that he took the wife and wealth of a prince of Amyklai who was away on business in Crete at the time, and that the Trojans touched Egypt or the Levant on their way back to Anatolia. It is possible that, after a suitable interval for collecting troops, a massive expedition of mainland aristocracy sailed out under the flag of Agamemnon of Mycenae, attacking Anatolia first near Pergamon where Hittite control was weak, then northward at Troy. The raids would have been well timed if they occurred during the riots in the southern seas against Merneptah, in the period of recrudescent mainland strength at the end of the thirteenth century. Troy fell, according to the guesses of later Greek savants, anywhere between 1334 (Douris of Samos) and 1135 (Ephoros). Eratosthenes' calculation by generations put it at 1184 B.C., which has always seemed an intelligent compromise. This was the ultimate period of Sea People disturbance, when Rameses III repelled them at the Delta and Suppiluliumas II won off Cyprus. The archaeological date for the burning of Troy VII A is unsettled at the moment because there was so little easily dateable Mycenaean pottery in that city. Professor Blegen has set it much earlier than other scholars, at 1240 or even 1270 B.C. in the generation of early III B prosperity after the battle of Kadesh, but most observers, noting the presence of III C sherds in the destruction level, would correlate the siege with the new period of Greek strength just before 1200 B.C.

Until this matter is definitely settled, it is permissible to imagine a setting of the vivid, internationally hybrid age of early III C as a background for the exhausted journeys homeward of the heroes which the poets report with a curious wealth of detail. There is no reason to doubt the unanimous verdict of the poets that mainland Greeks made no permanent foothold in Asia Minor and returned to insecurity at home.

Odysseus and Menelaos had a chance to visit Egypt around the time of the Delta battle against Rameses III when loot was everywhere and mercenaries in great demand. Nestor came home—to what? The palace at Pylos-Englianos is burned not much, if at all, later than Troy and its archaeology is difficult to correlate with its myths. Agamemnon came home to be murdered in his silver bathtub, and Mycenae entered a phase of weak kingship and dynastic savagery; after Orestes had killed Aigisthos he wandered all over the Aegean. Diomedes came home to the palace at Tiryns his father Tydeus had usurped in the days of the Theban war, to find that his wife had put another man in power; he escaped to Libya and the western seas. Achilles' son Neoptolemos moved from Thessaly to the west coast of Epeiros, where very late Mycenaean burials continue the princely tradition of tholoi. No one has ever put it better than Thucydides:

After the Trojan War Greece was in a state of constant movement and was being settled in a way that left her no peace to grow strong again. For the return of the Greeks from Troy took many years and brought many innovations, and civil wars happened in most cities, from which people escaped to found new places. . . . By the eightieth year after the war, the Dorians and the Herakleidai were in possession of the Peloponnesos (1.12).

This possession involved, among other things, the final sack of Mycenae.

The Dorians were of course Greeks, speaking a different dialect from the established Mycenaeans but sharing with them an energetic militarism and social organization which must have affected the late empire much as the arrival of the Shaft Grave princes affected the Minyans. It was not a question of a completely alien culture being imposed, only a question of submission and adaptation in certain limited districts the Dorians won for themselves. Their migration from the far northwest of Greece had taken many years and had passed along many routes; sometimes they joined forces with the Achaians and sometimes they burned them out. They reinforced the older Mycenaean settlers in Crete and Rhodes and eventually occupied most of the central and eastern Peloponnesos. Their dialect can be mapped quite precisely for classical times after inscriptions begin; how and when they originally settled is not so clear, but some crossed the Corinthian Gulf from Rhion into the Peloponnesos, some perhaps sailed along the west coast from Epeiros. Their move southward was perhaps a response to tribal shifts in the Balkans; their opportunity came when the Achaians and Sea Peoples had broken the older balances of power which offered stability to the mainland economy. They do not cause the fall of the Mycenaean empire; they profit by more general conditions which would have broken it up in any case.

No one knows what a Dorian looked like, what pots he made, or how to trace him archaeologically except by language. The innovations of the late empire which used to be attributed to him—iron, cremation, a new "spectacle" fibula, a broad sword type, and Protogeometric pottery—are now understood as changes from various sources which come mostly from the Near East through Mycenaeans in contact with other cultures, and are most characteristic of regions the Dorians never reached. It seems safe to say that the Dorians were not an important element of Greek society until the advanced twelfth century and are not primarily responsible for the wave of destructions in the late thirteenth. That destruction, involving so many distant sites of the Mediterranean, was a complicated series of migrations and counterattacks made possible by expanding population and great technological advance in a milieu of extreme political insecurity and self-interest.

Chapter IX

RELIGION: THEORY AND PRACTICE

As far as we know now there is a double stream of religious attention on the Greek mainland from the Shaft Grave period on. The pattern may be even more complicated than this, but scholars generally agree that the Mycenaeans managed somehow to fuse the double current of "Aegean" fertility- and mother-worship with their own Indo-European, masculine, "special-department" gods. They thus endowed the classical Greeks with a religious heritage combining both in somewhat unstable proportions.* The conventional view is that this "marriage" of nature worship and sky-god worship was symbolized through the various later Greek myths describing the marriage of Indo-European Zeus to one or another powerful female deities native to Aegean shores and islands. The gradual dominance of the Olympian dynastic gods then expresses a parallel dominance on the human scale of Indo-Europeans over native Aegean stock. While the older native beliefs never completely disappeared, they were

The
Mycenaean Heritage

lost to daily sight and only erupted in periodic spasms or were frozen in peculiar local cults, especially chthonic and mystery cults.

Theoretically this is an attractive and understandable explanation for a number of conflicts in classical religion, although it is hard to imagine exactly what it meant to an average Bronze Age prince or peasant. The archaeological evidence for Mycenaean religion is tenuous and contradictory. The sources of our knowledge are: (1) remains of buildings where worship was carried on; (2) representations of gods, worshipers, and holy symbols in statuettes or painting, or especially on gems; (3) the Linear B tablets (mostly from Pylos) naming gods and describing the details of what is offered to them; (4) the enormous amount of evidence for funeral practice with all its implications; (5) the testimony of Homer, and of the Greek myths which begin to assume canonical form in the period following the epic poems.

GREECE IN THE BRONZE AGE

With so many sources at the service of theory, it may be surprising that so little is known yet about religious beliefs in the Greek Bronze Age. But the defects in the sources are clear. As soon as one eliminates the evidence from Crete, the mainland evidence shrinks to a thimbleful. Most scholars take it for granted that the Mycenaeans borrowed Minoan religion along with Minoan art. There has been no study demonstrating this, and an historical parallel would be hard to find. The rites of Crete can have had no serious influence on Greece before Greeks had settled in one Cretan town in the fifteenth century, and even then it would be wrong to assume that Greeks returning from Knossos were able to proselytize the mainland from Thessaly to Kythera so successfully that a uniform, standard religion would emerge. It is extremely important to try to distinguish between the veneer of Minoan religious forms in mainland art, and the underlying tendencies of mainland religion. Next, there are practically no remains of public religious buildings in Greece. The representations of gods usually follow Minoan iconography and thus slight the divinities who have no precedent or counterpart in Crete; the images are overwhelmingly feminine, at odds with the tablets to some extent, and successfully ignoring the masculine Indo-Europeans. The interpretation of the Linear B texts is obviously uncertain, as in all departments, and that uncertainty combined with the poor scholarly manners which religious argument is apt to stimulate has led to a variety of subtle cross-purposes. It is easy to understand what Mycenaeans did at a funeral, but no amount of excavation will tell what they thought. And, finally, Homeric religion is one of the most complex fields of classical scholarship; to use the poetic evidence of an eighth-century *Iliad* and *Odyssey* for the prosaic practices of the thirteenth century needs learning, agility, and self-confidence. Nor is Greek myth a more reliable clue. It never stands still. It combines the personal temper of the narrator with an historically fluid content into a series of transformations more marvelous than Proteus'. We can guess linguistically and historically which myths *ought* to have a Bronze Age nucleus, but when we consider the great changes even the most stable myths experienced between Homer and Euripides, it is all too easy to guess how much they changed in double the time span before. So much for the warnings.

Public Shrines

The Greek situation is in stark contrast to Crete, where every major palace, villa, farmhouse, mountain top, and cave bears testimony to public cult. In

Greece there are no proven centers of cave or mountain worship, no independent rustic shrines have been found, and even within the palaces there are no rooms particularly constructed as sanctuaries. Cult was an integrated part of palace life, handled in palace halls which had other domestic functions as well. The focus of the palace was always the megaron with its huge fixed hearth. At Pylos a portable altar stood by the hearth; at Mycenae traces of an altar and offering tables were discovered in the porch of the megaron.[1] Everything suggests that throne, hearth, and movable altar formed a traditional complex, and that the hearth itself was the center of sacrificial ritual carried out or supervised by the prince or his palace priest.

The primary form of ritual must have been the sacrifice and burning of animals, just as in later Homeric cult. This is an essential difference from Minoan ritual; Cretans did not make burnt or blood offerings. No doubt the Greeks also made libations of wine and offered first fruits or cakes—a Pylos fresco shows cakes being carried in procession on a table—but their ancient habit of offering rams, calves, and pigs to divinity must have been deeply rooted in mainland tradition and too profound to be changed by Mycenaean fondness for Minoan religious symbols in art.

Other important differences in cult perhaps made it less necessary to build independent shrines in Greece. The Mycenaeans did not use the complex paraphernalia of Crete—the shrine models, the snake-goddess and dove-goddess images, the snake tubes, stepped altars, tables for liquid offerings, votive double axes and horns of consecration—and so did not need sanctuaries stocked with such equipment. The lack of separate housing for the gods is no index of lack of intensity in worship. Religion was apparently interwoven with daily routine, at least in the token sharing of a meal with divinity through sacrifice and libation at the heart of the palace. Even in the Homeric age when separate shrines were just beginning to be built, one offered meat and drink in one's own house to the protectors of the household as a matter of course. Ceremonies must have been simple and natural, carried out with little physical apparatus.

The palaces also had altars outside the throne room, both fixed and portable. The best example of a fixed altar occurs at Pylos, standing in the middle of the open courtyard in the northeast wing of the palace (p. 165). It is a solid block of limestone covered with plaster and painted with a winged or scalloped design in primary colors. It was placed axially before the façade of a simple, cell-like room one step higher than the court, empty of any kind of cult equipment but at least well placed to be a sanctuary annex. A round altar at Tiryns was built in the principal court on a line with the door of the megaron (Pl. XXIII B).[2] Portable altars which could also be used as braziers in cold weather are fairly common; several were found at Mycenae, stored in the closet where the ivory triad was kept (p. 220; Pl. XXXVIII). They occasionally appear in tombs as well. As with fixed hearths, their household and ceremonial functions are interchangeable, for it is the fire and not the fireplace that counts.

We do not know if private houses had the same arrangements as palaces. The most interesting candidate for an independent shrine during the palace age is a building on the citadel at Mycenae known as Tsountas' House.[3] A plaster ramp led directly down from a stepped street into a hall with a stuccoed floor. There were benches along the south and east sides of this hall, and a moon-shaped plaster hearth at the south. Beside the hearth a channel in the floor connected two hollows: the first was pointed, as though for a rhyton or libation vessel, the second contained a two-handled jar to receive liquid. An analogous arrangement is seen in the curious cuttings beside the throne at Pylos (p. 176), where an irregular channel connected two circular depressions, perhaps for ceremonial libation near the hearth. Tsountas' House has no megaron and is architecturally an original building. Three famous fragments of painting found in it seem to confirm some cult activity there: a limestone plaque painted with a shield goddess appearing between two dancers; a fresco of ladies sitting at a window where double axes are stuck into the embrasure; and a fresco of three ass-daimons carrying a pole. Apart from this house, there is no evidence that the Greeks on the mainland ever built independent shrines before the palaces were burned.[4] The Pylos texts do, however, mention one or two sanctuaries of gods, which may have been open-air precincts near the palace.

When the palaces and principal towns of Greece were destroyed near the end of the thirteenth century, the resulting instability of life seems to have provoked a new interest in cult. Crete also displays an intensification of worship in shrines. Most known Cretan cult idols were made in the late thirteenth and twelfth centuries, set on benches in shrines and surrounded with elaborate cult equipment such as altars and kernoi. At least one shrine flourished on the mainland at this time, in the harbor town of Asine which was not destroyed in the general catastrophe; her ships were still at sea (see Fig. 43 d), surely in touch with Crete and the east. The shrine at Hagia Eirene on Keos is older but also had a flourishing period after 1200 B.C.

Asine on the Gulf of Argos is a small rocky town whose houses sprawl over terraces above the sea. House G there was a particularly large and sturdy building with a main hall long identified as a shrine.[5] The simple rectangular room is punctuated by two columns on the long axis and has a rude stone bench along one wall. A group of late terracottas and vases was found spread on the bench. The figurines include the standard Φ-type (cf. Pl. XLI A) and a more tubular Cretan kind of goddess with upraised arms, one of whom wears a painted crown and necklace. The most interesting piece is a little terracotta head called the Lord, or Zeus, of Asine because its sharp jaw looks like a beard. In fact the flesh is painted white like a woman's, and the hair is worn in long twists; in general style the Lord resembles the painted stucco head from Mycenae (Pl. XL C) although much smaller and cruder. But there are other little bearded heads in the palace age and after, the majority from neighboring Mycenae, and a male statuette would certainly not be out of religious character for the times. From elsewhere in House G came very distinctive III C vases covering most of the first half of the twelfth century by current chronology, among them the stirrup jar painted with a ship (Fig. 43 *d*).

The temple or shrine on Keos is much more elaborate (pp. 118 and 217). It is the first major Aegean shrine which mainlanders knew. The great statues found in it seem to go back to the period of Kean prosperity in the fifteenth century, when the formal aspects of the temple were laid out, and early dedications include a splendid Minoan bronze figure of a youthful worshiper with long hair as well as good vases of the age when the Greeks were at Knossos. After the town was destroyed by earthquake about the time Knossos fell, a smaller and less trig settlement replaced it. Traces of the thirteenth-century town have been largely eroded, but the sacral building itself was cleared out and reused as well as remodeled; some of its walls still stand higher than a man's head. It shows at least five main periods of use, ranging from the fifteenth century to the classical period; one of the latest dedications is a fourth-century button representing the Athena Parthenos. There is no doubt that during the Dark Ages and after it was remembered as a place of holy antiquity even when no town remained to support it.

The temple was built of schist slabs and field stones like all houses on Keos. It is a long, narrow building divided into three main sections, the outer one close to the sea at the east, the inner one at the west the most holy part. Room V on the east was remodeled several times. At the end of the Mycenaean period it had a doorway with a stone threshold, jambs, and lintel, and two benches along the walls flanking the door. A massive stone podium occupied the center of the room, and here in the debris were found fragments of at least five of the great terracotta statues. Most of the pottery here was of the III C style, the earlier phases being now below sea level. The center section of the temple was subdivided into three rooms, two narrow compartments along the north wall serving as corridor or storage space, the larger room (IV) having a bench along its south wall. Here were more bits of the broken statues, and at the lowest levels early dedications including part of a bronze ship. The inner section, again subdivided into two rooms, preserved a better sequence of the shrine's history. The earliest floors ran just above the debris of the Middle Bronze Age town and were covered with sherds of the fifteenth century. The cell on the left (XI) seems to have been the inner sanctum or adyton. Many more pieces of the statues were discovered here, one body joining a head in the outermost room; they were battered and broken in the Mycenaean period, perhaps by the earthquake which destroyed the town. It is interesting that even the adyton contained no formal cult equipment of the Cretan kind.

The Keos statues were discussed above as examples of monumental sculpture which have no parallels on the mainland yet (p. 217; Pl. XL A–B). It is not certain that they were all made early in the history of Hagia Eirene, although this may be suggested by their stylistic similarities and by their dense grouping in the adyton in the middle of early remains. Perhaps some of them were resurrected in the later phases of the temple and displayed as holy objects, visible manifestations of the goddess in her epiphany to mortals, accompanied by attendant priestesses. Their very numbers puzzle. Cretan shrines often have multiple figures on a smaller scale, but in later Greek shrines it is rare to find more than one cult image of the same type. Possibly they delineate successive priestesses as each took office, like an official portrait, and thus represent a longer span of creation than our eyes discern in such provincial and unusual pieces. Possibly they were arranged in the adyton, or on the stone podium in the outer room, in a way that suggested a procession or dance in honor of the goddess, three-dimensional versions of procession frescoes. At any rate they represent for us vividly the impressive environment of Aegean religion when it was surrounded by formal architecture filled with ambitious works and dedications. They are not documents of Mycenaean religion, but illuminate the kind of cult center to which seafaring Mycenaeans were exposed. Mainlanders contributed to the dedications in the period of the Sea Peoples, among other things a ritual jar painted with red-robed figures marching in procession.

The afterlife of the temple on Keos is instructive for those considering possible continuity of belief from the Bronze Age to the classical age. No doubt the religious imagery it evoked in its devotees changed with the changing times. One of the most astonishing accidents in the fortunes of the goddesses, who had long been buried under debris, took place in the archaic period. The head of one goddess was somehow resurrected and installed in a new high level of the temple, nesting in a specially designed ring of terracotta. Nearby the base of a black-glazed cup recorded a dedication to the god Dionysos. Possibly the old head changed sex in the eyes of its later discoverers; possibly Dionysos was thought a fitting consort for an elder Aegean goddess. At least the incident seems to confirm the many stories attached to Greek sanctuaries, about their possessing images so antique that they must have fallen from heaven.

One remarkable but tenuous series of facts should be mentioned as a fragment of the evidence for public religious buildings: the strong pull on archaic Greeks to build temples or worship on the sites of former Mycenaean palaces. Aside from Keos, only two sites have positive claim to endurance as cult centers from the Bronze Age to the fully literate classical Greek age—the powerful holy places at Eleusis and Delos.[6] A small Mycenaean megaron at Eleusis, simply a long room and porch, lies exactly under the site of the later Telesterion where the mysteries of Demeter and Persephone were shown centuries after. The megaron was never part of a palace, but an isolated building inside a stone courtyard wall. It had two columns in the main room and perhaps two in the porch, and constitutes a possible example of architectural influence from the megaron upon the classical temple form. Thermon in Aitolia is another, although there the Mycenaean site beneath the classical Temple of Apollo seems purely secular. The building at Eleusis was too destroyed by later architecture to still hold any religious equipment, except one painted eye which might come from a ruined procession fresco, but in view of its position at the heart of the sanctuary and its peculiar isolated form it probably served as the "house" of some Bronze Age divinity. We have no right to call her Demeter yet; Potnia of Eleusis would be more accurate.

At Delos, the renowned classical sanctuary of Apollo around whom other divinities clustered as satellites, there had been habitation since the Early Cycladic period. The island was mildly influenced by Crete in the sixteenth and fifteenth centuries when its two famous Tombs of the Hyperborean Maidens were probably constructed. Legend records that the first pair of these girls from beyond the north wind came to the island at the same time as Apollo and Artemis, so that cult here does have an antique tradition, although clearly open to severe contamination from antiquarian research in later centuries. There is a late Mycenaean town by the harbor, but no formal sanctuary. One possible sacral building of the late Bronze Age lies under the archaic Artemision, and it was here that the famous group of Delian ivories, bronzes, gold, and seals was discovered (Pls. XXXVII C, XXXIX B). It must have been relaid as a foundation deposit when the Artemision was built on its predecessor's site, for it included Geometric and Orientalizing elements as well as Mycenaean. Later building has eroded any other evidence for a sanctuary flourishing on the island in Mycenaean times, although a gem with a scene of worship may be linked to Delian tradition (see Fig. 44).

Many other classical sanctuary sites claim a Mycenaean heritage, although it has not yet proved possible to find a Bronze Age cult building at any one of them. Scholars who believe in direct continuity between Mycenaean and Geometric religion build their case on sherds and idols from strata under later temples. If a mass of terracotta idols is found together without a domestic context they may indeed be relics of informal countryside worship, signs of the *temene* or outdoor precincts hinted at in the tablets. Formal relations between the two epochs of cult are harder to prove. Casual contact between Mycenaean villages and later cult centers is clear enough at sites like Delphi, Amyklai, Epidauros, or Aigina. At Delphi, sherds and idols were found below the east flank of the Apollo temple and in the Marmaria precinct later dedicated to Athene; much has always been made of a fragmentary marble ceremonial rhyton in the shape of a lioness' head which has a counterpart at Knossos; a Homeric Hymn tells how Apollo staffed his temple with a crew of kidnapped Cretans who had been sailing toward Pylos on business, and this has a good Bronze Age ring, although Apollo, on the evidence, is not a Mycenaean god. The Mycenaean settlement was wiped out by flood; it had no immediate successors.

At Amyklai the cult places of Hyakinthos with his pre-Greek name and of Helen who was partly divine in Spartan imaginations both covered Mycenaean house deposits. Figurines of women with children and of bulls lay in a rubbish dump near the classical temple of Aphaia on Aigina. Mycenaean sherds and idols near the sanctuary of Asklepios at Epidauros have been taken to prove antique worship there; a bronze dagger engraved with spirals and the steatite rhyton fragment (Fig. 20 b) add a strangely warlike temper under the temple of Apollo Maleatas. At Tiryns the round altar in the megaron courtyard was remodeled in Geometric times. The relation between the megaron and the first temple of Hera is badly complicated and must wait for further light from the new revelations of a rich III C period in the town. The first temple of Hera on Samos was erected about 800 B.C. near the site of a late Mycenaean walled town, but again the evidence of sacral continuity is tenuous.

Whether potsherds prove cult is perhaps a matter for individual judgment. It is simply not true that every great Mycenaean stronghold begot a later sanctuary, as some scholars claim—Pylos, Orchomenos, Gla, Thebes, and Iolkos are obvious exceptions. Yet memory of the Mycenaean past may have conditioned revival of interest in some towns, and each revival meant a temple to make the town complete and protected. Some later Greeks, hearing that divinity had once visited and feasted in the houses of the old kings, would then have been attracted toward these Bronze Age ruins when new divine houses were to be built. A god does not like to be shifted.

Representations of Gods

The earliest representations of divine figures appear on the gold rings and gems of the Shaft Grave–tholos age (Pl. XIX A, F). It is curious that most of the famous gold rings with what is accepted as Cretan religious iconography actually come from the mainland: Mycenae, Tiryns, Dendra, Thebes, and Pylos. Impressions of similar rings or gems with cult scenes are well represented in Crete, however; and the style is almost universally agreed to be Cretan. The usual scene is outdoors, with a tree enclosed by a little railed fence, before which women in flounced skirts or youths in loin cloths gesticulate in worship. Sometimes they pull the tree down toward them, or lean over it dreamily, or bring presents: flowers, fruit, a shield, a jar of liquid (Pl. XIX F). Other popular themes are the divinity making an epiphany before a worshiper, a goddess seated to receive a procession of votaries, a holy object such as a pillar or double ax which is set between favorite animals and monsters. An unusual example of the first type comes from the tholos tomb at Pylos. The signet ring shows an outdoor shrine on a mound of rocks at which a wild goat and a worshiper watch a young god descending in the middle air. This is the only ring with a male epiphany to match the male gods listed in the Pylos tablets. On a ring from Tiryns a goddess sits on a high-backed throne with a bird perched behind her, as on the Homage krater (Fig. 36), wearing a long Mycenaean robe. Four lion daimons approach with ewers to fill her lifted drinking cup. On a ring from Mycenae (Pl. XLIII F) the goddess sits on a low stool or altar in front of a rocky mountain, dwarfing the male consort or mortal prince who stands before her. He grasps a great spear in his left hand, and holds his right hand out with index finger pointing toward the divinity, perhaps a gesture of assent or promise which she accepts with a reciprocal motion. This *sacra conversazione* is often interpreted as a scene of a mainland prince communing with the source of his spiritual power, although the costumes are Minoan. All three rings seem to have an independent, mainland imagery.

One unique, appealing gem recently excavated on Naxos illustrates mainland worship on a more human level (Fig. 44). A prince or soldier stands before an altar, behind which a palm tree sways in the wind. He wears Mycenaean dress: a tunic cinched with a metal belt, a flat cap with a plume. His

Fig. 44.—Gem with a ceremonial scene, worshiper before altar, Naxos. (After Kontoleon, *Ergon* 1959, Fig. 135, from a cast.)

spear is held at arm's length in the left hand, while the right hand rises to the cheek in a gesture of respect. The simple equipment of the ceremony is piled upon the altar: the worshiper's sword in its scabbard, balanced upright on the hilt to give us a better view of it, a conical rhyton, a pitcher for pouring libations, and a jar to catch the liquid. This bloodless offering in an outdoor precinct beside a sacred tree recalls Minoan rite too, here transposed to the Mycenaean world. The most holy palm tree in the Aegean grew in the sanctuary on Delos: the tree which Leto grasped in pain when she gave birth to Apollo, the tree which Odysseus saw beside the altar there (*Odyssey* VI, 162). Perhaps the cylinder was brought home from Delos by a Naxian traveler who had himself paid worship there.

The great gold rings and gems must have been restricted to the aristocracy or priesthood, but cheap terracottas make it clear that the great goddess so familiar in Crete was also loved in Greece, and that her Cretan form satisfied Mycenaean imaginings about her. The Keos statues are the most monumental; they show the goddess benignly at home to worshippers in her island temple, but most Greeks had no such large images to worship. Possibly the little terra-cotta women found in quantity all over the mainland are popular substitutes (p. 221; Pl. XLI A–B). Some scholars interpret them as divine nurses, espe-cially if they hold children in their arms or are arranged with a child in a triad like the Mycenae ivory group (Pls. XXXVIII, XLI E). Others consider them simple votives. They are as generalized religiously as the plastic Virgin on the windshield of a Greek taxi. When the artist puts the figure on a throne, how-ever, or riding a quadruped (Pl. XLI F), he is probably expressing in popular shorthand some belief about the goddess as the ordinary Mycenaean liked to imagine her, queen of the visible and invisible world, or dominating her serv-ant monster.

One cannot doubt that the Mycenaeans strongly recognized the power of the goddess, and of the gods of local towns, and that to them, as to the Minoans or later Greeks, such divine figures could appear in many aspects: regal, be-nevolent, threatening, remote, protective. Their artistic expression of such feel-ings is weak, however, and clouded behind borrowed conventions. In the same way, the cult apparatus of the Minoans seems lifeless when it is borrowed on the mainland, because it is not integrated in mainland tradition. Horns of consecration are shown as architectural elements of palaces and in palace frescoes, but are not worshipped. The double ax is much less common than on Crete except as a working tool. Plastic kernoi are extremely rare (p. 223; Pl. XLII D), and so are pierced libation vessels (Fig. 51). The physical evidence for Mycenaean religion is scanty; what does exist, tends to distinguish My-cenaean from Minoan religion in a fundamental way, beneath the superficial likenesses in the world of art.

Gods and Ceremonies in the Tablets

In contrast to the missing or mute evidence of physical remains, the Linear B texts are rich in religion. The Knossos and Pylos tablets offer the names of many gods, both recognizable classical divinities and other more elusive names which have not yet been matched with classical counterparts or did not survive the Dark Ages. There is also evidence for the kinds of offerings made to divinities, the priests and slaves in attendance upon them, and the laymen and land controlled in their names. There is no trace of religious codification, except for references to holy days. There are no texts of religious law, no recorded prayers. Mycenaean religion seems singularly free from priestly dictation and from dogma. This kind of spontaneous individual worship continues among the Homeric descendants of the Bronze Age Greeks.

The following divine figures have been recognized in the texts.

Knossos	*Pylos*
Potnia Atana	
Potnia Dapu$_2$ritojo	
	Potnia Asia
	Potnia Iqeja
	Potnia Newopeo
	Potnia Upojo
	(Potnia Pakijania)
Pipituna	
Eleuthia	
Erinu	
Diwia	Diwia
Hera	Hera
	Wanasoi
	Mater Theia
	Artemis
	Manasa
	Peleia
	Iphimedeia
	Posideia
Poseidon (Enesidaone)	Poseidon
Zeus	Zeus
Ares (Enyalios)	Ares(?)
Paiawon	
	Hermes
	Dionysos
	Trisheros
	Dopota
	Dipsioi
	Wanax(?)
	Drimios(?)

At Knossos the religious texts are fewer in proportion to the whole number than at Pylos, but the presence of Greek deities is clear. The two Potnias are local forms of the great lady who existed all over Greece, apparently, with distinctive epithets for each place or aspect which she had. *Potinija* is the Linear B spelling for an Indo-European word which has become rather a common title by the Homeric age; it is not a name, but a form of respectful address—lady or mistress. The Knossos text referring to *Atanapotinija* (V 52.1) may mean the Potnia of Athens, Athene, just as Homer often uses the formula πότνι' 'Αθηναίη, or Atana may be a town in Crete. *Dapu₂ritojo Potinija* (Gg 702) is almost surely the Lady of the Labyrinth, that is, of the place of the *labrys* or double ax, the palace itself. The other goddesses are easily identified. Pipituna is probably classical Diktynna, a Cretan hunting goddess. Eleuthia is Eileithyia in classical Greek, and had an old cult center as goddess of birth and fertility in a cave above Amnisos, the harbor station for Knossos. Diwia dies out after the Mycenaean Age; she seems to be the female form of Zeus (Dieus), and was supplanted by Hera. Erinu may be Erinys, the Fury of Homeric poetry, perhaps here an epithet for Demeter who is sometimes addressed as Demeter Erinys later. Otherwise Demeter does not exist in Linear B.

Epithets seem more in vogue at Knossos than at Pylos, from the meagre records surviving; Poseidon has his title *Ennosigaion,* "Earth-Shaker," and Ares is *Enyalios,* "Battle God." Poseidon is mentioned four times at Knossos, and thus appears to be the most popular deity, as he is at Pylos later among his Neleid descendants, suiting warriors who had made their conquest by sea and were respectful of the sea's power.

The Knossos deities are known from lists made on the occasion of offerings to them. The schedule of offerings sometimes mentions the month when they are made, and mentions certain days as *outemi,* οὐ θέμις, "not customary" (V 280). Besides the gods, certain cult figures receive offerings, such as *anemo ijereja,* the "Priestess of the Winds," and *qerasija,* perhaps the Augur(?) or the Huntress(?). A very common offering is to *pasi teoi,* "All-the-Gods," especially at Amnisos where cults and names had perhaps proliferated among sailors of mixed background and language. Religious offerings are entirely bloodless in Crete. A jar of honey, jars of oil, barley and wine, spices like fennel and coriander, possibly wool and cheese are the only recorded gifts. Groups of sheep and shepherds are associated with Potnia but not in terms of sacrifice.

The Augur, if he existed at all, must have been the sort to interpret bird flights or tree noises, not entrails.

One misses the goddesses who seem in classical religion to have old Aegean characteristics: Aphrodite, Artemis, Britomartis, Demeter(?). One misses any reference to snake goddesses, bulls, built shrines, horns of consecration, double axes, altars, and ecstatic dances. The only cave sanctuary is Eileithyia's at Amnisos, in which people still offer; there is perhaps a peak sanctuary for Zeus on Mount Dikte; possibly a sanctuary called the Daidaleon, the place of Daidalos, existed in the Knossos palace. Otherwise the records seem tame compared to Minoan pictorial renditions of cult, and strongly mainland in character.

The classic mainland list of offerings is the great tablet Pylos *Tn* 316, which arranges many gods in a curious order (Zeus near the bottom) and records their gifts of gold bowls and cups, men and women:

Side A:	Potnia	1 gold cup	1 woman
	Manasa	1 gold bowl	1 woman
	Posideia	1 gold bowl	1 woman
	Trisheros	1 gold cup	
	Dopota	1 gold cup	
Side B:	Poseidon	1 gold cup	2 women
	Pere-*82	1 gold bowl	1 woman
	Iphimedeia	1 gold bowl	
	Diuja	1 gold bowl	1 woman
	Hermes	1 gold cup	1 man
	Zeus	1 gold bowl	1 man
	Hera	1 gold bowl	1 woman
	Drimios	1 gold bowl	[

Many of these figures are shadowy and did not survive the Dark Ages. Manasa is unknown. The Triple Hero is popular at Pylos, though he has no good classical counterpart; the name should mean Great Hero, Triply Great. Dopota is perhaps the Despot or Master of the House. Pere-*82 is variously translated Peleia, "Dove Goddess"; Pelekys, "Goddess of the Double Ax"; Persephone, "The Destroyer." Iphimedeia becomes a mere heroine later, a lover of Poseidon, a mother of giants. Diuja is the defunct Lady Zeus, Drimios is unknown. The tablet does not specify whether offerings are to be made in separate sanctuaries for each divinity, or in one communal sanctuary, perhaps the palace or the precinct of Poseidon. Among many curious aspects of the text one may single out the seeming dominance of women over men, the presentation of

human beings to gods, and the total lack of co-ordination between this ceremony and every standard scene in art except the procession frescoes (p. 193).

The major god at Pylos is Poseidon. He has a sanctuary, and perhaps a female consort, Posidaeja. He is closely associated with the great Potnia of Pylos,
whose sanctuary is at *Pakijana,* and with the Wanasoi or "Two Queens." He is
offered oil, boars and sows, bulls, sheep, rams' fleece, grain, wine, cheese, and
honey. Animals were expensive offerings, but blood sacrifice certainly existed,
to goddesses and gods alike.

There are many Potnias at Pylos, with different places or activities under
their command. The one at *Pakijana* is the richest and most often called upon.
Potnia *Iqeja* is connected with the horse chariots in the Pylos sheds (p. 178).
Smiths and other laymen are sometimes titled "Potnia people," as though
formed into a guild under divine protection. The nature of Potnia and of the
Wanasoi, the Two Queens, is left general. Everyone must have understood who
they were. The latter are the kind of figures out of whom Demeter and Persephone later crystallized. They are associated with a young Wanax, or "Lord,"
as in the ivory triad from Mycenae (Pl. XXXVIII), or with Poseidon who is a
normal husband for Demeter in that region. Offerings are also made to *Matere
teija,* "Mother of the Gods" or "Divine Mother," nameless in a sense but surviving into classical religion as the Magna Mater. These ladies are all distinguished by individual titles, just as Rhea and Demeter and Hera and the
Mother of the Gods were distinguished in classical belief but had overlapping
functions and images. Visitors from Mycenae or Eleusis with their comparable
strong cults would undoubtedly have recognized the Pylian goddesses, but have
been relieved, in the end, to get home safely to their own. Such a belief in local
goddesses who are all of commanding stature and alike in their natures, yet
personal in a way only a native can be, is exactly what one would predict in a
country of strong regional divisions before any real concept of a nation grew up.

The sanctuaries of Potnia at *Pakijana* and of Poseidon are not formally called
sanctuaries in the texts—there is no Mycenaean word for this—but they are
places where personnel serve the gods and where priests, servants of the gods, or
tereta (a noble religious title) hold extensive lands. There are no buildings
mentioned, which harmonizes with the archaeological evidence. So, in Homer,
Nestor makes his sacrifice of bulls to Poseidon simply on the shore, on the loose
sand (*Odyssey* III, 5) as he might in the fields, in the palace courtyard, or at
his own hearth. Cult environment and living environment seem the same, in-
terpenetrating, natural, and unpretentious. Presumably when gold vases or jars

of oil were offered to the gods, they were not left out in the open air but divided among the personnel or housed in the palace itself.

Pylos ceremonies are best known from the Olive Oil tablets, found in 1955, which had been stored upstairs in the palace or in the oil stores behind the megaron. A characteristic entry is "Olive oil for the *Upojo* Potnia, for annointing robes"(?) (Fr 1225). The distinctions among scents and qualities of oil are astonishing (batches with sage, rose, kuperos, and *eti-*) and so is the destination of so much of it to gods. The principal recipients are the *Asia* and *Upojo* Potnias, the Two Queens, the Lord, the Divine Mother, Poseidon, the Thirsty Ones or *Dipsioi,* the Triple Hero, and plain *theoi,* gods. The Thirsty Ones have been interpreted as the dead demanding libations in their tombs (though wine, not oil, should be offered to the dead), or as the little daimons in skin suits who keep appearing in art with hopefully lifted ewers, filling the Queen's cup or watering her altar. The occasions on which oil is offered to this divine company include the Season of New Wine (Fr 1202), the Spreading of the Couch (Fr 343-1212, 1217), and the Bringing Forth of the Throne (Fr 1222). The couch would be proper for some human celebration of the divine *hieros gamos* or sacred wedding, perhaps each year between Poseidon and Potnia. The throne is brought forth for the Two Queens; one can well imagine that an elaborate inlaid throne like those of the furniture tablets (p. 174) was exhibited to the people of Pylos once a year; the rite would harmonize with the scenes on gold rings showing the seated goddess accepting adoration. The offerings are sometimes described as *xeinion* or "gift of hospitality." The whole series, despite its mysteries, reflects sensible, respectful, and colorful practice, removed from the more dramatic cult scenes of Minoan iconography. Pylos offers what Pylos grows and exports best, to gods whose protection extends over the sea and the crops.

The gods and ceremonies were served by a variety of persons at Pylos. Both men and women have the role of priest, not necessarily matching the sex of the god. Eritha the priestess at *Pakijana* has a more vivid personality than most. She argues with the *damos* or community over the terms on which she holds her land; she hopes to get it declared the god's property (tax free) but the *damos* insists she must pay (Ep 704). She is quite a rich woman, with a personal slave girl and two male slaves; perhaps she is the priestess who was awarded fourteen girls "because of the sacred gold" (Ae 303), presumably to guard and polish those gold vessels in the cupboard. We have already met the priest *Newokito* (p. 252), charged to divide out land fairly. A priest at Prosymna in the Argolid came of a good and wealthy family, and was buried with the equipment of his trade (p. 300). Other functionaries are the servants of the gods, both male and female, who sometimes inherit the position and own land as substantial citizens; the Key Bearer (*karawiporo*); the Sacrificer (*ijero-woko*), Barley Sprinklers (*kiritewija*) and perhaps the Fire Tender (*pukowo*). The *Tereta* or Telestai are men of noble rank with mixed religious and military functions. Indeed the tablets illustrate a much greater diversity of officials than the physical remains of archaeology would lead one to suspect, and are a healthy antidote to the old belief in a Minoan priest-king with overwhelming divine and political powers. The king remained central, as he must, but understood how to delegate responsibility and avoid irritating vested interests.

On the whole the tablets present a complex, rather independent society in which religion plays an important but not massive role. The main concerns at Pylos are in the land and its wealth, in the outlying towns and the sea. The ceremonies are rich but not elaborately staged. It is pleasant to find the Mycenaeans relatively free of superstition, without temples, dogmatic laws, or penalties for transgression, not paying forced taxes to gods and priests or being cursed in their names, but offering the best of what they have to their local protectors.

BURIAL CUSTOMS

Early Ritual

This body of evidence is so well known, and has been so ably summarized elsewhere, that only a few interesting aspects need be commented on here. From the Shaft Graves onward, there are fixed rituals for burying a member of a Mycenaean family. Although the ornate funeral dress of the Shaft Graves does not seem to persist beyond the early fifteenth century, other elements in them do. They offer the prototypes for the association of chariot races with funeral games or corteges (p. 91). They show that a meal of meat and wine was shared by the survivors after the grave had been filled in (Circle B), and that the dead person was also given vases of ordinary domestic kinds, presumably filled with oil or wine. The tradition of filled vases, perhaps a weapon and beads as gifts, documented in Early Helladic and Cycladic graves, had persisted all through the Middle Helladic Age (p. 79). What is newly established in the Shaft Grave era is the conception of the grave as a family receptacle which could be opened many times for younger relatives.

Two other "firsts" in the Shaft Graves continue through the tholos period and after: the presence of scale balances (Pl. XLVII A) and of lamps. The Vapheio prince (p. 128) had with him bronze discs of scale pans, a sturdier version of the Shaft Grave gold foil examples. Stone vases in his cist functioned as lamps. Light and weighing machinery as a symbolic element in Mycenaean beliefs about the dead are matters we do not quite understand yet but cannot set aside. The need for light is the more understandable of the two, as with a child being sent into the dark. The scales are not regular equipment but are given only in richer tombs and are fairly rare even there. One could connect them with the symbol of measuring authority, or with the classical tradition of *psychostasia,* weighing the souls for life or death, or for their merits in the underworld, but nothing from tombs will confirm such guesses.[7]

The Myrsinochorion tholos adds further information about Early Mycenaean practice (p. 131). No tholos shows more clearly the family character of these buildings. Two cists under the floor were packed with earlier dead, four or five in one and a single princess wearing gorgeous beads in the other; the last figure lay in the center of the floor on a red and blue rug. A little tripod brazier painted with an octopus stood between the two cists as though a coal fire had been lit there to clear the air or punctuate some moment in the ceremony; on the floor nearby was a firehook of a kind mentioned later in the Pylos texts (*purautoro*). Fumigation and the burning of incense were common practice in reopened tombs, and highly desirable as a practical measure against the airless damp. A pair of scale pans was also present in this tomb. In a neighboring tomb a frying pan was found filled with decayed meat (lamb or kid) from the funeral meal.

The whole Pylos district is rich in funerary evidence, which Marinatos has collected. One interesting phenomenon is the deep cuts for wheels of a chariot or practical wagon in the door or dromos of some tombs, like the Tragana tholos. Persson noted the same in Dendra tombs in the Argolid, and was torn between interpreting them as ruts of carts, or marks of sledges on which a heavy coffin could ride. Coffins, of course, are extremely rare (p. 301), but even an unboxed corpse is heavy to carry decently on a bier or rug, and no doubt many contrivances were used to make work easier for pallbearers. Wagons were probably one, and the wheel ruts were made ahead of time to lower the cortege under the lintel block. Although the procession is illustrated occasionally in Mycenaean art (p. 205), the only genuine horse burial found in Greece so far is the pair at the outer end of the Marathon tholos dromos (Pl. XLVII B) where no traces of carriage or harness were reported. Horses were expensive and could not often be so spared. One dearly loved horse at Lerna was apparently offered a funeral toast by thirty-seven admirers when he died.[8] The west coast, an archer's district, also supplies examples of volleys of arrows being shot inward toward the tomb apparently in a last salute of honor. The more normal practice, everywhere in Greece, is to drink from a plain cheap kylix (see Fig. 51) and smash it against the door or drop it in the dromos.

Many of these tholos customs were shared by families using chamber tombs, so that there was no social distinction in the ceremonies, which must interest those who believe the new Mycenaean dynasts to be of different stock from their "subjects." The main difference between tholoi and chambers in the early period is money, sometimes also topography, when a district might have no suitable bedrock for carving out the one or stone for building the other. The first chamber tombs of Pylos, in LH I, are made to tholos specifications with vaulted roofs and incised lintels; in both east and west some chambers are as rich as tholoi until after LH III A:1, when a leveling out in quality prevails (p. 208). It is primarily the LH III chambers, so abundant and often intact, that allow almost certain reconstruction of an "empire" funeral.

A Normal Empire Funeral

The chamber tomb is a family vault. If the family outlives the Mycenaean Age the tomb, especially its dromos, may continue to be used into Geometric times. It is originally cut into a variety of shapes, square or round, with a flat or hip roof and as many as three or four side chambers for large families. In the early period it may be painted outside to resemble a house or palace door, with rosettes or feathered papyrus motifs in yellow, blue, black, and red (Fig. 45), but it is rare to take so much trouble.[9] The floor is normally the bedrock or a layer of beaten earth. Persson thought it might be whitened with plaster, but this is not regularly observed. The corpse is carried into the tomb, sometimes on a bier or catafalque of flimsy wood covered with a skin or cloth, or stuccoed over; traces are understandably rare but guaranteed. He is laid out on the freest part of the floor, fully clothed and usually on his back, less often contracted foetally to one side. His head may be slightly raised on a stone to counteract the awful lolling look of the dead; his hands are by his sides or crossed in his lap. There is no special orientation except a tendency to face the door. Ancestors are swept against rear or side walls to make room for newcomers, with some disregard for their arrangement. Their gifts may be taken back now, but more often they are left in peace, particularly if they are cheap gifts like pots. Infants are often set in niches in the dromos. Some tombs have benches, usually against the right-hand wall, on which older skeletons or extra gifts may be piled. The gifts are the common things from which our understanding of Mycenaean minor art is drawn; some districts specialize in stirrup jars (large for oil, small for perfume), others in jugs or kraters. Almost everyone is given a drinking cup in some form. Infants may be given special feeding bottles with spouts (see Fig. 51). A child who died with his mother during birth is laid in her arms; older children may be given lead-filled shells to play games with. A man is granted his knife, a woman her jewelry or comb; other dress objects like gems depend on the family resources.

Fɪɢ. 45.—Design on a door frame of a tomb at Argos, painted in black, red, yellow, and blue. (After Vollgraff, *BCH* 1904, Fig. 1.)

Only the richer tombs possess ivory boxes or other containers. The evidence for furniture in tombs is extremely tenuous (p. 175). Dendra and Mycenae among others yield the ivory plates from footstools, small curved ivory strips from Kakovatos and Asine perhaps came from bier frames, some inlays may have fallen off chairs and tables as well as boxes. Yet the overwhelming majority of chamber tombs hold no furniture of any large kind, and the new fashion of ascribing the Pylos furniture tablets to the inventory of a prospective tomb group will probably soon be adjusted to the evidence. However, lamps, braziers, and tableware of all sorts are vouched for. Sometimes a man's professional gear is buried with him, not just military gear, but the tools of a stone-cutter, or a carpenter. A priest's burial at Prosymna included, among other marks of rank, a gold signet ring corded to his wrist, a table of offerings, and five pierced vases for libation. The tomb was a very large one (5.0 m. deep) and had been in use since LH I; it was equipped with lamps, scales, grooves in the door, possibly a bier, gems, jewelry, arrowheads, knives, lead, ivory, and amber, all the signs of a prominent family.[10] The ivory lyre from the Menidi tholos may have belonged to a poet.

When the burial had been completed the doorway was painstakingly filled up again with stones (rarely brick), and the dromos filled in after farewells had been spoken or drunk.

Coffins and Cremation

Since the Mycenaeans traveled abroad so much (see Fig. 40) it is not surprising to find them bringing home occasional new customs, among which the use of coffins and cremation are most interesting. Coffins or sarcophagi when made of wood are susceptible to rapid disintegration, and when one finds traces of such rotted wood in tombs it takes nice judgment to ascribe it to a coffin, a bier, a box, or the fuel for fumigation. Persson was sure of an Early Mycenaean wooden coffin at Dendra, however, and considering the other close links to Knossos in that period he was likely right although in photographs it looks more like a bier. The use of wooden coffins in Crete begins about the time of the Warrior Graves; at Katsaba, where the Tuthmosis III vase was buried (p. 152), Alexiou found one painted bright blue. The Greeks tended not to use them, however, except in rare cases of addicts to foreign fashion. The Cretan stone or clay versions on legs with gabled lids are no doubt modeled on an original wooden prototype, and come into Greece again in the late thirteenth century in the unique series of painted larnakes already discussed (p. 210; Pls. XXXIV-XXXV). Very occasionally, one finds the other type, the bathtub larnax, used for a child whose size would make it easy to carry. This rarity of coffins is an element in the Mycenaean heritage which seems to continue, for the classical Greeks did not normally use them either.[11]

Cremations are equally a foreign innovation, which used to be attributed to the invading Dorians at the beginning of the Dark Ages but are now seen to be much older and particularly connected with the East.[12] The first example is perhaps in a tholos tomb at Tragana near Pylos where women were cremated just after 1400 in the fall of Knossos period. Perhaps, like coffins, this new fashion should be attributed to Crete, where it is known as early as MM II. It is, however, much more native to Anatolia and the Near East, and when it turns up in Greece in the late thirteenth and early twelfth centuries it is mostly associated with Levantine trade and the Close style. Whether it was brought by soldiers who had been fighting with the Hittites or merchants who had seen the cremation cemetery of Troy VI we cannot tell. It appears at the same time as the first iron weapons, the Hittite or Syrian bronze figurines, and the Syrian and Egyptian seals and scarabs (Pl. XLVIII; Fig. 29), and illustrates as well as any physical fact could the intense internationalism of the Sea Peoples period.

The principal cremations in the Mycenaean world were made at Ialysos in Rhodes and at Perati in Attica; there are instances also at Naxos, Argos, and several coastal sites in Crete which were receiving new settlers and sailors returning home. Ialysos and Perati testify dramatically to the new crosscurrents of the age. A single tomb at Ialysos was found to contain a Hittite seal, an iron bracelet, an ivory comb, two cremations and ten inhumations. Another peculiar feature of the cemetery is the use of little stone blocks, with geometric signs incised on them, set in the dromos or the chamber (see Fig. 47 *b*). These *cippi tombali* are not tombstones in the modern sense, since they could not be seen from outside the tomb, but one wonders whether they represent a vague trend toward identifying the dead through a primitive writing system. Sometimes late sarcophagi in Crete have such incised signs too. The few real grave stelai which survive from this period are simply scalloped or, in one case, painted with soldiers (p. 209; Fig. 47 *a, c*).[13]

Perati is one of the most interesting and extensive of all Mycenaean cemeteries. It lies above the harbor at Porto Raphti on the east coast of Attica and holds nearly two hundred tombs in an agreeable landscape (Pl. XLVIII A). The small rocky acropolis higher up was created as a town by people moving shoreward after the palace destructions, and the harbor brought it a strange mixture of overseas souvenirs. Different kinds of burials—shafts, cists, chambers —are mixed together; seven cremation burials have been discovered so far, six adults and a child. These cremations may be either in a jar or in the bare earth; in one case a cremated woman was given her jewelry as for a normal burial. One cremation is "dated" by a scarab of Rameses II who ruled during so much of the thirteenth century (1301–1234 B.C.); his scarabs are particularly popular in Greece. According to Iakovides' analysis of the chronology, the whole Perati cemetery begins just after the reign of Rameses II, in the age of mainland disasters, and lasts for perhaps three generations. During that time the local Mycenaeans acquired a good many Egyptian mementoes: scarabs, Bes figures, little faïence crocodiles. From Syria they got two hematite cylinders in the classic Mitanni style of two hundred years before (Pl. XLVIII C), a curved bronze blade, two iron daggers, and an iron pin. Their sea-going habits are represented by a fishing net with lead weights and bronze fishhooks, their superstition perhaps by a hematite seal with gibberish Linear B characters (Fig. 46). The apotropaic power of writing is specially felt among the illiterate. One cannot divorce the finds of this cemetery from the Achaian raids of the late Hittite empire and the Greeks in the Delta or at Troy (p. 273), as evidence of internationalism affecting the provinces.

Fig. 46.—Hematite amulet seal with gibberish Linear B signs, Perati Tomb 24. (Drawing by Sp. Iakovides.)

A little kalathos bowl from Perati has unusual figurines of mourning women mounted around the rim (Pl. XLII F). Their hands are raised to their heads as though to scratch their cheeks or tear their hair the way Homeric mourners do. Such figurines are rare, limited to exactly the kinds of places that have the other late innovations: Ialysos, Naxos, and possibly Tiryns with its iron sword and European gold. They are intimately linked in theme and emotion to the mourning women on the painted sarcophagi (Pls. XXXIV–XXXV), with the same long robes and classic gestures of grief. Such novelties are prompted partly

303

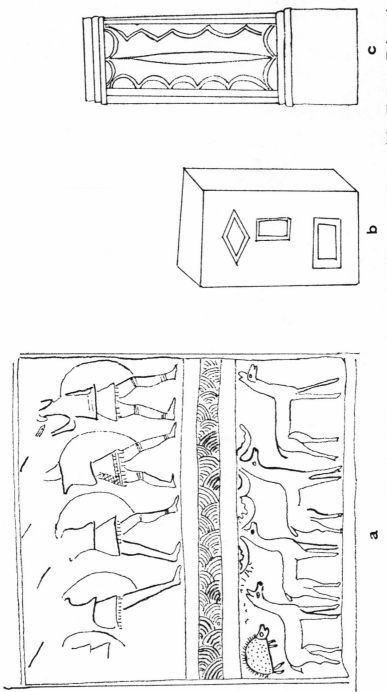

FIG. 47.—Gravestones and stelai: (a) painted stele, stucco over limestone, twelfth century, Mycenae (after Tsountas, *Ephemeris* 1896, Pl. 1); (b) incised block from a tomb at Ialysos, thirteenth century (after Maiuri, *Annuario* 1926, Fig. 131); (c) incised stone stele from a tomb at Mycenae, thirteenth century (after Tsountas, *Ephemeris* 1888, Fig. 4).

by the more general eruption of three-dimensional genre sketches of the age but also because it was a dangerous age to live in; any adventurous man was likely to die young.

As the Mycenaean world fades out and the people tend to scatter from the old urban centers, they take a variety of burial practices with them. Tholoi are newly built in the III B–C epoch in Epeiros, Thessaly, Crete, and even overseas in Caria (see chap. v bibliography). The Parga tholos in Epeiros shows the links between Hallstatt A Europe and the west provinces at this moment. Crete and Caria practice cremation inside the old chamber tomb form, and cover the whole with an earth tumulus. In Kephallenia, with its great influx of refugees, deep pits containing up to fifty persons are dug in the floor of the chamber. Athens switches almost exclusively to cremation at the beginning of the Proto-geometric period. This diffusion of practice is not reflected in Homer; he speaks only of cremation and an earth tumulus combined, another reason for discarding his testimony for normal Mycenaean behavior and belief before the Dark Ages.

Tourism and Mythology

What can one tell, from such descriptions, about Mycenaean religion or thoughts? The tombs suggest a strong sense of family solidarity. This harmonizes with the epic passion for genealogy, and probably on each opening the family could recite the names of the older skeletons. But there is nothing approaching ancestor worship. No cult of the dead was ever practiced in any Mycenaean tomb during the Bronze Age. This is reserved for later ages, from the late tenth century onward, when people were astonished at the size and solidity of the old tombs, the richness of gifts, and the apparent power of the men buried in them. Then they might add their own vases to tombs accidentally opened, or ones which had become centers of some sort of tourist curiosity.

The archaic and classical periods are especially susceptible to such feelings. The cult of Agamemnon was prominent at Mycenae and Sparta. The tholos tomb at Menidi received all sorts of humble archaic offerings in the dromos before the door. The tholos at Peristeria was visited from the early fifth century onward by people who lit fires and consumed a meal over the old dead. They took in lamps to light their way. In Athens a half-dozen white-ground funeral lekythoi were placed beside a Mycenaean skeleton whose legs had been accidentally chopped off in an urban renewal program. In Boiotia the Tomb of

Alkmene was opened and a marvelous bronze sheet with mysterious script signs on it became part of the fabulous heritage of the past. Some similar event may have prompted what sometimes seems like a revival of Linear B signs in late vase painting. The fantasies about these older tombs are rich. Likely bumps were chosen for the old heroes, and shown with pride to strangers: the tombs of Hippolytos, Aias, Talthybios, Kassandra, Menelaos and Helen, Lykos and Opheltes. It is the period which turned Thebes into a "wahres mythologisches Raritätenkabinett," as Belger put it, where the graves of Herakles' or Amphion's children vied with Alkmene's bedroom or Kadmos' cow as tourist come-ons. A tumulus in Arkadia had a stone marker supposed to be Orestes' petrified finger which he bit off and threw away as the Furies chased him. Old chambers between Tiryns and the sea, recently rediscovered, were thought to be the bedrooms of the lusty mad daughters of Proitos who were turned into cows. Skeletons were judged enormous by classical standards. "Orestes" proved to be seven cubits tall when exhumed in Tegea; "Asterios the son of Anax the son of Earth" was ten cubits long in his grave on an islet in front of Miletos. A grave by the shore on Salamis was attributed to Aias or one of his huge followers because the knee-pan was larger than a boy's discus.[14] The two tombs on Delos were believed the sepulchres of the fabulous Hyperborean Maidens. Without understanding the Mycenaeans their descendants obviously enjoyed them enormously, and found them a rich source for creating a national tradition of mythology.

Music and Poets

One of the first excitements upon the decipherment of Linear B was to see whether some genuine forefather of Homer had scratched his poems upon the tablets. In an essay of this sort, entirely unliterary, it would be wrong to discuss trivially the links between the Mycenaean and Homeric worlds; everyone has his own opinion. For the past thirty years, however, scholars have agreed that Homer was singing his own version of a traditional narrative poem which was in itself only a fraction of the poetic material inherited by Geometric Greeks from an earlier age. Some of the material is certainly Mycenaean, and the tradition may go back at least to *ca.* 1400 B.C. (p. 135). Opinions vary as to how much, which parts, and how. The evidence of Linear B is related to many Homeric fields: religion, warfare, social structure, furniture, weapons, ships, food. At first scholars overlooked the fact that this was raw material for Homer, not the poetic expression of that material, and the whole academic world turned out in an Easter egg hunt for hexameters on clay at Pylos. The results were poor. Certain words and names were also used by Homer and the rest of the epic school, and the inventories were held to be poetically sympathetic to the Homeric love of catalogues. But the prime quality of poetry, metrical form, was never found except by a few determined quantity-counters; the surprise was, how many people were disappointed.

What sensible poet, when he could sing with his lyre to a good audience, or in his off hours perfect formulae and think about character or effective incident, would abandon all that for the irritation of Linear B on clay tablets fit only for two to twelve lines of verse? There are many reasons to be astonished if one should discover poetry in Linear B, at least until some long papyrus or bronze roll should be found. Such a find is unlikely. Papyrus was used for certain communications, as one guesses from the string marks on clay sealings used to fasten thin packages, but it rarely survives in the Greek climate. More important, such a find would presuppose the poet to be literate, which is not usual among oral poets, or that one of the thirty men at Pylos who could write could also take dictation from a local versifier, or would be concerned to. This would imply a fear of losing the songs unless steps were taken, and thus a kind of antiquarian interest which especially marks a people whose history is behind it. Until after the Sea Peoples epoch the Mycenaeans had no thought that their world would shrink or disappear, or that their poets and adventures would not continue with the old success. Their own poetry was probably not primarily historical any more than their painting was, and their heroes only grew great in the imagination of posterity when it seemed impossible to breed new heroes to match them. Hesiod makes his feelings about this clear in the famous passage about human history, its steps from the Golden Age to the Iron Age: the heroes belong *after* the Bronze Age, and their wars at Thebes and Troy are later than the great anonymous wars of an age that knew no iron.[15] The later heroes are given immortality in soul and in poetry; the earlier ones "left no name." This historical perspective suits Aegean archaeology very well. The Sea Peoples period with its coming iron and cremation, its travels and internationalism, is prime material for mythical-historical poetry; the older days before *ca.* 1250 remain still pretty anonymous.

This does not deny the presence of many genuine Mycenaean elements in later epic; it merely suggests a distinction between Mycenaean poetry of the early period and of the palace age, and poetry from the late thirteenth century onward. The earlier poetry is not recoverable. The later poetry mentions none of the salient features of the early period: tholos tombs, frescoes, writing. But poetry and song certainly existed from the beginning, and one can tell something about it without written documents. From the first Cycladic harper past the singing mouths on the Harvester Vase to the poet of the Pylos megaron song was a happy element in Aegean life. The natural Mycenaean instrument was the stringed lyre. The instrument itself is known, first with seven strings on the Hagia Triada sarcophagus, then in the ivory lyre from the Menidi tholos tomb which is tenuously reconstructed and may have had seven or eight strings. A little model bronze lyre from Amyklai by Sparta has eight strings, or places for them (Fig. 49); it was found with the late terracottas characteristic of the Sea Peoples epoch. The lyre-playing poet from Pylos uses only five strings (Pl. XXX A). Lyres imply a decent knowledge of scales and chords. The other two instruments known to the Cretans, the pipe and the *sistrum* (a sort of tambourine), have not yet been reflected in Mycenaean finds except for one bone flute from Mycenae.[16]

With the lyre and whatever other instruments were familiar, the Mycenaeans had both amateur and professional poets, but probably not "schools" or "guilds" in the later formal sense. The Pylos poet wears a distinctive, womanish costume; he is a professional. Amateurs in the villages and palaces no doubt used some of the fixed types of song which Homer says were traditional in his day: songs of harvest, of mourning at funerals, of procession in ceremonies, songs for work, weddings, war, and games. The professionals would produce more extensive and lively compositions, or they would not be invited to the palace twice.

The ancestor of all lyric poets, Orpheus, seems to have a Bronze Age type of name with the *-eus* ending. Tradition makes him a northerner. A fellow poet called Thamyris traveled from the north to Pylos; in his poignant entry to Homeric tradition he was "stopped" before he got there. He was arrogant enough to challenge the Muses to a contest, and "the angry goddesses crippled him—they took away his divine song and made him forget how to play the lyre" (*Iliad* II, 599). Perhaps this explains the apathetic posture of the Pylos poet—Thamyris looking wistfully at a bird for inspiration, with limp hands. If his story has Mycenaean content it implies again that there was no Bronze Age need for putting poems into writing; the mountain muses were guarantors enough of fact and truth, and memory was the poet's greatest gift. The story also implies Mycenaean singing contests among professionals. A third tenuous

Bronze Age song was attributed to the misty poet Musaios: a very archaic-sounding Hymn to Demeter which was thought to be his only original composition and thus of huge antiquity.[17]

These poets have left us only songs without words, and not much music, and cannot be forced to conform to our ideas about Homer's archaic prototypes. They may perfectly well have sung about famous hunts, overseas expeditions, sieges, foundations of foreign colonies, natural marvels like whirlpools and volcanoes, even apparitions of the gods and wars in heaven (if the Mycenaeans had a theology they would have committed some of its developmental aspects to forms easily memorized). We shall never know. The singers were probably itinerant experts like the best fresco painters, gem cutters, goldsmiths, or the prophets and doctors whom Penelope mentions in the *Odyssey*. Less reputed figures might have been trained and supported in each palace, like the minstrel Agamemnon left to keep an eye on his wife. The scanty information for early poetry is strongest in places of strong Mycenaean settlement: Pylos, the Attic-Boiotian border, Thessaly; to these must be added Mycenae, Argos, and Sparta for the centrality of their epic stories and the hints of old music there. From these areas with old traditions, the poets of the real Homeric age, *ca.* 850–700, inherited some material and spread it more widely abroad, but where the Mycenaean heritage remained least altered, in the mainland countryside after the palaces and in the new overseas towns founded by colonists, the potentialities for poetry were most ardent.

THE GREEK MEMORY OF THE MYCENAEANS

The oral tradition refracted in part to us through Homer and his contemporaries preserves Mycenaean dialect, vocabulary words, personal names, geography, genealogy, a few military aspects, a little cult. This is utterly normal. There was no break between the Mycenaean and Homeric worlds, only change. The degree of change is arguable. Lists of Mycenaean relics in Homer are constantly shifting from one epoch to another; breastplates, greaves, lamps, cult statues have all been removed recently from the Geometric-Orientalizing list and given back to the Mycenaeans. No doubt many other poetic objects would move the other way if necessary or comforting. The curious case of Nestor's *depas* is a nice example (Fig. 48). Schliemann thought he found it in gold in the Shaft Graves. In Linear B the depas is a large storage jar; in Homer, Nestor drinks from a bronze(?) one with gold trim; by the eighth century the depas

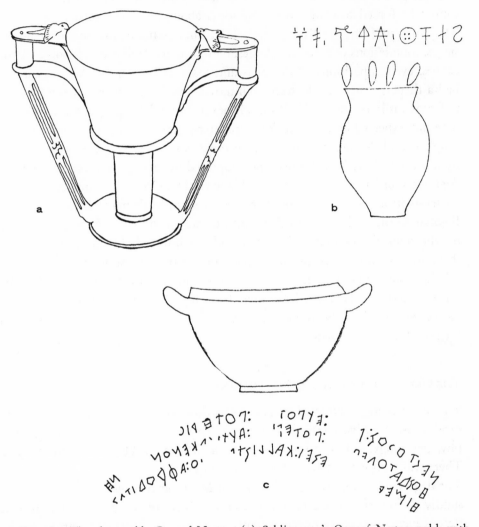

Fig. 48.—The changeable Cup of Nestor: (*a*) Schliemann's Cup of Nestor, gold, with hawks on the handles, Circle A, Grave IV, Mycenae, fifteenth century (after Bossert, *Alt-Kreta*[2], Fig. 212); (*b*) depas with four handles, sketched on Pylos tablet *Ta* 641, thirteenth century. The text says, "Dipa, of larger size, with four ears." (*c*) Skyphos from the Euboian colony at Pithecusai near Naples, eighth century. The text says, "I am Nestor's good drinking cup. Whoever drinks this cup, longing for lovely-crowned Aphrodite will get him quickly." (After Jeffery, *Local Scripts of Archaic Greece*, Pl. 47, 1.)

has become a clay cup of modest but refreshing capacity. These transformations warn us of the scholarly gymnastics demanded as knowledge of the Greek language changes, new archaeological finds are made, and emotional desires shift. It does not affect Nestor's depas in the least if we find physical parallels to it or not. Yet the desire to endow Homer with roots and ancestors to whom he is faithful is deeply felt by many, as though it were all we could do to repay him for his poetry.

What shall we grant Homer as "pure" Mycenaean? Epithets and myths of towns which faded out after 1200 B.C.—Pylos, Salamis, Dendra, Thebes, and Troy. Some of their visual charms painted by the epithets were meters under dust or overgrown with scrub when Homer was born, and their myths half-forgotten. Homer, like every good oral poet, guarded these by communal oral memory and reintroduced the Greeks to aspects of their own past which non-poets did not know of. Certain set pieces were preserved such as catalogues of ships, men, and treasures. The originals of many myths retold by Homer were Mycenaean since they refer to people and towns of the Bronze Age. We may be quite sure, however, that Homer's versions of these myths are not the versions the Mycenaeans knew, because myth changes with every telling and is constantly being improved, made more "modern" and "meaningful." Certain archaic features like chariot drill or *guala* or stone-walled cities, or foreign voyagers like Bellerophon in Lycia, may have been "remembered" in the professional sense by poets for four hundred years—rarely going back earlier than 1250, however.

The story-telling uses of this material no doubt varied remarkably from singer to singer. The real world was changing and its interests and desires naturally changed too. Both overseas and mainland poetry was moving away from its old formal character by Homer's and Hesiod's time. Lyric poetry, that is, short personal and sometimes bumptious compositions like Archilochos', was already respectable and admired before 700 B.C. The long heroic narrative and catalogue poems were going out of fashion. Perhaps this matched the change from shepherd life to large-scale agricultural and commercial life. The older poets like Hesiod met their muses because they were alone watching the animals on the hills. The Amyklai lyre was buried with a cow (Fig. 49) but Archilochos sold his cows, and with them his leisure to compose long reflective pieces in his head. Perhaps, if Hesiod was primarily concerned with teaching about a new depressing way to keep alive during the transition from meat to bread, that is from flock-watching to back-breaking farmwork, we may see the death of epic poetry in a corresponding loss of time and loneliness.[18] The creative period passes with the coming of progress, industry, and the formalization of the working man's role. In Yugoslavian tradition the young shepherd learned to sing in his field alone; he does not do so well on a collective farm where the grinding gears of the best machines and democratic bonhomie outdecibel the muse. The short poem and the public drama succeed epic in the Greek tradition, and with the epic dies the Mycenaean core of Greek memory.

Homer and Hesiod suffered relatively little change after their death because their poems were written down. Before that, the material they used had been subjected to four or five hundred years of creative change. Since 1100 B.C. at the very latest no one had seen a live Mycenaean or knew what he ate or wore, how he lived or sang. Occasionally the accidental discovery of a tomb gave impetus to myths about the past; sometimes traditions were kept alive in families. But whatever the Greeks knew about their own Bronze Age past was surely very different from past reality.

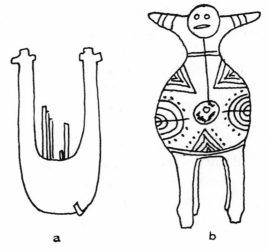

a   b

FIG. 49.—The lyre and the cow in poetry: (*a*) bronze votive lyre with eight strings, Late Helladic III C; (*b*) painted cow rhyton, Late Helladic III C. Both from a tomb at Amyklai (after Tsountas, *Ephemeris* 1892, Pl. 3).

FIG. 50.—The Wild style in Mycenaean painting: (*a*) bird in the process of laying four eggs(?), Koukounara, about 1400 B.C. (courtesy Sp. Marinatos); (*b, e*) prancing goat and dolphin from Ialysos (after Maiuri, *Annuario* 1926, Figs. 144 and 39); (*c, f*) astonished man and goose from Circus Pot, Mycenae (after Wace, *Chamber Tombs*, Pl. 18); (*d*) shy hedgehog, Mycenae (after Furtwängler-Loeschke, *MV*, Pl. 40); (*g*) bull-jumper upside down, Mycenae (after Reichel *HW*², Fig. 49); (*h*) creeping "saffron-gatherer," Perati (after *BCH* 1959, 598, Fig. 32); (*i*) dog chasing a hare, Mycenae (after Furtwängler-Loeschke, *MV*, Pl. 39); (*j*) armed warrior in a suit with a tail, Tiryns (after Lorimer, *HM*, Fig. 9).

CHRONOLOGICAL CHART OF REPRESENTATIVE MAINLAND POTTERY TYPES FROM THE NEOLITHIC AGE TO THE DARK AGES

6200
B.C.

NEOLITHIC

Rainbow ware (Early Neolithic, southern Greece); Sesklo period, flat dish (Otzaki); Dimeni period, open bowl (Dimeni).

Rainbow    Sesklo    Dimeni

3000

2900

EARLY HELLADIC

Early Helladic I bowl (Corinth); Early Helladic II sauceboat (Zygouries); Early Helladic III patterned tankard (Lerna).

I: Bowl 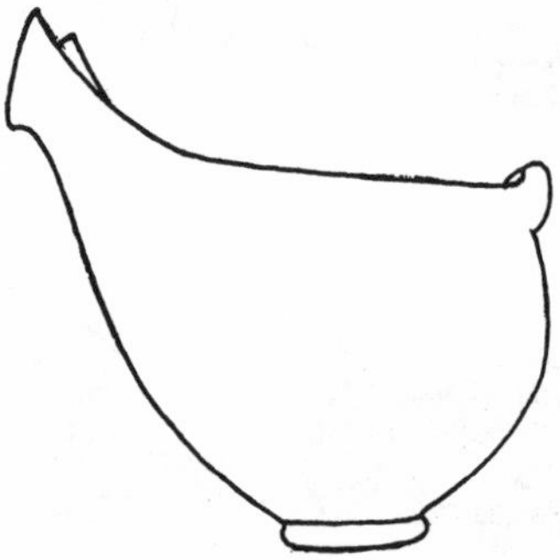   II: Sauceboat    III: Patterned Ware

2000

1900

MIDDLE HELLADIC

Minyan ware, two-handled goblet or kantharos (Eutresis); Matt-painted pithos (Aigina); Matt-painted cup (Shaft Grave Circle B, Mycenae).

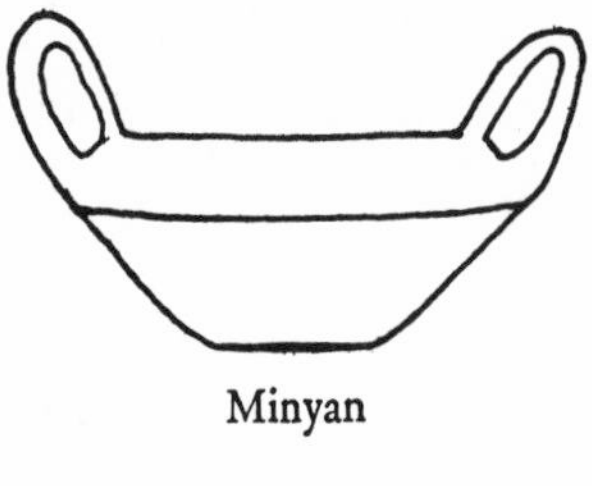

Minyan 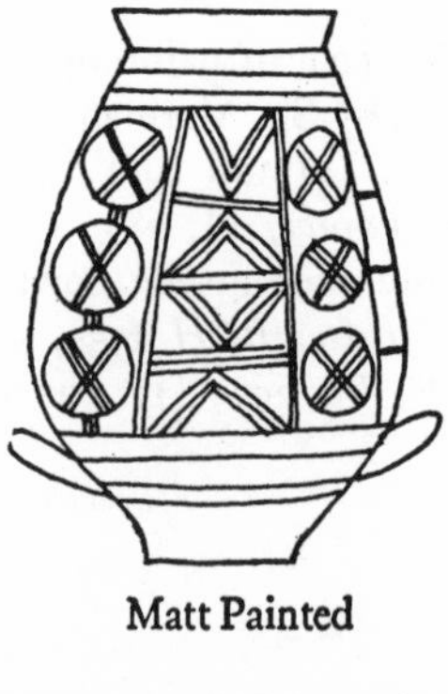   Matt Painted    Shaft Graves

1550

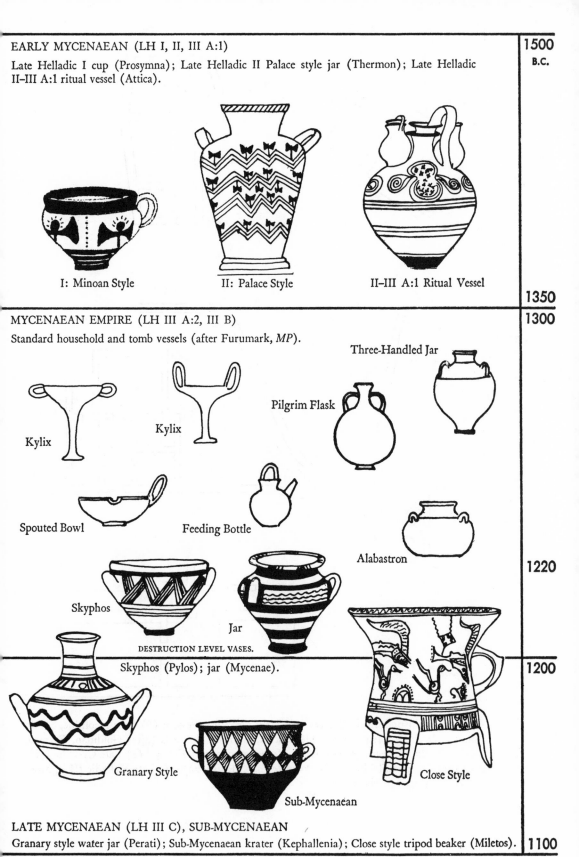

EARLY MYCENAEAN (LH I, II, III A:1)

Late Helladic I cup (Prosymna); Late Helladic II Palace style jar (Thermon); Late Helladic II–III A:1 ritual vessel (Attica).

1500 B.C.

I: Minoan Style II: Palace Style II–III A:1 Ritual Vessel

1350

MYCENAEAN EMPIRE (LH III A:2, III B)

Standard household and tomb vessels (after Furumark, *MP*).

1300

Three-Handled Jar

Pilgrim Flask

Kylix

Kylix

Spouted Bowl

Feeding Bottle

Alabastron

1220

Skyphos

Jar

DESTRUCTION LEVEL VASES.

Skyphos (Pylos); jar (Mycenae).

1200

Granary Style

Sub-Mycenaean

Close Style

LATE MYCENAEAN (LH III C), SUB-MYCENAEAN

Granary style water jar (Perati); Sub-Mycenaean krater (Kephallenia); Close style tripod beaker (Miletos).

1100

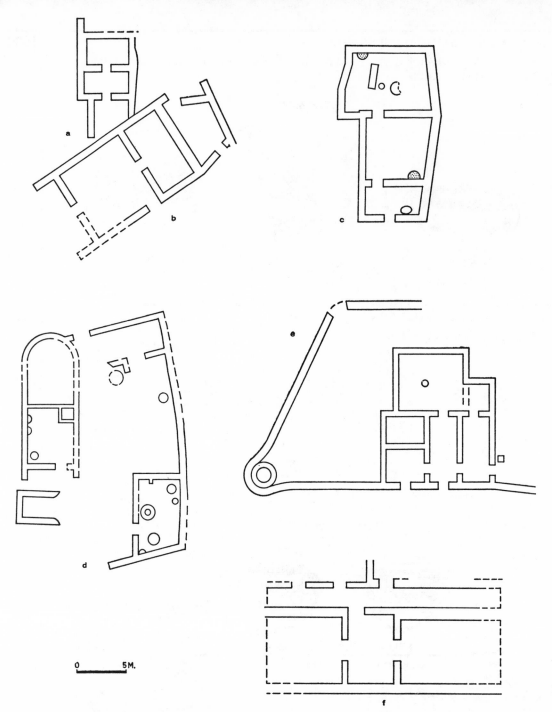

FIG. 52.—House types in prehistoric Greece: (a) Early Neolithic, Sesklo; (b) Late Neolithic, Sesklo (both after Tsountas, *D–S,* Pl. 3); (c) Early Helladic II, Eutresis House L (after Goldman, *Eutresis,* Fig. 13); (d) Middle Helladic, Lerna (after Caskey, *Hesperia* 1957, 149, Fig. 4); (e) Late Cycladic I(?), Therasia, Thera (after Perrot and Chipiez, *Histoire de l'art* VI, Fig. 29); (f) Late Helladic III B, Mouriatada Megaron A (courtesy Sp. Marinatos).

Appendix I
The Physical World

Excavation	Art	Linear B	Homer
			Trees
		ash? box?	alder ash boxwood cedar cornel
		cypress elm	cypress elm laurel
acorn date	palm	oak-cutter palm? (poniki)	oak, acorn palm pine fir

sycamore			plane
			poplar
			  black
			  white
			tamarisk

		yew? willow	willow
			Fruit Trees
almond			apple
fig olive, fruit pear (wild) plum pomegranate	olive, tree pomegranate	figs olive oil pomegranate?	fig, tree and fruit olive, tree, fruit, and oil pear pomegranate
			Shrubs, Plants
	bush grass reed		bush grass reed asphodel
	crocus fern		crocus fern hyacinth
	ivy lily lotus papyrus (plant) poppy rose iris	rose iris root	ivy-wood (lily-like) lotus papyrus (rope) poppy (rosy) violet

EXCAVATION	ART	LINEAR B	HOMER
		Edible Plants	
aniseed			
		cardamon	
		celery-seed	celery
coriander		coriander	
		cress	
		cumin	
		fennel	(Marathon)
		galingale	galingale
		gingergrass	
		mint	
			moly
			onion
		pennyroyal	
		safflower	
		red	
		white	
	saffron	saffron	
		sage	
		sesame	(sesame)
			bitter roots
unguents		unguents	unguents
		(beet-root?)	

		Crops	
barley		barley	barley
	clover		clover
	linen	flax, linen	linen
		(linseed?)	
millet			
rye			
wheat		wheat?	wheat
(N.B.: one grain of Middle Helladic oats is recorded, probably fallen from a workman's trousers)			
grapes		wine, vines?	grapes, vineyards, wine
beans			beans
broad			black
Ervum ervilia			
peas	pea plant?		chickpeas
vetch			
lentils			
parsnip			
pumpkin seed			
			"vegetables"

		Wild Beasts	
boar	boar		boar
	wild bull		
elephant-ivory	ivory	ivory	ivory
elk			

318

EXCAVATION	ART	LINEAR B	HOMER
	Wild Beasts—*Continued*		
hare (agrimi)	fox? hare hedgehog ibex		hare goat, wild
mouse? deer, antlers tortoise	leopard lion mouse? stag, doe, fawn toad griffin sphinx	lion deer? griffin? (poniki)	jackal (?) leopard lion marten mouse stag, doe, fawn (frog) wolf
	Birds and Insects		

goose eggs	cock, hen
	
	crow (raven?)
	
	dove
	duck (mallard?)
	  waterfowl
	eagle
	
	egret
	goose
	
	hawk
	heron
	
	ostrich egg
	owl
	partridge
	
	blue roller
	
	(bustard)
	(fantastic birds)
	bee
	butterfly
	
	snake
			crane
			crow
			  sea crow
			daw
			dove
			
			eagle
			  sea eagle
			
			goose
			halcyon
			hawk
			heron
			nightingale
			
			owl
			
			pigeon
			chalkis-kymindis
			sparrow
			starling
			swallow
			vulture
			bee, honey
			
			cicada
			fly
			locust
			snake
			  water-snake
			worm
			  maggot

		honey	

EXCAVATION	ART	LINEAR B	HOMER
	Fish, Shells		
	argonaut		
	barnacle		
bream			
cardium shell			
	catfish		
	coral		
crab			
	(crocodile)		
dentalia elephantina			
	dolphin		dolphin
			eel
	flying fish		
heartshell			
mullet?			
murex	murex	purple dye	purple dye
mussel	mussel		
	octopus		octopus?
oyster			oyster
pinna, fan	fanshell		
scallop	scallop		
	cockle		
	sea anemone		
			seal
	seaweed		seaweed
shark-tooth			(dangerous sea beasts)
	sponge		sponge
	squid		squid
	starfish		(schools of fish, little fishes)
tridacna	tridacna		
	tuna?		
turretshell	turretshell		
	Domestic Animals		
ass?	ass		
bull	bull	bull	bull
cow	cow	cow	cow
		ox	ox
			calf
dog	dog		dog
	hunting		hunting
			house ("table")
	donkey		donkey
goat		goat	goat
horse	horse	horse	horse
	red		red
	white		white
	brown		brown
			race
			mule
pig	boar	pig	pig
		fatted hog	fatted hog
		sow	sow
sheep	ram	sheep	sheep
		ram	ram
		ewe	ewe
			lamb

Appendix II
Note on Neolithic Pottery

The following list gives in shorthand form the traditional categories of Neolithic pottery in Greece, classified usually by color. For further detail, see Tsountas, Wace and Thompson, Hansen, Weinberg, and Schachermeyr. The new categories of Miløjčič have been set at the beginning, without any firsthand knowledge of the sherds.

Nea Nikomedia: red burnished
                     brown coarse, fingernail impressed
                     red-on-cream geometric
                     white-on-red with Balkan links

Thessaly:
Pre-pottery
     Early pottery: red burnished
                     red-on-white linear

     Proto-Sesklo: mottle burnished (variegated, Rainbow), barbotine

     Pre-Sesklo: cardium-rocker, fingernail, and other impressed ware

     Sesklo I–III: red polished A 1
                     incised red A 2
                     white-on-red painted, geometric A 3 α
                     red-on-white painted: oblique lines, flames, pyramids A 3 β *
                     red-on-red biscuit, A 3 γ
                     red-on-white splinter-scraped (Lianokladi) A 3 δ
                     red-on-buff (Tsangli) A 3 ε
                     pink-on-red (Rachmani) A 3 ζ
                     white polished (imitating stone) A 4
                     black polished (Rachmani) A 5 (Schachermeyr groups this with Thessalian III [Gamma], contemporary with Early Bronze in the south)
                     red-brown on gray-black, some incised dots and linear patterns A 5 β
                     brown-on-white linear (Rachmani) A 6
Dimeni or Thessalian B:*
                     monochrome red (B 1)—may have plastic knobs, spirals
                     incised gray-brown, may have spirals, dots (B 2)

Classic Dimeni:

         B 3 α: white-on-red polished, chocolate-on-blond, black-on-white; these may have meanders, spirals, bunched lines

* As Miløjčič had refined the Thessalian phases before classical Sesklo, so has he distinguished phases preceding and following Dimeni, according to the mounds where variant pottery types are found; before Dimeni come "Middle Greek" Matt-painted (Arapi) and the polychrome and the curvilinear Otzaki wares; after it (Thessalian Γ) the Larissa black-polished and Rachmani crusted wares. The sherds are not fully published yet, and so it is not clear whether these are really chronological culture phases or local variations within an essentially homogeneous era.

three-color: red-on-white or white-on-red, outlined in black B 3 β
black and red on white B 3 γ
black-on-red matt, linear B 3 δ
brown-on-buff like γ and δ, B 3 ε
three-color linear (Tsani, Tsangli) like A 3 β, B 3 ζ

Late Thessalian or Thessalian Γ

white-on-black, polished black-on-gray, rippled Γ 1 α; relations
to Cyclades and Troy
gray-on-gray Γ 1 β, anciently mended, valued
crusted red-on-white Γ 1 γ
crusted white Γ 1 δ
matt black-on-buff Γ 1 ε
red-gray-black incised Γ 2, linear or spirals, may be filled with white
monochrome gray, brown, black Γ 3, may have plastic lugs or handles

Elateia:
Early Neolithic (*ca.* 5500–5100 B.C.):

spongy brown-gray monochrome
spotted red-gray on brown
reddish slip, some plastic ornament

Middle Neolithic (*ca.* 5000–4000):

black burnished
cream and yellow slips
red-brown on buff-gray
red-on-white (Chaironea ware)
Urfirnis (brown lustrous, red slip, some incision)
black-on-red
gray-black burnished like Thessalian Γ 1 a
rarely, white or gray on gray

Late Neolithic (*ca.* 4000–3200):

Matt-painted
polychrome, somewhat like Thessalian B 3 β
gray-black burnished

Central and Southern Greece (broad categories not allowing for local variations):
Early Neolithic: monochrome polished—red, gray, dark
Rainbow or variegated—usually red, varying through yellow and
brown

Late Neolithic: lustrous glazed ("Neolithic *Urfirnis*") red-brown
1. glazed all over
2. incised with simple scratches through glaze
3. pattern-glazed (purple-brown paint on red-brown slip) like
Sesklo A 3 β designs
white on gray-black, or white-filled on incised black like Cyclades or
Sub-Neolithic Crete

Appendix III

Building Activities and Destruction Levels in the Late Mycenaean World

The sites listed are principally those with walls, excavated houses, or large groups of tombs which indicate extensive settlement. Dates are approximate. Often the publication is too sketchy, or the remains too worn, to give a precise historical fix for events in the life of the town. More detailed surveys in Ålin, *Fundstätten*, or Desborough, *The Last Mycenaeans*.

Site	Late Helladic III A	Late Helladic III B	Late Helladic III B-C	Late Helladic III C	Sub-Mycenaean	Continuity
ARGOLID						
Mycenae	palace redesigned north wall, circuit outer houses, tholoi	palace *burned* Lion Gate, south circuit, Granary houses *burned*, tholoi	palace redesigned? *burned?* northeast extension, postern, fountain, Granary *burned* houses *burned*	citadel *destroyed*	yes	yes
Tiryns	city, palace palace redesigned walls	palace *burned* walls, gates	palace *burned* palace redesigned extension wall, galleries water system	megaron altar?	robber hoard	yes
Argos	walls?	walls, burials	burials	habitation	habitation	
Heraion	habitation	habitation	*abandoned*			
Lerna		habitation	*abandoned*			
Kandia		habitation, walls	*destroyed*	burials	yes	yes
Berbati	habitation, tholoi	habitation	*abandoned*			
Iria		habitation	*abandoned?*			
Epidauros	habitation	habitation	habitation?	habitation		
Nauplion	habitation	habitation, unwalled?	habitation	habitation	yes	yes
Asine	habitation	habitation, walls	habitation	burials	yes	yes
Dendra	habitation	habitation, walls			yes	yes
LAKONIA						
Amyklai	habitation	habitation, unwalled	influx			
Menelaion	habitation	habitation, unwalled	*burned*	yes	yes	yes
Epidauros (Monemvasia)	habitation	habitation	influx	burials, *abandoned?*		

APPENDIX III—*Continued*

Site	Late Helladic				Sub-Mycenaean	Continuity
	III A	III B	III B–C	III C		
MESSENIA						
Pylos	habitation, *burned*	palace, unwalled	*burned*	no	no	burials
Nichoria	habitation	habitation	*destroyed*		yes	yes
Koukounara	tholoi	habitation	*abandoned*	burials	?	?
Tragana	burials	burials	burials	*abandoned?*		
Volimidia		habitation	*abandoned*			
Peristeria		habitation, walls	*abandoned*			
Mouriatada	walls	habitation	*abandoned*			
Malthi	walls	habitation	*abandoned*			
Kakovatos		walls?				
Klidi						
ACHAIA						
various tomb sites			influx, refugees	yes	yes	yes
Dyme		walls?	*abandoned?*	burials	yes	?
KEPHALLENIA			influx, refugees	yes	yes	?
ITHAKA		habitation	influx	yes	yes	yes
CORINTHIA						
Corinth		habitation	*abandoned?*	traces	yes?	yes?
Isthmos	habitation	habitation	wall	*abandoned?*		
Korakou	habitation	habitation, walls?	unharmed	*abandoned?*		
Gonia		habitation	habitation, unharmed?			
Zygouries			*abandoned, burned?*			
ATTICA						
Athens	palace? habitation	palace, walls	wall extension, fountain	outer houses *abandoned*, habitation on citadel	yes	yes
Salamis	habitation	habitation	*abandoned?*	no	yes	yes
Hagios Kosmas		habitation	walls	*abandoned*		
Perati			influx, walls	burials, *abandoned?*		
Thorikos	tholoi	habitation?	?	*abandoned*		
Brauron		walls?	?	*abandoned*		
Spata	habitation	habitation	influx	habitation, *abandoned?*		
Eleusis	habitation	habitation, walls?	habitation	yes	yes	yes

APPENDIX III—Continued

LATE HELLADIC

Site	III A	III B	III B-C	III C	Sub-Mycenaean	Continuity
BOIOTIA, PHOKIS						
Thebes	palace	*palace burned?* walls built?	burials	burials	?	yes?
Gla	habitation, palace	habitation, walls, gates	*burned, abandoned*			
Haliartos	habitation	habitation, walls?	*abandoned*			
Orchomenos	habitation	habitation, walls	*abandoned?*	traces		
Eutresis	habitation	habitation	*abandoned?*			
Delphi	habitation	habitation	*burned?*	habitation, *flood?*	yes	yes?
Krisa	habitation	habitation	*burned*			
Drachmani		habitation, walls?	*burned?*			
THESSALY						
Iolkos	palace?	palace? walls?	*burned*	traces, *abandoned?*	?	yes?
CYCLADES, DODEKANESE						
Keos	habitation?	habitation, unwalled?	shrine	shrine	?	yes?
Naxos	habitation	habitation	influx	influx	yes	yes
Delos	habitation	habitation, unwalled?	unharmed?	traces	?	?
Paros	habitation	habitation	habitation			
Melos	*abandoned*	habitation, walls?	influx	habitation?	*abandoned?*	
Rhodes, Trianda Ialysos	burials	burials	influx	yes		
Kos	habitation	habitation, unwalled?	influx	burials, *abandoned?*		
Kalymnos	habitation	habitation	influx	habitation, *abandoned?*		
ASIA MINOR, NORTHERN ISLANDS						
Samos	habitation	habitation? walls?	influx, walls?	*abandoned?*	?	?
Chios				habitation, *destroyed*		
Kolophon				*abandoned?*		
Miletos	habitation	habitation, *burned*	tholos; habitation, walls, towers; burials	habitation, *destroyed?*	yes	yes
Müskebi Assarlik		influx, unwalled?		*abandoned*		
Tarsus		unharmed	destroyed, influx	yes	influx, burials; *abandoned?*	yes

325

Abbreviations

Periodicals

AA	Archäologischer Anzeiger
AJA	American Journal of Archaeology
AM	Mitteilungen des Deutschen Archäologischen Instituts, Athenische Abteilung
AnatSt	Anatolian Studies
Annuario	Annuario della Scuola Archeologica di Atene
AnzWien	Anzeiger der Akademie der Wissenschaften, Wien, philologische-historische Klasse
BASOR	Bulletin of the American Schools of Oriental Research
BASPR	Bulletin of the American Schools of Prehistoric Research
BCH	Bulletin de Correspondance Hellénique
BdA	Bollettino d'Arte
Belleten	Belleten Türk Tarih Kurumu
BICS	Bulletin of the Institute of Classical Studies, University of London
BMFA	Bulletin of the Museum of Fine Arts, Boston
BSA	Annual of the British School at Athens

BullLund	Bulletin de la société royale des lettres de Lund
CAH	Cambridge Ancient History
CJ	Classical Journal
Deltion	Ἀρχαιολογικὸν Δελτίον
Ephemeris	Ἀρχαιολογικὴ Ἐφημερίς
Ergon	Τὸ Ἔργον τῆς Ἀρχαιολογικῆς Ἑταιρείας
HSCP	Harvard Studies in Classical Philology
ILN	Illustrated London News
JdI	Jahrbuch des Deutschen Archäologischen Instituts
JEA	Journal of Egyptian Archaeology
JHS	Journal of Hellenic Studies
JNES	Journal of Near Eastern Studies
JOAI	Jahreshefte des Österreichischen Archäologischen Instituts
JRGZM	Jahrbuch des Römisch-Germanischen Zentralmuseums, Mainz
KChron	Κρητικὰ Χρονικά
MonAnt	Monumenti Antichi
OpArc	Opuscula Archaeologica
OpAth	Opuscula Atheniensia
PEQ	Palestine Exploration Quarterly
PP	La Parola del Passato
PraktAkAth	Πρακτικὰ τῆς Ἀκαδημίας Ἀθηνῶν
Praktika	Πρακτικὰ τῆς ἐν Ἀθήναις Ἀρχαιολογικῆς Ἑταιρείας
ProcPhilSoc	Proceedings of the American Philosophical Society
ProcPS	Proceedings of the Prehistoric Society
PZ	Prähistorische Zeitschrift
RE	Pauly-Wissowa, Real-Encyclopädie der klassischen Altertums-wissenschaft
REG	Revue des Études Grecques
RGK	Deutsches Archäologisches Institut, Bericht des Römisch-Germanischen Kommissions
RHA	Revue Hittite et Asianique
RhM	Rheinisches Museum für Philologie
VIIArcCong	Atti del VII Congreso Internazionale di Archeologia Classica (1961)
TAPA	Transactions of the American Philological Association
ZVS	Zeitschrift für Vergleichende Sprachforschung

BOOKS

AAAE	W. S. Smith, *The Art and Architecture of Ancient Egypt* (1958)
AAAO	H. Frankfort, *The Art and Architecture of the Ancient Orient* (1954)
AC	J. D. S. Pendlebury, *The Archaeology of Crete* (1939)
Aegean and Near East	S. Weinberg (ed.), *The Aegean and the Near East: Studies Presented to Hetty Goldman* (1956)
AegOrient	H. J. Kantor, *The Aegean and the Orient in the Second Millennium B.C.* (1948; = *AJA* 51 [1947] 1)

Abbreviations

AK	G. E. Mylonas, *Aghios Kosmas* (1959)
AncMyc	G. E. Mylonas, *Ancient Mycenae* (1957)
Archaion Taphon	G. Papavasileiou, Περὶ τῶν ἐν Εὐβοίᾳ ἀρχαίων τάφων (1910)
Chron	A. Furumark, *The Chronology of Mycenaean Pottery* (1941)
CMG	Sp. Marinatos and M. Hirmer, *Crete and Mycenae* (1960)
Companion	A. J. B. Wace and F. Stubbings, *Companion to Homer* (1962)
CT	A. J. B. Wace, *Chamber Tombs at Mycenae* (*Archaeologia* 82 [1932])
CVA	*Corpus Vasorum Antiquorum*
Dawn	S. Piggott (ed.), *The Dawn of Civilization* I (1961)
DMR	*Studies Presented to David M. Robinson* I (1951), II (1953)
Documents	M. Ventris and J. Chadwick, *Documents in Mycenaean Greek* (1956)
D-S	Chr. Tsountas, Ἀι προϊστορικαὶ ἀκροπόλεις Διμηνίου καὶ Σέσκλου (1908)
ECT	H. Hansen, *Early Civilization in Thessaly* (1933)
Epitumbion Tsountas	Ἐπιτύμβιον Χρήστου Τσούντα (1941)
Fimmen	D. Fimmen, *Die kretisch-mykenische Kultur*² (1924)
Fundstätten	P. Ålin, *Das Ende der mykenischen Fundstätten auf dem griechischen Festland* ("Studies in Mediterranean Archaeology," Vol. I [Lund, 1962])
Geras Keramopoullou	Γέρας Ἀντωνίου Κεραμοπούλλου (1953)
GP	O. Montelius, *La Grèce préclassique* (with O. Frödin, 1924–28)
HM	H. Lorimer, *Homer and the Monuments* (1950)
Kirrha	L. Dor, J. Jannoray, H. and M. van Effenterre, *Kirrha: Étude de préhistoire phocidienne* (1960)
Kuppelgrab	H. Lolling, R. Bohn, A. Furtwängler, and U. Köhler, *Das Kuppelgrab bei Menidi* (1880)
Levant	F. Stubbings, *Mycenaean Pottery from the Levant* (1951)
Matz I	F. Matz, "Die Ägäis," *Handbuch der Archäologie* II (1954) 179
Matz II	F. Matz, *Kreta, Mykene, Troia* (1956)
Matz III	F. Matz, *The Art of Crete and Early Greece* (1962)
MMR²	M. P. Nilsson, *The Minoan-Mycenaean Religion*² (1950)
MP	A. Furumark, *The Mycenaean Pottery* (1941)
MV	A. Furtwängler and G. Loeschke, *Mykenische Vasen* (1886)
MycAge	Chr. Tsountas and J. Manatt, *The Mycenaean Age* (1897)
Mycenae	A. J. B. Wace, *Mycenae, An Archaeological History and Guide* (1949)
NDA	*Neue Deutsche Ausgrabungen im Mittelmeer Gebiet* (1959)
NT	A. Persson, *New Tombs at Dendra near Midea* (1942)
PC	R. W. Hutchinson, *Prehistoric Crete* (1962)
PM	A. Evans, *The Palace of Minos* (1921–36)
PT	A. J. B. Wace and M. Thompson, *Prehistoric Thessaly* (1912)
PTK	A. Evans, *The Prehistoric Tombs of Knossos* (1905)

329

Rodenwaldt I	G. Rodenwaldt, "Die Fresken," *Tiryns* II (1912)
Rodenwaldt II	G. Rodenwaldt, *Der Fries des Megarons von Mykenai* (1921)
RT	A. Persson, *Royal Tombs at Dendra near Midea* (1931)
Schachermeyr I	F. Schachermeyr, "Die prähistorischen Kulturen Griechenlands," *RE* 22 (1954), 1350
Schachermeyr II	F. Schachermeyr, *Die Ältesten Kulturen Griechenlands* (1955)
Schachermeyr III	F. Schachermeyr, "Forschungsbericht zur ägäischen Frühzeit," *AA* 1962, 106
SG	G. Karo, *Die Schachtgräber von Mykenai* (1930–33)
SME	N. Valmin, *The Swedish Messenia Expedition* I (1938)
Troy	C. Blegen, C. Boulter, J. Caskey, and M. Rawson, *Troy* I–IV (1950–58)

Notes

1. The dates may be too high, or those of other sites not high enough; there is no pre-pottery level. A recent C-14 date for the first settlement at Knossos is 6100 ± 150; Elateia in Phokis had early pottery by 5520 ± 70.

Since this account of Nea Nikomedia was written, publication (*ILN* 11 and 18 April 1964, 564 and 604) has affirmed two distinct Early Neolithic building periods without marked change in culture. One house of the early phase is 8.50 × 6.0 m., two rooms with hearth and porch. Nearby a larger shrine, divided into three aisles by posts, contained at least five fertility idols, one with red hair, another with a fan-shaped headdress. The later settlement was built in the same style, oak framework plastered with reeds and mud, gable roofs, woven matting on the mud floors. Pistachio nuts and acorns are identified among the food remains. Twenty-one burials, usually single interment without gifts, offer good anthropological material. The anthropomorphic vases seemed linked to western Asiatic cultures.

2. This book will not give as much detail about pottery as would be proper in a more technical account. Prehistory often becomes an exercise in ceramics at the expense of architecture and art. A general survey of types of Neolithic pottery by major sites and periods is given in Appendix II.

3. There were sherds of pottery in the pre-pottery level at Gremnos, discounted by the excavators as strays; cf. Weinberg, *Gnomon* 1963, 630. Painted human figure, Miløjčič, *NDA* 229, Fig. 2; clay stamp, *AA* 1956, 146, Fig. 4; cf. *AA* 1933, 315.

4. Southern Neolithic is still less well known than Thessalian, and although linked directly to the cultural attainments of Thessaly and central Greece it has local distinctiveness. The dividing line may be put near Orchomenos. Principal sites in central Greece are Orchomenos, Elateia (Drachmani), Chaironea, Halai, Hagia Marina. In Attica, Athens, Nea Makri, the Cave of Pan, and Kokkinia are important. Southern Greece is best known from Corinth, Gonia, Prosymna, Lerna, Hagiorgitika, and Asea.

The south has no pre-pottery level so far. The earliest levels produce animal bones and a few sherds; next simple mottled or burnished Rainbow ware appears. Most houses have straight walls supported by posts, roofs made of poles and reeds, and an interior hearth. Some obsidian is imported. As agricultural life becomes more secure the villages experiment with painted pottery, in a lustrous glaze called Neolithic *Urfirnis* (to distinguish it from Early Helladic *Urfirnis*). Colors are red or dark purple-brown, quite unlike the dull rich orange of the north; patterns resemble simpler Thessalian ones. The fabric is hard, refined, and musical when dropped.

5. Dimeni origins and parallels are analyzed in Schachermeyr II, 93; Childe, *The Danube in Prehistory* (1929); Weinberg in *Relative Chronologies in Old World Archaeology;* Gimbutas, *Prehistory of Eastern Europe* I, 51, 99, 114; French, "Late Chalcolithic Pottery in North-West Turkey and the Aegean," *AnatSt* 1961, 99; Garašanin, "Zum Problem der Dimini-Wanderung," *AM* 1954, 1; C. Delvoye, *BCH* 1949, 29.

6. Angel's analyses (see bibliography) are the best and most vivid introduction to characteristic features of prehistoric Greek skulls. His basic types, usually found mixed, are Basic White (A), Classic Mediterranean (B), Alpine (C), Nordic-Iranian (D), Dinaric Mediterranean (F). A typical Neolithic skull from Attica might be Type A:1 (Megalithic) moving toward Type F: a man thirty to thirty-five years old, with a medium ovoid skull, sloping forehead, big crude face, good teeth. The late Neolithic period introduces more D and F tendencies. Neolithic burials to 1954 in Matz I, 185 note 6; Elateia, Lerna, and Nea Nikomedia have contributed several since.

7. A fine general discussion of the principles of linguistic archaeology in H. Hencken, *Indo-European Languages and Archaeology* (American Anthropological Association Memoir 84) 1955. The classic ancient text on the Pelasgians is Herodotos I.57, cf. A. Gomme, *Historical Commentary on Thucydides* I, 94. References to recent resurrections of Pelasgians in A. van Windekens, *Études Pelasgiques* (*Bib. Muséon* 1960), or F. Lochner-Hüttenbach, *Die Pelasger* (1960); cf. Laroche, *RHA* 1960, 40, and chap. ii, note 10.

8. See bibliography for studies of Neolithic figurines; unconforming mainland examples in Tsountas, *D-S*, Pls. 31 and 33; thrones and altars, Hansen, *ECT* 44 and note 17. Hacilar, J. Mellaart, *AnatSt* 1961, 39, Çatal Hüyük, *AnatSt* 1962, 41, *ILN* 1 February 1964, 158; 8 February 1964, 194; 15 February 1964, 232; 22 February 1964, 272. Knossos: J. Evans, *ILN* 8 July 1961, 60, *JHS Reports* 1961, 27, *BSA* 1964 (forthcoming).

9. Cave of Eileithyia: Marinatos, *Praktika* 1929, 94; 1930, 91; Nilsson, *MMR*², 53.

NOTES TO CHAPTER II

1. Caskey, *Hesperia* 1960, 301. Other sites burned in EH II: Asine, Tiryns, Zygouries, perhaps Corinth, and Hagios Kosmas. Eutresis and Orchomenos in central Greece passed peacefully from EH II to EH III, and then were burned.

2. The contents of the tower, the only good evidence for the date of Chalandriani's destruction, have recently been increased by a spearhead (Bossert, *JdI* 1960, 2); the Trojan jar is probably Troy III; a seal impression relates to the First Intermediate Period in Egypt. The fort is certainly Early Cycladic, not Mycenaean, perhaps abandoned near 2200 B.C.

3. Hesperia 1959, Pl. 42; *Tiryns* IV, Pl. XIX; *Zygouries* Fig. 114.

4. W. McLeod will publish the Lerna pot marks and has kindly sent drawings (see Fig. 6 here); see *Hesperia* 1955, Pl. 15; *BCH* 1955, 240; *Archaeology* 1960, 132.

5. Good bibliographies in Mylonas, *AK* 152, Schachermeyr III 189. Corinth shaft with two side chambers, *AJA* 1930, 404. Up to fifteen skeletons may be stuffed in rock cavities (*Zygouries* 43, cf. *Prosymna* 46, *Asine* 338, *SME* 186, *D-S* 125). Occasionally a child is buried in a coarse jar or covered with a broken one, a custom better known in MH (*Kirrha* 50, *PT* 41, *Ephemeris* 1937, 46 note 5; see chap. iii note 3). Sometimes cist graves are made in groups in flat land (Hagios Stephanos in Lakonia, *JHS Reports* 1960, 9; 1961, 32) or in caverns (*Ergon* 1961, figs. 177 and 179). The Cyclades also have rare pithos burials, and multiple ossuaries (*Hesperia* 1962, 265, on Keos). See also chap. iii, note 3.

6. The problem of chronological and cultural relations between the Cyclades and the mainland is hard because no good stratified EC site has been excavated, and the mainland transition from EH II to EH III needs further study. Apart from the exchange of grave gifts, communication is suggested by the presence of dark gray stamped or incised wares in both areas; the designs are such typically Cycladic concentric circles and spirals that some scholars have considered the possibility of a Cycladic invasion of the mainland (cf. Schachermeyr II 138). More recently Bossert has distinguished between mainland and island designs, and suggested that the gray ware is made locally on the mainland, perhaps even earlier than on the islands (*JdI* 1960, 1). A tentative equation of historical phases might be: Pelos = Neolithic and EH I; Kampos = EH I and II; Syros = EH II (the later, House of the Tiles, phase) to EH III = the First Intermediate Period in Egypt; Phylakopi I = EH III and MH I.

7. The appeal of Cycladic idols to collectors of modern sculpture has created a greater demand than supply; ateliers in Athens and Naxos happily respond. Most forgeries have a dull, oily imitation of the yellow patina on originals; if the purchaser hesitates, the tale that it was smuggled out of Greece in a barrel of oil will calm him. One should be cautious of peddlers with Cycladic accents, and test by fluoroscope before buying; avoid idols with painted red diadems and necklaces, marble saucers with crushed red pigment in them, and carved steatite boxes. Otherwise the new Cycladic art is as good as the old, same marble, same island make.

8. See bibliography, Ships and Sailing. Egypt, the Levant, Anatolia, and Crete all illustrate their ships in this period. Even if the sword-blade inlaid with ships from the mysterious Dorak Treasure contemporary with Troy II should prove genuine, the ships do not look quite Cycladic (*ILN* 28 November 1959, 754).

9. See note 1 above.

10. The tentative hypothesis toward which some Anatolian linguists seem to be working is that "pre-Greek" elements in the Aegean are actually relics of a rich Indo-European culture which included several earlier branches of the same stock as the Greeks and the Hittites. Good recent summaries of the Luvian situation in E. Laroche, *Mnemes Charin* II (Kretschmer, 1959), *Dictionnaire de la langue Louvite* (1959), "Études de toponymie anatolienne," *Bulletin de la Société Linguistique* 1960, 156; see also *RHA* 1961, 57; A. Kammenhuber, "Zur Stellung der Hethitisch-Luvisch innerhalb der indogermanischen Gemein-

sprache," *ZVS* 1961, 31; see also *RHA* 1956, 1. Cf. H. Stoltenberg, *Das Minoische und andre larische Sprache* (1961), V. Ševoroškin, *Nestor* 258, 263, 282, 293, 318. Archaeological summary in Mellaart, *CAH* I² xxiv. For the Greek side, see J. Chadwick, "Prehistory of the Greek Language," *CAH* II², xxxix, A. Beattie, "Aegean Languages," *Companion* 311, P. Chantraine, *Traité de morphologie grecque²* (1961), A. Heubeck, *Praegraeca* (1961), W. Merlingen, "Zum 'Vorgriechischen,'" *Linguistique Balkanique* 1962, 25, and note 11 below.

The proposal to link Cretan Linear A to an Indo-European Anatolian tongue, Luvian or Palaic, probably began with A. Furumark's circulated typescript (Berlin, 1956); the argument whether the Linear A phrase *Jasasara(me)* on cult objects is a Luvian goddess or a Semitic gentleman still provides a certain gaiety in archaeological circles. The identification of Cretans and Luvians argued at length by L. Palmer in *Transactions of the Philological Society* 1958, 75, and *Mycenaeans and Minoans* (1962) 226; by G. Huxley in *Crete and the Luwians* (1961). The need for a flexible, rational position is well-stated by Schachermeyr, "Luwier auf Kreta?" *Kadmos* 1962, 27; he finds Palmer's and Huxley's conclusions unscientifically based on "kling-klang Ähnlichkeiten." Mylonas reviews the evidence for no Luvians in Greece, *Hesperia* 1962, 284. For the Semitic nature of the language of Linear A, at least at Hagia Triada, see C. Gordon, *JNES* 1962, 207.

11. It is old-fashioned to believe in all these things as part of the Early Helladic world; many no doubt reached the Greeks later through cultural osmosis or were survivals in backward districts, but they are still pleasant to think about. An old, full, deceptive list in G. Glotz, *Aegean Civilization* (1925) 386; cf. Schachermeyr I, 1517; a collection can be made up from C. Buck, *Reverse Index of Greek Nouns and Adjectives* (1939). Place names best in A. Fick, *Vorgriechische Ortsnamen* (1905); J. Haley and C. Blegen, "The Coming of the Greeks: The Geographical Distribution of Pre-Greek Place Names," *AJA* 1928, 141. See also Schachermeyr I, 1494; D. Hester, "Pre-Greek Place Names in Asia Minor," *RHA* 1957, 107; A. Carnoy, "Les suffixes toponymiques pré-grecs," *L'Antiquité Classique* 1960, 319.

NOTES TO CHAPTER III

1. The two characteristic wares of the Middle Bronze Age in Greece are Minyan and Matt-painted. There are three technically distinct classes of Minyan ware which spring from a single tradition: True, Argive, and Yellow. True Minyan ware is typically northern, the earliest class and the best made. Its soapy surface can be recognized by touch. Its color varies from blue through steel gray and olive to near black, depending on firing. Most Minyan vases are made on the wheel. Decoration is limited to thin incised lines or garlands. Argive Minyan is a southern imitation or reflection; it is more often hand-made; its dark surfaces conceal a buff or red core, sandwich fashion, showing less absolute control of kiln temperature than in the north. It may be incised or even stamped with concentric circles like Early Helladic and Cycladic wares. Yellow Minyan is the latest of the three classes, and provides the tradition for all later light-ground pottery in Greece; it continues into the Late Helladic period. It may be plain and elegant (the rounded stemmed goblet is a typical shape), or painted. Painted examples seem to reflect two influences: the fusion of Minyan with Matt-painted pottery, and the contemporary shift in Crete from a dark to a light ground for painted vases; the designs are first stiff imitations of Matt-painted patterns, then more curvi-

linear as in the Cyclades or Crete. The three principal Minyan colors are sometimes thought to imitate metal prototypes; gray = silver, yellow = gold, and red (rare) = copper.

Matt-painted pottery appears in slightly later strata than the first gray wares, and accompanies them through most of the Middle Bronze Age. Its origins are obscure; some connoisseurs understand it as a revival of the painting traditions among submerged EH elements in Greece, some as an imitation of current styles in Cycladic pottery, some as a natural experiment of a simple kind. Most important sites have it; it is best on the east and west coasts of the Peloponnesos. Aigina, a fine production center, specialized in large pithoi with black geometric patterns on a rough greenish ground (Fig. 51) and exported them as far as Boiotia. Aiginetan potters knew the wheel, perhaps through Crete; one disc survives. Aigina also imitates Minoan Kamares ware with chalk-white patterns on black. Small shapes in Matt-painted ware are rare at first, but by the Shaft Grave period (see chap. iv; Fig. 51) cups and goblets have been adapted from the Minyan repertory. This late phase also sees the introduction of polychrome vases, black and red on buff, directly influenced by Crete through the Cyclades (cf. Pl. IX E–F).

Aside from these principal fabrics some provinces in Greece produce poor local handmade wares, black, red, or gray, and at all sites coarse kitchen ware is voluminous but undistinguished.

Gray, metallic-looking wares have a longer history in Anatolia than in Greece, though the pure type of Minyan ware does not appear until the new city of Troy VI, where it runs concurrent with the gray of Troy V for a while and then supersedes it; this is like Lerna (see chap. ii), where gray ware appears casually toward the end of EH III, but real Minyan shapes wait until MH. Other Anatolian sites like Beycesultan or Kusura are rich in their own varieties of "Minyan," but Anatolian and Greek fabric and color are quite different; the likeness is closest at Troy. See Mellaart, *AnatSt* 1957, 55 and *CAH* I² xxiv; Mylonas, *Hesperia* 1962, 284; Blegen, *Troy* III, 35 and *Korakou* 15; Schachermeyr I, 1463.

2. See note 1 above.

3. Variations of Middle Helladic grave types not mentioned in the text include cists with mudbrick walls (*Kirrha* Pl. 17); single pithos burials without tumuli especially for infants (*Korakou* 101, *PT* 196 [Orchomenos], *PT* 161 [Zerelia], *Kirrha* 50, *SME* 206, *BCH* 1958, 777 [Kos], *BSA* 1910–11, 8 [Phylakopi], *BSA* 1934–35, 14 [Ithaka]). A rectangular tumulus on the Athenian Acropolis contained several burials (Skias, *Ephemeris* 1902, 123; Gropengiesser, *Gräber von Attika* (1907) 2; Mylonas, *AK* 3); the one at Samikon is not published yet but may have stone walls inside. In a prominent tumulus at Drachmani a single woman was buried with many pots; extra cists contained ashes and grain, and the whole was crowned by a Matt-painted pithos invisible from the surface; an interesting cult explanation was offered by the excavator, see also Blegen and Wace 34. Ordinary cists may reuse stone slabs with drawings or graffiti (cf. chap. viii, note 6).

Offerings to the dead in Middle Helladic, in such forms as vases deposited on the cover slab, are a debated matter; for opposed positions see Blegen and Wace, and Mylonas, *DMR* I. The custom is sporadically attested and continues in the Shaft Grave period (Mycenae Circle B Tomb *Nu*, Lerna). Asine's "tomb altars" are not generally accepted as evidence for cult (*Asine* 347). A primitive "grave circle" at Malthi is felt by most scholars to be really part of the city gate built over earlier MH graves *versus* Mylonas, *DMR* I, 69. An increasing number of tholos tombs are being found with late MH pottery (see chap. v, bibliography, Major Tholos Tombs, *under* Delos, Dramesi, Karditsa, Osman Aga).

1. Collection de Bosset, Neuchâtel, late, awkward vases from the Ionian Islands: P. Dessoulavy, *Revue Archéologique* 1900, 128; S. Benton, *BSA* 1931–32, 222; the collection is no longer accessible. De Bosset also brought back a bronze nail from the Treasury of Atreus, perhaps one which held a rosette to the wall (chap. vii, note 15). Late Mycenaean vases from Attica came to London through Lord Elgin early in the nineteenth century.

2. Other shaft graves of the early period: Lerna: Caskey, *Archaeology* 1960, 130; Mycenae: Wace, *Mycenae* 51, cf. *BSA* 1954, 273; Berbati: Caskey, *Hesperia* 1955, note 16; Staphylos (?): Platon, *KChron* 1949, 534. There are related types at Eleusis, Knossos, and on Skyros, developments of cists rather than true shafts. In later Mycenaean times shafts with dromoi occur on Cyprus and in Attica (Perati), cheaper and more compact than chambers, never royal. Many scholars discern a prototype for the Mycenae shafts in the third-millennium Royal Tombs at Alaca Hüyük in central Anatolia, especially for their depth, construction, and hoards of advanced jewelry and weapons, though there are specific differences in rite: R. Arik, *Alaca Hüyük 1935;* H. Koşay, *Les Fouilles d'Alaca Höyük* (1951); T. Özgüç, *Die Bestattungsbrauche im vorgeschichtlichen Anatolien* (1948); M. Mellink, "The Royal Tombs at Alaca Hüyük," *Aegean and Near East* 39; E. Akurgal, *Kunst der Hethiter* (1961), Pls. 1–23; T. Özgüç, *Horoztepe* (1958). Continuity of general burial type farther north from the third millennium to the classical period, from Maikop to Trebenischte, M. Rostovtzeff, *Iranians and Greeks in South Russia* (1922); B. Filow, *Die archaische Nekropole von Trebenischte* (1927); A. Mongait, *Archaeology in the U.S.S.R.* (1961) 129 (Trialeti, Kirovakan). Mylonas' argument for shafts developing from simple Middle Helladic cists, *Proceedings of the American Philosophical Society* 1955, 37; *Hesperia* 1962, 298; no development is observable at Mycenae, the two contrasting forms simply existing side by side in both Grave Circles.

3. The numbers of weapons reported by Schliemann and Karo do not coincide. New additions to the catalogue for Grave IV: A. Xenaki-Sakellariou, *Ephemeris* 1957 (1961) Chron. 1, large silver shield; handle inlaid with gold argonauts; high-footed goblet with rosettes made up of Karo's numbers 122, 155 *b*. Ivory statuette of a woman in flounced dress found in a box from Grave IV, but belonging to a later period, *ibid.*, Pl. 2, 1. New cleaning of a copper cauldron revealed the inscription, Grumach, *Kadmos* 1962, 85.

4. F. Bisson de la Roque, *Le Trésor de Tôd* (1950). Cretan influence is evident in some shapes, but Cretan metalwork scarcely survives until the early Mycenaean period, with the bronze vessels of Knossos and Tylissos, and the gold Vapheio Cups. Silver is much rarer on Crete than on the mainland, which had sources in Anatolia. No niello work has been found in Crete to date; until a collection is known, it seems more correct to call the Shaft Grave examples mainland, not Minoan, though Cretan skill, color sense, and style are somewhere in their background.

5. S. Chapman's new drawing of the Siege Rhyton includes the fragments inserted since the war but not yet published, most of them plain or with scale-pattern; the whole scene has been arranged in consultation with W. Smith; the famous fragment with the sea monster no longer discernible, only seen in Gilliéron's drawing, Evans, *PM* III, 96, Fig. 54, Karo, *SG* 176, Fig. 85.

6. Pottery from Circle B, mainly unpublished, is on view in Nauplion and Athens. See Mylonas, *AncMyc*, and for the Knossos faïence vase Wace, *Companion* 341. Circle A: *SG* plates 166–75, Furtwängler-Loeschke, *Mykenische Thongefässe* (1879); the span dated

by Furumark from MH II (Grave VI) to LH I B/LM II (Grave I), *OpArc* 1950, 190. Minyan sherd at Knossos, Evans, *PM* II 309, Pendlebury, *AC* 175, Scholes, *BSA* 1956, 9. Disputed MM III sherds from Circle A, Graves IV and V, Evans, *Shaft Graves and Bee-Hive Tombs* 24, Pendlebury, *AC* 174 note 5. Cycladic sherds quite common in the early Shaft Grave period (see chap. iii bibliography under Kirrha, Samikon) but give way to massive Minoan imports in the later phases.

7. J. Myres, *Who Were the Greeks?* (1930) 308; Blegen, "Mycenaean Age," *Semple Lecture* 1962, 31; Nilsson, "Prehistoric Migrations of the Greeks," *Opuscula Selecta* III, 467.

8. Translation combined from M. Hammad, "Découverte d'une stèle du Roi Kamose," *Chronique d'Égypte* 1954–55, 198, and L. Habachi, "Preliminary Report on the Kamose Stele," *Annales de la Service* 1956, 195. Persson's revival of Meyer's theory that the Siege Rhyton scene is in the Delta convinces few, *NT* chap. vi; there is no hippopotamos. For Hyksos rule see R. Engberg, *The Hyksos Reconsidered* (1939); T. Säve-Söderbergh, "Hyksos Rule in Egypt," *JEA* 1951, 53; Frankfort, *AAAO* 138; W. Helck, *Mitteilungen des Deutschen Archaeologischen Instituts Kairo* 1961, 110 (fall of Avaris no later than 1542 B.C.) and *Die Beziehungen Ägyptens zur Vorderasien* (1963). Egyptian gold in Mycenae, Marinatos, *CMG* 82. Aegean connections of Ah-hotep's dagger and ax, Kantor, *AegOrient* 64, Smith, *AAAE* 126, Furumark, *OpArc* 1950, 219 among many. Apophis dagger, G. Daressy, *Annales de la Service* 1906 Fig. 2, Frankfort, *AAAO* 139.

NOTES TO CHAPTER V

1. Late Helladic I in Shaft Graves, tholoi, and early chamber tombs co-ordinates with the reign of Hatshepsut and the infancy of Tuthmosis III, *ca.* 1504–1480 B.C. The best mainland evidence is a seal in Prosymna Tomb 14, here Fig. 29 *a* (Blegen, *Prosymna* 169, 261, Fig. 597). The next datable Egyptian finds are the alabaster vase with the cartouche of Tuthmosis III, *ca.* 1460–50, in a tomb by the harbor at Katsaba (Alexiou, *KChron* 1952, 9) in a context just before 1400; then scarabs of Queen Tiy, consort of Amenhotep (Amenophis) III (1417–1379) at Hagia Triada Tomb 5 and Mycenae, and of both the pharaoh and his queen at Ialysos. At Mycenae a newly discovered faïence plaque with the cartouche of Amenhotep III seems to be in a III B context (*Nestor* 295). See Hayes, Rowton, and Stubbings, *CAH* I², vi, for the latest standard chronology, and chap. viii bibliography under Trade and Foreign Relations.

2. Glanville, "Records of a Royal Dockyard of the Time of Tuthmosis III," *Zeitschrift für Aegyptische Sprache und Altertumskunde* 1931, 105, chief workmen building Keftiu ships from local timber before *ca.* 1469; Prince Amenhotep was in charge of the yard. Keftiu ships go to Keftiu, no more odd than the Boston packets of Liverpool. See also Breasted, *Ancient Records* II, 206/492, for Tuthmosis III's harbors being filled with Keftiu, Byblos, and Sektu ships; cf. note 16 below.

3. For fifteenth-century Aegean exports to the Near East see Figure 22; major sites are Troy, Miletos, Byblos, Ugarit; in Palestine, Tell el Duweir, Lachish, Gezer; in Cyprus, Enkomi, Maroni, possibly Sultan Hala Tekke; sherds are scanty in all. See Blegen, *Troy* III, Fig. 383; Furumark, *Chronology* 46, 110, *MP* site list; Kantor, *AegOrient* 36; Stubbings, *Levant* 53; Weickert, *Istanbuler Mitteilungen* 1959–60. Aegean influence sensed on such metal objects as a Hittite silver belt inlaid with gold wire, Frankfort, *AAAO*, Fig. 58, or a peculiar group of gold bowls "from near Ugarit" now circulating on the art market in all styles, periods, prices, e.g., *Bulletin of the Metropolitan Museum of Art* October 1960, 38.

4. J. Cook suggests that *Minoa* sites without Bronze Age remains may be named so later as mysterious citadels the peasants did not understand, just as ancient sites are now often called *Helleniko*.

5. The early period shows local living styles with Minoan overlays at Phylakopi, Thera, Trianda, Keos, Miletos, possibly Maroni in Cyprus and Pigadia on Karpathos; in the transitional period *ca.* 1400 Mycenaean pottery begins to predominate and Minoan houses are often abandoned. See Furumark, *OpArc* 1950, 185, and note 17 below.

6. The gold foil façade from the Volo (Kapakli) tholos tomb (Fig. 32 *a*) is one of the earliest architectural documents. The early acropolis at Englianos had a large poros building, defensive wall, and stepped gate, Blegen, *AJA* 1960, 155; 1961, 154; other palace sites yield mostly debris of the early period without substantial architectural remains.

7. The origin of the tholos tomb in Greece has not been settled to anyone's satisfaction. Often the theories are more complicated than the problem. The Minoan school derives all mainland examples from the much earlier round low community tombs of EM–MM Crete, best known in the Mesara plain, also on the south coast and sparsely in the northeast (Hood, *Antiquity* 1960, 166; Matz III, 196); principal differences are that Cretan tholoi are never cut into the ground, have low roofs which may sometimes be constructed of overlapping fieldstones, but are never corbeled to a high vault as in Greece, and go out of fashion well before Greek tholoi begin. Mylonas believes tholoi imitate a grave circle with the vault rendering more permanently the vault of the sky over an open precinct (*AncMyc* 100), and the occasional interior pits a reduction of original shafts. Wace believed the tholos was a native development, partly influenced by round Early Bronze tombs in Euboia, the Cyclades, the Ionian Islands; he did not point to any tradition surviving through the intervening Middle Helladic phase (*Mycenae* 119). Marinatos suggests that the stone tholos is a translation of the round chamber tomb into more princely and lasting form (*CMG* 91); this simple solution leaves as the only puzzle why the Mycenaeans shifted generally from individual cists to large family vaults. Round or vaulted chambers are known at Volimidia, Monemvasia, Palaiochori, and Delphi (see bibliography, Major Tholos Tombs). The change may be rooted both in social evolution and in international contacts: early Mycenaean confidence in new dynastic foundations and family continuity, and acquaintance with permanent stone family vaults in Canaan and Egypt.

The earliest monumental tombs in Crete seem contemporary with the beginning of tholos structures in Greece, but the first, the Temple Tomb, has nothing in common with tholoi except quality of masonry (Evans, *PM* IV 965, Pendlebury, *AC* 194). The tholoi on the Kephala ridge at Knossos and at Maleme on the north coast (see Major Tholos Tombs) both probably belong to the mid-fifteenth century when the Greeks were already controlling Knossos; so does the Royal Tomb. For parallels between *Rho* at Mycenae and underground vaults at Ugarit, see e.g., C. Schaeffer, *Ugaritica* I (1939) 56, 90, Pl. 17, Figs. 75 ff., some of which are certainly before 1500; Enkomi in Cyprus across from Ugarit also adapts the type, A. Westholm, *OpArc* 1941, 43, Fig. 15. *Rho* is briefly published in Mylonas, *AncMyc* 158. Its whimsical likeness to great Etruscan tombs eight hundred years later, like Regolini-Galassi and La Montagnole (Van Buren, *AJA* 1961, 385) is heightened by their "throwback" displays of gold, bronze, ivory, ostrich eggs.

8. See chap. vii, note 15. Wace explored the stratigraphy from many angles and was convinced that the treasury had been built in a "good" period, mid-fourteenth century; others make it mid-thirteenth, contemporary with the Lion Gate (Marinatos, Matz, Mylonas).

9. Wace, *Mycenae* 44; Pausanias 9.37.5; Herodotos 2.121. The space over the lintel is also often penetrated by dogs chasing rabbits, and by wintering tortoises, whose remains are thus found in early Mycenaean contexts (see chap. ix, note 8). High points of tomb robbing, tourism, and worship in tholos tombs seem to come in late Mycenaean, Protogeometric, Archaic, Hellenistic, and Roman Republican times. See Blegen, "Post-Mycenaean Deposits in Chamber Tombs," *Ephemeris* 1937, 377, and Marinatos, "Palaipylos," *Das Altertum* 1955, 140.

10. Kampos lead figurines: Tsountas, *Ephemeris* 1891, 189, *MycAge* 160, Marinatos, *CMG* 224–25, Hope-Simpson, *BSA* 1957, 236. Vourvoura-Analipsis: see bibliography under Tholos Tombs.

11. Recent discussions: Blegen, "Pylos," *Companion* 422; Kiechle, "Pylos und der pylische Raum," *Historia* 1960, 1, and *RhM* 1960, 335; Marinatos, "Problemi omerici e preomerici in Pilo," *PP* 1961, 219, and *AnzWien* 1961, 235; E. Meyer, *RE* 23-2 (1959) 2113; Hope-Simpson and McDonald, *AJA* 1961, 221; see also chap. vi bibliography for sites.

12. Marinatos, *VII ArcCong.* I, Pl. 2; Munich Antiquarium, Loeb Bequest, through A. Sanborn, who found it on the dump.

13. Cuirass and tomb, Verdelis, *Ephemeris* 1957 (1961) Chron. 15; Daux, *BCH* 1961, 671; Vanderpool, *AJA* 1963, 281; pottery, Åström, *Deltion* 1960 (1963) Pl. 73. Connection with Knossos ideograms, Marinatos, *PraktAkAth* 1962, 72, provenience for tablet from Little Palace, with caution, Chadwick and Huxley, *BSA* 1957, 147. Homeric references to *guala*, *Iliad* 4.132, 5.99 (as shoulderpiece for *thorax*), 15.529 (Meges wears an heirloom, perhaps made in Corinth), 13.507 and 587, with plates over belly or chest. Pausanias gives a clear description: "They were made of two bronze pieces one fitting the chest and parts around the belly, the other meant to protect the back. They were called *guala* . . . fastened together with buckles . . . thought to give safety even without a shield" (10.26.5).

Kallithea greaves, *AJA* 1960, 1, no. 48; see also bibliography, chap. vii, Metalwork and Weapons, von Merhardt, Yalouris, and Catling. Swords from *Ars Antiqua* auction catalogue (Lucerne) April 1961, now in Copenhagen.

Previous denials of possibility of Mycenaean bronze armor, e.g., Lorimer, *HM* 250, or Page, *History and the Homeric Iliad* 246. European examples are later; Hencken refers to Točnika and Paulik, *Slovenska Archaeologia* 1960, 59; see also von Merhardt, "Panzerstudie," *Rivista Archeologica delle provincia di Como* 1954, 33, and Müller-Karpe, "Spätbronzezeitlichen Bewaffnung," *Germania* 1962, 255; the earliest ca. 1250–1000. Fifteenth-century representations of cuirasses in Crete: Levi, *BdA* 1959, 257; Hutchinson, *BSA* 1956, Pl. 8 (Platon's identification). Pre-Dendra bronze armor in the Near East well-documented; see Breasted, *Ancient Records* II 501, loot in the tenth campaign of Tuthmosis III: "10 living prisoners, 180 horses, 60 chariots, 13 inlaid corselets, 13 bronze (suits) of armor, 5 bronze helmets for the head. . . ." The bronze helmet at Knossos seems distantly linked with European types, Hood, *BSA* 1952, 256; Hencken, *ProcPS* 1952, 36, *AJA* 1953, 107; reverse trade is suggested by the discovery of a Cretan bronze cup in fifteenth-century Germany, Sprockhoff, *Germania* 1961, 11.

14. Hood, *ILN* 17 February 1962, 261, *JHS Reports* 1962, 25; *KChron* 1961–62, 92.

15. Find-spots of LM II vases: Evans, *PM* IV, 299, II 513, 619, IV 49; cf. Vermeule, *AJA* 1963, 195; Furumark, *Chronology* 83, *OpArc* 1950, 261; Fimmen 90.

16. Theban tombs with Keftiu and Syrians: full re-evaluation and bibliography in J. Vercoutter, *L'Égypte et le monde Égéen préhéllenique* (1956), B. Porter and R. Moss, *Topographical Bibliography* I², *Theban Necropolis* I (1960). See also Kantor, *AegOrient* 41;

Furumark, *OpArc* 1950, 203; N. Davies, *Tomb of Menkheperrasonb* (1933); Pendlebury, *JEA* 1930, 75; Wace and Blegen, *Klio* 1939, 131; W. S. Smith, *AAAE* 145; Schachermeyr "Das Keftiu-Problem," *JOAI* 1960, 44; T. Säve-Södebergh, *Private Tombs at Thebes* (1957—). The chief tombs are those of Senmut (Senenmut), chief steward and architect (Thebes 71, late Hatshepsut); anonymous (Thebes 119, late Hatshepsut–Tuthmosis III); Antef, great herald (Thebes 155, early Tuthmosis III); User(amon) (Amenuser), vizier (Thebes 131, also Thebes 61, early Tuthmosis III); Puyemra, prophet of Amon (Thebes 39, Tuthmosis III); Menkeperrasoneb, prophet of Amon (Thebes 86, also Thebes 112, Tuthmosis III); Rekhmire, vizier (Thebes 100, Tuthmosis III–Amenhotep (Amenophis) II); Amenmose, captain of troops (Thebes 42, Tuthmosis III–Amenhotep II; here Syrians and Lebanese are labeled Keftiu, as in Thebes 85); Kenamon, chief steward (Thebes 93, Amenhotep II). Thebes 41 and 91 also show Mitanni and Hittites.

17. Sample mixed contexts: Marine style/LH III A, Attica, Theochares, *Antiquity* 1960, 266; vases ranging from Circle A Grave I to LH III A with one little girl in Athens, Thompson, *Hesperia* 1952, 107, Townsend, *Hesperia* 1955, 195 note 11; LH I and III A:1 with one burial, Tragana tholos, Furumark, *Chronology* 55, and bronzes matching both Shaft Grave and Dendra finds, Marinatos, *Ergon* 1955, 88, Daux, *BCH* 1956, 283; Marine style and LM III A in single deposit at Hagia Triada, Halbherr, *MonAnt* 1903, 66; Hagia Triada sarcophagus mixing LM II and III A, Pendlebury, *AC* 248; sherd mixtures at Trianda and Phylakopi, Furumark, *OpArc* 1950, 178, 194, Edgar, *Phylakopi* Pls. 25–31; Staphylos Shaft Grave with LM III A pottery, Platon, *KChron* 1949, 534; Gortyna cuirassed terracotta with LM I and III A pottery, Levi, *BdA* 1959, 253. Cretan imports *ca.* 1400 at Troy, Blegen, *Troy* III, Fig. 330, Immerwahr, *AJA* 1956, 455; at Ugarit, Schaeffer, *Ugaritica* I 72, *ILN* 10 April 1954, 574; see also Benson, *Berytus* 1961, 37.

18. Pindar *Paian* IV, 30 (Turyn; the oaks still grow on Keos); see also Bacchylides *Ode* I, 112 (Snell).

NOTES TO CHAPTER VI

1. Beginning with Schliemann's delightful observation at Tiryns, "The surface of the citadel is scantily strewn with potsherds of the Middle Ages, and probably of the time of the Frank dominion, for that period seems indicated by the chalk floors of a villa and its dependencies," *Mycenae and Tiryns* 14; see also Pausanias 2.16.2, "Traces of the residence of Proitos at Tiryns remain to the present day."

2. Tripod hearths are also called tables of offerings, a term better reserved for those with hollows around the lip for libations and seeds. Porphyry table from Mycenae's palace, *Praktika* 1955, Pl. 79 *a;* from the Treasury of Atreus, Curtius, *Peloponnes* II 408. Schliemann mentions the long bronze chain suspended from the dome, *Mycenae and Tiryns* 50. Inlaid stone table at Pylos, *AJA* 1955, 34.

3. See chap. viii bibliography, Linear B. Pylos Furniture tablets, among others, Ventris, "Mycenaean Furniture on the Pylos Tablets," *Eranos* 1955, 109; Higgins, "The Archaeological Background to the Furniture Tablets from Pylos," *BICS* 1956, 39; Gray, "Linear B and Archaeology," *BICS* 1959, 47; Lang, *AJA* 1958, 189 (Ta 709 and 712); Palmer, "A Mycenaean Tomb Inventory," *Minos* 1957, 58, and *Mycenaeans and Minoans* 149. Glass-paste inlays, T. Haevernick, "Mykenisches Glas," *JRGZM* 1960, Pls. 3–7, and *Archaeology* 1963, 190. Ivory inlays may be seen on Plate XXXIX D. Laboriousness as an aesthetic value for Mycenaeans, Persson, *RT* 62. Midas furniture, Young, *AJA* 1958, Pl. 27. Two translations

here are abnormal: *greenwood* where others guess *crystal* for *uarejo,* on the analogy of green-heart or other special woods in modern cabinetry (a crystal chair would be shattering); *butterflies* for others' *rosettes* or *speech-symbols,* for **85-depi,* perhaps from σᾶτες, σῆτες, see Pl. XLIV C, XLVI A.

4. Lang, *AJA* 1958, 191; Chadwick, *AJA* 1959, 137. ἡνίαι may be reins, bridle, or both. *Teukepi* seems to mean "with τεύχεα," battle-plates, metal fittings, or buckles. *Rousewija* perhaps from ῥούσιος, russet; Lang prefers "white." *Ampux* is the frontlet or headband of a bridle, or perhaps here the whole bridle, in single or double form (for teams). *Studded with nail-heads,* perhaps from ἡλοπαγής, ἡλοπαῖον or *braided black-and-white thongs,* from εἰλέα (= χαλινοί) or εἶλος (= δεσμός) and φαῖος, dusky, black-and-white. *Poqewija* from *phorbeia,* halter or manger strap, more likely than πόρπαι (*porpax* a regular part of horse headgear) or πόκος (lined with) fleece; see Killen, *BICS* 1962, 10, KN X 997 + D 7206.

5. Recorded spices and condiments are: *kadamija* (cardamum), *kanako* (safflower, red and white), *korako* (pennyroyal), *kono* (gingergrass?), *korijadana* (coriander), *kumino* (cummin), *kuparo* (galingale), *maratuwo* (fennel), *mita* (mint), *sasama* (sesame), *serino* (celery), *pako* (sage), *wodo* (rose), *sapida* (?), *eti-* (?); there are also wine, honey, iris-root, garden cress, poppy. See bibliography under Food and Industry, and Appendix I.

Notes to Chapter VII

1. The destruction of Thebes is dated by Furumark to the early fourteenth century (*OpArc* 1950, 264, note 4), and by Mylonas to the mid-thirteenth. The later date seems more likely on grounds of general chronology, the large III B population buried in tombs outside the palace, and the inscribed stirrup jars from the storerooms (Fig. 42) which are usually III B in other palaces (Bjørck, *Eranos* 1954, 120; Caratelli, *MonAnt* 1944–45, Pls. 30–40).

The recent probe of the Kadmeion by building contractors initiated the discovery of over thirty inscribed Oriental cylinder seals and some Linear B tablets. One of the seals published in the Greek newspaper account has been read as containing the name of Burnaburiash II, the Kassite king who reigned *ca.* 1375–47 B.C. As well as assuring Thebes' links to the Near East, the seal suggests that the destruction of Thebes cannot have taken place before the latter fourteenth century. See Boardman, *On the Knossos Tablets* 75 ff. The Theban tablets should be the oldest surviving ones on the mainland even if the palace is not destroyed before *ca.* 1250 B.C.

2. Tiryns is being reinvestigated stratigraphically by Verdelis; preliminary results show a long III B phase interrupted by one remodeling of the palace without violence, one mild burning, and one serious burning; then an unexpectedly rich III C phase. Ålin, *Fundstätten* 25 is the best discussion. Fragments of both Rodenwaldt's "older" and "younger" series of frescoes were found with the same style of III B pottery; there are new fragments of the procession scene, *Ephemeris* 1956 Chron. 5–8, Fig. 16.

3. Procession frescoes: Knossos, Evans, *PM* II 655–757, Supplementary Plates 25–27; Hagia Triada, *MonAnt* 1908, 69, Nilsson, *MMR²*, Fig. 198, Pernier and Banti, *Guida degli Scavi,* Fig. 21, and a forthcoming publication by L. Banti; Thebes, Reusch (see bibliography) with full references, Keramopoullos, *Ephemeris* 1909, Pls. 1–3; Tiryns, Rodenwaldt I, 69–96; Mycenae, Lamb, *BSA* 1919–21, 194–6, Pl. 8, 1921–23, Pl. 28, Wace, *Mycenae* 71; Pylos, Blegen, *AJA* 1962, 147 and Pl. 40, *AJA* 1963, 159; Eleusis, Mylonas, *Eleusis and the Eleusinian Mysteries* 40 (one eye).

4. R. Carpenter, "Archaeology Now and Then," *Phoenix* 1959, 2.

5. Main group of megaron frescoes found by Tsountas in 1886; these and further fragments found in 1914 published by Rodenwaldt between 1911 and 1921 in a reconstruction of masterful good sense; a third lot, mainly architectural, by Lamb in 1923. One Tsountas fragment from the aithousa represents in rough style a boar or dog pursuing an ibex (*Ephemeris* 1887, 164, 168, Pl. 11; not Skylla as Studniczka, *AM* 1906, 50); perhaps hunting and siege themes were mixed as at Pylos. A fragment of arm and torso formerly in Bucharest is illustrated by Evans, *PM* II, Fig. 484, from B. Pharmakowsky, *Revue Archéologique* 1897, 374 (Fig. 34 here).

6. The earliest Egyptian scene of chariot horses leaping over falling enemies seems to be on the chariot of Tuthmosis IV; the perspective is different, tumbled Asiatics and horses rising in a confused tangle from Pharaoh's wheels to his horses' plumes (Carter and Newberry, *Catalogue Général du Musée de Caire* 15 [1904] 24; see also W. Smith, *BMFA* 1952, 74, A. Groenewegen-Frankfort, *Arrest and Movement* 114). Though the parallel for Mycenae most often quoted is the Battle of Kadesh relief (e.g., Rodenwaldt II, Fig. 29), scenes carved for Seti I seem closer, with the presence of cities on hills, soldiers among trees and plants below, or chariot horses stationed over cities (Wreszinski, *Atlas II*, Pls. 34, 39). The Egyptian and Aegean series are probably both early thirteenth century; "influence" may have been mutual reinforcement, for the Aegean tradition of sieges in city landscapes seems older, with the Town Mosaic and Siege Rhyton. I am indebted to W. S. Smith for a preview of his monograph on such interrelations.

7. Miss Lang reports fragments of black men from Pylos. Evans once thought to detect racial differences between red men and yellow men at Tiryns, *JHS* 1912, 283.

8. An imported Mycenaean vase at Tell Beit Mirsim proved to have been fired at 1030° C, far higher than the average or necessary 800–890° C. For lists of exports to the Near East see bibliography on Trade and Foreign Relations, chap. viii, under Immerwahr, Kantor, Furumark, Sjøqvist, Stubbings; Schachermeyr III 375.

9. Chariot scenes as funerary, Lorimer, *HM* 48 and index; Furumark disagrees, *MP* 430–70.

10. Chariot and goats on larnax from Zafer Papoura, Evans, *Prehistoric Tombs of Knossos* 29, Fig. 26; Episkopi larnax with many figures, quasi-mythological scenes, to be published by N. Platon. The two other figured larnakes from Crete have single floating human figures: from Milatos (Evans, *ibid.* 98), and Vatheianos Kampos (Marinatos, *AA* 1934, 247, Fig. 1, Zervos, *Art de la Crète*, Fig. 778); cf. Alexiou, *KChron* 1958, 218. See also note 13 below, and chap. ix, note 11.

11. Hagia Triada sarcophagus most recently in color in D. Levi, *Archaeology* 1956, 192, and Marinatos, *CMG*, Pls. XXVIII–XXX; Nilsson, *MMR*² 426 gives bibliography to 1950. Homage Krater, Pottier, *BCH* 1907, 232, Figs. 11–12, Karageorghis, *AJA* 1958, Pl. 99. Griffin and sphinx chariot, and altar with horns, Immerwahr, *Archaeology* 1960, Figs. 7, 15.

12. Window Krater newly pieced out, Karageorghis, *JHS* 1957, 269; the curiously similar Hittite polychrome relief vase from Bitik, Akurgal, *Kunst der Hethiter*, Pl. XIV. Some community of tradition is further illustrated here by Figure 20 *b*, the steatite relief vase from Epidauros (*Praktika* 1950, 200). The Window Vase may be later than 1400, see Immerwahr, *AJA* 1945, 534; it is probably not women worshiping in a pillar shrine, Hutchinson, *PC* 215. For the Warrior Vase, among many, see Lorimer, *HM* 146, Furumark, *MP* 452, Schliemann, *Mycenae and Tiryns* 132.

13. It is not yet possible to provide a complete list of these larnakes. Examples are known

in Geneva, Paris, Kassel, New York, and Athens; see *Munzen und Medaillen* Auktion 18 (1958) no. 74 (Niarchos Collection), and von Bothmer, *Ancient Art in New York Private Collections* (1961) no. 102 (Pomerance Collection). See Vermeule, *JHS* 1965. Permission to illustrate the example exhibited in Kassel (Pl. XXXIV here), from the owner; permission to discuss two of the three examples in Athens, from the late J. Threpsiades and N. Platon. One on the Paris market in 1956 had a conventional decoration of flowers; apart from the men and bird illustrated here (Pl. XXXV), the others all show mourners, both male and female, with architectural detail and occasional religious symbols such as horns of consecration. For other fragments of sarcophagi in Mycenaean burials see chap. ix, note 11. A fragmentary bathtub larnax from Mycenae is painted with horse and chariot, flowers and octopus, but considered a household piece, since there were no burial traces in the area (French, *BSA* 1961, 88). Household larnakes are usually painted red-on-buff or white-on-dark, rarely polychrome like the Boiotian group or the Pylos bathtub.

14. Lion Gate composition discussed fully in Mylonas, *AncMyc* 24 with bibliography, Nilsson, *MMR*[2] 252, Wace, *Mycenae* 53, Marinatos, *CMG* no. 141. Wace proposed a dove, Marinatos a lily, to fill the apex of the slab, from parallel compositions on gems. For the scheme in minor arts, Reusch, *Minoica*, Pls. 3–5.

15. Restorations of the Treasury of Atreus façade and discussions of its date: Wace, *Mycenae* 28, 119, *Antiquity* 1940, 233, *JHS* 1926, 110, *Geras Keramopoullou* 310, *BSA* 1956, 116; Marinatos, *Ephemeris* 1953–54, I, 9; Mylonas, *AncMyc*, Pl. 26; Graham, *Palaces of Crete* 38, *Archaeology* 1960, 46; Robertson, *JHS* 1941, 14; Thiersch, *AM* 1879, 177; Durm, *JOAI* 1907, 41; Perrot and Chipiez, *Histoire de l'Art* VI, 2, 46. Wace thought the Elgin slabs might have come from the Tomb of Clytemnestra, which uses some gypsum in its decor, *Mycenae* 36. The fragments in Pl. XXVI C, from casts in Sir John Soane's Museum, are pieces once in Dodwell's possession, the larger from the side bands flanking the triangle, the smaller from the band above the discs, cf. Pryce, *BM Catalogue of Sculpture* I, A 54, or Marinatos, *op. cit.*, Fig. 7. The decoration is distributed among the British Museum (Sligo), the Munich Antiquarium (Dodwell), and Athens. Parts of the columns were once built into the courthouse in Nauplion, Michaelis, *AM* 1896, 121. For a bronze nail, chap. iv, note 1; for original furnishings of tables and a chain, chap. vi, note 2.

16. "Everybody obviously knew long ago about ivory, at least for arts and crafts, but until the Macedonians crossed over to Asia no one had seen the elephants themselves. . . . Homer proves this by singing about couches and rooms belonging to the wealthier princes all decorated with elephant ivory, but never making a single mention of the elephant-animal. If he had ever seen one, or even heard about one, I am sure he would have put it in his poetry much more eagerly than the pygmies and the cranes" (Pausanias 1.12.4).

17. Agora pyxis, with a brilliant description, Shear, *Hesperia* 1940, 274. It is 0.16 m. high, 0.11 m. broad, the double handles made up of prostrate fawn and crouching lion are pierced for cords, the interior is lined with tin strips to prevent ointment or oily liquid from staining the ivory.

18. Many of the best Mycenae ivories come from Tsountas' excavations of chamber tombs and are not fully published yet, though Staïs, *Mycenaean Collection*, is helpful. *Ephemeris* 1888, Pl. 8 offers a good selection. Certain tombs were treasuries of ivory, like No. 27 of that year: it yielded a woman in a flounced skirt, a naked woman pressing her breasts, a griffin, a horse(?), conjoined headless animals, a pyxis fragment with a griffin attacking a bull, fluted and unfluted miniature columns, a relief with architectural split rosettes and triglyphs, discs with rosettes, "headbands" and miscellaneous decorations. When

such quantities are buried in a single tomb like this, or Spata (see bibliography), one may be justified in imagining elaborate chests or inlaid biers (compare the Dendra footstool, Persson, *NT* Pl. 2 and chap. ix, note 11 below), but there is not enough even here for a whole set of furniture such as the Pylos texts describe (chap. vi, note 3).

19. Mycenae sealings: Wace and Bennett, *Mycenae Tablets* II, Fig. 67; the pot names include *kanato, qetija, atara*. See bibliography under Chadwick, Lang. The Pylos sealings will be published by Mme. Xenaki-Sakellariou.

20. Keramopoullos, *Ephemeris* 1930, 40.

21. G. McFadden, "A Late Cypriote III Tomb from Kourion," *AJA* 1954, 131. This extraordinary tomb, robbed before the First World War and redug after fifty years, also contained famous bronze handles with paired daimons, a bronze cremation urn, an iron knife, and rod-tripods like one in the late robber's hoard at Tiryns; see also Karageorghis, *Kypriakai Spoudai* 1961, Pl. 8, and Higgins, *Greek and Roman Jewellery,* 24. Aristophanes may have known such sceptres: the birds "ruled with so strong a rule that any king in the cities of the Hellenes, Agamemnon or Menelaos, had a bird sitting on top of his sceptre, who shared in all the gifts" (*Birds* 508).

22. See chap. viii, note 7 for foreign weapons in Mycenaean contexts.

23. Pylos Jn tablets; *Documents* 351, Lejeune, *Historia* 1961, 409; see bibliography, Metalworking and Weapons, chap. viii.

NOTES TO CHAPTER VIII

1. The best discussion of Bronze Age literacy, S. Dow, *AJA* 1954, 120; the problem of language and script acutely reviewed, with historical parallels, by J. Alsop, *From the Silent Earth* 203–44. Alsop thinks Linear B may have been invented on the mainland, not at Knossos; M. Pope argues for an early invention, in the Shaft Grave period, *KChron* 1961–62, I, 310. For scribes in the palaces, E. Bennett, *Archaeology* 1960, 26 and *Mycenae Tablets* II, 89.

2. Herodotos 5.58; Sp. Marinatos, "Καδμήια Γράμματα," *University of Athens Philosophical Faculty* 1955–56, 531; J. Forsdyke, *Greece before Homer* (1956); J. Bérard, *Syria* 1952, 41. The goddess Eris and a girl from Pedasos wrote on apples (Hyginus *Fabulae* 92, Hesiod frag. 85 [Rzach]). A papyrus letter from Sarpedon brother of Minos was preserved in Lycia (Marinatos, *op. cit.* 536). Phaidra wrote on papyrus to Theseus, perhaps, or scratched her message on wax (Euripides, *Hippolytos* 856). Bellerophon's folding tablet from King Proitos was probably wood and wax (Homer, *Iliad* 6, 168). Its distressing signs, σήματα λύγρα, are in a formulaic phrase modeled on κήδεα λύγρα, φάρμακα λύγρα, λύγρης ἀγγελίης, and need not be early. Philomela wove her message in wool, perhaps simple pictures (Scholiast on Aristophanes' *Birds* 212). The bronze plate with incised barbaric signs from a prehistoric tomb in Boiotia is well known (Plutarch, *On the Genius of Socrates* 577 c, J. Schwartz, "Le Tombeau d'Alcmène," *Revue Archéologique* 1958, 76). Could the famous trident mark of Poseidon under the Erechtheion on the Athenian Acropolis be a mason's mark from the Mycenaean palace? On the whole, classical Greeks were unaware that their ancestors wrote a different script; myths are silent about clay tablets and scribes. Most of the early writing myths have widespread folklore motifs. Papyrus was certainly used for Bronze Age documents; fiber and string impressions on sealings show how the sheets were tied and dispatched.

3. The definitive studies of these tablets are: E. Bennett, "Notes on Two Broken Tablets

from Pylos," *Minos* 1957, 113–16, Pls. 8–11; M. Ruipérez, "Une charte royale de partage des terres à Pylos," *Minos* 1956, 146–64, and "Notes on Mycenaean Land-Division and Livestock Grazing," *Minos* 1957, 174–206. Related articles: E. Bennett, "The Land-Holders of Pylos," *AJA* 1956, 103–34; M. Finley, "The Mycenaean Tablets and Economic History," *Economic History Review* 1957, 128–41; cf. L. R. Palmer, *ibid.* 1958, 87–96; W. Brown, "Land Tenure in Mycenaean Pylos," *Historia* 1956, 385–400; M. Lang, "Es Proportions," *Mycenaean Colloquium* 1961, 37–55; L. Palmer, *Achaeans and Indo Europeans* (1955); M. Ruipérez, "*Koretere* et *Porokoretere* à Pylos," *Études Mycéniennes* (Gif-sur-Yvette 1956) 105–20; M. Ventris and J. Chadwick, *Documents* 175–77; E. Will, "Aux origines du régime foncier grec: Homère, Hésiode, et l'arrière-plan mycénien," *RevEtAnc* 1957, 24–50.

Commentary: I have reversed the texts, since *odaa₂* is an opening formula. Although the proper way to transcribe ideograms is now through Latin equivalents, in this case ZE = *Iugerum* and *171* = *Actus,* the older Greek-English style has been retained for non-specialists' convenience. *Moroqa:* there is no agreement about what kind of *moira, moros* these people hold. Some think it is a religious privilege, some a pragmatic piece of land. *Iterewa, Timitija:* either genitives or locatives. They are neighboring towns, near *Pi-82 (Pija,* Risowa's town?), on Jn 438.25. Klymenos is commander of his own regiment, An 654.1. *i-65: Docs'.* suggestion was *inis,* more often a cub but with the strained meaning "son." Chadwick later suggested *i-ju* = υἱύς. Ruipérez connects *teranija* with *therapon,* "servant." *Eqeo atomo:* frustrating; it looks so easy to solve, but Mühlestein's link with horses and joining (*hippias arthmon,* "chariot joiner") is still generally repudiated after seven years and there are no good new proposals. Lines 64.7 and 13 have extra words written in; what with the erasing and reruling, as bad a morning for the scribe as a problem for us. Priests: Risowa comes first, perhaps older and more important; Newokito is to do the real work; he is a "military" priest in Waparos' regiment (An 656); the other three officers are in regiments but do not command them (Ruipérez I.151). *Marateu* may be a profession, not a name; it seems connected with *marathon* the Pylian place and the plant. For *apuka* as an ethnic, Ruipérez I.159, but all spelled *apu₂.*

Since this section was written (spring 1962) a new discussion has appeared in L. Palmer's *Mycenaean Greek Texts* (1963) 140. Palmer also reverses the tablets, and almost entirely rejects Ruipérez' interpretation; he connects the texts with the *oka* tablets for military arrangements where several names also appear (Klymenos, Newokito, Poikilops, Aeriphoitas, Aiqota, Dewijo, Erkhomenatas[?]). The purport of the texts baffles him; he designates them as "arrangements of a predominantly religious character" (145). This difference of opinion among specialists is symptomatic of the state of Linear B now.

4. The prefixes to these tablets, An and Sn, denote ideograms of STANDING MAN and YOKE respectively. A synopsis of classifications of Linear B tablets according to ideograms is given in Bennett, *A Minoan Linear B Index,* xii–xiii; Ventris and Chadwick, *Documents* 50–51; Palmer, *Mycenaean Greek Texts* 5. Only a few modifications have been introduced into the original list, such as the discrimination of sex in domestic animals. In general terms, A = men, women, boys, girls; B = seated figure; C = wild and domestic animals, often mixed; D = rams and ewes; E = measures of grain and concerns landholding; F = various other commodities like cereals, oil, olives, figs; G = processed commodities (honey, wine, spices) and offerings; J = bronze and gold; K = vessels; L = cloth; M = wool (usually by weight) plus mixed commodities including hides, often in fixed proportions; N = flax, linen, saffron; O = wool and other uncertain signs including ingots; P = tools; R = weapons; S = chariots, wheels, yokes; T = furniture, vessels, gold luxu-

ries; U is reserved for miscellaneous lists; V is for numbers without ideograms; W = writing not on tablets, that is, labels and sealings; X = unidentifiable fragments; Z = records in paint and other abnormal media.

5. The importance of the foreign grain trade is often disputed; see Vermeule, *Archaeology* 1960, 66; Howe, *TAPA* 1958, 44 for post-palatial agricultural development; *Documents* 132, 237 for predominance of livestock over grain at Pylos, and meagerness of recorded grain to support the calculated population. Montelius, *GP* I gives a good survey of tools; selected types from the Gelidonya wreck, Bass, *AJA* 1961, 267. Land improvement: Aristotle, *Meteorology* 1.14, "At the time of the Trojan War the land of Argos, being swampy, could only feed a scanty population, while the land of Mycenae was good and therefore highly prized." Drainage of Lake Kopaïs must have corrected swampy conditions around Gla.

6. Stele from Dramesi (ancient Hyria?), Blegen, *Hesperia* Supplement 8 (1949) 39; from Enkomi, without funerary significance, Schaeffer, *Enkomi-Alasia,* Pl. 10, Fig. 38. The Dramesi stele is probably MH–LH I, like the pots there, not Trojan War period; there are other MH doodles in the same ΣΠΑΠ or railroad track style.

7. Selected foreign weapons (see also bibliography, chap. vii, Metalwork and Weapons; chap. viii, Trade and Foreign Relations): Peschiera daggers in Crete and the islands: *PM* IV, 857 (Zafer Papoura), *BSA* 1910, Pl. 14, 60 (Phylakopi). Cut-and-thrust swords in Cyprus, Mycenae, Tiryns, Phokis, Athens, Achaia: Catling, *ProcPS* 1956, 111; Vermeule, *AJA* 1960, 14; Cowen, *VI Internationale Kongress d. Vor- und frühgeschichte* (1958) 207; Miløjčič, *AA* 1948–49, 12; Schaeffer, *Enkomi-Alasia,* Fig. 105. European spearheads in Ithaka, Kephallenia, Thesprotia, Epeiros, Achaia: *BSA* 1934–35, 71, Fig. 20, *Ephemeris* 1933, 92, Fig. 41, *Deltion* 1920, 176, *Ephemeris* 1956, 114, *Ergon* 1960, 110. Helmets and greaves: chap. v, note 13. Italian winged ax mold at Mycenae: Stubbings, *BSA* 1954, 297, cf. *Ephemeris* 1932, Pl. 14. Iron blades: *Praktika* 1954, 98 (Perati), *Ergon* 1960, 191 (Naxos) *AM* 1930, 135 (Tiryns).

8. Home Guard tablets (An): *Documents* 183, Mühlestein, *Die Oka-Tafeln von Pylos* (1957), Palmer, *Mycenaeans and Minoans* 132. Military gear: *Documents* 351, 375, Lorimer, *HM passim,* Marinatos, *CMG* 99. Rations: Palmer, *op. cit.* 109. Roads and chariots, note 9.

9. Horses, chariots, and roads: J. Anderson, *Ancient Greek Horsemanship* (1961); E. Delebecque, *Le Cheval dans l'Iliade* (1951); R. Forbes, *Notes on the History of Ancient Roads* (1934); F. Hançar, *Das Pferd in prähistorischer und früher historischer Zeit* (1956); A. Kammenhuber, *Hippologia Hethitica* (1960, cf. Goetze, *JCS* 1962, 30); von Mercklin, *Der Rennwagen in Griechenland* (1909); Childe, *History of Technology* I, 716; *Documents* 361; Foltiny, *AJA* 1959, 53; Gray, "Swords, Rapiers, and Horse Riders," *Antiquity* 1953, 66; Hood, "A Mycenaean Cavalryman," *BSA* 1953, 84, with good bibliography; Hope-Simpson, "Mycenaean Highways," *Minutes of the Mycenaean Seminar* 31 January 1962, 257 and Chadwick, *ibid.* 260; Lorimer, *HM* 307; *PM* IV, 786; Moortgat, "Kampf zu Wagen," *Orientalische Literaturzeitung* 1930, 842; Schachermeyr, "Streitwagen und Streitwagenbild," *Anthropos* 1951, 705. The earliest finds or representations of horses seem to be: a sealing from Kültepe *ca.* 1850 (Hançar, *Pferd* 455), bones from Troy VI *ca.* 1800 (Blegen, *Troy* III 10), bones from Buhen in the Sudan *ca.* 1700 (Emery, *ILN* 12 October 1959, 250), the Shaft Grave stelai after 1600, and perhaps a borderline MH–LH set of bones from Dorion (Valmin, *SME* 58, 138). The Marathon and Lerna horse-burials should help identify the mainland breed (chap. ix, note 8). Horse bits: Anderson, *op. cit.* 48. One wonders if "sceptre" knobs are not sometimes the tops of whips.

10. That chariot horses often got out of control is clear from Nestor's nervous advice to his troops at Troy, to hang on tight and try to keep formation (*Iliad* 4.303), and we hear of horses "painful to drive in a chariot" (*Iliad* 10.402).

11. Almost every identification of the Sea Peoples has been argued, like the other facts about them. The *Denyen* or *Danuna* may illustrate. Page believes they cannot be Danaan Greeks because they seem to operate from a non-Mycenaean base in the Levant (*History and the Homeric Iliad* 22). Huxley believes Palestinian Joppa was in fact connected with Mycenaeans as a home of the tribe of *Dan* with whom *Danaos, Danaë,* and Perseus of Mycenae were linked (*Crete and the Luwians* 35). Wainwright, acknowledging the Palestinian background, suggests that a branch of *Danuna* settled on islands near Tarsus in Cilicia (*JEA* 1961, 71). See also his articles in *JEA* 1939, *AJA* 1952, *AnatSt* 1954, *JHS* 1963. *Aḫḫiyawa / Aqiyawasa*: normally identified with Achaia (the mainland—not the classical province) and the Achaians; Page, *op. cit.* 21, splits these apart, retaining the first as a Hittite transcription for ᾽Αχαιάϝα, a kingdom he localizes on Rhodes (but see Dow, *AJP* 1962, 96), and repudiating the second as Achaians because they seem to have no foreskins (*qrnt*); Page thinks proper Achaians should not be circumcised. Desborough conceives of the Achaians in more mobile terms, as a mixed party of mainlanders and non-Mycenaeans raiding eastward and southward in the late thirteenth century, sparing Mycenaean centers (*Minutes of the Mycenaean Seminar* 30 May 1962, 263). Cornelius suggests persuasively that they are Argives (*Argeiwoi, Argaioi*), which would be a generic tribal name extending beyond frontiers of local kingdoms (*Historia* 1962, 112). Others settle Achaioi near Bodrum (Halikarnassos) and Kos, where cemeteries of the right period are known.

In inconsistent orthography, the Sea Peoples in the Amarna Letters include *Shardana* (Sardinoi?), *Shekel* (Shekelesh, Sikels or men of Sagalassos?), *Danuna, Lukki* (Lukka, Lycians); in the records of Rameses II, *Dardana* (Dardanians from Troy?), *Iliunna* (men of Ilion? Ariunna? Oroant?), *Kalikisha, Masa, Mushant, Pidasa* (men of Pedasos?); in the records of Merneptah, *Akaiwasha* or *Ekwesh* (Achaians? circumcised unknowns?), *Lukka, Shardana, Shekelesh, Tjekker* (Teukroi from Cyprus?), *Tursha* or *Teresh* (Tyrsenians, pre-Etruscan stock from Lydia?); in the records of Rameses III, *Danuna, Pulesati* (Philistines), *Shardana, Shekesh, Tursha, Weshasha, Zakaray*. The Libyan tribes of *Retennu* and *Tehenu*, perhaps also *Meshwesh*, are not strictly Sea Peoples but become steadily more closely associated with them. Pindar speaks of the Trojan Sons of Antenor migrating to Libya with their chariots (*Pythian* 5, 82), and there are two Aegean sherds at Cyrene according to S. Stucchi; J. Boardman considers them East Greek.

12. Emigrants and adventurers: Sarpedon, the brother of Minos, from Crete to Milyas (Milas) in Lycia or Miletos; Bellerophon from Corinth to Lycia in the reign of King Proitos; Tlepolemos from Dendra (Midea) to Rhodes before the Trojan War after murdering a relative; Telephos from Arkadia to Pergamon as an infant, long enough before the Trojan War to fight Agamemnon when he landed there by mistake; Kadmos from Thebes to the Encheleis in the west (not the eel-eaters of Gla in Lake Kopaïs?); followers of Kadmos to Ialysos on Rhodes at an early date; the prophet Kalchas to Kolophon after the War; the prophet Mopsos from Kolophon to Cilicia (Mopsouestia?); Podaleirios the Greek doctor at Troy to Syrnos in Caria; Teukros the brother of Aias from Salamis and Troy to Salamis in Cyprus. See on the problem in general, Huxley, *Achaeans and Hittites* (1960), *Crete and the Luwians* (1961), N. Hammond, *CAH* II², xxxvi, 22.

13. The text of King Suppiluliumas II (only newly discovered himself at the end of the Hittite king list) relating to the great sea battle off Alasia *ca.* 1180, in G. Steiner, "Neue

Alašija-Texte," *Kadmos* 1962, 130; H. Otten, *Mitteilungen der deutschen Orientgesellschaft* 1963, 1. The king dedicates a statue and temple for Tudhaliyas IV, and describes how he beat back the ships and exacted a tribute of copper and gold from Cyprus. Cyprus was usually a nominal Hittite ally, used as a place of political exile but rich and independent; Enkomi revives after this battle with a new colony. This is the last action of the Hittites at sea.

14. Greek legend is clear about the first war against Troy: Herakles came "with fewer ships and men, destroyed the city of Ilion and widowed her streets," *Iliad* 5.640, see also 5.265, 20.145. Pindar elaborates the role of the sons of Aiakos; over four generations, seven members of the family fought at Troy, none with marked success but all with a certain brilliance—Aiakos, Telamon, Achilles, Neoptolemos, Aias, Teukros, and Epeios (*Olympian* 8.31, 9.70, *Nemean* 3.36, *Isthmian* 5.34, 6.27, 8.52). Furumark, reviewed through Nylander (*Antiquity* 1963, 6) puts the Mycenaean sherds of the crucial period at Troy in the III B–III C period; Blegen has recently proposed *ca.* 1270, which seems curiously high to many. The first war against Troy should be approximately contemporary with the Battle of Kadesh and perhaps the voyage of the Argonauts; the final sack of Troy, according to pottery, matches the sacking of a dozen other great cities on eastern shores, including Ugarit, Atchana, and Hazor. A proposal for all the disturbance of the age being caused by epidemics of bubonic plague, Watson-Williams, *Greece and Rome* 1962, 109.

NOTES TO CHAPTER IX

* As Guthrie remarks, "Given two sets of gods [the Greeks] would happily worship both and even unite representations of both under the same name. . . . Given contrasting rites which seem to us to call for a different approach and a different conception of the relations between heaven and earth, the same man, if he is a Greek, will enter with equal zest into both" (*CAH* II² xl, 4).

1. Altar in Mycenae vestibule: Papademetriou, *Praktika* 1955, 230, Fig. 7, *JHS Arc Reports* 1956, 11. At Pylos, by hearth: Blegen, *Guide* 9, cf. *AJA* 1960, 157. Pylos' fixed altar and "shrine" considered below. Mycenae's "shrine" seems rather to have been a storeroom or closet, guarding the ivory triad (Pl. XXXVIII), a Levantine cylinder seal, a painted plaster head, terracotta figurines, fragments of ivory and gold: Wace, *Mycenae* 82–86, 114; *BSA* 1957, 197.

2. Fixed altar at Pylos: Blegen, *AJA* 1958, 176; Tiryns, K. Müller, *Tiryns* III 136, 215, plan 5, Pl. 42; cf. Lorimer, *HM* 435, C. Yavis, *Ancient Altars,* Fig. 20.

3. Tsountas, *Ephemeris* 1887, 160, Pl. 10; Wace, *Mycenae* 66; *JHS Arc Reports* 1951, 254; 1961, 31.

4. I have eliminated the so-called shrine at Berbati because it has only a bench and some fragments of idols like many secular rooms: *AA* 1938, 553. Swedish excavations in the Argolid are likely to be rich in religious mysteries. Marinatos suggested the propylon at Mouriatada might be a shrine, but there was no bench or religious equipment. The "Ceremonial Room" at Dorion-Malthi has half a hearth but no cult equipment, and the "Sanctuary of the Double Ax" there was only a closet (1.0 m. × 0.80 m.); it contained one double ax and a quantity of pottery: Valmin, *SME* 78, 126, 178.

5. Frödin and Persson, *Asine* 75 (plan), 89, 104, 298 (pottery), 308 (small finds); Nilsson, *MMR*² 110. Other bearded heads: Mycenae, Wace, *Mycenae,* Pl. 104 *b;* Athens National Museum nos. 2595 and another (Tsountas), cf. Staïs, *Mycenaean Collection* no. 76

(lead), 2471 (ivory). See G. Mylonas, "A Mycenaean Figurine at the University of Illinois," *AJA* 1937, 237 for one with a moustache; Schliemann, *Mycenae* 73. If the plaited stone object Schliemann found at Mycenae is hair as Evans thought, and not an ominous liver in the Hittite manner, it would be from a stone statue nearly life size, but it makes unconvincing locks: Evans, *PM* IV, 480; Staïs, *Mycenaean Collection* no. 2656. Large clay head reported from Tiryns: *Asine* 308. A stone head at Corinth is probably medieval, Broneer, *AJA* 1936, 204.

6. Eleusis: Mylonas, *Eleusis and the Eleusinian Mysteries* (1961) 33–49. Delos: H. Gallet de Santerre, *Délos primitive et archaïque* (1959) 89, 165. Cf. *BCH* 1947–48, 148, Nilsson, *MMR²* 611. Lists of connections between Mycenaean habitations and classical temple sites, not always critical of evidence for continuity: Ch. Picard, *Les Religions préhelleniques* 207, 282; Nilsson, *MMR²* 473; Gallet de Santerre, *Délos* 96. Epidauros (uncertain): Papademetriou, *Praktika* 1949, 91; 1950, 194. Continuity in Cypriote sanctuaries: J. du Plat Taylor, *Myrtou-Pigadhes* (1957), P. Dikaios, *Kypriakai Spoudai* 1960, 1–30, under Hagios Iakovos, Idalion, Hagia Irini. Cf. also Lorimer, *HM,* under Cults, Temples; J. Wiesner, *Olympos passim;* Blegen, "The So-Called Temple of Hera at Tiryns," *Korakou* 130.

7. Scales in tombs: among others, Shaft Grave III, Karo, *SG* Pl. 34, 3 pairs; Vapheio, Tsountas, *MycAge* 144, 5 pairs; Dendra, *NT* T. 10, 73; Myrsinochorion; Mycenae, Wace, *Chamber Tombs* 58, Tomb 515; Prosymna, *Prosymna* 351 (Tombs 2, 25, 26, 43, 44, LH I–LH III A:1); Argos, Deiras Tomb 24, *JHS Arc Reports* 1955, 9; Pylos, Blegen, *AJA* 1958, 178; cf. also Mavrospilio cemetery by Knossos, Forsdyke, *BSA* 1926–27, 253, *PM* III, 151, II, 556. For the chariot krater with "Zeus and the Scales of Fate," Nilsson, *Bull Lund* 1932–33; Vermeule, *CJ* 1958, 103; Wiesner, *JdI* 1959, 35.

8. Lerna horse, one of the rare skeletons: Caskey, *Hesperia* 1954, 11. Marathon horse burial: *Ergon* 1958, 23; the excavators mention no trace of harness or wood, but did not clear the whole dromos. Parts of the skeletons have been filled in with clay for photography. Artificial ruts at Tragana: *Praktika* 1956, Pl. 95 *a*. Horse burials in Cyprus, of Iron Age, complete with cart: V. Karageorghis, *ILN* 2 June 1962, 894; *BCH* 1963, 265, 357. One horse tried to run away but was knocked down with stones. Dogs not considered as burial companions in noble Homeric style, because they are reported especially from tholoi where it is easy to creep in chasing rabbits: Asine Tomb 1; Thebes; Dendra Tomb 6 and tholos pit; Vapheio (teeth only); Mycenae (Tsountas, *MycAge* 152). The large beef bone buried at Prosymna (Tomb 12) was likely food, not a pet cow.

9. Painted doors: Mycenae, Tsountas, *MycAge* Figs. 16, 49 (elaborate rosettes, disc, roof beams), *Ephemeris* 1888, 122, Fig. 3; 1891, Pl. 1; *Praktika* 1890, 36. Prosymna: Blegen, *Prosymna* plan 39 (rosettes). Argos: Vollgraff, *BCH* 1904, 369 (Fig. 45 here); *JHS Arc Reports* 1954, 8; *BCH* 1955, 310 (yellow with alternate blue and red rectangles).

10. Blegen, *Prosymna* 206, Tomb 44. Lead, in wires or sheets, has been found in many tombs; use uncertain. Blegen suggests for trussing the corpse, Persson suggested dress-weights for improving hang of funeral costume (*Prosymna* 255, *NT* 50).

11. Biers: Prosymna Tombs 10, 26, 29, 42. Coffins: Dendra Tomb 8 (*NT* 111); Katsaba (Alexiou, *KChron* 1952, 10); Hagios Ioannis (Hood, *BSA* 1952, 248). Sarcophagi: see chap. vii, note 13; Mycenae: *Chamber Tombs* 9, 139, 184; *BSA* 1961, 88; *Prosymna,* Fig. 101; Thebes: *Deltion* 1917, 92; Kephallenia: *Ephemeris* 1933, 79, Fig. 22 (Kontogenada); *Praktika* 1951, 186 (Parisata); *Aghios Kosmas* 61; Pylos: tholos, *AJA* 1954, 31; Assarlik: *JHS* 1887, 67; Naxos: Grotta (Kontoleon).

12. Cremations: *Prosymna* 143, 242 in urn; Argos: *BCH* 1957, 537; Naxos: *Ergon* 1960,

191; Ialysos (see bibliography) Tombs 15, 17, 32, 37, 45, 71, 87; Perati (see bibliography) Tombs 1 (two examples), 36, 38, 46, 75, 122; Tragana: *BCH* 1956, 285; Ailias (Crete) MM II: *JHS Arc Reports* 1956, 32; Troy: Blegen *et al.*, *Troy* III, 370; in late Crete cremation occurs at Dreros, Karphi, Kavousi, Mouliana, Olous, Tylissos, Vrokastro. The early example in Leukas not certain: Dörpfeld, *Alt-Ithaka* 216, P. Goessler, *Ergebnisse der Ausgrabungen auf Leukas* (1927).

13. *Cippi tombali: Annuario* 1926, 208, Fig. 131. Inscribed sarcophagus from Karteros (Amnisos): *Deltion* 1927–28, 68. Stelai from Mycenae: *Ephemeris* 1896, Pl. I; 1888, 127, Fig. 4. Cf. chap. viii, note 6.

14. Chr. Belger, *Die mykenischen Lokalsage* (1893) *passim*. Cf. Herodotos 1. 68, 4. 34; Pausanias 1. 35. 5–6; 2. 25. 9.

15. Hesiod, *Works and Days* 142–69 b.

16. Schliemann, *Mycenae* 78, Figs. 128–30.

17. Pausanias 1.22.7.

18. N. Kontoleon, *Ephemeris* 1952, 32–95; cf. T. Howe, *TAPA* 1958, 44–65.

General Bibliography

This book does not try to list every title in Greek prehistory. The chapter bibliographies offer recent general works in particular fields, from which older references may be tracked down, as well as classic articles and reports on the sites discussed in the text. In most sections, the best or most complete sources are put at the beginning; the others are grouped by subject or by site.

SURVEYS OF BRONZE AGE GREECE

Chr. Tsountas and J. Manatt, *The Mycenaean Age* (1897).

H. R. Hall, *The Civilization of Greece in the Bronze Age* (1928).

G. Karo, "Mykenische Kultur," *RE* Supplement 6 (1935) 584.

H. Lorimer, *Homer and the Monuments* (1950)

O. Montelius, *La Grèce préclassique* (with O. Frödin, 1924–28).

G. Perrot and C. Chipiez, "La Grèce primitive," *Histoire de l'Art dans l'Antiquité* VI (1894).

F. Schachermeyr, "Die prähistorischen Kulturen Griechenlands," *RE* 22 (1954) 1350 (= Schachermeyr I).

V. Staïs, *Mycenaean Collection of the National Museum* (Athens) (1926).

351

GREECE IN THE BRONZE AGE

SURVEYS OF CRETE, THE AEGEAN, AND GREECE

Sp. Marinatos and M. Hirmer, *Crete and Mycenae* (1960).

F. Matz, "Die Ägäis," *Handbuch der Archäologie* II (1954) 179 (= Matz I); *Kreta, Mykene, Troia* (1956) (= Matz II); *The Art of Crete and Early Greece* (1962) (= Matz III).

H. Th. Bossert, *Alt-Kreta*² (1935); *The Art of Ancient Crete* (1937).

J. Charbonneaux, *L'Art Égéen* (1929).

R. Dussaud, *Les Civilisations préhelléniques dans le bassin de la Mer Égée*² (1914).

A. Evans, *The Palace of Minos* (1921–36).

D. Fimmen, *Die kretisch-mykenische Kultur*² (1924).

G. Glotz, *La civilisation Égéen*³ (1952).

R. Hutchinson, *Prehistoric Crete* (1962).

J. D. S. Pendlebury, *The Archaeology of Crete* (1939).

A. Severyns, *Grèce et Proche-Orient avant Homère* (1960).

Chr. Zervos, *L'Art de la Crète néolithique et minoenne* (1956).

SHORT GENERAL ARTICLES AND BIBLIOGRAPHIES

H. Biesantz, *Die kretisch-mykenische Kunst* (= Illustrierte Weltkunstgeschichte, 1959).

C. W. Blegen, "The Mycenaean Age," *Semple Lecture* 1962; "Pre-Classical Greece: A Survey," *BSA* 46 (1951) 16.

S. Dow, "The Greeks in the Bronze Age," *XIe Congrès International des Sciences Historiques* (1960).

M. S. F. Hood, "The Aegean before the Greeks," *Dawn of Civilization* (1961).

B. Moon, *Mycenaean Civilization: Publications since 1935* (1957); *Publications 1956–60* (1961).

F. Schachermeyr, "Forschungsbericht zur ägäischen Frühzeit," *AA* 1962, 106 (= Schachermeyr III).

F. Stubbings, "The Rise of Mycenaean Civilization," *CAH*² II (1963) chap. xiv; "Chronology of the Aegean Bronze Age," *CAH*² I (1962) chap. vi.

A. J. B. Wace, "The History of Greece in the Third and Second Millenniums B.C.," *Historia* 2 (1953) 74; "Crete and Mycenae," *CAH*¹ II (1926) 431.

POPULAR BOOKS AND NOVELS

J. Alsop and A. Frantz, *From the Silent Earth* (1964).

L. Cottrell, *The Bull of Minos* (1956); *Realms of Gold* (1963).

M. Renault, *The King Must Die* (1958); *The Bull from the Sea* (1961).

Chapter Bibliographies

I. Greece in the Stone Age

LANDSCAPE AND GEOGRAPHY

A. Philippson, *Die griechischen Landschaften* (with E. Kirsten) (1950–59).
N. Hammond, *Companion* 269.

ANTHROPOLOGY

J. Angel, "Ancient Cephallenians," *Amer. J. Physical Anthropology* 1 (1943) 229; "Skeletal Change in Ancient Greece," *ibid.* 4 (1946) 69; "The Neolithic Ancestors of the Greeks," *AJA* 49 (1945) 252; "Skeletal Material from Attica," *Hesperia* 14 (1945) 279; "The First Cypriotes," *AJA* 54 (1950) 261; "Kings and Commoners," *AJA* 61 (1957) 181; "The People of Lerna," *AJA* 62 (1958) 221; *Troy,* Supplementary Monograph I, *The Human Remains* (1951, good bibliography); *Aghios Kosmas* (1959) 169.
R. Charles, "Étude anthropologique des nécropoles d'Argos," *BCH* 82 (1958) 268; *Le Peuplement de Chypre dans l'Antiquité* (= École Française d'Athènes, *Études Chypriotes* II [1962]).
C. Fürst, "Zur Anthropologie der prähistorischen Griechen in der Argolis," *Lunds Universitets Årsskrift* 16, 8 (1930).

353

GREECE IN THE BRONZE AGE

PALAEOLITHIC AND MESOLITHIC

P. Kokkoros and A. Kanellis, "Découverte d'un crâne d'homme paléolithique dans la péninsule chalcidique," *L'Anthropologie* 64 (1961) 438; E. Vanderpool, *AJA* 65 (1961) 303.

P. Bialor and M. Jameson, "Palaeolithic in the Argolid," *AJA* 66 (1962) 181.

E. Higgs, "A Middle Palaeolithic Industry in Greece," *Man* 63 (1963) 2; *JHS* Reports 1962–63, 22, Fig. 27 (Pantanassa, Epeiros).

Sp. Marinatos, "Λίθινα 'Εργαλεῖα ἐκ Κεφαλληνίας," *Deltion* 16 (1960–62) 41.

V. Miløjčič, "Die neuen mittel- und alt-paläolithischen Funde von der Balkanhalbinsel," *Germania* 36 (1958) 319; *AA* 1960, 153.

J. Servais, "Outils paléolithiques d'Élide," *BCH* 85 (1961) 1.

R. Stampfuss, "Die ersten altsteinzeitlichen Höhlenfunde in Griechenland," *Mannus* 34 (1942) 132 (Lake Kopaïs).

NEOLITHIC

GENERAL

Chr. Zervos, *Naissance de la Civilisation en Grèce* (1962).

F. Schachermeyr, *Die Ältesten Kulturen Griechenlands* (1955) (= Schachermeyr II); cf. A. Wace, "Aegean Prehistory: A Review," *Antiquity* 32 (1958) 30.

V. Childe, *The Dawn of European Civilization*[6] (1957).

C. Delvoye, "Remarques sur la seconde civilisation néolithique du continent grec et des îles avoisinantes," *BCH* 73 (1949) 29.

J. Mellaart, "The Beginnings of Village and Urban Life," *Dawn of Civilization* I (1961) 55.

G. Mylonas, 'Η Νεολιθικὴ 'Εποχὴ ἐν 'Ελλάδι (1928).

CHRONOLOGY AND RADIOCARBON DATING

E. Kohler and E. Ralph, "C-14 Dates for Sites in the Mediterranean Area," *AJA* 65 (1961) 357.

W. Libby, *Radiocarbon Dating*[2] (1955); "The Accuracy of Radiocarbon Dates," *Antiquity* 37 (1963) 213.

V. Miløjčič, *Chronologie der jüngeren Steinzeit Mittel- und Südosteuropas* (1949); "Chronologie der jüngeren Steinzeit und Bronzezeit," *Germania* 37 (1959) 65; see also *JdI* 65–66 (1950) 1; "Zur Anwendbarkeit der C-14 Datierung in der Vorgeschichtsforschung," *Germania* 35 (1957) 102; 36 (1958) 409; 39 (1961) 434.

H. Müller-Beck, "C-14 Daten und absolute Chronologie im Neolithikum," *Germania* 39 (1961) 420.

S. Weinberg, "Aegean Chronology: Neolithic Period and Early Bronze Age," *AJA* 51 (1947) 165; "Relative Chronology of the Aegean," in R. Ehrich, *Relative Chronologies in Old World Archaeology* (1955).

MACEDONIA AND THE BALKANS

A. Benac, "Studien zur Stein- und Kupferzeit im nordwestlichen Balkan," *RGK* 42 (1961) 1.

Dikeli-Taş: D. Theochares and J. Deshayes, *BCH* 86 (1962) 912; D. Lazarides, *Ergon* 1961, 82.

M. Garašanin, "Neolithikum und Bronzezeit in Serbien und Makedonien," *RGK* 39 (1958) 1; "The Neolithic in Anatolia and the Balkans," *Antiquity* 35 (1961) 276; "Zur Chronologie und Deutung einiger frühneolithischer Kulturen des Balkans," *Germania* 39 (1961) 142.

M. Gimbutas, *The Prehistory of Eastern Europe* I (= *BASPR* 20 [1956]).

J. Gaul, *The Neolithic Period in Bulgaria* (= *BASPR* 9 [1948]).

W. Heurtley, *Prehistoric Macedonia* (1939).

V. Milojčič, "Southeastern Elements in the Prehistoric Civilization of Serbia," *BSA* 44 (1949) 258.

G. Mylonas, *Olynthos I, The Neolithic Settlement* (1929); "The Site of Akropotamos," *AJA* 45 (1941) 557; *Praktika* 1938, 103.

L. Rey, "Observations sur les sites préhistoriques et protohistoriques de la Macédoine," *BCH* 40 (1916) 257; "Observations sur les premiers habitats de la Macédoine," *BCH* 41 (1917) 1.

R. Rodden, "Excavations at the Early Neolithic Site at Nea Nikomedia," *ProcPS* 28 (1962) 267.

THESSALY

H. Hansen, *Early Civilization in Thessaly* (1933).

Chr. Tsountas, Αἱ προϊστορικαὶ ἀκροπόλεις Διμηνίου καὶ Σέσκλου (1908).

A. Wace and M. Thompson, *Prehistoric Thessaly* (1912).

H. Biesantz, "Bericht über Ausgrabungen im Gebiet der Gremnos-Magula," *AA* 1957, 37; "Soufli-Magula," *AA* 1959, 56.

K. Grundmann, "Aus neolithischen Siedlungen bei Larisa," *AM* 57 (1932) 102; cf. *AM* 59 (1934) 123; 62 (1937) 56.

V. Milojčič, "Versuchsgrabung an der Otzaki-Magula bei Larisa," *AA* 1954, 1; see also *AA* 1955, 182; 1956, 141; 1959, 36; 1960, 150; *JRGZM* 6 (1959) 1; *NDA* (1959) 225; "Präkeramisches Neolithikum auf der Balkanhalbinsel," *Germania* 38 (1960) 320.

V. Milojčič, J. Boessneck, and M. Hopf, *Die Deutschen Ausgrabungen auf der Argissa-Magula in Thessalien* I, *Das präkeramische Neolithikum* (1962); see S. Weinberg, *Gnomon* 35 (1963) 629.

D. Theochares, " 'Εκ τῆς προκεραμεικῆς Θεσσαλίας," *Thessalika* 1 (1958) 70; "Pyrasos," *Thessalika* 2 (1959) 39.

WEST COAST (see also under Palaeolithic, and chap. ii bibliography for Leukas, Ithaka)

S. Benton, "Haghios Nikolaos near Astakos in Akarnania," *BSA* 42 (1947) 156.

H. Zapfe, "Spuren neolithischer Besiedlung auf Zante," *Wiener Prähistorische Zeitschrift* 24 (1937) 158.

CENTRAL GREECE (see also chap. ii)

E. Kunze, *Orchomenos* II, *Die Neolithische Keramik* (1931).

G. Sotiriades, "Fouilles préhistoriques en Phocide," *REG* 25 (1912) 253; see also *Ephemeris* 1908, 63; *Praktika* 1910, 159; 1911, 205.

S. Weinberg, "Excavations at Prehistoric Elateia," *Hesperia* 31 (1962) 158; "Solving a Prehistoric Puzzle," *Archaeology* 15 (1962) 262.

GREECE IN THE BRONZE AGE

ATTICA AND SOUTHERN GREECE (see also chap. ii)

Cave of Pan: J. Papademetriou, *Ergon* 1958, 15; C. Daux, *BCH* 82 (1958) 681; 83 (1959) 587.

D. Theochares, "Nea Makri, eine grosse neolithische Siedlung in der Nähe von Marathon," *AM* 71 (1956) 1; *Praktika* 1954, 114; *Kokkinia: Praktika* 1951, 93.

C. Blegen, "Gonia," *Metropolitan Museum Studies* 3 (1930) 55; "Hagiorgitika," *AJA* 32 (1928) 533; *Prosymna* (1937).

L. Walker-Kosmopoulos, *The Prehistoric Inhabitation of Corinth* I (1948); *DMR* II (1953) 1.

S. Weinberg, "Remains from Prehistoric Corinth," *Hesperia* 6 (1937) 487; "Excavations at Corinth," *Hesperia* 29 (1960) 240.

Knossos

A. Furness, *BSA* 48 (1953) 94; J. Evans, *ILN* 8 July 1961, 60; 2 September 1961, 366; *JHS* Reports 1961, 27; Schachermeyr III, 110.

See chap. ii bibliography for Asea, Asine, Korakou, Lerna, Malthi, Zygouries.

SPECIAL TOPICS

J. Boessneck, "Zu den Tierknochen aus neolithischen Siedlungen Thessaliens," *RGK* 36 (1955) 1; *Germania* 38 (1960) 336.

J. Caskey and M. Eliot, "A Neolithic Figurine from Lerna," *Hesperia* 25 (1956) 175.

J. Geroulanos, "Οἱ ὀψιανοὶ τῆς Συλλογῆς Τραχώνων," *Ephemeris* 1956, 73 (useful survey of obsidian types).

K. Grundmann, "Figürliche Darstellungen in der neolithischen Keramik Nord- und Mittel-griechenlands," *JdI* 68 (1953) 1; "Eine steinzeitliche Hausnachbildung aus Chaironea," *Mitteilungen des Deutschen Archäologischen Instituts* 6 (1953) 7.

H. Möbius, "Über zwei prähistorische griechische Tonfiguren," *AA* 1954, 207.

V. Müller, *Frühe Plastik in Griechenland und Vorderasien* (1929).

A. Wace, "Prehistoric Stone Figurines from the Mainland," *Hesperia* Supplement 8 (1949) 423.

S. Weinberg, "Neolithic Figurines and Aegean Interrelations," *AJA* 55 (1951) 121.

F. Zeuner, *A History of Domesticated Animals* (1963); "The Domestication of Animals," "The Cultivation of Plants," in C. Singer, *History of Technology* I (1954) 327.

II. Early Bronze Age Greece and the Islands

EARLY HELLADIC ON THE MAINLAND

J. Caskey, "The Early Helladic Period in the Argolid," *Hesperia* 29 (1960) 285; *CAH* I² (1964) xxvi.

S. Fuchs, *Die griechischen Fundgruppen der frühen Bronzezeit* (1937); cf. F. Matz, *Gnomon* 15 (1939) 65.

F. Matz, "Zur ägäischen Chronologie der frühen Bronzezeit," *Historia* I (1950) 173.

J. Mellaart, "The End of the Early Bronze Age in Anatolia and the Aegean," *AJA* 62 (1958) 9.

G. Mylonas, " Ἡ Πρώτοελλαδικὴ καὶ ἡ Μεσοελλαδικὴ 'Εποχή," *Ephemeris* 1937, 40.

A. Wace and C. Blegen, "The Pre-Mycenaean Pottery of the Mainland," *BSA* 22 (1916–18) 175.

SITES

Asea: E. Holmberg, *The Swedish Excavations at Asea in Arcadia* (1944).

Asine: O. Frödin and A. Persson, *Asine, Results of the Swedish Excavations 1922–1930* (1938).

Askitario and Raphina: D. Theochares, *Ergon* 1954, 12; 1955, 30; *Praktika* 1951, 77; 1952, 129; 1953, 105; 1954, 104; 1955, 109; *Ephemeris* 1953–54, III (1961) 59.

Corinth: C. Blegen, *AJA* 24 (1920) 1; S. Weinberg, *Hesperia* 6 (1937) 515; 29 (1960) 240; F. Waage, *Hesperia* Supplement 8 (1949) 415; *AJA* 2 (1897) 314.

Eutresis: H. Goldman, *Excavations at Eutresis in Boeotia* (1931); J. and E. Caskey, "The Earliest Settlements at Eutresis," *Hesperia* 29 (1960) 126.

Hagios Kosmas: G. Mylonas, *Aghios Kosmas, an Early Bronze Age Settlement and Cemetery in Attica* (1959); *AJA* 38 (1934) 258; *Ephemeris* 1952, 117.

Korakou: C. Blegen, *Korakou, a Prehistoric Settlement near Corinth* (1921).

Lerna: J. Caskey, "Excavations at Lerna," *Hesperia* 23 (1954) 3; 24 (1955) 25; 25 (1956) 147; 26 (1957) 142; 27 (1958) 125; 28 (1959) 202; *ILN* 12 January 1957, 68; *BCH* 82 (1958) 708; *Archaeology* 8 (1955) 116; *Geras Keramopoullou* 24.

Malthi (Dorion): N. Valmin, *The Swedish Messenia Expedition* I (1938).

Nemea: J. Harland, "The Excavations at Tsoungiza," *AJA* 32 (1928) 63.

Orchomenos: H. Bulle, *Orchomenos I, Die älteren Ansiedlungsschichten* (1907); E. Kunze, *Orchomenos III, Die Keramik der frühen Bronzezeit* (1934).

Tiryns: K. Müller, *Tiryns III, Die Architektur der Burg und des Palastes* (1930); *Tiryns* IV, *Die Urfirniskeramik* (1938).

Zygouries: C. Blegen, *Zygouries, a Prehistoric Settlement in the Valley of Cleonae* (1928).

SPECIAL TOPICS

J. Caskey, "The House of the Tiles at Lerna," *Archaeology* 8 (1955) 116.

V. Childe, "A Gold Vase of Early Helladic Type," *JHS* 44 (1924) 163.

J. Harland, "The Peloponnesos in the Bronze Age," *HSCP* 34 (1923) 1.

M. Heath, "Early Helladic Clay Sealings from the House of the Tiles at Lerna," *Hesperia* 27 (1958) 81.

E. Holmberg, "Some Notes about the Ethnical Relations of Prehistoric Greece," *OpArc* 6 (1950) 129.

M. Hopf, "Pflanzenfunde aus Lerna/Argolis," *Der Zuchter* 31 (1961) 239.

Sp. Marinatos, "Greniers de l'Helladique Ancien," *BCH* 70 (1946) 337.

N. Valmin, *Das adriatische Gebiet in Vor- und Frühbronzezeit* (1939).

A. Xenaki-Sakellariou, "Τὰ σφραγίσματα τῆς Λέρνας" *KChron* 15–16 (1961–62) I, 79.

THE CYCLADES AND OTHER ISLANDS

Chr. Zervos, *L'Art des Cyclades* (1957).

J. Bent, "Researches among the Cyclades," *JHS* 5 (1884) 42; *The Cyclades* (1885).

S. Benton, "The Ionian Islands," *BSA* 32 (1931–32) 213.

Fimmen 80.

GREECE IN THE BRONZE AGE

A. Philippson, "Beiträge zur Kenntnis der griechischen Inselwelt," *Petermanns Geographischen Mitteilungen,* Ergänzungsheft 134 (1901) 34.

Chr. Tsountas, "Κυκλαδικά," *Ephemeris* 1898, 136; 1899, 74 (Amorgos, Despotiko, Naxos, Paros, Syros).

Aigina: A. Furtwängler, *Aigina* (1906); J. Harland, *Prehistoric Aigina* (1925); G. Welter, *Aigina* (1938); *AA* 1954, 40.

Amorgos: F. Dümmler, "Mittheilungen von den griechischen Inseln," *AM* 11 (1886) 15; E.-M. Bossert, "Zur Datierung der Gräber von Arkesine auf Amorgos," *Festschrift P. Goessler* (1954) 23; P. Wolters, *AM* 16 (1891) 46.

Antiparos: J. Bent, "Notes on Prehistoric Remains in Antiparos," *Journal of the Anthropological Institute* 14 (1884) 134.

Cape Krio: J. Bent, *JHS* 9 (1888) 82.

Chios: J. Boardman, *Archaeology* 8 (1955) 245; S. Hood and J. Boardman, *Antiquity* 29 (1955) 32; *BCH* 80 (1956) 326; A. Furness, *ProcPS* 22 (1956) 194; *JHS* 74 (1954) 162; *JHS* Reports 1954, 20.

Delos: H. Gallet de Santerre, *Délos primitive et archaïque* (1958) with bibliography; A. Plassart, *Fouilles de Délos* XI, 11.

Despotiko: see Tsountas above, and *BCH* 84 (1960) 814.

Euboia: G. Papavasileiou, *Archaion Taphon* (1910); D. Theochares, *Ephemeris* 1945–47, Chron. 1; *Archeion Euboïkōn Meletōn* 6 (1959) 279.

Ithaka: J. Partsch, *Kephallenia und Ithaka* (1890); S. Benton, *BSA* 39 (1938–39) 1 with bibliography; W. Heurtley, *BSA* 35 (1934–35) 1; 40 (1939–40) 1; F. Stubbings, *Companion* 398.

Keos: G. Welter, "Von griechischen Inseln," *AA* 1954, 48; J. Caskey, "Excavations in Keos," *Hesperia* 31 (1962) 263; *Archaeology* 16 (1963) 284.

Lemnos (Poliochni): L. Bernabo Brea, "A Bronze Age House at Poliochni (Lemnos)," *ProcPS* 21 (1955) 144; *BdA* 36 (1951) 31; 37 (1952) 339; 42 (1957) 193; *BCH* 81 (1957) 612; D. Levi, *ILN* 3 August 1957, 197; 18 April 1959, 662.

Lesbos: W. Lamb, *Excavations at Thermi in Lesbos* (1936).

Leukas: W. Dörpfeld, *Alt-Ithaka* (1927); P. Goessler, *Ergebnisse der Ausgrabungen auf Leukas* (1927).

Melos (Pelos and Phylakopi): T. Atkinson, R. Bosanquet *et al., Excavations at Phylakopi in Melos* (*JHS* Supplement I, 1904); C. Edgar, "Prehistoric Tombs at Pelos," *BSA* 3 (1896–97) 35; 4 (1897–98) 1; 5 (1898–99) 3; R. Dawkins and J. Droop, "Excavations at Phylakopi in Melos," *BSA* 17 (1910–11) 1; *JHS* 17 (1897) 122.

Naxos: Cl. Stephanos, "Les tombeaux prémycéniens de Naxos," *Congrès Internationale d'Archéologie* (1905) 216; *Praktika* 1908, 114; N. Kontoleon and N. Zapheiropoulos, *Praktika* 1949, 112; 1950, 269; 1951, 214; *Ergon* 1958, 165; 1959, 125; 1960, 185; 1961, 196; G. Welter, *AA* 1930, 132; G. Papathanasopoulos, *Deltion* 17 (1961/1963) 104.

Paros: O. Rubensohn, *AM* 42 (1917) 1; *Das Delion von Paros* (1962) 83; I. Varoucha, *Ephemeris* 1925, 98.

Rhodes and the Dodekanese: A. Maiuri, *Annuario* 6–7 (1926) 83; G. Jacopi, *Annuario* 13–14 (1933/1940) 253; G. Monaco, *Clara Rhodos* 10 (1941) 42; F. Stubbings, *Levant* (1951) 5; A. Furumark, *OpArc* 6 (1950) 150; *CVA* Copenhagen 1 and 2; *CVA* British Museum 1; *Clara Rhodos* 6–7 (1932) 133.

R. Dawkins, *BSA* 9 (1902–1903) 176; R. Dawkins and A. Wace, *BSA* 12 (1905–1906) 151; *Clara Rhodos* I (1928) 60; *Annuario* 8–9 (1929) 235; *BdA* 35 (1950) 316; P. Frazer and G. Bean, *The Rhodian Peraea* (1954); A. Furness, *ProcPS* 22 (1956) 194; G. Bean and J. Cook, *BSA* 52 (1957) 116; *Ergon* 1959, 131; R. Hope Simpson and J. Lazenby, *BSA* 57 (1962) 154 with bibliography; D. Levi, *Annuario* 39–40 (1961–62) 555; J. Benson, *Ancient Leros* (1963); S. Charitonides, *Deltion* 17 (1961/1963) 32.

Samos: R. Heidenreich, "Vorgeschichtliches in der Stadt Samos," *AM* 60 (1935) 125; V. Milǫjčič, "Die prähistorische Siedlung unter dem Heraion," *Samos* I (1961), with references.

Siphnos: J. Brock and G. Mackworth Young, "Excavations in Siphnos," *BSA* 44 (1949) 1; *Praktika* 1920, 147.

Skyros: H. Hansen, "Prehistoric Skyros," *DMR* I (1951) 54; see also Euboia.

Syros: see Tsountas above, E.-M. Bossert below.

Thera: F. Fouqué, *Santorin et ses eruptions* (1879); F. Hiller von Gaertringen *et al., Thera* III (1904) 37; Perrot and Chipiez, *Histoire de l'Art* VI (1894) 139; L. Renaudin, "Vases Préhelléniques de Théra," *BCH* 46 (1922) 113; *AA* 1930, 136.

SPECIAL TOPICS

E.-M. Bossert, "Die gestempelten Verzierungen auf frühbronzezeitlichen Gefässen der Ägäis," *JdI* 75 (1960) 1.

Ch. Dugas, *La céramique des Cyclades* (1925).

A. Furness, "Some Early Pottery of Samos, Kalymnos, and Chios," *ProcPS* 22 (1956) 173.

D. Hogarth, "Aegean Sepulchral Figurines," *Essays in Aegean Archaeology Presented to Sir Arthur Evans* (1927) 55.

U. Kahrstedt, "Zur Kykladenkultur," *AM* 38 (1913) 148.

G. Kaschnitz-Weinberg, "Zur Herkunft der Spirale in der Ägäis," *PZ* 1949, 193.

D. Theochares, "Νέοι κυκλαδικοὶ τάφοι ἐν Ἀττικῇ," *Νέον Ἀθηναῖον* I (1955) 283.

W. Zschietzschmann, "Kykladenpfannen," *AA* 1935, 652.

THIRD MILLENNIUM SHIPS AND SAILING

R. Barnett, "Early Shipping in the Near East," *Antiquity* 32 (1958) 220.

R. Bowen, "Egypt's Earliest Sailing Ships," *Antiquity* 34 (1960) 117; "Third Millennium B.C. Egyptian Sails," *Mariner's Mirror* 45 (1959) 332.

G. Clowes, *Sailing Ships* (1951 reprint) Part I.

A. Evans, *Palace of Minos* II, 239.

R. Hutchinson, *Prehistoric Crete* (1962) 92.

W. Hyde, *Ancient Greek Mariners* (1947).

A. Köster, *Studien zur Geschichte des Antiken Seewesens* (1934).

Sp. Marinatos, "La marine créto-mycénienne," *BCH* 57 (1933) 170.

H. Ormerod, *Piracy in the Ancient World* (1924).

GREECE IN THE BRONZE AGE

III. The Opening of the Middle Bronze Age

MIDDLE HELLADIC SITES AND POTTERY

SITES

See chap. i for Prosymna; chap. ii for Aigina, Asea, Asine, Eutresis, Korakou, Lerna, Leukas, Orchomenos, Zygouries; chap. vi for Mycenae and Tiryns.

Brauron: V. Staïs, *Praktika* 1893, 17; *Ephemeris* 1895, 196; D. Theochares, *Praktika* 1950, 88; J. Papademetriou, *Praktika* 1955, 119; 1956, 77; *Ergon* 1957, fig. 22; C. Daux, *BCH* 82 (1958) 677; Schachermeyr III, 210.

Dorion-Malthi: N. Valmin, *The Swedish Messenia Expedition* I (1938); "Malthi-Epilog," *OpAth* I (1953) 29.

Kirrha: L. Dor, J. Jannoray, H. and M. van Effenterre, *Kirrha: Étude de préhistoire phocidienne* (1960).

Orchomenos (see also chap ii): Pausanias 9.38; H. Schliemann, "Exploration of the Boeotian Orchomenus," *JHS* 2 (1881) 122.

POTTERY

Schachermeyr, III, 209.

C. Blegen, *Korakou* (1921) 15, the best analysis of the pottery.

C. Blegen and J. Haley, "The Coming of the Greeks: The Geographical Distribution of Prehistoric Remains in Greece," *AJA* 32 (1928) 146 (see also chap. ii, notes 10, 11).

V. Childe, "On the Date and Origin of Minyan Ware," *JHS* 35 (1915) 196.

J. Forsdyke, "The Pottery Called Minyan Ware," *JHS* 34 (1914) 126.

J. Myres, *Who Were the Greeks?* (1930).

A. Wace and C. Blegen, "The Pre-Mycenaean Pottery of the Mainland," *BSA* 22 (1916–18) 175.

GRAVES AND BURIALS (see also chap. ix)

J. Wiesner, *Grab und Jenseits* (1938).

C. Blegen and A. Wace, "Middle Helladic Tombs," *Symbolae Osloenses* 9 (1930) 28.

G. Mylonas, "The Cult of the Dead in Helladic Times," *DMR* I (1951) 64, with bibliography.

Schachermeyr I, 1461.

Aphidna: S. Wide, *AM* 21 (1896) 385; A. Gropengiesser, *Die Gräber von Attika* (1907).

Argos: R. Charles, "Étude anthropologique des nécropoles d'Argos," *BCH* 82 (1958) 268.

Athens: A. Skias, *Ephemeris* 1902, 123; *AJA* 7 (1903) 372.

Corinth: T. Shear, *AJA* 34 (1930) 403.

Drachmani: S. Sotiriades, *Ephemeris* 1908, 93; *AM* 31 (1906) 401.

Eleusis: G. Mylonas, "The Cemeteries of Eleusis and Mycenae," *ProcPhilSoc* 99 (1955) 57; *Praktika* 1953, 77; 1955, 67; 1956, 57.

Hagios Ioannis / Papoulia: Sp. Marinatos, *Praktika* 1954, 311.

Lerna: J. Caskey, *Hesperia* 26 (1957) 154 (Grave J4), pl. 40 d, f (Bubanj pots); *Hesperia* 25 (1956) pl. 43 c (MM I A cups).

Prosymna: C. Blegen, *Prosymna* (1937) 30.

Samikon: N. Yalouris, *JHS* Report 1955, 17; *BCH* 79 (1955) 253.

IV The Shaft Graves

THE SHAFT GRAVES AT MYCENAE

CIRCLE A

H. Schliemann, *Mycenae* (1878); *Mycenae and Tiryns* (1880).
G. Karo, *Die Schachtgräber von Mykenai* (1930–33), with bibliography to 1930.

CIRCLE B

G. Mylonas, *Ancient Mycenae* (1957) 103–75, with bibliography to 1956.

MAJOR ESSAYS AND PUBLICATIONS

C. Newton, "Dr. Schliemann's Discoveries at Mycenae," *Essays on Archaeology* (1880).
W. Schuchhardt, *Schliemann's Excavations* (1891).
G. Perrot and C. Chipiez, *Histoire de l'Art* VI, 1 (1894) 311.
Chr. Tsountas and J. Manatt, *The Mycenaean Age* (1897) chap. 5.
A. Keramopoullos, "Περὶ τῶν βασιλικῶν τάφων τῆς 'Ακροπόλεως τῶν Μυκηνῶν," *Ephemeris* 1918, 52.
H. Hall, *Civilization of Greece in the Bronze Age* (1928) 140.
A. Evans, *Shaft Graves and Bee-Hive Tombs of Mycenae* (1929).
A. Wace, "The Grave Circle," *BSA* 25 (1921–23) 103; *Mycenae* (1949) 59; see also *BSA* 49 (1954) 244.
N. Åberg, *Die Chronologie der Bronze- und Früheisenzeit* III (1932) 113.
G. Mylonas, "Οἱ βασιλικοὶ τάφοι τῶν Μυκηνῶν καὶ ἡ 'Αθηναϊκὴ παράδοσις," *Epitumbion Tsountas* (1941) 415; "'Η 'Ακρόπολις τῶν Μυκηνῶν," *Ephemeris* 1958 (1961) 159.
J. Papademetriou, *Praktika* 1951, 197; 1952, 427; 1953, 205; 1954, 242; 1955, 225; 1957, 105; *Ergon* 1957, 63; 1958, 125.
G. Mylonas and J. Papademetriou, "The New Shaft Graves at Mycenae," *Archaeology* 5 (1952) 194; "The New Grave Circle at Mycenae," *Archaeology* 8 (1955) 43.
Sp. Marinatos, "Περὶ τοὺς νέους βασιλικοὺς τάφους τῶν Μυκηνῶν," *Geras Keramopoullou* 3 (1953) 54; *CMG* 81.
J. Caskey, "Royal Shaft Graves at Lerna," *Archaeology* 13 (1960) 130.

SPECIAL TOPICS

G. Rodenwaldt, "Mykenische Miscellen," *Epitumbion Tsountas* (1941) 428.

STELAI

W. Heurtley, "The Stelae," *BSA* 25 (1921–23) 126.
Sp. Marinatos, *Geras Keramopoullou* 54.
G. Mylonas, "The Figured Mycenaean Stelai," *AJA* 55 (1951) 134.
K. Müller, "Frühmykenische Reliefs," *JdI* 30 (1915) 242.

MASKS AND PORTRAITURE

H. Biesantz, "Die minoischen Bildnisgemmen," *Marburger Winckelmann-Programm* 1958, 9.

C. Blegen, "Early Greek Portraits," *AJA* 66 (1962) 245.
E. Fischer, "Anthropologische Bemerkungen zu den Masken," *SG* 320.
Sp. Marinatos, "Minoische Porträts," *Festschrift Max Wegner* (1962) 9.

WEAPONS, JEWELRY, DRESS (see also chap. vii bibliography)

H. G. Buchholz, "Der Pfeilglätter aus dem VI. Schachtgrab von Mykene und die hella-
dischen Pfeilspitzen," *JdI* 77 (1962) 1.
H. Lorimer, *HM* (1950) *passim*.
M. Meurer, "Der Goldschmuck der mykenischen Schachtgräber," *JdI* 27 (1912) 208.
A. Persson, "Garters—Quiver Ornaments?" *BSA* 46 (1951) 125.
W. Reichel, *Homerische Waffen*² (1901).
N. Sandars, 'The First Aegean Swords and Their Ancestry," *AJA* 65 (1961) 17.

POTTERY (see also *SG* and note 6)

A. Furtwängler and G. Loeschke, *Mykenische Thongefässe* (1879).
A. Furumark, *Chronology* 46.

THE SILVER SIEGE RHYTON

Chr. Tsountas, *Ephemeris* 1891, 11; *MycAge* 213.
W. Reichel, *Homerische Waffen*² (1901) fig. 17.
H. Hall, *JHS* 31 (1911) 119.
G. Rodenwaldt, *Tiryns* II (1912) 203; *Fries des Megarons* (1921) 51.
V. Staïs, *AM* 40 (1915) 45.
K. Müller, *JdI* 30 (1915) 319.
A. Evans, *Palace of Minos* I 308, 668, 698; II pl. 24, figs. 129, 501; *III 81, figs. 50–56.
V. Müller, *JdI* 40 (1925) 112.
Sp. Marinatos, *Deltion* 10 (1926) 78.
G. Karo, *SG* no. 481, 106 ff., figs. 83–85, pl. 122.
A. Persson, *New Tombs at Dendra* (1942) chap. 6.

V. The Early Mycenaean Age

EARLY MYCENAEAN SITES

See also chap. vi, Empire Sites. For sites with tholos tombs not discussed in the text, see
bibliography below on Major Tholos Tombs.
Dendra/Midea: A. Persson, *Royal Tombs at Dendra near Midea* (1931); *New Tombs at
Dendra near Midea* (1942); N. Verdelis, *Ephemeris* 1957 (1961) Chron. 15 (the Dendra
Cuirass); *Deltion* 16 (1960/63) Chron. 93; R. Hägg, "Research at Dendra 1961,"
OpAth 4 (1962) 79.
Eutresis: H. Goldman, *Eutresis,* House B, 64.
Kakovatos: W. Dörpfeld, "Alt-Pylos," *AM* 32 (1907) vi; 33 (1908) 295; K. Müller, "Alt-
Pylos II: Die Funde aus den Kuppelgräbern von Kakovatos," *AM* 34 (1909) 269;
G. von Merhart, "Die Bernsteinschieber von Kakovatos," *Germania* 24 (1940) 99;
see also Hachmann and Sandars under Trade and Foreign Relations, chap. viii, bibli-
ography.

Myrsinochorion/Rutsi: Sp. Marinatos, *Ergon* 1956, 90; *Praktika* 1956 (1962) 202; 1957 (1963) 118; *ILN* 6 April 1957, 540; 27 April 1957, 690; *Antiquity* 31 (1957) 97; see also chap. ix, Burials.

Peristeria/Moira/Muron: Sp. Marinatos, *Ergon* 1960, 152; 1961, 164; 1962, 110; *AA* 1962, 903; see also chap. ix, Burials; E. Vermeule, *Boston University Graduate Journal,* 1961, 119.

Pylos/Englianos: C. Blegen, *AJA* 58 (1954) 30; 62 (1958) 178; 63 (1959) 125; 64 (1960) 155; 66 (1962) 145; 67 (1963) 159; see also chap. vi, Empire Sites.

Thermon: K. Rhomaios, *Deltion* 1 (1915) 225; 2 (1916) 179.

Vapheio: Chr. Tsountas, *Ephemeris* 1888, 197; 1889, 130; *MycAge* 130, 144; H. Leake, *Travels in the Morea* III (1830) 4; H. Waterhouse and R. Hope Simpson, *BSA* 55 (1960) 76; Sp. Marinatos, "The 'Swimmers' Dagger from the Tholos Tomb at Vaphio," *Essays in Aegean Archaeology* (Evans, 1927) 63; see also chap. vii, Gems.

ISLAND AND OVERSEAS SITES (see also chap. ii, Cyclades; chap. viii, Trade and Foreign Relations)

K. Scholes, "The Cyclades in the Later Bronze Age," *BSA* 51 (1956) 9 ff.

Enkomi: C. Schaeffer, *Enkomi-Alasia* (1952); P. Dikaios, Κυπριακαὶ Σπουδαί, 1954—.

Keos: J. Caskey, "Excavations in Keos 1960–1961," *Hesperia* 31 (1962) 263–83; *ILN* 19 May 1962, 801; *Archaeology* 16 (1963) 284.

Miletos: C. Weickert, "Die Ausgrabungen beim Athena-Tempel in Milet," *Istanbuler Mitteilungen* 7 (1957) 102; 9–10 (1959–60) 1; *NDA* 181–197.

Phylakopi: T. Atkinson, R. Bosanquet et al., *Excavations at Phylakopi in Melos, JHS* Supplement I (1904); *BSA* 16 (1910–11) 1.

Trianda: G. Monaco, "Scavi nella zona micenea di Jaliso," *Clara Rhodos* 10 (1941) 42–199; A. Furumark, "The Settlement at Ialysos and Aegean Prehistory," *OpArc* 6 (1950) 150–271.

MAJOR THOLOS TOMBS

GENERAL

Chr. Belger, *Beiträge zur Kenntnis der griechischen Kuppelgräber* (1887); "Die mykenische Lokalsage von den Gräbern Agamemnons und der Seinen," *Programm Friedrichs-Gymnasium* 54 (1893).

A. Evans, *Shaft Graves and Bee-Hive Tombs of Mycenae* (1929).

S. Hood, "Tholos Tombs of the Aegean," *Antiquity* 34 (1960) 166.

N. Valmin, "Tholos Tombs and Tumuli," *Acta Inst. Romani Regni Sueciae* 2 (1932) 216.

A. Wace, "The Tholos Tombs of Mycenae: Structural Analysis," in Persson, *RT,* 140; *BSA* 25 (1921–23) 283–402; *Mycenae* 16 and Appendix I; "The Treasury of Atreus," *Antiquity* 14 (1940) 233; *BSA* 50 (1955) 194; see also below, *s.v.* Mycenae, and chap. vii, n. 15.

THESSALY

Ano Dranista: *Praktika* 1911, 351.

Dimeni: *AM* 1884, 97; 1886, 435; 1887, 136; *Praktika* 1901, 37; *D-S* 27.

Gonnos: Stählin, *Thessalien* 32.

Gritsa: *Praktika* 1951, 141; 1952, 171.
Gura: *AM* 1896, 247; *MycAge* 395; *PT* 208.
Karditsa (Giorgikon): *AJA* 1958, 324; *Thessalika* 1959, 69; *Deltion* 1960, 171.
Larissa: *JHS* Report 1962–63, 24.
Marmariani: *D-S* 121; *Praktika* 1899, 101; *PT* 214; *BSA* 1930–31, 1.
Pharsala (H. Theodoroi): *Praktika* 1951, 157; 1952, 185.
Sesklo: *AM* 1884, 103; *D-S* 75, 115; *PT* 68, 215.
Volo (Kapakli): *Ephemeris* 1906, 211; *Praktika* 1900, 72; 1912, 229.

EPEIROS, AKARNANIA, LOKRIS, PHOKIS, BOIOTIA

Delphi: *Fouilles de Delphes* 5, 5 (vaulted chambers).
Dramesi: *Hesperia* Supplement 8 (1949) 9.
Kalbaki: *Ephemeris* 1956, 114.
Koronta: *Praktika* 1908, 100.
Orchomenos: Pausanias 9.38; *JHS* 1881, 134; *MV* 42; *BCH* 1895, 177; *Orchomenos* I, 85; *Deltion* 1915, 51; *AA* 1915, 204.
Parga: *Ergon* 1960, 110.

ATTICA

Eleusis: *Ephemeris* 1898, 29; 1912, 1, 18; Gropengiesser, *Gräber von Attika* 14; Perrot-Chipiez vi, 317.
Marathon: *Praktika* 1933, 35; 1934, 29; 1935, 92, 105; *AA* 1934, 148; 1935, 179; *Ergon* 1958, 23; *BCH* 1959, 583.
Menidi: *AM* 1887, 139; *Kuppelgrab;* Gropengiesser 13; *GP* 158; *MV* 39; *BSA* 1958–59, 292.
Thorikos: *Praktika* 1890, 159; 1893, 12; *Ephemeris* 1895, 193, 223; *MycAge* 383 (elliptical).

ARGOLID

Argive Heraion (Prosymna): *AM* 1878, 271; *Mykenische Thongefässe* pl. 12; *BSA* 1921–23, 330.
Berbati: *AA* 1938, 552; *ILN* 15 February 1936, 276.
Dendra: *RT* 8; *AA* 1927, 371.
Mycenae: *BSA* 1921–23, 283 (bibliography for each); *Mycenae* (index); *RT* 140; *Praktika* 1892, 56; *JHS* 1926, 110; *Antiquity* 1940, 233; *BSA* 1953, 69; 1955, 194; 1956, 116; see chap. vii, note 15.
Tiryns: *AM* 1913, 347.

LAKONIA, ARKADIA

Analipsis (Vourvoura): *Praktika* 1954, 270; 1956, 185; *Ergon* 1954, 38; 1956, 81; *BCH* 1955, 254.
Arkines: *Ephemeris* 1889, 132; *Praktika* 1910, 277.
H. Ioannes (Monemvasia): *Ergon* 1956, 96; *Praktika* 1956, 207 (vaulted chambers).
Kalyvia: *Deltion* 1926, Par. 41; *JHS* 1927, 257 (chamber with relieving triangle).
Kampos: *Ephemeris* 1891, 189; *MycAge* 229; *BSA* 1957, 236; *CMG* pl. 224.
Palaiochorion: *Deltion* 1924–25, Par. 18; *BSA* 1956, 168 (elliptical).
Sarandopotamos (Tegea): Fimmen 10; *BCH* 1901, 256.
Vapheio: *Ephemeris* 1888, 197; 1889, 136; *AM* 1909, 71; *MycAge* 144; see site bibliography.

MESSENIA, TRIPHYLIA

Chandrinos: *BCH* 1960, 701.

Charokopion: *Ergon* 1958, 154.

Koryphasion, Osman Aga: *Praktika* 1925, 140; *AA* 1927, 384; *Hesperia* 1954, 158.

Koryphasion, Voïdokoilia: *Ergon* 1956, 90; 1958, 148; *CMG* pl. XXXII.

Koukounara: *Ergon* 1958, 150; 1959, 117; 1960, 145.

Malthi (Bouga, Bodia, Vasiliko-Kopanaki): *BullLund* 1927–28, 190, 201, 31, 46; *SME* 207.

Mouriatada: *Ergon* 1960, 149.

Myrsinochorion (Rutsi); see site bibliography, above.

Nichoria: *ILN* 20 April 1960, 740.

Peristeria (Moira, Muron): see site bibliography.

Pylos (Englianos): *AJA* 1954, 30; 1958, 178; *ILN* 5 December 1953, 932.

Pylos (Kakovatos): see site bibliography.

Tragana: *Praktika* 1909, 274; *Ephemeris* 1912, 268; 1914, 99; *Praktika* 1955, 247; 1956, 202; *Ergon* 1955, 88; 1956, 90; *BCH* 1956, 283.

Volimidia (Chora): *Ergon* 1954, 42; 1960, 146 (vaulted chambers).

ACHAIA

Chalandritsa: *AA* 1930, 120 (tumuli).

Pharai: *Ergon* 1956, 89; *Praktika* 1956, 193; 1957, 114.

ISLANDS

Delos: *Délos* 15; 5, 63; *BCH* 1924, 247; *MMR*² 611; Gallet de Santerre, *Délos* 89, 165.

Euboia: Papavasileiou 21 (Chalkis), 24 (Oxylithos), 39 (Katakolou), 42 (Enoria, Bellousia); *Praktika* 1909, 207 (Livadi-Aliveri).

Kephallenia: *Comptes-Rendus de l'Académie* 1911, 7; 1919, 382; *Praktika* 1899, 17; 1912, 115; *AM* 1894, 486; *Deltion* 1915, Par. 59; *Ephemeris* 1912, 268; 1932, 1; 1933, 68 (vaulted chambers).

Mykonos: *AM* 1898, 362.

Naxos: *Praktika* 1908, 118.

Zakynthos: *AA* 1934, 161.

CRETE (mostly sub-Minoan and Protogeometric)

Achladia (Seteia): *Praktika* 1952, 643.

Anavlochos: *BCH* 1931, 374.

Anogeia: *MonAnt* 1890, 203.

Apodoulou: *JHS* Report 1962–63, 33.

Damanio: *Deltion* 1916, 171.

Erganos: *AJA* 1901, 261.

Gournia: *AC* 243.

Hagia Triada: *MonAnt* 1904, 678; *Annuario* 1930–31, 155.

Kamares: *AJA* 1901, 270, 439.

Karphi: *BSA* 1937–38, 111, 138.

Kavousi: *AJA* 1901, 125.

Knossos: *BSA* 1956, 68.

Kourtes: *AJA* 1901, 290; *Annuario* 1931, 558.

GREECE IN THE BRONZE AGE

Maleme: *AM* 1910, 150.
Massara: Perrot-Chipiez vi, 434.
Mouliana: *Ephemeris* 1904, 21.
Palaikastro: *BSA* 1901, 303.
Papoura: Fimmen 18.
Rotasi: *JHS* Report 1955, 17.
Vasiliki: Seager, *Transactions PennU* 1907, 207.
Vrokastro: *AJA* 1913, 91.

ANATOLIA (late or Protogeometric)

Assarlik: *JHS* 1887, 64; *BM Catalogue of Vases* I, 21.
Dirmil: *AJA* 1963, 357.
Kolophon: *AJA* 1923, 68.

THE KNOSSOS PROBLEM

S. Hood, "The Knossos Tablets: A Complete View," *Antiquity* 36 (1962) 38, with bibliography of quarrel to date; "Stratigraphic Excavations at Knossos 1957–61," *KChron* 15–16 (1961–62) I, 92.

J. Alsop, *From the Silent Earth* (1964) 176.

C. Blegen, "A Chronological Problem," *Minoica* (Sundwall, 1958) 61.

J. Boardman, "The Date of the Knossos Tablets," *KChron* 15–16 (1961–62) I, 167; *Antiquity* 38 (1964) 45; *On the Knossos Tablets* (1963).

D. Levi, "Ricerca scientifica e polemica sull'evoluzione della civiltà minoica," *PP* 84 (1962) 206; "La Villa rurale minoica di Gortina," *BdA* 44 (1959) 253.

L. Palmer, "The Truth about Knossos," *Observer Weekend Review* 3 July 1960, 17; *Mycenaeans and Minoans* (1962) 156, no references; "The Documentation of the Knossos Excavations," *KChron* 15–16 (1961–62) I, 162.

J. Pendlebury, *Archaeology of Crete* (1939) 222.

N. Platon, "Συγκριτικὴ χρονολογία τῶν τρίων Μινωϊκῶν ἀνακτόρων," *KChron* 15–16 (1961–62) 127.

J. Raison, "Une Controverse sur la chronologie des tablettes cnossiennes," *Minos* 7, 2 (1963) 151; *BCH* 85 (1961) 408.

E. Vermeule, "The Fall of Knossos and the Palace Style," *AJA* 67 (1963) 195.

ANALYSES OF LATE MINOAN CHRONOLOGY AND POTTERY (see also chap. vii, Mycenaean Pottery)

St. Alexiou, "Νέα Στοιχεῖα διὰ τὴν ὑστέραν Αἰγιακὴν χρονολογίαν," *KChron* 6 (1952) 9.

R. Bosanquet, "Some 'Late Minoan' Vases Found in Greece," *JHS* 24 (1904) 317.

A. Evans, *Palace of Minos* II (1928) 359, 423, 511; IV (1935) 259, 297.

A. Furumark, *The Mycenaean Pottery* (1941); *The Chronology of Mycenaean Pottery* (1941); "The Settlement at Ialysos and Aegean Prehistory," *OpArc* 6 (1950) 261.

D. Mackenzie, "The Pottery of Knossos," *JHS* 23 (1903) 190.

M. Mackeprang, "Late Mycenaean Vases," *AJA* 42 (1938) 537.

Sp. Marinatos, "The Volcanic Destruction of Minoan Crete," *Antiquity* 13 (1939) 425.

F. Matz, "The Minoan Civilization: Maturity and Zenith," *CAH*² II (1962) iv, xii.

K. Müller, "Alt-Pylos," *AM* 34 (1909) 302.

J. Pendlebury, *Archaeology of Crete* (1939) 201.

L. Pernier and L. Banti, *Il Palazzo Minoico di Festòs* II (1950) 515.

F. Stubbings, "Chronology of the Aegean Bronze Age," *CAH²* I (1962) vi, 69.

A. Wace, "Ephyrean Ware," *BSA* 51 (1956) 123.

Warrior Graves and Related Burials

A. Evans, *Prehistoric Tombs at Knossos* (1906), especially the Chieftain's Grave and Zapher Papoura Nos. 44, 68; *The Tomb of the Double Axes* (1914), especially the name tomb and the Mace-Bearer's Tomb.

F. Halbherr, "Le tombe dei nobili," *MonAnt* 14 (1904) 505.

S. Hood and P. de Jong, "Late Minoan Warrior Graves," *BSA* 47 (1952) 243; "Another Warrior Grave," *BSA* 51 (1956) 81.

S. Hood, G. Huxley, and N. Sandars, "A Minoan Cemetery on the Upper Gypsades," *BSA* 53–54 (1958–59) 194.

R. Hutchinson, "A Late Minoan Tomb at Knossos," *BSA* 51 (1956) 68; "A Tholos Tomb on the Kephala," *ibid.* 74.

N. Platon, " 'Ο Τάφος τοῦ Σταφύλου καὶ ὁ Μινωϊκὸς ἀποικισμὸς τῆς Πεπαρήθου," *KChron* 3 (1949) 534.

St. Alexiou, "Νέα Στοιχεῖα διὰ τὴν ὑστέραν Αἰγιακὴν χρονολογίαν," *KChron* 6 (1952) 9; *Praktika* 1953, 299; 1954, 369; 1955, 311; see also *BCH* 84 (1960) 838.

VI. Life in a Mycenaean Palace

EMPIRE SITES*

Athens and Attica

Sp. Iakovides, 'Η Μυκηναϊκὴ 'Ακρόπολις τῶν 'Αθηνῶν (1963).

P. Ålin, *Fundstätten* 99.

C. Blegen, "Athens and the Early Age of Greece," *HSCP* Supplement I (1940) 1.

O. Broneer, "Athens in the Late Bronze Age," *Antiquity* 30 (1956) 9; "The Dorian Invasion: What Happened in Athens?" *AJA* 52 (1948) 111; "A Mycenaean Fountain on the Athenian Acropolis," *Hesperia* 8 (1939) 317; "Excavations on the North Slope of the Acropolis," *Hesperia* 2 (1933) 329; rev. Iakovides, *Gnomon* 35 (1963) 707.

B. Graef, *Die Antiken Vasen von der Akropolis* I (1909).

A. Gropengiesser, *Die Gräber von Attika* (1907).

* This site list is restricted to places discussed in the text. More detailed site bibliographies in Fimmen; Karo *RE* Supplement 6, 604; Furumark *MP;* Matz I, 275; Schachermeyr III, 220; Moon, *Mycenaean Bibliography;* the extremely valuable annual "Chronique des Fouilles" by G. Daux in *BCH,* or Archaeological Reports by J. Cook, S. Hood, or A. Megaw in *JHS.*

Recently area studies have formed a more important part of Mycenaean research; e.g., H. Waterhouse, "Prehistoric Laconia," *BSA* 1956, 168; with R. Hope Simpson, *BSA* 1960, 67; 1961, 114; cf. "Identifying a Mycenaean State," *BSA* 52 (1957) 231; Pylos: McDonald and Hope Simpson; Phthiotis, Hope Simpson and Lazenby, *Antiquity* 1959, 102; the Dodekanese, Hope Simpson and Lazenby, *BSA* 57 (1962) 154; the Cyclades, K. Scholes, *BSA* 51 (1956) 9.

GREECE IN THE BRONZE AGE

H. Hansen, "The Prehistoric Pottery on the North Slope," *Hesperia* 6 (1937) 539.

I. Hill, *The Ancient City of Athens* (1953) 8.

S. Immerwahr, *Prehistoric Remains from the Athenian Agora* (forthcoming).

D. Levi, "Abitazioni preistoriche sulle pendici meridionale dell'Acropoli," *Annuario* 13–14 (1933/40) 411.

G. Mylonas, "Athens and Minoan Crete," *HSCP* Supplement I (1940) 11.

C. Nylander, "Die sog. mykenische Säulenbasen auf der Akropolis in Athen," *OpAth* 4 (1962) 31.

F. Stubbings, "The Mycenaean Pottery of Attica," *BSA* 42 (1947) 1.

L. Talcott, "Athens: A Mycenaean Necropolis under the Agora Floor," *Archaeology* 4 (1951) 223.

E. Townsend, "A Mycenaean Chamber Tomb under the Temple of Ares," *Hesperia* 24 (1955) 187, and notes 3–4.

J. Travlos, Ἡ πολεοδομικὴ ἐξέλιξις τῶν Ἀθηνῶν (1960).

W. Wrede, *Attika* (1934).

For Marathon, Menidi, and Thorikos see chap. v, Tholoi; for Spata, chap. vii, Ivories; for Hagios Kosmas, chap. ii; for Brauron and Eleusis, chap. iii; for Perati, chap. ix.

See also Furtwängler-Loeschke, *MV;* Montelius, *GP;* Karo, *RE* Supplement 6, 608.

CORINTH AND THE ISTHMOS

C. Blegen, "Corinth in Prehistoric Times," *AJA* 24 (1920) 1, 274; *Corinth* I (1932) 107.

O. Broneer, "The Isthmus of Corinth at the End of the Bronze Age," *VII ArcCong* I (1961) 244; see also *Hesperia* 27 (1958) 1; 28 (1959) 298; *Antiquity* 32 (1958) 80.

S. Weinberg, *Hesperia* 18 (1949) 156.

See also chaps. i and ii, esp. Korakou and Zygouries.

GLA-ARNE

A. de Ridder, "Fouilles de Gha," *BCH* 18 (1894) 271, 446.

U. Kahrstedt, "Die Kopaissee im Altertum," *AA* 1937, 1.

N. Kambanis, "Le Déssechement du Lac Copaïs par les anciens," *BCH* 16 (1892) 121; 17 (1893) 322.

E. Kenney, "The Ancient Drainage of the Copaïs," *Liverpool Annals of Art and Archaeology* 22 (1935) 189.

F. Noack, "Arne," *AM* 19 (1894) 405; *Homerische Paläste* (1903) 19.

I. Threpsiades, *Praktika* 1955, 121; 1956, 90; 1957, 48; *Ergon* 1955, 34; 1956, 32; 1957, 25; 1958, 42; 1959, 20; *1960, 37.

IOLKOS (see also chap. v, Tholoi [Kapakli])

D. Theochares, *Praktika* 1956, 119; 1957, 54; *Ergon* 1956–61, *1961, 51; *Archaeology* 11 (1958) 13.

MOURIATADA

Sp. Marinatos, *Ergon* 1960, 149; *Deltion* 16 (1960/63) 116.

E. Vermeule, *Boston University Graduate Journal* 1961, 73, 119.

MYCENAE (see also chap. iv, Shaft Graves, chap. v, Tholoi, chap. vii, Frescoes)

H. Schliemann, *Mycenae* (1878); *Mycenae and Tiryns* (1880); *Catalogue des trésors de Mycènes au Musée d'Athènes* (1882).
L. Steffen, *Karten von Mykenai* (1884).
Chr. Tsountas, *Praktika* 1886, 59; 1888, 29; *Ephemeris* 1887, 155; 1888, 119; 1891, 1; 1896, 1; 1897, 97; 1902, 1; *JdI* 10 (1895) 143; Μυκῆναι καὶ μυκηναῖος πολιτισμός (1893); and J. Manatt, *The Mycenaean Age* (1897).
A. Wace, *Chamber Tombs at Mycenae* (= *Archaeologia* 82 [1932]); *Mycenae: An Archaeological History and Guide* (1949) with bibliography; *BSA* 24 (1919–21) 185;* *BSA* 25 (1921–23); *Antiquity* 10 (1936) 405; *BSA* 45 (1950) 203; 48 (1953) 3; 49 (1954) 231; 50 (1955) 175; 51 (1956) 103; 52 (1957) 193; "The Last Days of Mycenae," *Aegean and Near East* (Goldman, 1956) 126; "Pausanias and Mycenae," *Festschrift B. Schweitzer* (1954) 19; *Companion* 386.
A. Wace and E. Bennett (eds.), *The Mycenae Tablets* II (1958).
H. Wace and C. Williams, *Mycenae Guide* (1961).
E. Wace French, *BSA* 56 (1961) 81; 58 (1963) 44; *Mycenae Tablets* III (1963).

J. Chadwick (ed.), *The Mycenae Tablets* III (1963).
G. Karo, *RE* Supplement 6 (1935) 605, bibliography; *RE* 16 (1935) 1015; *AJA* 38 (1934) 123.
G. Mylonas, *Ancient Mycenae* (1957); " Ἡ Ἀκρόπολις τῶν Μυκηνῶν," *Ephemeris* 1958 (1961) 153; *Ergon* 1959, 93; 1961, 148; 1962, 92.
J. Papademetriou, *Praktika* 1952, 427; 1953, 205; 1954, 242; 1955, 217; 1957, 105; *Ergon* 1954, 53; 1955, 69; 1957, 63; 1958, 118.
J. Papademetriou and Ph. Petsas, *Praktika* 1950, 203; 1951, 192.
W. Taylour and J. Papademetriou, *Deltion* 16 (1960–63) Chron. 89; *Mycenae Tablets* III (1963) 35.
N. Verdelis, *Ergon* 1959, 100; 1961, 156; 1962, 99; "A Private House Discovered at Mycenae," *Archaeology* 14 (1961) 12; *Mycenae Tablets* III (1963) 13.
P. Ålin, *Fundstätten* 10.

ORCHOMENOS (see also chaps. i, ii, v, Tholoi, vii, Frescoes)

H. Schliemann, "Explorations at the Boeotian Orchomenus," *JHS* 2 (1881) 122.
A. de Ridder, "Fouilles d'Orchomène," *BCH* 19 (1895) 136.
H. Bulle, *Orchomenos* I (1907).

PYLOS AND MESSENIA (see also chap. v, Tholoi and n. 11, and chap. ix, Burials)

C. Blegen and K. Kourouniotes, "Excavations at Pylos," *AJA* 43 (1939) 557.
C. Blegen, "The Palace of Nestor Excavations," *AJA* 57 (1953) 59; 58 (1954) 27; 59 (1955) 31; 60 (1956) 95.
C. Blegen and M. Lang, *AJA* 61 (1957) 129; 62 (1958) 175; 63 (1959) 121; 64 (1960) 153; 65 (1961) 153; 66 (1962) 145; 67 (1963) 155; 68 (1964) 95.
C. Blegen, "Nestor's Pylos," *ProcPhilSoc* 101 (1957) 379; "King Nestor's Palace," *Archaeology* 6 (1953) 203; *Companion* 422; *A Guide to the Palace of Nestor* (1962).

GREECE IN THE BRONZE AGE

J. Alsop, *From the Silent Earth* (1964) 38.
W. Dörpfeld, "Alt-Pylos," *AM* 38 (1913) 97.
F. Kiechle, "Pylos und der pylische Raum in der antiken Tradition," *Historia* 9 (1960) 1.
W. McDonald and R. Hope Simpson, "Prehistoric Habitation in Southwestern Peloponnese," *AJA* 65 (1961) 221; 68 (1964) 229.
Sp. Marinatos, "Περὶ τὸν πρῶτον Ἀχαϊκὸν ἐποικισμὸν τῆς Κρήτης," *KChron* 15–16 (1961–62), III, 177; "Problemi omerici e preomerici in Pilo," *PP* 16 (1961) 219.
N. Valmin, *Études Topographiques sur la Messénie* (1930).
H. Wade-Gery, "The Dorian Invasion: What Happened in Pylos?" *AJA* 52 (1948) 115.

Sparta-Amyklai (see also chap. v, Vapheio and Tholoi)

Chr. Tsountas, *Ephemeris* 1889, 130; 1892, 1.
R. Dawkins, *BSA* 16 (1910) 1; E. Fiechter, *JdI* 33 (1918) 123; E. Buschor and A. von Massow, *AM* 52 (1927) 1; H. Waterhouse and R. Hope Simpson, *BSA* 55 (1960) 74.

Thebes (see also chap. vii, Frescoes)

A. Keramopoullos, *Ephemeris* 1907, 205;* 1909, 57; 1910, 177; 1930, 29;* *Deltion* 1917, 1; *Praktika* 1910, 152; 1911, 143; 1912, 85; 1921, 32; 1922–24, 28; 1927, 32; 1928, 45; 1929, 60.

Tiryns (see also chap. v, Tholoi; chap. vii, Frescoes)

G. Rodenwaldt, "Die Fresken des Palastes," *Tiryns* II (1912).
H. Dragendorff, "Tiryns," *AM* 38 (1913) 329.
A. Arvanitopoullos, "Tiryns," *Praktika* 1915, 201.
K. Müller, "Die Architektur des Burg und des Palastes," *Tiryns* III (1930).
G. Karo, *Führer durch Tiryns* (1934); "Tiryns," *RE* VI² (1937) 1453.
N. Verdelis, *Ephemeris* 1956, Par. 5; *Archaeology* 16 (1963) 129; *AJA* 67 (1963) 281.
P. Ålin, *Fundstätten* 25.

ARCHITECTURE

W. Dinsmoor, *The Architecture of Ancient Greece* (1950) 16.
A. Lawrence, *Greek Architecture* (1957) 65.
Chr. Tsountas and J. Manatt, *The Mycenaean Age* (1897) 12.

Å. Åkerström, "Zur Frage der mykenischen Dacheindeckung," *OpArc* 2 (1941) 164.
E. Bell, *Prehellenic Architecture in the Aegean* (1926).
C. Blegen, "The Roof of the Mycenaean Megaron," *AJA* 49 (1945) 35; *Zygouries* (1928) 28.
A. Boethius, "Mycenaean Megara and Nordic Houses," *BSA* 24 (1919–21) 161.
M. Bowen, "Some Observations on the Origin of Triglyphs," *BSA* 45 (1950) 113.
R. Demangel, "La Frise du Socle du Palais de Tirynthe," *BCH* 68–69 (1944–45) 404; "Fenestrarum Imagines," *BCH* 55 (1931) 117.
W. Dinsmoor, "Notes on Megaron Roofs," *AJA* 46 (1942) 370.
W. Dörpfeld, "Die kretischen, mykenischen, und Homerischen Paläste," *AM* 30 (1905) 257; cf. *AM* 32 (1907) 576.

J. Durm, "Über vormykenische und mykenische Architekturformen," *JOAI* 10 (1907) 41.

J. Graham, "Mycenaean Architecture," *Archaeology* 13 (1960) 46; *The Palaces of Crete* (1962).

E. Heinrich, "Die 'Inselarchitektur' des Mittelmeergebietes," *AA* 1958, 89.

L. Holland, "Primitive Aegean Roofs," *AJA* 24 (1920) 323.

H. Lorimer, *HM* 406.

M. Meurer, "Form und Herkunft der mykenischen Säule," *JdI* 29 (1914) 1.

V. Müller, "The Development of the 'Megaron' in Prehistoric Greece," *AJA* 48 (1944) 342.

F. Noack, *Homerische Paläste* (1903).

L. Palmer, "The Homeric and the Indo-European House," *Transactions of the Philological Society,* 1948, 92.

A. Schott, "Minoische und mykenische Palasthöfe," *JOAI* 45 (1960) 68.

B. Schweitzer, "Megaron und Hofhaus in der Ägäis," *BSA* 46 (1951) 160.

E. Smith, "The Megaron and Its Roof," *AJA* 46 (1942) 99.

A. Wace (see Empire Sites, Mycenae, above); "Notes on the Homeric House," *JHS* 71 (1951) 203.

CLOTHES

G. Karo, *Schachtgräber* 173.

H. Lorimer, *Homer and the Monuments* 336.

FOOD (see also chap. ii, Special Topics, and Appendix I)

K. Vickery, *Food in Early Greece* (1936).

J. Chiva, "Cypro-Mycenaean and Early Agriculture," *Man* 1960, 40.

H. Helbaek, "Late Cypriote Vegetable Diet at Apliki," *OpAth* 4 (1962) 171, with references.

T. Howe, "Linear B and Hesiod's Bread-Winners," *TAPA* 89 (1958) 44.

A. Keramopoullos, "Μυκηναϊκά," *Deltion* 4 (1918) 88.

M. Möbius, "Pflanzenbilder der minoischen Kunst," *JdI* 48 (1933) 1.

F. Stubbings, *Companion* 323.

INDUSTRY AND ECONOMY (see also chap. vii, Pottery and Metalwork, and chap. viii)

Å. Åkerström, "Das mykenische Topferviertel in Berbati in der Argolis," *Bericht der VI International Kongress,* Berlin (1939) 296.

M. Finley, "The Mycenaean Tablets and Economic History," *Economic History Review* 10 (1957) 128; cf. L. Palmer, *ibid.* 11 (1958) 87.

A. Keramopoullos, "Βιομηχαναὶ καὶ 'Εμπόρειον τοῦ Κάδμου," *Ephemeris* 1930, 29.

Sp. Marinatos, "Βασιλικὰ μυρεψεῖα καὶ ἀρχεῖα ἐν Μυκήναις," *PraktAkadAth* 1958, 161.

L. Palmer, *Mycenaean Greek Texts* (1963) *passim.*

F. Stubbings, *Companion* 531.

F. Tritsch, "The Women of Pylos," *Minoica* (Sundwall, 1958) 406.

M. Ventris and J. Chadwick, *Documents* (1956) *passim.*

A. Wace, *Mycenae* 102.

VII. Art in the Palaces

FRESCOES* (see also Pictorial Vases, below)

G. Rodenwaldt, "Die Fresken des Palastes," *Tiryns* II (1912) (= Rodenwaldt I); *Der Fries des Megarons von Mykenai* (1921) (= Rodenwaldt II).

M. Swindler, *Ancient Painting* (1929) 71–108.

SITES

GLA-ARNE (see chap. vi, Empire Sites)

J. Threpsiades, *Ergon* 1961, 46, fig. 49.

MYCENAE (see Rodenwaldt II)

Chr. Tsountas, *Praktika* 1886, 59; *Ephemeris* 1887, 155; 1891, 1

G. Rodenwaldt, "Fragmente mykenischer Wandgemälde," *AM* 36 (1911) 221; "Votivpinax aus Mykenai," *AM* 37 (1912) 129; "Die Fussböden des Megarons," *JdI* 34 (1919) 87; Rodenwaldt II (1921); "Mykenische Miscellen," *Epitumbion Tsountas*, 434.

W. Lamb, "Frescoes from the Ramp House," *BSA* 24 (1919–21) 189; "Palace Frescoes," *BSA* 25 (1921–23) 164, 249.

A. Wace, *Mycenae* 70, 79, 90, 104, 126.

H. Reusch, "Vorschlag zur Ordnung der Fragmente von Frauenfriesen aus Mykenai," *AA* 1953, 26.

ORCHOMENOS

H. Bulle, *Orchomenos* I (1907) 72.

PHYLAKOPI

R. Bosanquet, "The Wall Paintings," *Excavations at Phylakopi in Melos* (= *JHS* Supplement I) (1904) 70.

PYLOS (see chap. vi, Empire Sites)

M. Lang, "Picture Puzzles from Pylos: First Steps in the Study of Frescoes," *Archaeology* 13 (1960) 55.

THEBES (see chap. vi, Empire Sites, Keramopoullos)

H. Reusch, "Die Zeichnerische Rekonstruktion des Frauenfrieses im Boötischen Theben," *Abhandlungen der Deutschen Akademie des Wissenschaften, Berlin* 1956 (= 1955, no. 1) with bibliography; "Der Frauenfries von Theben," *AA* 1948, 240; "Ein Frauenfries der kretischen-mykenischen Epochen aus dem Boötischen Theben," *Forschungen und Fortschritte* 1957, 82; "Ein Schildfresko aus Theben," *AA* 1953, 16.

*There are astonishingly few modern special studies, least of all for the mainland. The books in the General Bibliography offer résumés; only Rodenwaldt has studied the subject in depth. See also Tsountas, *MycAge;* Marinatos, *CMG;* Matz III.

Tiryns (see Rodenwaldt I)

N. Verdelis, *Ephemeris* 1956, Par. 5.
R. Hinks, *Catalogue of Paintings and Mosaics in the British Museum* (1933) no. 4.

Trianda

G. Monaco, "Scavi nella zona micenea di Jaliso," *Clara Rhodos* 10 (1941–49) plates 7, 9, 11.

Zygouries

C. Blegen, *Zygouries* (1928) pl. 3.
See also note 2 (Eleusis).

STYLE AND SPECIAL TOPICS

A. Evans, *Palace of Minos, passim,* through Index.

L. Banti, "Il sentimento della Natura nell'Arte Minoica e Micenea," *Geras Keramopoullou*
119.
J. Forsdyke, "Minoan Art," *Proceedings of The British Academy* 15 (1931).
E. Hall, *The Decorative Art of Crete in the Bronze Age* (1907).
H. Hall, *The Civilization of Greece in the Bronze Age* (1928).
F. Matz, *The Art of Crete and Early Greece* (1962) 204.
M. Möbius, "Pflanzenbilder der minoische Kunst," *JdI* 48 (1933) 1.
N. Platon, "Συμβολὴ εἰς τὴν σπουδὴν τῆς μινωϊκῆς τοιχογραφίας," *KChron* 1 (1947) 505;
13 (1959) 319.
M. Robertson, *Greek Painting* (Skira, 1959) 19–33.
W. Schiering, "Steine und Malerei in der minoischen Kunst," *JdI* 75 (1960) 17.
G. Snijder, *Kretische Kunst* (1936) 27, 153.
O. Walter, "Studie über ein Blumenmotiv als Beitrag zur Frage der kretisch-mykenischen
Perspektive," *JOAI* 38 (1950) 17.

Mycenaean Pottery (see also chap. v bibliography and n. 15, chap. vi and ix, site bibliographies; and Pictorial Vases, below)

A. Furumark, *The Mycenaean Pottery, Analysis and Classification* (1941); *The Chronology
of Mycenaean Pottery* (1941).

Basic Excavations, Collections, and Discussions (see also chap. vi, Mycenae)

C. Blegen, *Prosymna* (1937); *Korakou* (1921); *Zygouries* (1928).
Ch. Blinkenberg and K. Friis Johansen, *CVA* Denmark I, Copenhagen National Museum
I (1924), II (n.d.).
R. Bosanquet, "Some 'Late Minoan' Vases found in Greece," *JHS* 24 (1904) 317.
O. Broneer, "Excavations on the North Slope of the Acropolis," *Hesperia* 2 (1933) 356.
H. Catling, "Spectrographic Analysis of Mycenaean and Minoan Pottery," *Archaeometry*
4 (1961) 31.
H. Catling, E. Richards, and A. Blin-Stoyle, "Composition and Provenience of Mycenaean
and Minoan Pottery," *BSA* 55 (1963) 94.

GREECE IN THE BRONZE AGE

P. Devambez, *Greek Painting* (1962) 8.

V. Desborough, *The Last Mycenaeans and Their Successors* (1964).

J. Forsdyke, *British Museum Catalogue of Vases* I, i, ii (1912, 1925).

O. Frödin and A. Persson, *Asine* (1938).

A. Furumark, "The Mycenaean III C Pottery and Its Relation to Cypriote Fabrics," *OpArc* 3 (1944) 194.

A. Furtwängler and G. Loeschke, *Mykenische Vasen* (1886).

M. Lang, "Pylos Pots and the Mycenaean Units of Capacity," *AJA* 68 (1964) 99.

M. Mackeprang, "Late Mycenaean Vases," *AJA* 42 (1938) 537.

A. Smith, *CVA* Great Britain I, British Museum I (1925).

F. Stubbings, "The Mycenaean Pottery of Attica," *BSA* 42 (1947) 1; *Mycenaean Pottery from the Levant* (1951).

A. Wace, *Chamber Tombs at Mycenae* (= *Archaeologia* 82, 1932); "Middle and Late Helladic Pottery," *Epitumbion Tsountas* (1941) 345; "Late Helladic III Pottery and Its Subdivisions," *Ephemeris* 1953–54 (1955) 137; "The Chronology of Late Helladic III B," *BSA* 52 (1957) 220.

SITES WITH ABUNDANT MYCENAEAN POTTERY (see also chaps. ii, v, vi, ix, bibliographies for Athens, Cyclades, Dendra, Dodekanese, Eutresis, Ialysos, Kakovatos, Miletos, Mycenae, Perati, Pylos, Thebes, Troy)

Amarna (Egypt): F. Petrie, *Tell el-Amarna* (1894); H. Frankfort and J. Pendlebury, *The City of Akhenaten* II (1933).

Argos: J. Deshayes, "Les Vases Mycéniens de la Deiras (Argos)," *BCH* 77 (1953) 59, with older bibliography of the site.

Chalkis: V. Hankey, "Late Helladic Tombs at Chalkis," *BSA* 47 (1952) 49.

Enkomi (Cyprus): C. Schaeffer, *Enkomi-Alasia* (1952); also in *Comptes Rendus de l'Académie des Inscriptions et Belles-Lettres,* 1948——; P. Dikaios in *FA* 1946——; E. Sjøqvist, *Problems of the Late Cypriote Bronze Age* (1940); J. Forsdyke and H. Walters, *British Museum Catalogue of Vases* I, ii (1925); E. Coche de la Ferté, *Essai de classification de la ceramique mycénienne d'Enkomi* (1951).

Ionian Islands: P. Dessoulavy, "Vases Mycéniens du Musée de Neuchâtel," *RA* (1900) 128; Sp. Marinatos, *Ephemeris* 1932, 1; 1933, 68; S. Benton, "The Ionian Islands," *BSA* 32 (1931–32) 213.

Müskebi (Turkey): G. Bass, "Mycenaean and Protogeometric Tombs in the Halicarnassus Peninsula," *AJA* 67 (1963) 353.

Patras district: E. Vermeule, "The Mycenaeans in Achaia," *AJA* 64 (1960) 1.

Salamis: S. Wide, "Gräberfunde aus Salamis," *AM* 35 (1910) 17; C.-G. Styrenius, "The Vases from the Submycenaean Cemetery on Salamis," *OpAth* 4 (1962) 103.

Tarsus (Turkey): H. Goldman, *Tarsus* II (1956) 220.

PICTORIAL VASES (see also Forsdyke, Furumark, Furtwängler-Loeschke, and Smith above, and Sjøqvist, chap. viii, Trade)

V. Karageorghis, *The Mycenaean Vases of the Pictorial Style* (forthcoming).

Å. Åkerström, "Some Pictorial Vase Representations from the Mainland in Late Helladic Times," *OpAth* 1 (1953) 9.

374

J. Benson, "Observations on Mycenaean Vase-Painters," *AJA* 65 (1961) 337; "Pictorial Mycenaean Fragments from Kourion," *AJA* 65 (1961) 53.

S. Charitonides, "Μυκηναῖος ἀγγειογράφος," *Ephemeris* 1953–54, II, 101; " 'Ο Μυκηναῖος ἀγγειογράφος τῶν παπύρων," *Deltion* 16 (1960) 84.

J. Forsdyke, "A Late Mycenaean Vase from Cyprus," *Essays in Aegean Archaeology* (Evans, 1927) 27.

A. Furumark, "A Scarab from Cyprus," *OpAth* 1 (1953) 47.

S. Immerwahr, "Three Mycenaean Vases in the Metropolitan," *AJA* 49 (1945) 534; "The Protome Painter and Some Contemporaries," *AJA* 60 (1956) 137.

V. Karageorghis, "Deux peintres de vases mycéniens," *Syria* 34 (1957) 81; "A Mycenaean Chalice and a Vase Painter," *BSA* 52 (1957) 38; "Myth and Epic in Mycenaean Vase-Painting," *AJA* 62 (1958) 383; "A Mycenaean Horse-Rider," *Bulletin van de Vereeniging tot Bevordering der Kennis van de Antieke Beschaving te 'S-Gravenhage* 33 (1958) 38; "Some Mycenaean Vases in the G. G. Pierides Collection, Cyprus," *Kypriakai Spoudai* 1956; "Les personnages en robe sur les vases mycéniens," *BCH* 83 (1959) 193; "Supplementary Notes on the Mycenaean Vases from the Swedish Tombs at Enkomi," *OpAth* 3 (1960) 135; "Le cratère mycénien aux taureaux des Musées de Berlin," *BCH* 86 (1962) 11; *CVA* Cyprus Museum I (1963).

F. Stubbings, "Some Mycenaean Artists," *BSA* 46 (1951) 168.

J. Wiesner, "Hochzeit des Polypus," *JdI* 74 (1959) 35.

IVORIES

H. Kantor, "Ivory Carving in the Mycenaean Period," *Archaeology* 13 (1960) 14.

A. Dessenne, *Corpus of Cretan and Mycenaean Ivories* (forthcoming).

MAJOR PUBLISHED GROUPS

P. Chantraine and A. Dessenne, "Quelques termes mycéniens relatifs au travail de l'ivoire," *Comptes Rendus de l'Académie des Inscriptions et Belles-Lettres* 1957, 241.

P. Demargne, "Ivoires comparés," *La Crète Dédalique* (1947) 188.

A. Dessenne, "Le Griffon créto-mycénien," *BCH* 81 (1957) 203.

H. Gallet de Santerre and J. Tréheux, "Rapport sur le dépôt égéen et géométrique de l'Artémision à Délos," *BCH* 71–72 (1947–48) 148.

B. Haussoullier, "Catalogue descriptif des objets découverts à Spata," *BCH* 2 (1878) 185; cf. Koumanoudis, "Οἱ ἐν Σπάτα τῆς Ἀττικῆς ἀρχαῖοι τάφοι καὶ τὰ ἐν αὐτοῖς ἀνευρεθέντα." *Athenaion* 6 (1887) 167; Milchhöfer, *AM* 2 (1877) 261.

G. Loud, *The Megiddo Ivories* (1939).

Ch. Picard, "Sur un groupe d'ivoire de Mycènes," *Epitumbion Tsountas* (1941) 446.

J. Schäfer, "Elfenbeinspiegelgriffe des 2. Jahrtausends," *AM* 73 (1958) 73.

V. Staïs, *Mycenaean Collection of the National Museum* (Athens) (1926).

H. Taylor, "Chemical Investigations on Ivory," *BSA* 50 (1955) 248.

A. Wace, "Ivory Carvings from Mycenae," *Archaeology* 7 (1954) 149; *Mycenae* 83, 115; *BSA* 52 (1957) 197.

H. Wace, "The Ivory Triad," *Ivories from Mycenae* I (1962).

GREECE IN THE BRONZE AGE

TERRACOTTAS AND OTHER SCULPTURE (see also chap. ix, n. 5)

E. Wace French, *The Development of Mycenaean Terracotta Figurines* (dissertation, London, 1962).

O. Broneer, "A Sandstone Head from Corinth," *AJA* 40 (1936) 204.

A. Furumark, *Chronology* 86.

G. Hafner, "Eine submykenische Stierplastik," *JdI* 58 (1943) 183.

F. Jones, "Three Mycenaean Figurines," *Aegean and Near East* (1956) 122.

G. Karo, "Minoische Rhyta," *JdI* 26 (1911) 249.

V. Müller, "The Beginnings of Monumental Sculpture," *Metropolitan Museum Studies* 5 (1934–36) 157.

G. Mylonas, "Cycladic and Mycenaean Figurines," *Bulletin of the City Art Museum* (St. Louis), 1955, 1; "A Mycenaean Figurine at the University of Illinois," *AJA* 41 (1937) 237; "Seated and Multiple Mycenaean Figurines," *Aegean and Near East* (1956) 110.

M. Nilsson, *MMR*² (1950) *passim*.

Chr. Tsountas, *Ephemeris* 1902, 1.

N. Valmin, "Spätmykenische Steinreliefs aus Messenien," *OpAth* 2 (1955) 66.

GEMS AND RINGS

F. Matz (ed.), *Corpus of Minoan and Mycenaean Seals* (in progress).

H. Biesantz, *Kretisch-mykenische Siegelbilder* (1954).

A. Evans, *The Palace of Minos* IV (1935) ii, 484 and *passim*, through Index.

V. Kenna, *Cretan Seals* (1961).

M. Nilsson, *MMR*² (1950) *passim* (iconography).

SPECIAL STUDIES

H. Biesantz, "Die minoische Bildnisgemmen," *Marburger Winckelmannsprogramm* 1958.

M. Gill, "The Minoan Dragon," *BICS* 10 (1963) 1.

A. Persson, *The Religion of Greece in Prehistoric Times* (1942) (iconography of gold rings).

IMPORTANT PUBLISHED GROUPS

Vapheio: Ephemeris 1889, pl. 10; Evans, *Palace of Minos,* Index *s.v.* Vaphio Tomb; Kenna, *Cretan Seals* 52, 79; Karo, *AM* 35 (1910) 182.

Mycenae: Ephemeris 1888, pl. 10; Kenna, *Cretan Seals* 81; Wace, *Chamber Tombs* pl. 28.

Dendra: Persson, *RT* pl. 19.

Myrsinochorion: Marinatos, *Ergon* 1956, fig. 92.

Mixed: Marinatos and Hirmer, *CMG* pls. 206–12; Kenna, "Cretan and Mycenaean Seals in North America," *AJA* 68 (1964) 1.

Sealings: J. Chadwick, *Eranos* 57 (1959) 1; M. Lang, *AJA* 63 (1959) 134; A. Xenaki-Sakellariou, '"Ενα σφράγισμα ἀπὸ τὴν Πύλο," *Festschrift F. Matz* (1962) 19; Wace and Bennett, *The Mycenae Tablets* II, 12, 65, 103.

JEWELRY (see also chap. iv)

R. Higgins, *Greek and Roman Jewellery* (1961) 68, with full bibliography of sites and references.

G. Becatti, *Oreficerie antique dalle minoiche alle barbariche* (1955).

E. Blegen, *Prosymna* (1937) 265 (survey of normal Mycenaean types).

V. Staïs, *Ephemeris* 1907, 31.

GLASS

T. Haevernick, "Beiträge zur Geschichte des antiken Glases III, Mykenisches Glas," *JRGZM* 7 (1960) 36; "Mycenaean Glass," *Archaeology* 16 (1963) 190.

FAÏENCE (see also Stone and Thomas, chap. viii, Trade and Foreign Relations)

H. Hall, *The Civilization of Greece in the Bronze Age* (1928).

METALWORK AND WEAPONS (see also chap. iv, chap. v, n. 13; chap. viii, n. 7)

St. Alexiou, "The Boars's Tusk Helmet," *Antiquity* 28 (1954) 211.

G. Bass, "The Cape Gelidonya Wreck," *AJA* 65 (1961) 267.

S. Benton, "No Tin from Kirrha in Phokis," *Antiquity* 38 (1964) 138.

C. Blegen, *Prosymna* (1937) 328 (survey of normal Mycenaean types).

H.-G. Büchholz, "Der Kupferhandel des 2 vorchristlichen Jahrtausends," *Minoica* (Festschrift Sundwall, 1958) 92; see also *PZ* 1959, 1; "Die helladischen Pfeilspitzen," *JdI* 77 (1962) 1.

E. Caley, "On the Prehistoric Use of Arsenical Copper in the Aegean Region," *Hesperia* Supplement 8 (1949) 60.

H. Catling, *Cypriot Bronzework in the Mycenaean World* (1964); *The Metal Industry in Cyprus* (Diss. Oxford 1957); "Bronze Cut-and-Thrust Swords," *ProcPS* 22 (1956) 102; "A Bronze Greave from a Thirteenth Century B.C. Tomb at Enkomi," *OpAth* 2 (1955) 21; "A New Bronze Sword from Cyprus," *Antiquity* 35 (1961) 115.

J. Cowen, "Einführung in die Geschichte der bronzenen Griffzungenschwerter," *RGK* 36 (1955) 52.

S. Dakaris, "Προϊστορικοὶ τάφοι παρὰ τὸ Καλμπάκι—'Ιωαννίνων," *Ephemeris* 1956, 114.

O. Davies, "Two North Greek Mining Towns," *JHS* 49 (1929) 89; "The Copper Mines of Cyprus," *BSA* 30 (1928–30) 74.

J. Deshayes, *Les Outils de Bronze de l'Indus au Danube* (1960).

R. Forbes, *Metallurgy in Antiquity* (1950).

A. Hertz, "Iron: Prehistoric and Ancient," *AJA* 41 (1937) 441; H. Richardson, *ibid.* 447.

R. Higgins, *Greek and Roman Jewellery* (1961).

G. Karo, "Schatz von Tiryns," *AM* 55 (1930) 119.

M. Lejeune, "Les forgerons de Pylos," *Historia* 10 (1961) 409.

H. Lorimer, *Homer and the Monuments* (1950) *passim*.

Sp. Marinatos, "The 'Swimmers' Dagger from the Tholos Tomb at Vaphio," *Essays in Aegean Archaeology* (Evans, 1927) 63.

H. Maryon, *Metalwork and Enamelling*[4] (1959); "Metalworking in the Ancient World," *AJA* 53 (1949) 93; "Early Near Eastern Steel Swords," *AJA* 65 (1961) 173.

G. von Merhart, "Geschnürte Schienen," *RGK* 37–38 (1956–57) 91; see also chap. v, n. 13.

A. Moss, "Niello," *Studies in Conservation* 2 (1953) 49.

H. Müller-Karpe, "Zur spätbronzezeitlichen Bewaffnung in Mitteleuropa und Griechen-land," *Germania* 40 (1962) 255; "Metallbeigaben der Kerameikos-Gräber," *JdI* 77 (1962) 59.

G. Mylonas, "Three Late Mycenaean Knives," *AJA* 66 (1962) 406.

W. Reichel, *Homerische Waffen*[2] (1901).

N. Sandars, "The Antiquity of the One-Edged Knife in the Aegean," *ProcPS* 21 (1955) 174; "The First Aegean Swords and Their Ancestry," *AJA* 65 (1961) 17; "Later Aegean Bronze Age Swords," *AJA* 67 (1963) 117.

C. Schaeffer, "La coupe en argent incrustée d'or d'Enkomi-Alasia," *Syria* 30 (1953) 51; cf. Ch. Picard, "De Midea à Salamis," *Geras Keramopoullou* 1.

F. Stubbings, "Arms and Armour," *Companion* 504; "A Bronze Founder's Hoard," *BSA* 49 (1954) 292.

H. Thomas, "The Acropolis Treasure from Mycenae," *BSA* 39 (1938–39) 65.

M. Ventris and J. Chadwick, "Metals and Military Equipment," *Documents* 351.

N. Verdelis, *Ephemeris* 1957 (1961) Chron. 15 (Dendra Cuirass); sub-Mycenaean Helmet, Tiryns, in G. Daux, *BCH* 82 (1958) 706.

G. Wainwright, "Early Tin in the Aegean," *Antiquity* 17 (1944) 57.

A. Xenaki-Sakellariou, "La représentation du casque en dents de sanglier," *BCH* 77 (1953) 46.

N. Yalouris, "Mykenische Bronzeschutzwaffen," *AM* 75 (1960) 42.

VIII. Society and History in the Mycenaean World

TRADE AND FOREIGN RELATIONS (see also chaps. v, vi)

St. Alexiou, "Ζητήματα τοῦ προϊστορικοῦ βίου. Κρήτο-Μυκηναϊκὸν Ἐμπόριον," *Ephemeris* 1953–54, III (1958) 135.

J. Benson, "Coarse Ware Stirrup Jars of the Aegean," *Berytus* 14 (1961) 37.

A. Burn, *Minoans, Philistines, and Greeks* (1930).

E. Capovilla, "L'Egitto e il mondo miceneo," *Aegyptus* 40 (1960) 3.

F. Cassola, *La Ionia nel mondo miceneo* (1957).

H. Catling, "Patterns of Settlement in Bronze Age Cyprus," *OpAth* 4 (1962) 129.

H. Catling and V. Karageorghis, "Minoika in Cyprus," *BSA* 55 (1960) 109.

M. Cavalier, "Les cultures préhistoriques des Iles Éoliennes et leur rapport avec le monde Égéen," *BCH* 84 (1960) 319.

V. Childe, "The Relations between Greece and Prehistoric Europe," *Acta Congressi Mad-vigiani* 1 (1958) 293; "A Bronze Dagger of Mycenaean Type from Pelynt, Cornwall," *ProcPS* 17 (1951) 95; "Lausitzische Elemente in Griechenland," *Mannus* Ergänzungs-band 6 (1928) 236.

J. Cook, "Greek Settlements in the Eastern Aegean and Asia Minor," *CAH*[2] II (1961) xxxviii.

T. Dunbabin, "Minos and Daidalos in Sicily," *Papers of the British School in Rome* 16 (1948) 8.

D. Fimmen, *Die kretisch-mykenische Kultur*[2] (1924) 152–209.

A. Furumark, "The Settlement at Ialysos and Aegean Prehistory," *OpArc* 6 (1950) 150.

V. Grace, "The Canaanite Jar," *Aegean and the Near East* (1956) 80.

R. Hachmann, "Bronzezeitliche Bernsteinschieber," *Bayrische Vorgeschichtsblätter* 22 (1957) 1; cf. N. Sandars, *Antiquity* 33 (1959) 292.

H. Hall, *The Civilization of Greece in the Bronze Age* (1928) 199.

H. Hencken, "Beitzsch and Knossos," *ProcPS* 18 (1952) 36.

R. Hope Simpson and J. Lazenby, "Notes from the Dodecanese," *BSA* 57 (1962) 154.

S. Immerwahr, "Mycenaean Trade and Colonization," *Archaeology* 13 (1960) 4.

H. Kantor, *The Aegean and the Near East in the Second Millennium B.C.* (1948).

H. Lorimer, *Homer and the Monuments* (1950) 52.

Sp. Marinatos, "The Minoan and Mycenaean Civilisation and Its Influence on the Mediterranean and Europe," *VI Congreso delle Scienze Pre/Protoistoriche* I (1961) 161; "La marine créto-mycénienne," *BCH* 57 (1933) 170; "La Sicilia e la Grecia nell'eta preistorica," *Kokalos* 5 (1959) 3; "Lausitzer Goldschmuck in Tiryns," Θεωρία (Festschrift Schuchhardt, 1960) 151.

R. Merrillees, "Opium Trade in the Bronze Age Levant," *Antiquity* 36 (1962) 287.

V. Miløjčič, "Einige 'Mitteleuropaische' Fremdlinge auf Kreta," *JRGZM* 2 (1955) 153; "Neue Bernsteinschieber aus Griechenland," *Germania* 33 (1955) 316.

P. Pecorella, "Aspetti e problemi della espansione micenea verso l'Oriente," *Accademia Toscana "La Columbaria"* 27 (1962–63) 3 (complete list of Mycenaean finds in Anatolia to 1962).

J. Pendlebury, "Egypt and the Aegean in the Late Bronze Age," *JEA* 16 (1930) 75; *Aegyptiaca* (1930); "Egypt and the Aegean," *DMR* I (1951) 184.

S. Piggott, "A Late Bronze Age Wine Trade?" *Antiquity* 33 (1959) 122.

K. Polyani *et al.*, *Trade and Markets in Early Empires* (1957).

C. Schaeffer, *Enkomi-Alasia* (1952) 350.

E. Sjøqvist, *Problems of the Late Cypriote Bronze Age* (1940).

E. Sprockhoff, "Nordische Bronzezeit und frühes Griechentum," *JRGZM* 1 (1954) 28; "Eine mykenische Bronzetasse aus Dohnsen," *Germania* 39 (1961) 11; *Zur Handelsgeschichte der germanischen Bronzezeit* (1950).

L. Stella, "La scoperta del greco-miceneo e la preistoria della Sicilia," *Archeologia Classica* 10 (1958) 279; "Il problema etnico dei Greci dopo il deciframente delle tavolette micenee," *Rivista di antropologia* 47 (1960) 3.

J. Stone and L. Thomas, "The Use and Distribution of Faience in the Ancient East and Prehistoric Europe," *ProcPS* 22 (1956) 37.

F. Stubbings, *Mycenaean Pottery from the Levant* (1951); "Chronology of the Aegean Bronze Age," *CAH²* I, vi, 69.

W. Taylour, *Mycenaean Pottery in Italy and Adjacent Areas* (1958).

J. Vercoutter, *L'Égypte et le Monde Égéen Préhellenique* (1956).

K. Völkl, *Die achaische Expansion und die äolische Kolonisation* (1959).

A. Wace and C. Blegen, "Pottery as Evidence for Trade and Colonization in the Aegean Bronze Age," *Klio* 32 (1939) 131.

A. Wace and C. Blegen, "The Determination of Greek Trade in the Bronze Age," *Proceedings of the Cambridge Philological Society* 1938, 119.

LINEAR B

Minimum equipment includes the journals *Minos* (1951——), *Nestor* (1957——), perhaps *Kadmos* (1962——), technical discussions in the successive *Mycenaean Colloquia*, archaeological and linguistic discussions in the *Minutes of the Mycenaean Seminar* (University of London), and the following volumes or special studies.

E. Bennett, *A Minoan Linear B Index* (1953); *The Pylos Tablets*[2] (1955); *The Olive Oil Tablets of Pylos* (= *Minos* Supplement 2, 1958).

M. Ventris and J. Chadwick, *Documents in Mycenaean Greek* (1956); "Evidence for Greek Dialect in the Mycenaean Archives," *JHS* 73 (1953) 84.

E. Bennett, J. Chadwick, M. Ventris, and F. Householder, *The Knossos Tablets*[2] (= BICS Supplement 7, 1959).

E. Bennett, J. Chadwick, A. Wace, *The Mycenae Tablets II* (= *Transactions of the American Philosophical Society* 48, 1, 1958).

J. Chadwick *et al.*, *The Mycenae Tablets III* (= *Transactions of the American Philosophical Society* 52, 7, 1963).

M. Lang, "Palace of Nestor Excavations Part II," *AJA* 62 (1958) 181; 63 (1959) 128; 64 (1960) 160; 65 (1961) 158; 66 (1962) 149; 67 (1963) 160.

J. Chadwick, L. Palmer, M. Ventris, *Studies in Mycenaean Inscriptions and Dialect*, 1956——.

L. Palmer, *Mycenaean Greek Texts* (1963), with bibliography to 1962.

HELPFUL COMMENTARIES AND SOURCES

J. Chadwick, *The Decipherment of Linear B* (1958); "The Prehistory of the Greek Language," *CAH*[2] II, xxxix (1963).

L. Deroy, *Initiation à l'epigraphie mycénienne* (1962).

D. Diringer, *Writing* (1962).

S. Dow, "Minoan Writing," *AJA* 58 (1954) 77.

A. Evans and J. Myres, *Scripta Minoa* II (1952).

C. Gallavotti and A. Sacconi, *Inscriptiones Pyliae* (1962).

L. Jeffery, "Writing," *Companion* 545.

O. Landau, *Mykenisch-griechische Personennamen* (1958).

M. Lejeune, *Mémoires de philologie mycénienne* (1958).

A. Morpurgo, *Mycenaeae Graecitatis Lexikon* (1963).

L. Palmer, *Mycenaeans and Minoans* (1961); "The Language of Homer," *Companion* 75.

E. Risch, "Frühgeschichte der griechischen Sprache," *Museum Helveticum* 16 (1959) 215.

C. Ruigh, *Tabellae Mycenenses Selectae* (1962).

E. Vilborg, *A Tentative Grammar of Mycenaean Greek* (1960).

THE LATE EMPIRE, THE TROJAN WAR, THE DORIAN INVASION

P. Ålin, *Das Ende der mykenischen Fundstätten auf den griechischen Festland* (1962).

M. Andronikos, "The 'Dorian Invasion' and Archaeology," *Hellenika* 13 (1954) 221.

J. Bérard, "Le Mur pelasgique de l'Acropole," *DMR* I (1951) 135; *Recherches sur la chronologie de l'époque mycénienne* (1950).

C. Blegen, "The Mycenaean Age," *Semple Lecture* 1962; *Troy and the Trojans* (1963).

C. Blegen, C. Boulter, J. Caskey, and M. Rawson, *Troy III* (1953), *Troy IV* (1958).

O. Broneer, "Athens in the Late Bronze Age," *Antiquity* 30 (1956) 9.

J. Bury, "The Achaeans and the Trojan War," *CAH*[1], II (1926) 473.

S. Casson, "Excavations in Macedonia," *BSA* 24 (1919–21) 1.

V. Childe, "The Final Bronze Age in the East and Temperate Europe," *ProcPS* 14 (1948) 177.

J. Cook, "The Dorian Invasion," *Proceedings of the Cambridge Philological Society* 1962, 16.

F. Cornelius, "Zum Aḫḫijawaa-Problem," *Historia* II (1962) 112.

J. Daniel, O. Broneer, and H. T. Wade-Gery, "The Dorian Invasion," *AJA* 52 (1948) 107.

P. Demargne, *La Crète dédalique* (1947) 35–101.

V. Desborough, *The Last Mycenaeans and Their Successors* (1964).

V. Desborough and N. Hammond, "The End of Mycenaean Civilization and the Dark Ages," *CAH²* II (1962) xxxvi.

J. Garstang and O. Gurney, *The Geography of the Hittite Empire* (1959).

O. Gurney, *The Hittites²* (1962).

N. Hammond, *A History of Greece* (1959) 72; "Prehistoric Epirus and the Dorian Invasion," *BSA* 32 (1931–32) 131.

F. Hampl, "Die Chronologie der Einwanderung der griechischen Stämme," *Museum Helveticum* 17 (1960) 57.

W. Heurtley, "A Site in Western Macedonia and the Dorian Invasion," *BSA* 28 (1926) 158.

G. Huxley, *Achaeans and Hittites* (1960).

P. Kretschmer, "Achäer in Kleinasien zur Hethiterzeit," *Glotta* (1954) 1.

F. Matz, "Die Katastrophe der mykenischen Kultur," *VII ArcCong* I (1961) 197; cf. *AA* 1961, 74.

V. Miløjčič, "Die dorische Wanderung im Lichte der vorgeschichtlichen Funde," *AA* 1948, 12.

G. Miltner, "Die dorische Wanderung," *Klio* 27 (1934) 54.

G. Mylonas, ''Οἱ χρόνοι τῆς ἁλώσεως τῆς Τροίας,'' *University of Athens Philosophical Faculty* 1960, 408.

C. Nylander, "The Fall of Troy," *Antiquity* 37 (1963) 6.

H. Otten, "Neue Quellen zum Ausklang des Hethitischen Reiches," *Mitteilungen der deutschen Orientgesellschaft* 94 (1963) 1.

D. Page, *History and the Homeric Iliad* (1959) i–iii; "The Historical Sack of Troy," *Antiquity* 33 (1959) 25.

M. Sakellariou, *La migration grecque en Ionie* (1958).

F. Schachermeyr, *Hethiter und Achäer* (1935).

T. Skeat, *The Dorians in Archaeology* (1934).

F. Sommer, "Die Aḫḫijava-Urkunden," *Abhandlungen der Bayerischen Akademie der Wissenschaften* 6 (1932) 2.

G. Steiner, "Neue Alašija-Texte," *Kadmos* I (1962) 130.

E. Vermeule, "The Fall of the Mycenaean Empire," *Archaeology* 13 (1960) 66; "The Mycenaeans in Achaia," *AJA* 64 (1960) 1; *AJA* 63 (1959) 203; *Gnomon* 35 (1963) 495.

K. Völkl, "Achchijawa," *La Nouvelle Clio* 4 (1952) 329.

A. Wace, "The Last Days of Mycenae," *Aegean and Near East* (1956) 126.

H. Wade-Gery, "The Dorians," *CAH¹* II (1926) 518.

G. Wainwright, "Some Sea Peoples," *JEA* 47 (1961) 71; "A Teucrian at Salamis in Cyprus," *JHS* 83 (1963) 146; cf. *AJA* 56 (1952) 196; *AnatSt* 4 (1954) 33.

E. Will, *Doriens et Ioniens* (1956).

IX. The Mycenaean Heritage

RELIGION

M. Nilsson, *The Minoan-Mycenaean Religion*[2] (1950); *Geschichte der griechischen Religion*[2] I (1941).

W. Guthrie, "The Religion and Mythology of the Greeks," *CAH*[2] II (1961) 45.

St. Alexiou, "Ἡ μινωϊκὴ Θεὰ μεθ᾽ ὑψωμένων χειρῶν," *KChron* 1958, 178; cf. *KChron* 1951, 346.

E. Bennett, *The Olive Oil Tablets of Pylos* (= *Minos* Supplement II, 1958).

J. Chadwick, "Potnia," *Minos* 5 (1957) 117.

P. Dikaios, "The Bronze Statue of a Horned God from Enkomi," *AA* 1962, 2.

A. Evans, *The Mycenaean Tree and Pillar Cult* (1901); *The Earlier Religion of Greece* (1931).

M. Gill, *The Minoan Genius* (dissertation, Birmingham, 1962).

W. Guthrie, "Early Greek Religion in the Light of the Decipherment of Linear B," *BICS* 6 (1959) 35.

E. Herkenrath, "Mykenische Kultszenen," *AJA* 41 (1937) 411.

M. Lejeune, "Prêtres et Prêtresses dans les documents mycéniens," *Coll. Latomus* 45 (1960) 129.

F. Matz, "Göttererscheinung und Kultbild im Minoischen Kreta," *Abhandlungen Mainz* 1958.

G. Mylonas, *Eleusis and the Eleusinian Mysteries* (1961).

L. Palmer, *Mycenaeans and Minoans* (1962) 119; "New Religious Texts from Pylos," *Transactions of the Philological Society* 1958, 1.

A. Persson, *The Religion of Greece in Prehistoric Times* (1942); cf. A. Nock, *AJA* 47 (1943) 492.

Ch. Picard, *Les religions préhelléniques* (1948).

N. Platon, "Τὰ μινωϊκὰ ἱερά," *KChron* 1954, 428.

H. Rose, "Religion," *Companion* 463.

L. Stella, "La religione greca nei testi micenei," *Numen* 5 (1958) 18.

M. Ventris and J. Chadwick, "Mycenaean Religion," *Documents* 125; "Proportional Tribute and Ritual Offerings," *Documents* 275.

E. Vermeule, "Götterkult," *Archaeologia Homerica* (1964).

J. Wiesner, *Olympos* (1960).

C. Yavis, *Greek Altars* (1949) 29.

BURIALS

G. Mylonas, "The Cult of the Dead in Helladic Times," *DMR* I (1951) 64; "Homeric and Mycenaean Burial Customs," *AJA* 52 (1948) 56; "Burial Customs," *Companion* 478; "Τὰ μυκηναϊκὰ ἔθιμα ταφῆς," *University of Athens Philosophical Faculty* 1961–62, 291.

J. Wiesner, *Grab und Jenseits* (1938).

M. Andronikos, "Ὁμηρικὰ καὶ μυκηναϊκὰ ἔθιμα ταφῆς," *Hellenika* 17 (1962) 40.

C. Blegen, *Prosymna* (1937) 228.

V. Karageorghis, " 'Αρχαιολογικαὶ παρατηρήσεις ἐπί τινων Ὁμηρικῶν ἐθίμων ταφῆς," *Stasinos* I (1963) 31.

H. Lorimer, "Cremation," *Homer and the Monuments* (1950) 102.

Chr. Tsountas, " 'Ανασκαφαὶ τάφων ἐν Μυκήναις," *Ephemeris* 1888, 119.

A. Wace, *Chamber Tombs at Mycenae* (1932) 121.

Ialysos: A. Maiuri, *Annuario* 6–7 (1926) 83; G. Jacopi, *Annuario* 13–14 (1933–40) 253.

Perati: V. Staïs, *Ephemeris* 1895, 199; *Deltion* 11 (1927–28) Par. 59; Sp. Iakovides, Περὶ ἀνασκαφῆς τοῦ μυκηναϊκοῦ νεκροταφείου τῆς Περατῆς (1961); *Praktika* 1953, 88; 1954, 89; 1955, 100; 1956, 63; 1957, 35; *Ergon* 1954, 10; 1955, 25; 1956, 21; 1957, 17; 1958, 27; 1959, 9; 1960, 16; 1961, 13; 1962, 21.

Pylos District (see also chap. v, Tholoi; chap. vi, Empire Sites): Sp. Marinatos, *Praktika* 1952, 473; 1953, 238; 1954, 299; 1955, 245; 1956, 202; 1957, 118; *Ergon* 1954, 41; 1955, 88; 1956, 90; 1957, 70; 1958, 148; 1959, 117; 1960, 145; 1961, 164; 1962, 110; *Antiquity* 1957, 97; "Palaipylos," *Das Altertum* I (1955) 140; "Die messenischen Grabungen," *Anz Wien* 25 (1961) 235; "Die Pylosforschungen," *VIIArcCong* I (1961) 221; *La Parola del Passato* 16 (1961) 219; *Deltion* 16 (1960/62) 112.

MEMORY AND POETRY

L. Banti, "Myth in Pre-Classical Art," *AJA* 58 (1954) 307.

C. Blegen, "Post-Mycenaean Deposits in Chamber Tombs," *Ephemeris* 1937, 377.

M. Bowra, "Homeric Epithets for Troy," *JHS* 80 (1960) 16.

R. Carpenter, *Folktale, Fiction and Saga in the Homeric Epic* (1946).

J. Cook, "The Cult of Agamemnon at Mycenae," *Geras Keramopoullou* (1953) 112.

G. Hafner, "Kretisch-Mykenisches in der späteren griechischen Kunst," *Festschrift, Römisch-Germanisches Zentralmuseums, Mainz* III (1952) 83.

T. Howe, "Linear B and Hesiod's Bread-Winners," *TAPA* 89 (1958) 44.

V. Karageorghis, "Myth and Epic in Mycenaean Vase-Painting," *AJA* 62 (1958) 383; "Some Mycenaean Survivals in Cyprus during the First Millennium b.c.," *Kadmos* I (1962) 71.

G. Kirk, *The Songs of Homer* (1962); "Dark Age and Oral Poet," *Proceedings of the Cambridge Philological Society* 7 (1961) 34.

A. Lord, *The Singer of Tales* (1960).

H. Lorimer, "Music," *HM* 455.

J. Myres, "Homeric Art," *BSA* 45 (1950) 229.

M. Nilsson, *The Mycenaean Origin of Greek Mythology* (1932); "Mycenaean and Homeric Religion," *Archiv für Religionswissenschaft* 33 (1936) 84.

J. Notopoulos, "Homer, Hesiod, and the Achaean Heritage of Oral Poetry," *Hesperia* 29 (1960) 177.

D. Page, *History and the Homeric Iliad* (1959).

A. Persson, "Legende und Mythen," *Dragma M. P. Nilsson* (1939) 379.

A. Sacconi, "Il mito nel mondo miceneo," *PP* 15 (1960) 161.

C. Starr, *The Origins of Greek Civilization* (1961).

E. Vermeule, "Mythology in Mycenaean Art," *Classical Journal* 54 (1958) 97.

A. Wace and F. Stubbings, *Companion passim*.

T. Webster, *From Mycenae to Homer* (1958) 64.

S. Wide, "Nachleben mykenischer Ornamente," *AM* 22 (1897) 233.

Glossary

aithousa: the outer portico of a megaron (Pls. XXII A, XXIII B)

alabastron (pl. *alabastra*): a low baggy vase in clay or stone, usually with three miniature handles on the upper shoulder, designed for fine oil or perfume

argonaut: paper nautilus in Aegean designs (Pls. XXIX D, XLIV A)

askos (pl. *askoi*): a vase in the shape of a sack, skin, or animal (Pls. VIII A, XLII A-B)

bothros (pl. *bothroi*): a pit in the ground, often used for garbage, sometimes for chthonic offerings

cartouche: Egyptian oval or oblong frame containing hieroglyphs for the names of members of the royal family (Fig. 29)

cist: a boxlike grave sunk below ground surface, often lined with stone rubble or plaques, with cover slabs (Fig. 11 *b*)

cut-and-thrust sword: a new sword type in the Late Mycenaean world, with the hilt-attachment so strengthened that slicing attacks could be made as fearlessly as puncturing attacks

daimon: the Greek term for a strange or divine being usually applied to grotesque lion-men wearing skin garments like a crocodile hide (Fig. 25)

depas (pl. *depas*): usually the *depas amphikupellon*, a Homeric term for a two-handled drinking cup misapplied by Schliemann to a peculiar Trojan (Early Bronze) shape, and used in Linear B for a large jar (Fig. 48 *b*) *dromos* (pl. *dromoi*): the runway, or sloping entrance cutting, to a tholos or chamber tomb (Fig. 24)

fabric: the composition or quality of clay in a vase, which varies in color, firing, levigation, surface finish

fibula: a brooch, often of the safety-pin type (Fig. 39)

flange-hilted: descriptive of swords or daggers whose hilt-plates are flanged toward the shoulder for greater security

flying gallop: an artistic convention for rendering a running animal with his legs stretched parallel to the ground or kicking upward behind (Pls. XII, XXXVI B–C; Fig. 21 *b*)

frying pan: a peculiar shape of Cycladic vase whose use is uncertain; possibly made for the kitchen but practically never used there; thought by some to be a mirror-case (Pl. VIII C)

horns of consecration: Evans' name for clay or stone architectural elements usually used on palace or shrine entablatures, of "divine significance" (Figs. 19, 32)

ideogram: an incised picture on Linear A or B tablets, schematically representing an object, creature, weight, or measure (Pl. XLVI; Fig. 41)

kernos (pl. *kernoi*): ritual vessel with small vases attached in a ring, for libations (Pl. XLII D)

koiné: a common, international, or intercultural, standardized use of an achievement (language, design, technology)

krater: a mixing-bowl, or any large wide-mouthed bowl (Pl. XXXIII)

kylix (pl. *kylikes*): a stemmed drinking goblet; the standard Mycenaean kylix is a product of the thirteenth century (Fig. 51)

larnax (pl. *larnakes*): a chest or coffer, used of chest-shaped sarcophagi in clay or stone (Pls. XXXIV–XXXV)

lentoid: bean-shaped, descriptive of gems (Pl. XLIII)

liparite: a type of brescia from the Lipari Islands

megalithic: an architectural preference for building with great boulders or ashlar blocks; by extension, descriptive of several prehistoric cultures which use this architecture (Pl. XXVI A)

megaron (pl. *megara*): a "big room," used loosely for any long narrow structure with a single door in the narrow end; used more precisely for the three-unit Mycenaean building consisting of aithousa, prodomos, and inner megaron with a central hearth surrounded by four columns (Pls. XXII A, XXIII B, XXV A; Fig. 51 f)

naturalism: used loosely in Aegean aesthetics for any imitation of natural birds, plants, fish, no matter how stylized or unreal the representation may be

peribolos: a surrounding wall (Fig. 16)

pithos (pl. *pithoi*): a large storage jar for oil or wine, usually clay; sometimes used as a burial jar (Fig. 15)

poros: Greek archaeological term for local limestone of a certain pale spongy quality (Pl. XVI B)

Potnia (pl. *Potniai*): Greek "lady," "mistress," used for goddesses (Pl. XXXVIII)

prodomos: the second unit of a three-room megaron, the enclosed vestibule (Pl. XXII A)

propylon (pl. *propyla*): outer gateway, either an independent entrance building or an element in a wall, usually with a double door and columns supporting a porch on both fronts (Pls. XXIII B, XXX C)

pyxis (pl. *pyxides*): a closed boxlike vessel with a lid (Pls. XXVIII A, XXXVI B) *relieving triangle:* the triangular hollow space above a lintel in tholoi or other massive lintel-and-post structures such as gates; loosely used for the concealing slabs on either end, or for non-triangular spaces with the same function in provincial tholoi (Pls. XVII A–B, XXVI A; Fig. 24)

rhyton (pl. *rhyta*): (1) a vase in the shape of a funnel or cone; (2) a vase in the shape of an animal or animal head (Pls. XI D, XIV, XLII; Fig. 28)

sacral knot: Evans' term for the rigid double loop of cloth worn at the back of the neck by Minoan female figures or used alone as a symbol; in Greece it occurs in faïence imitating tartan cloth in the Shaft Graves, and as a design element in vase painting

schist: laminated, easily splitting rock like slate; the Cycladic island variety (Pl. XVI A)

slip: a peptized colloidal solution of fine clay applied over the surface of a vase, between body and paint

stele (pl. *stelai*): any marker or object set standing over a tomb, particularly the worked tall slabs over the Shaft Graves (Figs. 17, 18, 47 *a*)

stirrup jar: a form of closed oil vessel with a false spout rising on top to support two handles in the shape of a stirrup, and a real spout farther down the shoulder (Pl. XLV B–C). The first two fingers slip through the stirrup, the thumb closes the spout

stoa: an independent porch with columns and a rear wall

stomion: the mouth or door passage of a tholos tomb (Pl. XVI B; Fig. 24)

table of offerings: properly, an altar in tripod or table shape with cuttings in the top surface for libations or solid offerings; loosely, of the tripod-brazier with a sunken top (Fig. 44)

theatral area: Evans' term for a sunken court with surrounding tiers of steps for dances and other performances; in Greece, applied to any open area with provision for an audience, like the court in the northeast wing at Pylos (Pl. XXII A)

tholos (pl. *tholoi*): a round building, in particular a beehive-shaped underground tomb, or the inner chamber of such a tomb; also used for non-funerary architecture like granaries (Pls. XVI B, XVII A; Fig. 24)

tumulus: an earth mound over a tomb, whether a tholos or a circular communal precinct; any round heap of earth (cf. Pl. III A)

Urfirnis: a forerunner of proper glaze paint, descriptive of certain classes of Neolithic and Early Helladic lustrous painted vases (Pl. VIII A; Fig. 51)

Index

Achaia: pottery, 223; refugees, 270
Achaian; *see* Aḫḫiyawa; Mycenaean
Achilleus, 252, 276, 278
Agamemnon of Mycenae, 174, 213, 237, 277, 278, 305, 309
Aghios Kosmas; *see* Hagios Kosmas
Aḫḫiyawa, 260, 272 ff.
Aigina (Saronic Gulf), 26; EH walls, 29, 32; Cycladic trade, 45, 55; MH pottery, 75; LH trade, 145, 288
Alaca Hüyük (Anatolia), royal burials, 26, 42
Alalakh (Syria), 107, 207, 270
Alexiou, St., 301
altars: Neolithic, 8, 16, 20; Shaft Graves, 86; Mycenaean, 165, 182, 206, *283–84*, 290; *see also* Mycenaean Greece, religion
amber, 89, 114, 127, 128, 131, 147, 227, 231, 257, 301
Amnisos (Crete), cave of Eileithyia, 21, 293–94
Amorgos (Cyclades), 47, 54; burials, 58; daggers, 64

Amyklai (Lakonia), Mycenaean town, 160, 183, 270, 288, 308, 311
Analipsis; *see* Vourvoura
Anatolia: Neolithic settlements and Greek parallels, 2, 15, 19, 21; raw materials and resources, 12, 22, 25, 56, 89, 128; migrations, 26, 59; Cycladic affinities, 47; languages, 61; Early Bronze chronology, 64; Shaft Grave connections, 89, 95; contacts with Mycenaean Greece, 222, 254–56, 257, 263–64, 265, 301; destructions, 270; *see under* individual sites; *see also* Levant; Mycenaean Greece, trade
Angel, L., 18
animals, Appendix I
—domestic: Neolithic, 4, 8, 12; EH, 37; Mycenaean, 180, 195, 257; *see also* chariots and horses
—wild: Neolithic, 8, 12; EH, 37; in Shaft Grave art, 95–100; Mycenaean, 194–95
Aphidna (Attica), 81
Archilochos, 311

389

Plate List

Plate I. Early Neolithic burial of mother and children, Nea Nikomedia. Courtesy, R. Rodden.

Plate II. Neolithic sculpture
   A. Amulet of greenstone in the form of a seated goddess, Malthi. *SME*, Pl. 1.
   B. Ritual vase in the form of a woman's belly and legs, Elateia. Courtesy S. Weinberg.
   C. Neolithic (or later Bronze Age?) stone menhir, costumed goddess, over life size, Souphli Magoula. Courtesy H. Biesantz.
   D. Terracotta female figurine, Lerna. Courtesy J. Caskey and University of Cincinnati.

Plate III. Lerna in Early Helladic II
   A. Plan of the town.
   B. House of the Tiles from the northwest; photograph by A. Frantz. Courtesy J. Caskey and University of Cincinnati.

Plate IV. Aspects of Early Helladic civilization at Lerna
   A. Fortification wall with towers.
   B. Decorated band from a jar, rolled out with a cylinder seal carved with beasts running among spirals.

C. Ceremonial clay hearth with cavity in the form of a double ax. Courtesy J. Caskey and University of Cincinnati.

Plate V. Selected stamped clay sealings, Early Helladic II, Lerna. Courtesy J. Caskey and University of Cincinnati.

Plate VI. Vases of the Early Aegean world

A. Gold sauceboat from Arkadia; photo Giraudon. Courtesy Musée du Louvre.
B. Silver bowl from a Cycladic island. Courtesy Metropolitan Museum of Art.
C. Marble vases from Herakleia in the Cyclades. Private collection.

Plate VII. Cycladic idols

A. Female idol from Amorgos, in Athens. Zervos, *L'Art des Cyclades*, Pl. 293.
B. Male idol from Antiparos. Zervos, *L'Art des Cyclades*, Pl. 105.
C. Head from Amorgos, in Athens. Zervos, *L'Art des Cyclades*, Pl. 178.
D. Double idol, mother and child, in Karlsruhe. Zervos, *L'Art des Cyclades*, Pl. 319.

Plate VIII. Vases of the Early and Middle Bronze Ages

A. Painted askos, Early Helladic II, Lerna. Courtesy J. Caskey and University of Cincinnati.
B. Patterned-ware jar, Early Helladic III, Lerna. Courtesy J. Caskey and University of Cincinnati.
C. Cycladic frying pan or mirror, Syros, in Athens. Zervos, *L'Art des Cyclades*, Pl. 210.
D. Steatite model of a walled compound with granaries(?), perhaps a spice or cosmetic box, Melos, in Munich. Zervos, *L'Art des Cyclades*, Pl. 29.
E. Red Minyan fruit bowl, Eutresis. H. Goldman, *Eutresis*, Pl. 10.
F. Spouted jug with flowers, Middle Cycladic, Phylakopi. Zervos, *L'Art des Cyclades*, Pl. 283.

Plate IX. Vases of the Middle Bronze Age

A. Matt-painted kantharos, Lerna Grave J4. Courtesy J. Caskey and University of Cincinnati.
B. Bridge-spouted jar, Middle Minoan II, Lerna Grave J4. Courtesy J. Caskey and University of Cincinnati.
C. Matt-painted jar, dromos of Tomb of Clytemnestra, Mycenae. Courtesy L. MacVeagh and Museum of Fine Arts, Boston.
D. Matt-painted bridge-spouted jar, Athens. Courtesy Agora Excavations, Athens.
E. Jar painted with roses, Circle B, Grave *Omicron*, Mycenae; photo Tombazis. Courtesy the late J. Papademetriou.
F. Jug in the Cycladic bird style, Samikon tumulus; photograph from German Archaeological Institute. Courtesy N. Yalouris.

Plate X. The Shaft Graves

A. Cist burial with Middle Helladic vases, Circle B, Grave *Eta;* Photo Tombazis. Courtesy J. Papademetriou.
B. Gold funeral suit for a child, Circle A, Grave III; photograph by J. McCredie. Courtesy National Museum, Athens.

Plate XI. Shaft Grave Art

    A. Gold funeral mask, Circle A, Grave IV. G. Karo, *Schachtgräber*, Pl. 47.

    B. Gold funeral mask from an archaic burial at Trebenischte, Bulgaria. B. Filow, *Die archaische Nekropole von Trebenischte*, Pl. I.

    C. Amethyst portrait-gem of a prince, Circle B, Grave *Gamma*. Courtesy National Museum, Athens.

    D. Gold rhyton in the form of a lion's head, Circle A, Grave IV. G. Karo, *Schachtgräber*, Pl. 118.

Plate XII. Inlaid Daggers from the Shaft Graves, Circle A, Graves IV and V; Photo Hirmer.

Plate XIII. Princely weapons from Shaft Graves and Tholos Tombs

    A. Gold and ivory sword hilt with lions' heads, Circle B, Grave *Delta;* Photo Tombazis. Courtesy J. Papademetriou.

    B. Inlaid dagger blade with leopards in landscape, Myrsinochorion. Courtesy Sp. Marinatos.

    C. Inlaid sword blade with gold battle-axes, Thera. Courtesy Danish National Museum, Copenhagen.

    D. Damaged inlaid dagger blade with flying birds. Private collection.

Plate XIV. Silver Siege Rhyton, Circle A, Grave IV; drawing by S. Chapman.

Plate XV. Sites of the fifteenth century

    A. Rubble houses at Peristeria. Courtesy Sp. Marinatos.

    B. Town at Hagia Eirene, Keos. Courtesy J. Caskey and University of Cincinnati.

Plate XVI. Architecture of the Early Mycenaean Age

    A. Stone house at Hagia Eirene. Courtesy J. Caskey and University of Cincinnati.

    B. Façade of tholos tomb at Peristeria, with masons' marks. Courtesy Sp. Marinatos.

    C. Interior of Tomb *Rho* at Mycenae, with red painted bands; drawing by A. Boyatsis. Courtesy J. Papademetriou.

Plate XVII. Pioneers at Mycenae

    A. Madame Schliemann excavating the Tomb of Clytemnestra; photograph from German Archaeological Institute.

    B. The Lion Gate before Schliemann's excavations. E. Dodwell, *Views and Descriptions of Cyclopian Remains in Greece and Italy* (1834), Pl. 6.

Plate XVIII. Vases of the Early Mycenaean Age

    A. "Vapheio" cup, Late Helladic I, Keos. Courtesy J. Caskey and University of Cincinnati.

    B. "Vapheio" cup, Late Helladic I, Peristeria. Courtesy Sp. Marinatos.

    C. "Ephyrean" goblet, Late Helladic II, Mycenae. A. Wace, *BSA* 1956, Pl. 32; drawing by P. de Jong. Courtesy Trustees of the British School at Athens.

    D. Palace style jar, Late Helladic II, Analipsis (Vourvoura). K. Rhomaios, *Ergon* 1954, Fig. 48.

    E. Palace style jar, Late Helladic II, Kakovatos. K. Müller, *AM* 1909, Pl. 17.

    F. Palace style jar, Late Helladic II, Koukounara. Courtesy Sp. Marinatos.

    G. Jar of the early fourteenth century (LH III A:1), Royal Tomb, Athens. Courtesy Agora Excavations, Athens.

H. Jar of the early fourteenth century (LH III A:1), Troy. Courtesy C. Blegen and University of Cincinnati.
I. Jar of the early fourteenth century (LH III A:1), Warrior Graves, Knossos. Courtesy S. Hood and Trustees of the British School at Athens.

Plate XIX. Gems from Mycenaean Tombs

A. Vapheio no. 34, sard, goddess and wild goat.
B. Vapheio no. 2, yellow jasper bound with gold, two dolphins playing.
C. Vapheio no. 38, dark jasper bound with gold, two men binding a lion.
D. Vapheio no. 15, chalcedony, man battling a wild boar among rocks.
E. Vapheio no. 1, sardonyx bound with gold, warrior racing a two-horse chariot. Tsountas, *Ephemeris* 1889, Pl. 10 and Zervos, *L'Art en Grèce*[2] (1936), Pl. 36.
F. Myrsinochorion, sard, votary at altar. Marinatos, *Ergon* 1956, Fig. 92.
G. Myrsinochorion, sard, two heroes or divinities mastering lions. Marinatos, *Ergon* 1956, Fig. 92.
H. Tragana, amethyst, three heroes in battle. Marinatos, *VIIArcCong* I (1961), Pl. 2.
I. Myrsinochorion, amethyst, two ducks in flight. Marinatos, *Ergon* 1956, Fig. 92.
J. Mycenae, sard, lioness playing with cub. Tsountas, *Ephemeris* 1888, Pl. 10, no. 17.
K. Mycenae, two lions with single head, posed heraldically on altar. Tsountas, *Ephemeris* 1888, Pl. 10, no. 2.
L. Mycenae, jasper, two winged lion-goats(?) posed heraldically on altar, with Linear B sign, *Wheat*. Tsountas, *Ephemeris* 1888, Pl. 10, no. 30.

Plate XX. Metalwork from Dendra

A. Silver goblet with flying birds (extended drawing); photograph from German Archaeological Institute.
B. Set of silver vases from Tomb 10; photograph from German Archaeological Institute.

Plate XXI. Mycenaean Armor and Weapons

A. Bronze cuirass about 1400 B.C., Dendra Tomb 13. Courtesy N. Verdelis.
B. Gold and bronze swords contemporary with Dendra Tomb 13. *Ars Antiqua Auktion* 3 (1961), frontispiece.
C. Bronze greaves about 1200 B.C.; photograph by C. Vermeule. Courtesy N. Yalouris and Patras Museum.

Plate XXII. Plans of Mycenaean Palaces

A. Pylos in the thirteenth century. Courtesy C. Blegen and University of Cincinnati.
B. Gla in the thirteenth century; drawing by J. Travlos. Courtesy the late J. Threpsiades.

Plate XXIII. Plans of Mycenaean Palaces

A. The Acropolis of Athens in the thirteenth and twelfth centuries. Courtesy Sp. Iakovides.
B. The Upper Citadel of the Third City at Tiryns, about 1250 B.C. K. Müller, *Tiryns* III, Pl. 4.

Plate XXIV. Mycenae in the Thirteenth Century

A. Air view of the citadel. Courtesy Royal Hellenic Air Force and M. Paraskevaïdes.
B. Plan of the houses outside the citadel; plan by A. Petronotes. Courtesy N. Verdelis.

402

Plate XXV. The Megaron at Pylos

A. View of the main block from the storerooms at the back; photograph by A. Frantz. Courtesy C. Blegen and University of Cincinnati.
B. The painted floor and hearth of the megaron; drawing by P. de Jong. Courtesy C. Blegen and University of Cincinnati.

Plate XXVI. The Treasury of Atreus

A. The Treasury of Atreus after "excavation" by Veli Pasha. E. Dodwell, *Views and Descriptions of Cyclopian Remains in Greece and Italy* (1834), Pl. 10.
B. Base of a column from the façade. E. Dodwell, *A Classical and Topographical Tour through Greece* (1819), 232.
C. Fragments of the sculptured façade (from a cast). Courtesy Trustees of Sir John Soane's Museum, London.

Plate XXVII. Procession Fresco in the House of Kadmos, Thebes. H. Reusch, *Zeichnerische Rekonstruktion des Frauenfrieses,* Pl. 15.

Plate XXVIII. Procession Frescoes at Tiryns and Pylos

A. Detail of woman carrying a carved box, Tiryns; drawing by E. Gilliéron. G. Rodenwaldt, *Tiryns* II, Pl. 8.
B. Embroidered skirt, Pylos. Courtesy C. Blegen and University of Cincinnati.
C. Detail of the upper body of a woman or goddess, Pylos. Courtesy C. Blegen and University of Cincinnati.

Plate XXIX. Hunters, Servants, and Animals

A. Huntsman, horse, and hound, Tiryns. M. Swindler, *Ancient Painting,* Fig. 176.
B. Hunter fighting a stag, Pylos. Courtesy M. Lang and University of Cincinnati.
C. Servant carrying a sedan chair, House of the Oil Merchant, Mycenae. Courtesy H. Wace and Trustees of the British School at Athens.
D. Horse and argonaut frieze, propylon, Pylos. Courtesy C. Blegen and University of Cincinnati.

Plate XXX. Excerpts from Pylos Frescoes

A. Musician and bird, from the King's megaron.
B. Griffin fragment, from the Queen's megaron.
C. Sphinx Gate, from the propylon.
Courtesy C. Blegen and University of Cincinnati.

Plate XXXI. Siege scene from the megaron at Mycenae

A. Warrior plunging below chariot on a hillside; drawing by A. Kontopoulos. Courtesy National Museum, Athens.
B. Palace façade with women watching from the window. W. Lamb, *BSA* 1921–23, Pl. 42.

Plate XXXII. Scenes from chariot kraters of the fourteenth and thirteenth centuries

A–C. From Enkomi in Cyprus. E. Sjøqvist, *Problems of the Late Cypriote Bronze Age,* Figs. 20,1, 20,3, and 21,1.
D. From Suda Bay in Crete. F. Matz, *Forschungen auf Kreta,* Pl. 3, 2.

GREECE IN THE BRONZE AGE

Plate XXXIII. Pictorial Vases
  A. The Window Krater, Enkomi. Courtesy Trustees of the British Museum.
  B. The Warrior Vase, Mycenae; photograph by J. McCredie. Courtesy National Museum, Athens.

Plate XXXIV. Three views of a Late Mycenaean sarcophagus with mourning women. Private collection.

Plate XXXV. Two Late Mycenaean painted sarcophagi.
  A. Mourning women.
  B. Warriors and bird.
    Private collections.

Plate XXXVI. Early ivory
  A. Wooden (sycamore?) box with ivory architectural details and watchdogs, Circle A, Grave V, Mycenae; photograph from German Archaeological Institute. Courtesy National Museum, Athens.
  B. Pyxis and lid, carved with griffins hunting deer, Royal Tomb, Athens. Courtesy Agora Excavations, Athens.
  C. Drawing of the pyxis by P. de Jong. Courtesy Agora Excavations, Athens.

Plate XXXVII. Ivory plaques with monsters
  A. Griffin sleeping among flowers, Mycenae; photograph from German Archaeological Institute. Courtesy National Museum, Athens.
  B. Plumed sphinxes on column above horns of consecration, Mycenae. Courtesy H. Wace and Trustees of the British School at Athens.
  C. Cutout inlay of lion devouring flying griffin, Delos. Courtesy Director of the French School at Athens.
  D. Griffin with stretched wings, Megiddo. Courtesy Oriental Institute, Chicago.

Plate XXXVIII. Ivory group, triad of divinities(?), Mycenae; photo Hirmer. Courtesy Trustees of the British School at Athens.

Plate XXXIX. Ivory figures, tusk, and inlays
  A. Woman in bodice and flounced skirt, Prosymna. Courtesy C. Blegen and University of Cincinnati.
  B. Plaque of warrior with helmet, shield, and spear, Delos. Courtesy Director of the French School at Athens.
  C. Tusk section (libation horn?) carved with goats lying beside a formal plant, a bird rising overhead, Mycenae, probably imported from Syria; photograph by J. McCredie. Courtesy National Museum, Athens.
  D. Furniture inlays, dolphin, and columns, House of the Sphinxes, Mycenae. Courtesy H. Wace and Trustees of the British School at Athens.

Plate XL. Monumental Sculpture
  A. Terracotta statue from a shrine, Keos. Courtesy J. Caskey and University of Cincinnati.
  B. Head of a similar statue, Keos. Courtesy J. Caskey and University of Cincinnati.
  C. Painted stucco head of a goddess(?), Mycenae; photo Hirmer. Courtesy National Museum, Athens.

Plate XLI. Terracotta figures of the palace age

  A. Φ-Figurine.

  B. Ψ-Figurine.
     Courtesy Trustees of the British School at Athens.

  C. Man reclining in a comfortable chair.

  D. Chariot group, Prosymna. Courtesy C. Blegen and University of Cincinnati.

  E. Woman cradling child, Mycenae. Courtesy National Museum, Athens.

  F. Goddess riding a beast sidesaddle. Courtesy National Museum, Athens, Stathatos Collection.

Plate XLII. Plastic vases from the late Mycenaean world

  A. Pack horse with pilgrim flasks strapped on, Ialysos. G. Jacopi, *Annuario* 13–14 (1933), Pl. 22.

  B. Duck with eyebrows, Achaia; photograph by C. Vermeule. Courtesy Patras Museum.

  C. Bull's-head drinking cup, Karpathos. Courtesy Trustees of the British Museum.

  D. Ritual *kernos* with bull's head, doves, and ceremonial vases. Courtesy Museum of Fine Arts, Boston.

  E. Fish head, Tiryns. Courtesy N. Verdelis.

  F. *Kalathos* bowl with figurines of mourning women on the rim, Perati. Courtesy Sp. Iakovides.

Plate XLIII. Masterpieces of Mycenaean gem carving

  A. Sard, lion and bull in combat.

  B. Sard, heraldically poised lions killing a stag.

  C. Sard, bull and lioness.
     Courtesy Museum of Fine Arts, Boston.

  D. Dark agate, lion and bull, from inside the king's gold cup, Dendra tholos tomb. A. Persson, *Royal Tombs at Dendra,* Pl. 19.

  E. Amethyst, warrior stabbing a lioness, Pylos tholos tomb. Courtesy C. Blegen and University of Cincinnati.

  F. Gold ring, goddess and prince or consort, Mycenae. Marinatos and Hirmer, *Crete and Mycenae,* Pl. 206.

Plate XLIV. Mycenaean jewelry

  A. Beads of a necklace in gold with enamel, each two argonauts heraldically arranged, Mycenae; photograph by A. Frantz. Courtesy National Museum, Athens.

  B. Gold-foil spray of flowers, Peristeria. Courtesy Sp. Marinatos.

  C. Gold-foil wasps, Peristeria. Courtesy Sp. Marinatos.

  D. Gold sceptre mounted with gold and cloisonné hawks on an orb, Kourion. Courtesy V. Karageorghis and Nicosia Museum, Cyprus.

  E. Stone mold for casting gold ornaments, Mycenae. Schliemann, *Mycenae and Tiryns,* Fig. 162.

Plate XLV. Vases from Egypt and the islands

  A. Mycenaean vases found in Egypt, fifteenth to thirteenth centuries. Courtesy Museum of Fine Arts, Boston, Hay-Way Collection.

  B. Egyptian alabaster copy of a Mycenaean stirrup jar, reign of Seti I(?). Photograph by C. Vermeule.

  C. Close style stirrup jar. Courtesy Danish National Museum, Copenhagen.

Plate XLVI. Pair of Linear B "page" tablets from Pylos
 A. An 218.
 B. Sn 64.

Plate XLVII. Rare funeral customs
 A. Pair of gold scales and balance, Mycenae, Circle A, Grave III; photograph by J. McCredie. Courtesy National Museum, Athens.
 B. Pair of horses buried in the dromos of the Marathon tholos tomb; photo Tombazis. Courtesy J. Papademetriou.

Plate XLVIII. Cemeteries and foreign imports at the end of the Mycenaean world
 A. The cemetery at Perati.
 B. Near Eastern cylinder seal, probably Mitanni, Tiryns; photograph from German Archaeological Institute.
 C. Near Eastern cylinder seal, Perati. Courtesy Sp. Iakovides.
 D. Bronze figurine, probably from north Syria, Tiryns; photograph from German Achaeological Institute.

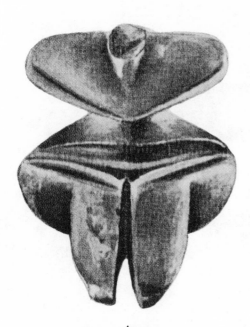

A

B

D

C

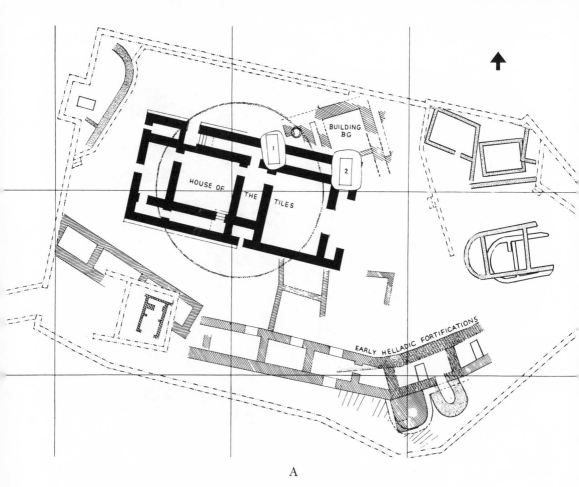

A

III. Lerna

B

A

IV. Aspects of EH Culture

B

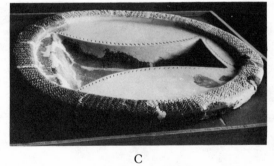

C

A

B

C

A

B

C

D

A

B

C

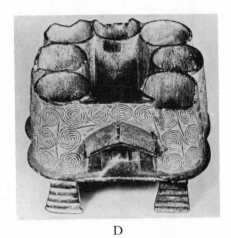

D

E

F

A

C

B

E

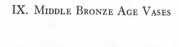

IX. Middle Bronze Age Vases

D

F

A

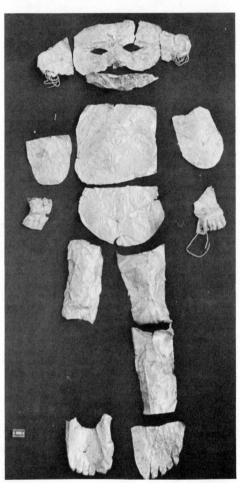

B

B

A

C

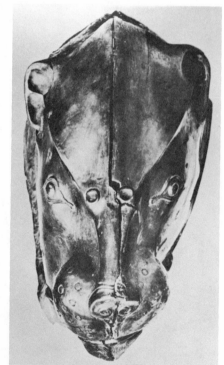

D

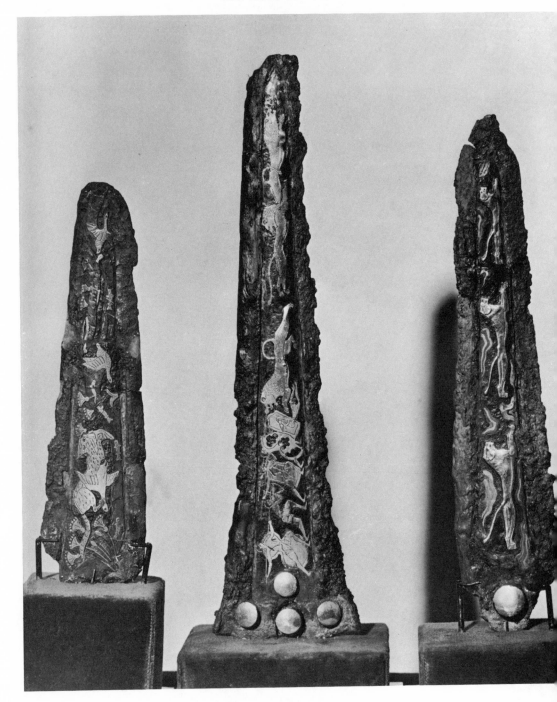

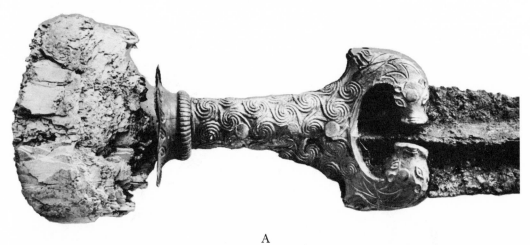

A

B

C

D

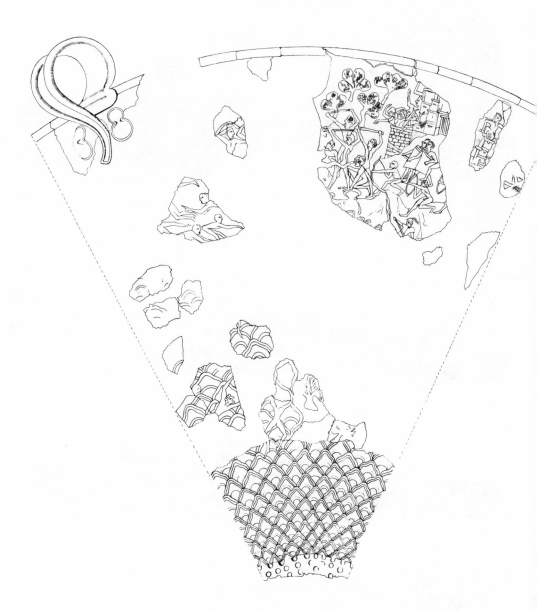

A

B

A

C

XVI. Early Mycenaean Architecture

B

A

XVII. Pioneers at Mycenae

B

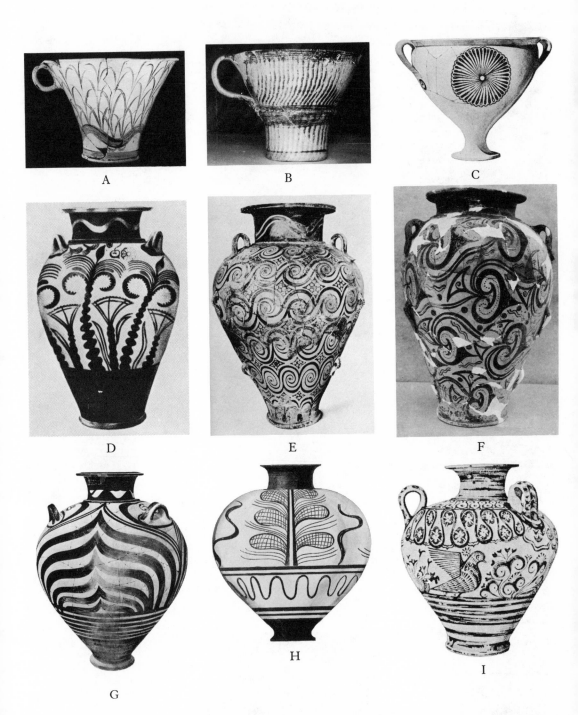

A

B

C

D

E

F

G

H

I

A

B

C

D

E

F

G

H

I

J

K

L

A

XX. Dendra Metalwork

B

A

XXI. Armor and Weapons

B

C

A

XXII. Pylos and Gla

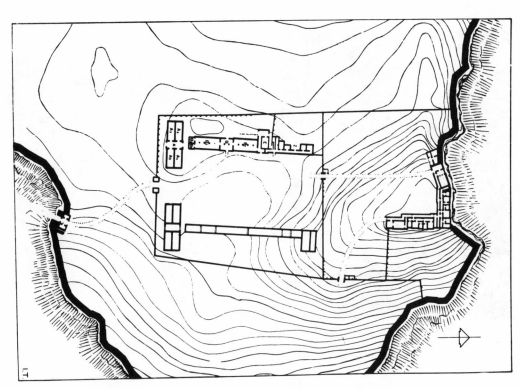

B

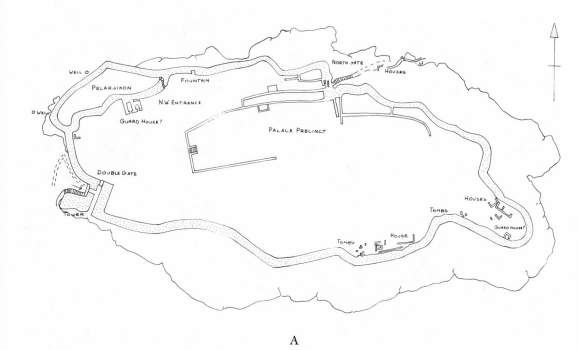

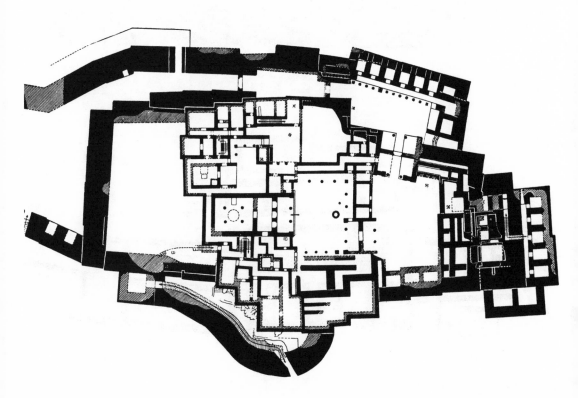

A

XXIII. Athens and Tiryns

B

A

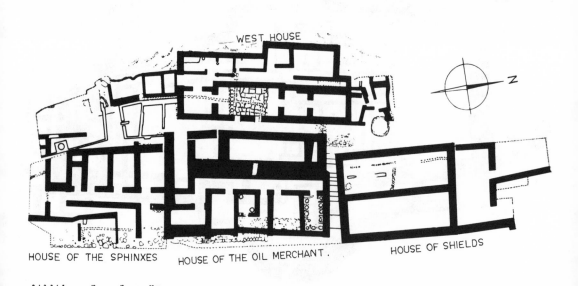

WEST HOUSE

HOUSE OF THE SPHINXES   HOUSE OF THE OIL MERCHANT.   HOUSE OF SHIELDS

0 1 2 3 4 5   10   15   20 m.

B

A

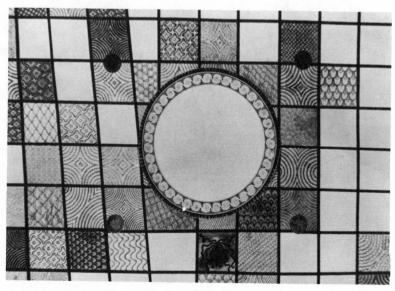

B

A

C

B

XXVII. Procession from Thebes

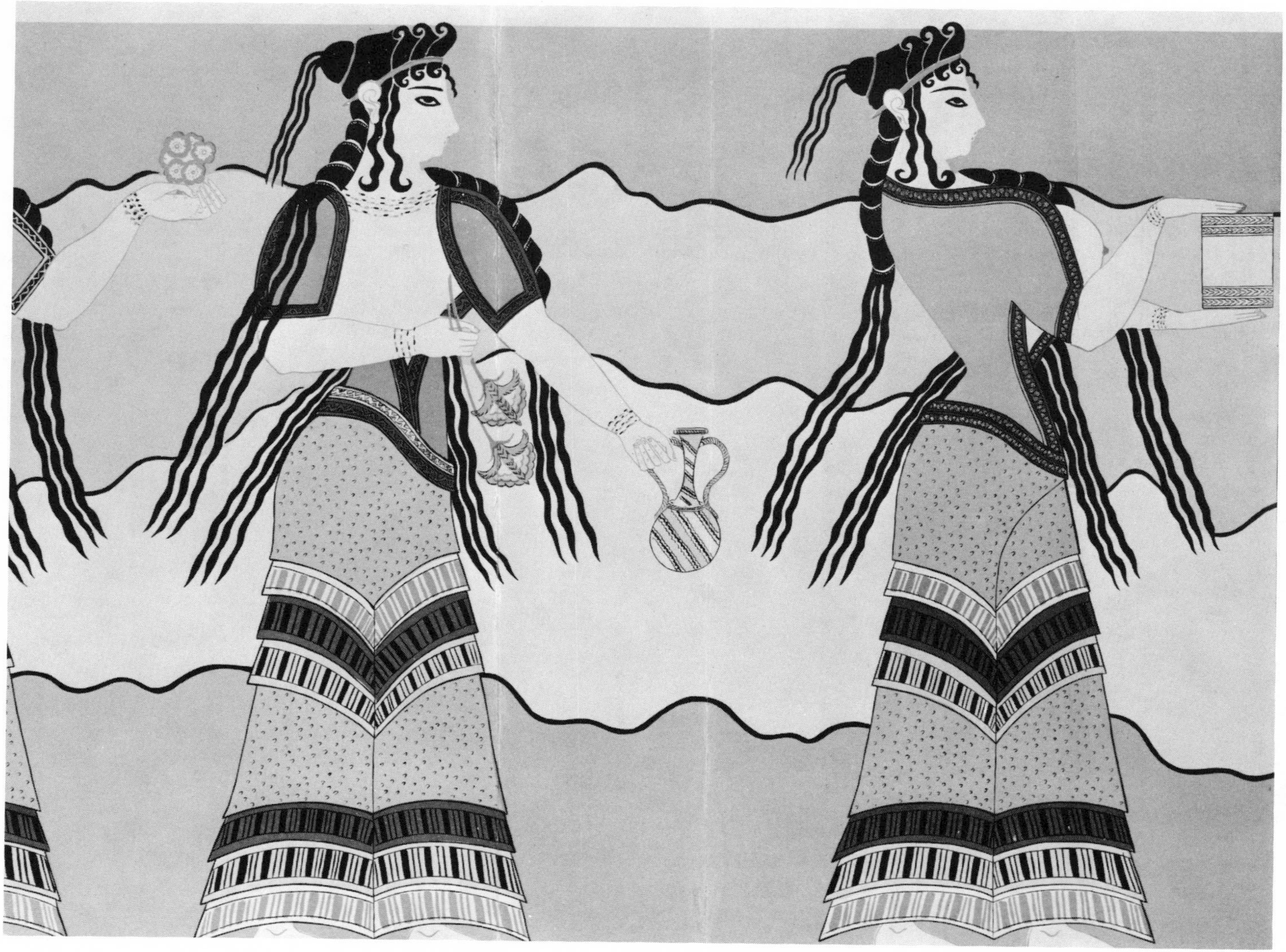

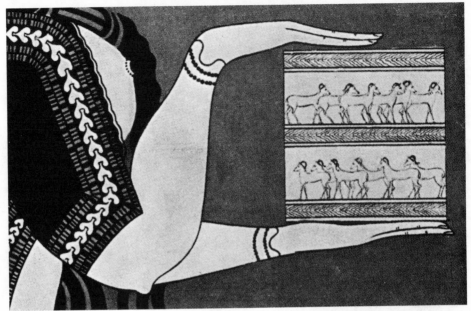

A

C

XXVIII. Procession Frescoes

B

A

XXIX. Hunters, Servants, and Animals

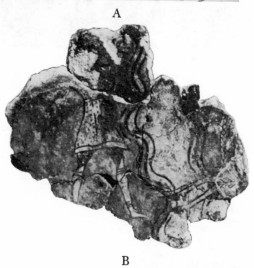

B

C

D

A

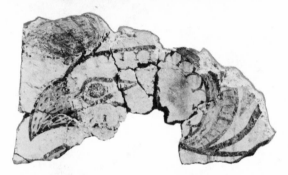

B

XXX. Pylos Frescoes, Excerpts

C

XXXI. Siege Scene, Mycenae

A

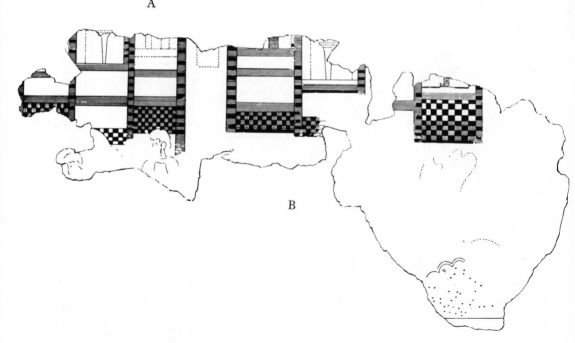

B

A

B

XXXII. Chariot Kraters

C

D

A

XXXIII. Pictorial Vases

B

XXXIV. PAINTED SARCOPHAGUS

A

XXXV. Two Painted Sarcophagi

B

A

B

C

A

B

XXXVII. Ivory Plaques and Inlays

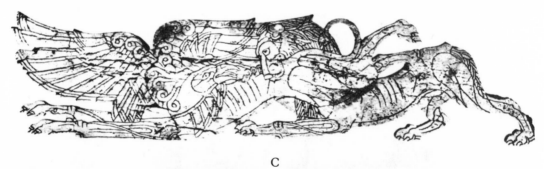

C

D

XXXVIII. Ivory Triad

A

B

C

D

XXXIX. Figures, Tusk,
and Inlays

A

B

C

A

B

C

D

E

F

A

C

B

D

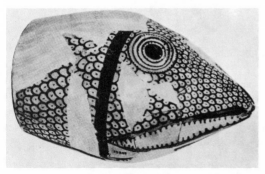

E

F

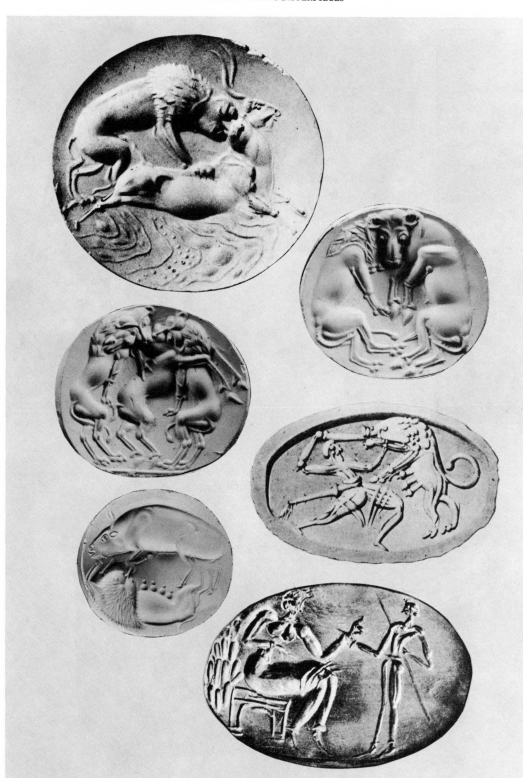

A

E

F

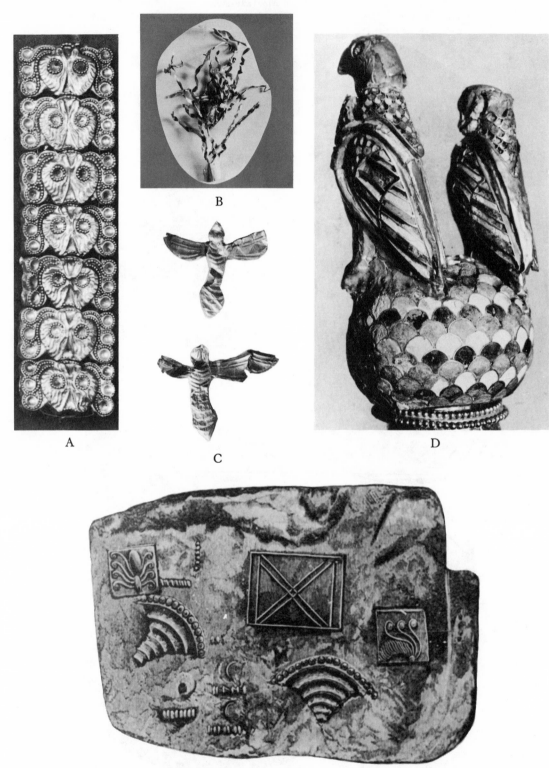

A

B

C

D

E

A

B

XLV. Vases from Egypt and the Islands

C

B

A

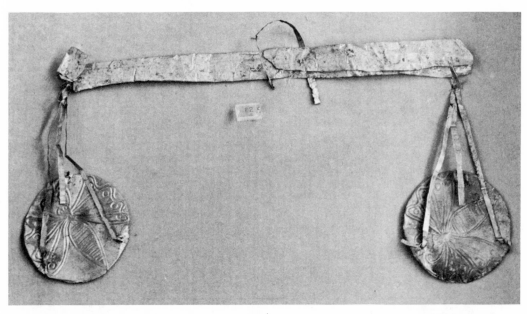

A

XLVII. Funeral Customs

B

XLVIII. Cemeteries and
Foreign Imports

A

D

B

C